Nelson Yuan-sheng Kiang

Neuropsychology and Neurolinguistics

JANUA
LINGUARUM
Studia Memoriae
Nicolai van Wijk Dedicata

Series Maior 78

edenda curat
C. H. van Schooneveld
Indiana University

Neuropsychology and Neurolinguistics

Selected Papers

Egon Weigl

In Collaboration with
M. Bierwisch, R. Böttcher, A. Fradis, A. Kreindler,
H.-J. Lander, E. Metze, L. Mihăilescu, I. Weigl

Mouton Publishers
The Hague · Paris · New York

ISBN 90 279 7956 1
 Typesetting: Georg Wagner, Nördlingen. – Printing: Karl Gerike, Berlin. – Binding: Lüderitz & Bauer, Berlin.
Printed in Germany

Contents

Part Three
Experimental Studies on Neuropsychological Mechanisms of Aphasic Disturbances of Speech Perception and Production

Editorial Note

Egon Weigl, the author and co-author of this collection of papers, one of the pioneers of what might be called the neurolinguistic branch of neuropsychology, died on June 4th, 1979 aged 78. the *Introduction* to this volume, which he had finished only few days before, was the very last of a huge number of studies he could bring to an end. The brief *Foreword* that A. R. Luria, the world-renowned Soviet neuropsychologist, added to the Selected Papers of his colleague and close friend of many years was written shortly before his own death in 1977. The book thus turned into a memorial volume for two grand old men of our century's neuropsychology.

A large amount of material has had to remain unpublished. It may be hoped, however, that at least part of it will appear in the future after being prepared for publication by some of Weigl's closest collaborators and friends.

Unfortunately, Egon Weigl was not allowed the time to give this collection of papers the final shape he had intended to. We are therefore left with the fact that in its present form the volume lacks the unification of terminology the author wanted to make before submitting the final version to the publishers. Since the English versions of the papers collected here have been prepared by different translators at different times, certain terminological inconsistencies were unavoidable. Nevertheless, we are confident that this will be no obstacle to the understanding of the main tenets. I am indebted to Ewald Lang, one of Egon Weigl's younger friends and linguistic co-workers, for his invaluable help in proof-reading and other editorial matters.

Berlin, December 1980 — Irina Weigl

Foreword

by A. R. Luria

It is both a great pleasure and a privilege to write a few words as a prefatory note to this volume of my old friend Egon Weigl on neuropsychological and psycholinguistic problems.

Egon Weigl became well-known when he – being a pupil and collaborator of the great neurologist Kurt Goldstein and of the outstanding psychologist Adhémar Gelb – published his investigations concerning the psychology of so-called abstraction processes. His experimentally ascertained observation that in brain lesioned patients an abstract classification of objects is easily replaced by a reproduction of a practical situation ("kategoriales Ordnen" vs. "sinnvolle Zusammengehörigkeit in einer Situation") made him a widely known psychologist in the 30s of our century.

Continuous studies on aphasia over several decades proved Egon Weigl's abilities as an outstanding neuropsychologist.

In the present collection of his papers, the reader will find lot of new ideas and well-prepared facts, among them analyses of the complex, highly specialized factors pertaining to the speech functional system as well as some well-founded indications of a partial independence of these factors. This offers new and promising ways for the further development of analytical neuropsychology. At the same time, Weigl's results impressively show how reliable facts can be obtained from a careful study of aphasic phenomena.

The reader will find as well a series of very important data concerning the mutual relationship of these factors, the general rules and the limits of transcoding processes, which no doubt will provide a new approach to synthetic neuropsychology.

All these data are merely the basic steps leading to the central idea of the author – the idea that aphasia does not only include symptoms of destroyed speech functions but that it also comprises the blocking of certain speech functions. Weigl has found new ways of restoring disturbed speech functions (mostly those of naming, understanding, reading and writing) by his method of "deblocking" temporary blocked components and reintegrating them into the system of preserved speech functions.

The general idea of "deblocking" aphasically disturbed components as well as the detailed elaboration of the various specific procedures that constitute the "deblocking method" belong to the most important achievements of this creative scholar.

Neurologists and psychologists, neuropsychologists and psycholinguists will gain many important insights and stimulating ideas when reading this book. I can only congratulate the author and the Mouton Publishers for opening to the readers the possibility to enter this field, which is of equal import for psychology, medicine, and linguistics.

Moscow, May 1976 A. R. L.

Prefatory Note

by M. Bierwisch

The work represented by this collection of essays covers two decades of past research, but it is still part of the future of linguistics and neuropsychology. Let me briefly indicate on three levels of increasing generality why I think that to be the case.

1. *Deblocking*. The first level concerns Weigl's work as an experimental neuropsychologist and it contains his most personal and unique footprint in the future of the field. Among the wealth of his experimental findings, with respect to which he compares to many other inventive experimenters, the discovery of a phenomenon that he rather felicitously called 'deblocking' will be the one that is unseparably linked to the name of Egon Weigl. In fact, the phenomenon has been noted various times, but it was considered as a curiosity before Weigl became aware of its remarkable character and began to investigate it systematically. What he discovered as a first step depends on two fairly general prerequisites: (a) There must be two different modes of speech processing, one of which is disturbed, while the other is intact. (b) There must be an invariant item to be processed on these two modes. What Weigl was able to establish is that processing the item on the intact mode made it available also on the disturbed one. This original finding expanded into a complex network of further questions. One series of problems concerns the relation among the involved modes of processing. Which coupling of different modes yields the deblocking effect? Does it spread automatically through more than one (possibly all) disturbed modes within a given type of aphasia? If so, does it run simultaneously or sequentially through a number of modes? Is there a difference in strength of the deblocking effect according to systematic conditions? Another series of problems concerns the nature of the item to be processed. How invariant has the item in the deblocking and the deblocked mode to be? How do different, though related items influence each other? Are semantic and phonetic properties of an item of equal importance for the deblocking effect? Weigl clarified many of those questions by systematic experimentation. The initial curiosity thus turned into an extremely revealing observation,

which is, moreover, deeply connected to the very nature of aphasic disturbances: The fact that deblocking is possible has crucial consequences for the explanation of the mechanisms involved in aphasia; the conditions by which this possibility is constrained provide further insights into the character of these mechanisms.

Weigl's contribution belongs to the future of the field for a number of reasons. First of all the nature and the importance of his discovery is still not fully recognized. Secondly, there are quite a number of questions of the kind mentioned above that are still to be answered, and some are not even raised so far. Thirdly, a different type of problem is totally unsettled, viz. a causal account of the observed phenomena in terms of the underlying physiological mechanisms. This problem is finally connected to the challenging problem inherent in Weigl's discovery: Why is it that disturbed modes of speech processing can (or must) be deblocked piecemeal, although the modes of processing as well as the items to be processed obviously belong to integrated systems?

2. *The Speech Functional System.* The second level I would like to consider concerns Weigl's work as a theoretical neuropsychologist. Here again he shares a wide range of interests and goals with influential contemporaries. There is, however, one area of his interests that gives him a special place in the field. I'm talking about his conception of the complex system of speech functions or modes of speech processing. Although Weigl's ideas in this respect are by no means as unique as his work on deblocking – he insisted all the time on the great influence of Vygotski and his students, notably Luria, on his theorizing –, there are still specific contributions that are particularly due to him. Instead of pursuing the important, though highly controversial issues of localization, he developed a higly articulate functional picture of the different receptive and productive modes of speech processing, their interdependencies and separate characteristics, with transcoding as one of the key principles organizing the interaction of the various modes of speech behavior. He thus ended up with the view that language behavior is based on a system of partially autonomous, but closely interacting functions in terms of which not only normal speech production and perception, but also the different patterns of interferences are to be accounted for. The particular point is that these views are closely related to his experimental work in two ways. On the one hand, he was able to justify highly specific assumptions about the relative autonomy and the type of connectedness and integration of the different components of the system. On the other hand, it was this growing conception that gave him the perspective within which experimental results, and particularly the observations about deblocking, became remarkable facts. In a sense, for

him the deblocking phenomena and the speech functional system were two ends of one domain.

Two points are important to note. The first is, that Weigl's view of the speech functional system, and particularly the way he related it to deblocking and other experimental evidence, provided a natural place for the distinction between the language system and the different modes of its realization: If the different functions are governed by, or realizations of, certain invariant structures, then their particular modes of operation cannot be identified with these invariant structures. This perspective is very much in line with the distinction between competence and performance (or *langue* and *parole*) independently developed in linguistics. When he became aware of this coincidence, he gladly accepted the principled relation between the knowledge of a language and the system of speech functions emerging from this reconciliation. The second point is, that this reconciliation of two lines of theorizing provided not only a kind of missing link for Weigl's conception of the speech functional system, but enriched at the same time the fairly unspecified notion of linguistic performance, turning it into a highly organized system of neuropsychologically motivated mechanisms. Even if a large amount of problems related to speech production and perception cannot be solved by means available in neuropsychology, the ideas about the speech functional system and the facts on which they are based provide a fruitful framework for further elaboration and modification.

This brings up the point that makes Weigl's ideas a part of the future. Recent developments in cognitive sciences in general and in linguistics in particular emphasized the importance of what Chomsky has called the modular approach, i. e. the insight that complex behavior is the result of closely interacting autonomous systems. This line of thinking is currently applied to many problems of linguistic (and other) knowledge. Seen in this perspective, Weigl's conception of the speech functional system is an early paradigm case of this kind of theorizing in the domain of linguistic performance. Irrespective of all the modifications and refinements that undoubtedly will be made in the future, a set of fruitful facts and ideas is available to guide further developments.

3. *Language and Biology*. The third level of consideration concerns Weigl's general background and attitudes, his position as a philosopher (a term he would have been reluctant to accept).

Although he had clear and definite views also in this general respect, they are to be found for the most part implicit in his particular theoretical and experimental work. Besides a firm materialist point of view and a distinctive concern for progress and enlightment, his personal attitudes were characterized by a strong curiosity for new facts and unorthodox ideas. These are important, though by no means unique characteristics.

A personal feature emerges, however, if one considers the influence of these attitudes on his scientific efforts. It is not only that he liked 'cunning' experiments, or that he was sceptical about familiar and obvious opinions and interpretations. A more particular point relates to basic assumptions of his proper field, assumptions concerning the biology of man, and more specifically the biology of language. It goes without saying that he considered language, like any other intellectual and emotional capacity of man, as based on particular biological structures amenable to rational scientific analysis. There are, however, many different forms such a view might take. And here we find, only apparently superseded by the careful and strict analysis of data or rigid theoretical argumentation, Weigl's personal ingredient: He never reduced the enormous complexity of speech behavior, even in its most disturbed form, to the mechanisms he was able to account for. He always insisted on complementing the succinct details of experimental data and theoretical analysis with the maintenance of a wider perspective acknowledging the unexplained mysteries inherent in the field he was so seriously concerned with. This general attitude made him sensible for new and unexpected facts, led him to try out alternative ideas and new explanations. It was this constantly developing character of his thinking – which he maintained until his death – that gave his work its particular dignity and inspiration. The problem of explaining how language and other mental capacities are related to physiological mechanisms and biological foundations will be one of the challenging problems of the future of quite a number of disciplines. The way in which Weigl approached this problem all his life, insisting on strict experimentation and clear-cut theorizing without reducing the problem to triviality, guarantees his work a secure place in that development, even if many of his particular proposals and ideas will have to be changed or modified in the light of new insights.

Let me close these considerations with a few remarks that go even more beyond the content of the present volume. They concern the way Weigl's work is related to his personality. I had the chance to cooperate with him for more than fifteen years, and it is hard to say how much I profited during that period of never ending discussions. What possibly best characterizes his personal attitudes as a scientist is the way he managed to become acquainted with what was going on in linguistics. Once he realized that this was a field that had something to offer for his domain of interest, he became the most intensive interlocutor one can think of. In trying to convey to him whatever I was able to adduce, I myself learned a lot about linguistics, leave alone neuropsychology.

Fate has turned this prefatory remarks into an obituary. There are many respects in which his friends will miss his sceptical, challenging and productive advice and cooperation. Yet his work and his ideas will be with us for a long time.

Berlin, December 1979 M. B.

Introduction

I.

I may be allowed the liberty of introducing myself to the reader by giving a brief portrayal of myself; for this will add to, and possibly bring alive, these Selected Papers, which very much constitute a kind of longitudinal section through my scientific career.

Encouraged by the success that my father, the inventor of the first "seeing" colour-sorting machine, had had in answering technological problems, I decided to start studying at Munich's Technische Hochschule (Technological University) when I had finished high school. No sooner had I done so when I found myself following in the wake of Adler's individual psychology, which was at the time engaged in a fierce controversy with Freud's psychoanalysis and seemed to me to be more progressive than the latter. My personal acquaintance with Adler, which was to turn into co-operation later on (I was a co-editor of the "Handbuch der Individualpsychologie" published in 1926), and his deep insights into the intricate mechanism of the " nervous character" – insights that I found extremely fascinating – were the main reasons for my interest in psychology to prevail over that in engineering.

However much I may have been captivated by depth psychology, I finally realized that I took a particular interest in research into natural sciences. On obtaining my Vordiplom (pre-diploma), I left Technische Hochschule to go to Berlin, where I enrolled at the town's university to study experimental psychology and also higher mathematics and physics.

I was completely enthralled by the tremendous strides that were being made in experimental psychology under the aegis of eminent scientists like Max Wertheimer, Wolfgang Köhler, Kurt Lewin, and others. So I soon turned into a most devoted "fellow-combatant" of these exponents of gestalt psychology in their passionate controversy with the proponents of association psychology, which was considered "reactionary". I maintained a close friendship with Wertheimer, which allowed me to gain profound insights into the concepts and methods adopted in gestalt-psychological research, which he had laid the groundwork for.

But this was not the end of my search for personal specialization in the field of psychology. Word came from Frankfort on the Main of epoch-making new discoveries by other exponents of gestalt psychology, experimental psychologist Adhémar Gelb and neurologist Kurt Goldstein. And this gave me the idea of looking for a new academic home. The reception that I was given by the circle of these "fathers" of neuropsychology and their excellent assistants surpassed all my expectations. A very intimate friendship sprang up between myself and Kurt Goldstein, Director of the Frankfurt Institute for Research into the After-Effect of Brain Injuries, a scholar who took an exceedingly keen interest in psychological matters. I frequented his house as often as a son would; and on long evenings he personally initiated me into the details of the intensive research work he was carrying on.

I was soon allowed to take an immediate part in investigations into cases of aphasia, agnosia and apraxia – most of them patients suffering from brain damage as a result of gunshot wounds received in World War One – cases that were to become famous in science literature later on; and I had the chance of following the subsequent animated discussions on the results obtained in these investigations – discussions that were often attended by illustrious guests like philosopher Ernst Cassirer, graphological scientist Ludwig Klages, and others.

In 1927 I finished studying at Frankfort's university, writing my doctor's thesis "On the Psychology of So-Called Processes of Abstraction", which has to this day been enjoying a measure of appreciation.

Soon after I had obtained the academic degree of Doctor of Natural Sciences, Géza Révész, who had a professorial chair for experimental psychology at Amsterdam university, made me assistant lecturer at his university. I have ever since remained profoundly grateful to this versatile scientist – who was well-known for his studies in very different branches of psychology – because he gave me many an impulse in my work in terms of both theory and method. At Amsterdam's Zoological Garden I was given a chance of conducting my own experiments on monkeys in the field of animal psychology – my study "Identical Modes of Behavior in Man and Monkey in Choice Action" [173] dates from those days –; at the industrial enterprises in the town I tried my hand at what was called techno-psychology and helped write the book "Psychology of Enterprise Life" (1935), which was published by Révész.

In the late 1920's I was hired by the Central Institute for Education and Teaching in Berlin to investigate practice-related spheres of pedagogical psychology. Simultaneously, I resumed my co-operation with K. Goldstein, who had meanwhile been called to the town's university and was head of the Neurological Department of Moabit Hospital. I was writing my paper "Language and Sorting" [174] at the time.

This renewed meeting with the phenomenal scholar was, however, fated to come to an abrupt end. Nazism drove us apart in opposite directions. Goldstein had to flee to Holland and subsequently to the United States, while I went via Prague to Romania into an exile that was to last nearly thirty years.

In my first few years in that unfamiliar country I worked mainly in the area of psychopedagogics, following the lines of individual psychology, and was no more than sporadically able to examine questions of aphasia. Then Romania fell victim to nazism and entered the war against the Soviet Union on Hitler's side. An active member of the anti-fascist resistance movement, I was arrested and court-martialled, and spent some of the war years in a fascist prison.

After Romania had been liberated, I was so busy teaching at several Bucharest institutions of higher education that I had little, if any, time for research. The road back to my "calf love" – neuropsychology – opened to me only in the late 1950's, when I was given the opportunity of resuming my research work in that field at the Neurological Institute of the Romanian Academy of Sciences in Bucharest. I received a great deal of warmest support from my friend A. Kreindler, Director of the Institute and himself a well-known aphasiologist, and his very capable assistants A. Fradis, L. Mihăilescu and N. Gheorghiţă. I made a number of joint studies with Romanian aphasiologists in that period (see ⟨8⟩, ⟨13⟩, [195–198]).

After I had gone through decades of severest strain, in which I was in no position whatsoever to continue my scientific research, I now faced the serious challenge to catch up with the development that had in the meantime taken place in a field that was really and truly my own. Neuropsychology had flourished in Europe and even more so in the United States; and it had done so to an extent never thought possible before. Some readers might be interested to learn that a man who was not young any more found that severest frustrations in his previous life did not at all succeed in dampening his craving for scientific knowledge. I managed to catch up in a comparatively short space of time, not only because I read the relevant technical literature, which had by then turned into a veritable flood, but also because I got in touch again with colleagues working in the same field, visited Europe's major aphasia centres, took an active part in a large number of conferences, symposia and meetings arranged by the Research Group on Aphasia of the World Federation of Neurology, which I had been elected a member of, and never lost contact with the newly formed International Society of Neuropsychology, which made me one of its honorary members – all of this providing important opportunities for me to put up for discussion my own concepts, research methods and research results.

Although I did not find it possible to visit the numerous centres of neuropsychology in the United States – centres that had developed so rapidly over the previous two decades that they had left those in Europe far behind – I received ample compensation for that through both a constant exchange of publications with those centres and visits paid to me by my American colleagues.

While trying to catch up, I was on the receiving end of a great deal of support from Soviet neuropsychologists, with whom I am linked in close friendship. I was given most valuable scientific advice by A. R. Luria, who wrote an amazing number of superb papers, which made him one of the classic writers on neuropsychology. Luria had been one of my fellow-students at Berlin university many years before and later on became a friend of mine. I met him again when he came to Bucharest in 1957. Since then I never stopped exchanging ideas with him, either in person or by correspondence, until his death in 1977, which was very painful to me. I have paid repeated visits to aphasia centres in Moscow and Leningrad to study the exemplary work done there in the area of aphasia and to give lectures and demonstrations to explain my own research work.

Nearly three decades had passed when I returned to Berlin (in what was now the German Democratic Republic) in 1961, just before I was sixty.

The conditions that the GDR's Academy of Sciences provided for my work could not have been better. I was given additional support by K. Leonhard, Director of the Neurological Clinic of Charité, and his present successor H. A. F. Schulze, both of them authors of remarkable aphasiological studies. This put me in a position to set up a research laboratory of my own in the building of the Neurological Clinic.

I would now have been able to achieve the goal of my life's ambition, had it not been for the shortness of the time left until my retirement. Yet those few years were some of the most productive I have ever had in my work on research projects. In 1958, at the end of my Bucharest period, I had already succeeded in discovering the *phenomenon of deblocking:* I managed to prove that aphasia-caused speech disorders can be removed in experiment (see my first joint publication with A. Kreindler ⟨8⟩, and also ⟨9⟩, ⟨10⟩, ⟨14⟩). I thus started a special line of neuropsychological research, which to pursue was the prime object of the laboratory run by me. I carried out joint investigations with my assistants, who included R. Böttcher and I. Weigl. We standardized new aphasia test procedures (see ⟨5⟩) and verified the effects of the deblocking method (see ⟨2⟩ and Böttcher et al. [19]).

Some of the publications and lectures of those days dealt with diverse aspects of deblocking as a research method, which was subsequently extended to application in aphasic therapy as a result of investigations made by I. Weigl (see [201]).

If any further proof was needed to support the thesis defended by me earlier on that man can be productive in advanced age, I was now able to supply it. Although the much-loathed moment of my retirement had arrived, I found myself facing the challenge of studying the fundamentals of a branch of learning that had until then been wholly unfamiliar to me: linguistics.

True enough, I had been concerned with speech disorders all my life; but I realized only now that I had to close the gap existing between my own experience and knowledge, on the one hand, and that gained in linguistics, on the other. Admittedly, psychologists had begun turning their attention to linguistics as early as the 1950's, when the new scientific discipline of psycholinguistics emerged. But a further step had now to be taken, a step that gave rise to what then went by the name of neuropsycholinguistics and is now called neurolinguistics.

In my efforts to bridge the gap I had the privilege to be assited by an outstanding linguist, M. Bierwisch, of the Central Institute of Linguistics of the GDR Academy of Sciences. His sincere interest in neuropsychological research, his wellnigh unparalleled readiness to take part in experiments on aphasics and help programme and carry out linguistically sound investigations for the purpose, and also the most admirable patience he displayed in initiating me into the secrets of his subject – in particular into those of generative grammar – all this made it possible for me to indeed become a neurolinguist in the end.

After my retirement I began to thoroughly enjoy the advantages of the life of what might be termed as a "free-lance scholar". The following research projects have since claimed most of my attention. I concerned myself with both the question of transcoding, to which I devoted a number of publications written either on my own or in co-operation with my friend A. Fradis, and with that of the written language, i.e. its origin, acquisition and disorders. These two subjects are also discussed in some of the articles below. Since modern research has for quite some time been giving increasing attention to the question of memory, I have myself, over the last few years been studying the semantic memory in aphasics, relying on experimental material collected on earlier occasions (see ⟨16⟩).

The description of the gerontological evidence provided by my life and work would be incomplete, were I not to mention yet another factor. If I have managed to this day to preserve my keenness of mind to the full despite the incessant, merciless advance of the clock of my life, then I owe this – last, but by no means least – to Irina Weigl, my one-time student and subsequent assistant and severe critic. In my thirty-odd years of marriage to her she has given me continuing encouragement, not only during my academic come-back, but also to this day through her co-operation in my research projects and, over and above that, through her creative continuation, extension and reorganization of these projects, with me, in turn, taking a lively, unflagging interest in her own research work, which is mainly in child psychology.

At this point I should like to acknowledge a debt of gratitude to R. Böttcher, my student and former assistant lecturer, who is today head of a department of speech pathology at a local hospital and has in the meantime published a number of remarkable neurolinguistic papers. I wish to thank her for many years of fruitful co-operation and unfailing loyalty.

II.

A selection of an author's writings extending over a fairly long period and dealing with a comparatively wide variety of subjects can easily look like a random sampling of more or less isolated studies. To forestall this impression, I have divided the book into a number of sections that are each devoted to a particular topic, instead of presenting my papers in their chronological order. Without in the least underrating the reader's ability to detect for himself the central ideas running through all the articles like an unbroken thread, I think it will be quite appropriate for me to give a brief outline of common denominators as I see them.

Part of the basic views reflected in the studies printed below are described in the articles in Part One. Yet the papers that came out later raise a number of further issues of principle. That is why I feel that it will be quite worth-while giving yet another summary of my theoretical points of departure to help the reader towards a better understanding of the overall ideas. I will be explaining these points of departure especially in the light of my research into deblocking, although it goes without saying that my conceptional radius of action goes far beyond the boundaries of this research. The overall neuropsychological issues involved are essentially related to speech and its aphasia-caused disorders and therefore fall within the competence of *neurolinguistics.*

1. Linguistic competence and aphasia

The phenomenon of deblocking, if properly understood, does not refer to performances by round-about ways or compensation, but to the reactivation of disturbed linguistic – and sometimes even extra-linguistic – performances, which the aphasic was capable of as much as everybody else before he was taken ill. To put it another way, the conditions allowing that kind of reactivable performance cannot have been "lost" forever: they are merely *blocked,* wholly or partially, as a result of brain injury. This means that the faculty of speech underlying the particular impaired linguistic performance has been maintained, with only the access to one or several forms of its applications barred, subject to the kind of cerebral lesion involved.

This is not the right place to defend this basic idea against a number of criticisms that have been levelled against it. A convinced materialist, I should merely like to confine myself to pointing out that I do not regard the various capabilities of man as generally resistant to cerebral damage. I rather believe that the faculty of speech and other capabilities originate from a cortical storage of rules that can only be "extinguished" – if that is the word – if cerebral destruction is much more far-reaching than that resulting from the more or less limited local lesions we come across in cases of predominantly aphasic syndromes.

There is no denying the fact that the possibilities I have discovered of experimentally rehabilitating seemingly lost performance in aphasics have confirmed my interpretation of the disorders caused by cerebral damage and have encouraged me to extend my research into deblocking. And this is the general idea behind most of the studies printed below and especially behind the use that has recently begun to be made of deblocking in the field of aphasic therapy (see I. Weigl [201]).

Incidentally, neuropsychological evidence of the intactness of the faculty of speech vis-à-vis the impairment of language application in aphasics proves the psychological reality of linguistic differentiation between competence and performance (see Chomsky [28], and Weigl and Bierwisch ⟨3⟩).

2. *The speech functional system. Analysis of functional and componential structures*

The analyses of speech functions and their components in cases of aphasia – analyses underlying the investigations explained below – are mainly based on the view that psychic functions have a system character, which Soviet neuropsychologists have made indisputably meritorious efforts to reveal (Vygotski, Bernshteyn, Anokhin, Leontyev et al.).

In what has gone before I expressed the view that blocks caused by local cerebral lesions do not mean loss of the storage of ontogenetically acquired systems of rules. And this, I think, shows that it is generally possible to deblock certain failures of performance. In my very first paper on deblocking, which I wrote jointly with A. Kreindler a comparatively long time ago (Weigl and Kreindler ⟨8⟩), a neuropsychological

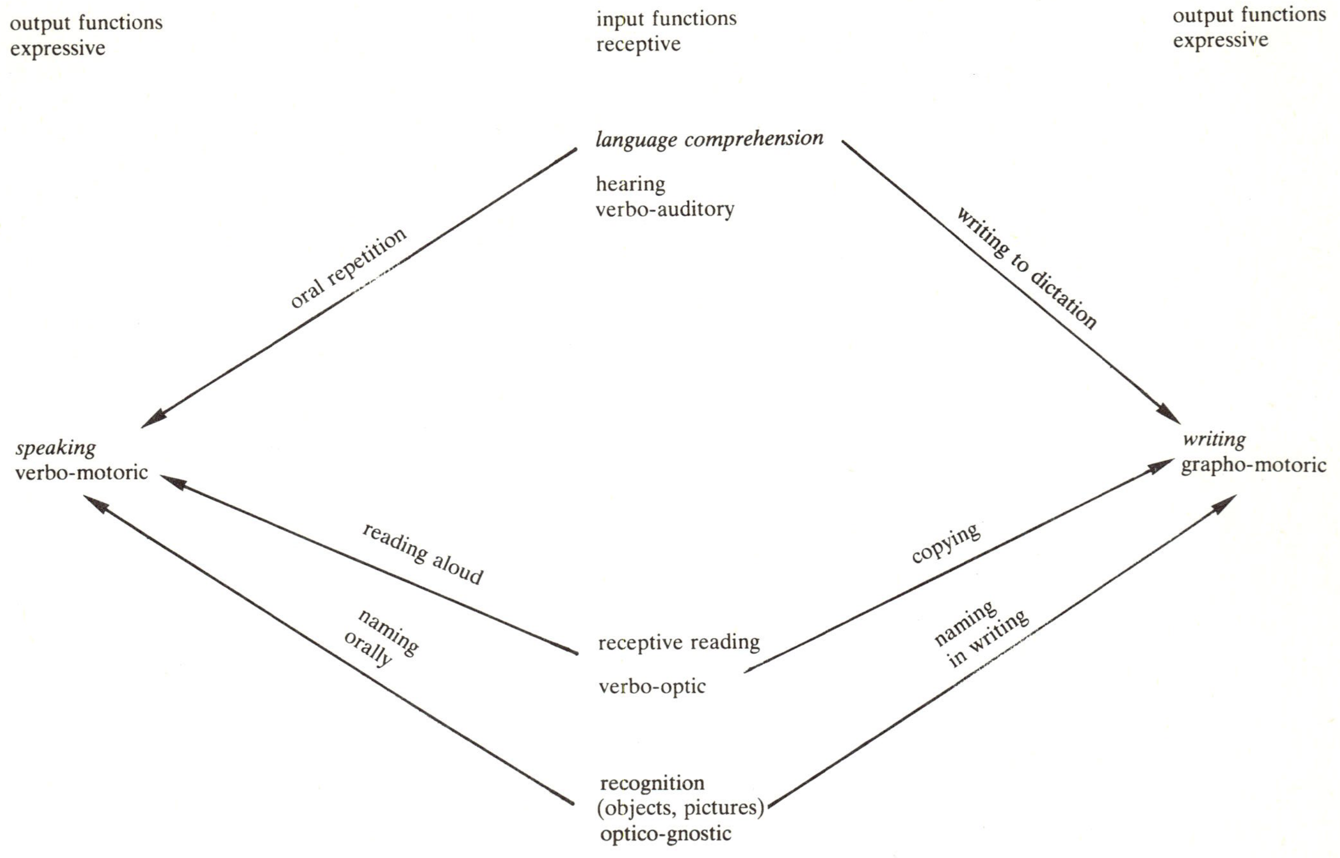

Fig. 1: *Componential structure of the system of reproductive speech functions*

interpretation of that phenomenon was attempted, which had been discovered by myself shortly before. Although the one-sided Pavlovist interpretation, which was made use of for the purpose, is now out of date, the idea of dynamic localization (cf. Luria [112]), i.e. the idea that the cortex is able to activate different morpho-functional structures in order to perform one and the same task, will, I think, continue to be valid. That means that pathological conditions resulting from focal lesion of the brain still permit a certain flexibility in the choice to be made from among alternative cerebral switching circuits, the very choice that deblocking makes use of.

The speech functional system is divided into sub-systems, which, for all their relative autonomy, are most closely interrelated (e.g. language comprehension and language production, the written and the spoken language) and have certain typical functional and componential structures (e.g. the sub-system of the spoken language has the functions of auditory language comprehension, spontaneous talking, oral repetition, naming, etc. and also verbo-auditory, verbo-motoric, grapho-motoric, etc. components) (see Fig. 1).

If you wish to understand aphasic syndromes you have to start from the selective disturbability of functional and componential structures, which results from their relative autonomy and is caused by local cortical damage (e.g. impairment of the verbo-expressive components of oral repetition, reading aloud and naming, with the verbo-receptive components of auditory, lexical and gnostic comprehension or recognition being intact).

The method of deblocking has to be seen as an appeal to the dynamics of the more or less seriously blocked overall speech functional system and its sub-systems with a view to reintegrating and reactivating the functions and components that have broken down.

Studying the papers on deblocking, the reader will be struck by the fact that my original views of the essence of the phenomenon have over the years undergone a considerable metamorphosis. Initially, I believed that the effects of deblocking are extremely short-lived and can only be brought about under severely restricted circumstances. Continuing my experiments, I realized, however, that the transience of the effects was merely due to an imperfection of method, of "simple" deblocking. A qualitative leap forward came when I made some in-depth research into my point of departure, which efforts culminated in my conceiving the principle of what might be called "stimulation on all channels". While the mere successive coupling of intact and disturbed performances (functions) produced nothing but limited deblocking effects, the incorporation of one or several disturbed performances in a "functional chain" raised the process of deblocking to a higher, more effective level.

It is a major success of this multi-functional method of stimulation – called *chain deblocking* – that its rehabilitating effects continue for months and years (see ⟨2⟩, ⟨20⟩, ⟨15⟩).

The implementation of the principle of multi-functional stimulation (on all channels) required a careful, systematic analysis of the state that the particular patient's functional and componential structures found themselves in (see ⟨6⟩). This, in turn, gave rise to the need for developing special test procedures that can be used to detect both the funtions that are intact and can therefore be employed as deblockants, and the functions that are disturbed and are to be deblocked. It will never be enough, just recording a patient's failure to perform one or several functions. What is needed is to take detailed stock of the state that all components are in, including those which certain different functions have in common. Only in this way is it possible to decide what components can act as suitable deblockants in a chain. In the case of a woman patient suffering from disorders of auditory word comprehension, oral repetition and writing to dictation (described in schematic form in Fig. 2), the intact verbo-optic components (reading comprehension) of expressive reading and copying served as deblockants for disturbed verbo-auditory components (comprehension in listening to words) of oral repetition and writing to dictation; expressive reading and copying here strengthened the verbo-motoric and grapho-motoric components, which were actually intact, but were subjected to secondary blocking in oral repetition and writing to dictation as a result of disorders in auditory word comprehension.

3. Processes of transcoding

Transitions within and between speech functional sub-systems (e.g. the spoken and the written language) take the form of processes of transcoding, whose probability of failure in the case of aphasia can be manifest in difficulties e.g. in changing from input to output functions (from intact language comprehension to oral repetition, reading aloud or writing to dictation, or from the spoken to the written language, etc.)

The need for aphasia-caused impairments of these transcoding processes to be taken account of can be instructively demonstrated when the method of chain deblocking is being used. There are cases when a patient, although he can be shown to have intact individual components of the functions in question, fails to effect certain switchings among them (see ⟨7⟩). In other words, these functional disorders differ from others in that they refer to the impairment of the processing operations going on between certain input and output functions that are in themselves

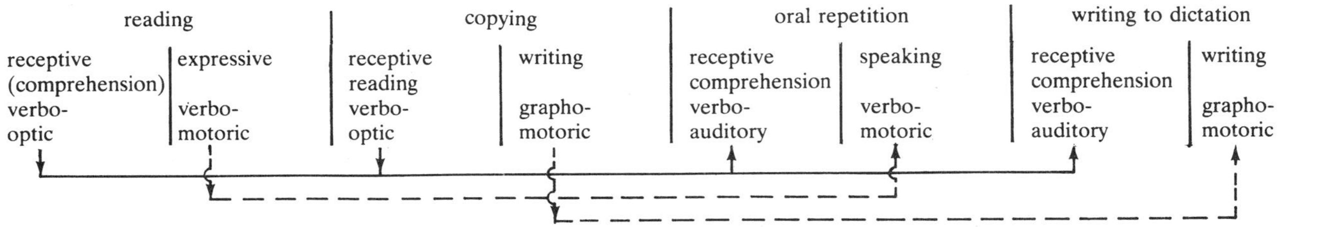

Fig. 2. *Pattern of deblocking in the case of sensory aphasia, with reading and copying intact*

Legend: unbroken lines: deblocking blocked components; broken lines: additional reinforcing of components that are under secondary blocking.

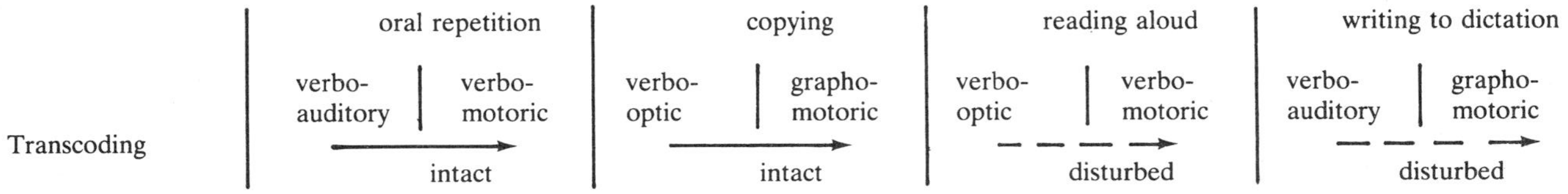

Fig. 3. *Selective transcoding disorders, with input and output functions intact*

intact. In consequence, it is necessary to deblock the particular transcoding disorders themselves. To illustrate, here is an example taken from hitherto unpublished investigations that I have made conjointly with I. Weigl. Patient W. suffered from disorders in reading aloud and writing to dictation, with his oral repetition and copying intact. Comparing the components of these functions (see Fig. 3), we found that both the verbo-auditory (language comprehension) and the verbo-motoric language components were intact (a fact that was revealed by his correct oral repetition, which contains either component). His correct copying proved that there were no disorders in the verbo-optic (receptive reading) and grapho-motoric (writing) components. But since reading aloud and writing to dictation are made up of these very components, his expressive-alexical and dictation-agraphic failures must have been due to impairments of the particular transcoding variants. These switching disorders were then deblocked by preceding blocked processes of transcoding with intact ones. The result was that patient W. was in this way capable of correctly reading aloud and writing to dictation the words in question.

4. Semantic fields and semantic memory

The utterances produced on the channels (modalities) of individual speech functions presuppose the storage not only of linguistic rules, but also of the lexically organized structural levels of the natural language in hand (semantic fields).

The experimental study of semantic fields – i.e. of the organization of the lexical structure of a language in the form of memory-stored relations among word units – was made possible by Luria and Vinogradova [118] by means of some neurophysiological (plethysmographic) method and by myself by means of a neuropsychological procedure (see ⟨15⟩, ⟨16⟩). Either method is well-suited to provide infallible evidence of the psycholinguistic reality of fields of this kind and, in consequence, to support corresponding psychological and linguistic hypotheses.

The neuropsychological method of deblocking semantic relations on the word level permits controlling these relations in a very special way in language comprehension and language production.

At this point the questions emerge of how these semantic fields are stored and how individual lexical units become retrievable (e.g. with regard to the naming of images in the case of aphasia). Such insights into semantic memory can be gained in investigations into aphasia-caused disorders in word finding and into ways of deblocking them (see Weigl ⟨16⟩). In investigations of this kind it is of special interest to establish what share short-term memory and what share long-term memory have in word retrieval that is controlled by the deblocking method (e.g. with regard to naming pictures).

5. Semantic, syntactic and functional radiation

Research into semantic fields did not only lead to the statements made above, but also proved the radiability of deblocking effects. As soon as a number of words from a certain field (e.g. clothing, food) are deblocked, a whole list of further, non-deblocked words from the same sphere can be released as a result of a process in which the retrievability brought about by the stimulation of partial areas of the semantic memory extends to ever larger lexically organized areas.

The deblocking method proved capable of stimulating analogous processes of radiation also on the semantic-syntactic level. When this was happening, patients did not only manage to provide an oral and written reproduction of a deblocked sentence, but also to subject it to spontaneous syntactic transformations (e.g. to turn a declarative sentence into an interrogative sentence, etc.) (see Bierwisch and I. Weigl [16], I. Weigl [202]).

This semantic radiation is matched by functional radiation. As mentioned above, chain deblocking is marked by intact and disturbed speech functions that relate to one and the same item following each other in this order (e.g. the correct auditory language comprehension, simultaneous oral repetition and writing to dictation of the word "skirt" is followed by the disturbed functions of the lexical comprehension, reading aloud and image naming of the word). In certain cases it is possible for blocked functions that have not been part of the chain before to share in the deblocking (e.g. the spontaneous reproduction of the word). In other words, the deblocking effect has in the particular patients radiated within the speech functional system because of existing interconnections in this system (functional radiation).

6. Forms of neurolinguistic interdependence

The handicap of patients vis-à-vis certain linguistic word classes (such as function words and particles) – an issue that already classic research workers in the field of aphasia, like A. Pick, hit upon when they were studying agrammatism, and that has never stopped being examined to this day (see Goodglass et al. [57], Marshall and Newcombe [119],

Böttcher [17], I. Weigl and Mihăilescu [201], Mihăilescu et al. [123], etc.) – this handicap is being shed new light upon by the research done into performance disorders of this kind on the individual channels (speech functions). Interdependence has been proved to exist (I. Weigl [202]) between the processing going on on linguistic levels (the lexical and syntactic levels) and the processing occurring within the different speech functions. To illustrate: a patient can fail when writing function words to dictation without, however, having any difficulty at all in reading them aloud or repeating them orally. In a similar vein, we can detect selective disorders relating only to certain functions, when word classes are being incorporated into the syntactic context (see I. Weigl, [202]).

Neurolinguistic evidence proving the existence of this kind of interdependence is of particular consequence for research into deblocking, since agrammatical disorders of the above description can here be eliminated with the aid of intact channels just because they are selective. (see I. Weigl [202])

A special explanation might be required for why I have added to this collection my paper "On the Psychology of So-Called Processes of Abstraction", my doctor's thesis, published in 1927. When I was writing it, I did not at all intend to turn those investigations into a "test procedure". Yet the experiments described there were later on gauged without my participation and were without any alteration included in a test battery to study "concrete and abstract behaviour" (they then figured as "the G.G.W.S. Object Sorting Test" and " the Weigl-Goldstein-Scheerer Colour Form Sorting Test" [see K. Goldstein and M. Scheerer: "Abstract and Concrete Behaviour. An Experimental Study with Special Tests", Washington 1941]). These procedures, which had been developed by myself, have to this day been used in the study of very different neuropsychological issues, starting from the dominance of the hemispheres right to matters of the psychologies of thought, development and language, and also for diagnostic purposes (see e.g. De Renzi et al. [32]).

Publishing this collection of writings, I pursue an aim quite different from that pursued by recently published treatises on the subject of neuropsychology and neurolinguistics. What I wish to do is to explain my personal contribution and that of my co-authors to this subject, thus familiarizing wider circles of public opinion with the concepts, methods and research results that I have produced over a fairly long period.

To compile this sampler, I did not only select papers written exclusively by myself. I also chose articles that are very much the result of my co-operation with neurologists, psychologists and linguists. In the latter articles my own views interlace with those of my co-authors in a most fruitful manner.

An anthology of this kind is of course bound to reveal that some of the views and conclusions in my earlier studies were added to, and occasionally even rendered obsolete, by later ones. But I feel that this will make it easy for the reader to gain an insight into the ways scientific concepts develop.

Naturally enough, the chapters and sections into which my writings have been sub-divided are only roughly in line with their contents; and there are a number of unavoidable repetitions.

Finally, I should like to extend my most cordial gratitude for the publication of this selection of my articles – all but one of them were written over the last twenty years – to Mouton Publishers and especially to C. H. van Schooneveld, editor of the Janua Linguarum series, on whose initiative this book has been published.

Note

Throughout the book we use the following method of bibliographical citation: numbers in '⟨. . .⟩' refer to papers contained in this volume, numbers in '[. . .]' refer to the cumulative bibliography at the end of the volume.

PART ONE

Neuropsychology and Neurolinguistics

⟨1⟩

E. WEIGL

On the Future of Neuropsychology

In a recently published work, A. R. Luria [113] made some observations on "The Future of Clinical Neuropsychology". I should like to expand these observations by attempting to draft a future picture of a possible structure for the scientific field of neuropsychology.

Like a number of disciplines which have come into existence in recent decades of this century in the course of the speedy development of modern science, neuropsychology has to wage a stubborn battle to prove and establish its independent character, its specific structure and method, and to ensure its prospects.

It is easy to understand that the attempt to clarify the position and the prospects of new disciplines can certainly not be rejected as theoretical speculation. Insofar as a recent branch of science receives recognition at all for its viability and its possibilities for development, questions immediately arise as to its institutional placing, the support it should receive from the state and public bodies, the integration of this field in the teaching structure of university studies, the establishment of certain practical fields of use, etc. In particular, branches of research which mainly base themselves upon experimental investigation raise concrete questions: the sponsorship of the planned activities, who approves and finances them, in which overall plan of scientific activity they should be included, etc. It is important, with regard to young scientists, to decide upon the overall professional status of such specialists, their academic standing and their institutional alignment, etc. [cf. also 152].

Decisions with regard to these questions must necessarily be of an empirical character as long as the subject of research of the relevant science, and its structure, have not been clarified or are even still in dispute.

All this, of course, holds true with regard to neuropsychology; its history extends back to the middle of the previous century, but it is only in the past few years that it has begun to win sharper contours under the name neuropsychology.

The difficulties which arise in the attempt to define this branch of science are clearly closely connected with the fact that the process of separation from its 'mother sciences' proceeded relatively slowly.

Stemming as it does from the medical brain research of the previous century, particularly brain pathology – in the more restricted sense, from the research into aphasia, agnosia, and apraxia – the neuropsychology of today has found it difficult to liberate itself from its 'medical eggshell' and the claim of medicine to have the sole rights in this science.

On the other hand, the intensive occupation of renowned psychologists (A. Gelb, L. W. Wygotski, etc.) with neuropsychological clinical pathological research since the 1920s has tended to lead psychology, the second 'mother science', to declare neuropsychology as a section of itself.

In attempting to justify neuropsychology as an independent discipline it is absolutely necessary to demarcate it clearly from the mother sciences mentioned.

The main task of medical brain research lies in the study of the anatomy, the histology, the physiology, and biochemistry of the brain, while the endeavours of psychology are devoted to research into the processes of the senses and of action, thought, and memory, etc.; the specific theme of neuropsychology, on the other hand, is research into the connections and the interdependence between the subjects of study of these two disciplines. As a result of the decisive role played by speech in connection with the higher psychic functions of man, one of the most important subfields of neuropsychology is the study of the relationship between speech attitudes and the underlying cerebral preconditions.

In accordance with this viewpoint, neuropsychology is *the science of the relationship between the brain, as the material basis, and the higher psychic functions, the psychic behavior of man and of animals (by way of comparison.)* In this sense Hécaen [62] defined neuropsychology as "la discipline qui traite des fonctions psychologiques supérieures dans leur rélations avec les structures cérébrales" (Abstr. 26, 110) in his lecture "Développement de la Neuropsychologie comme champ de recherches disciplinaires" at the XVIII International Congress for Psychology in Moscow (1966).

The subject of neuropsychology is defined in a similar manner in the *Bulletin of the International Society for Neuropsychology* (1965): "The interdisciplinary study of the relationship of central nervous system mechanisms and behaviour, including behaviour related to brain dysfunctions or pathology", and by Luria [113]: ". . . a new branch of science with the specific and unique aim of investigating the role of individual brain systems in complex forms of mental activity" (p. 16).

Many other neuropsychologists have defined the subject of their discipline in a similar manner, though as a rule the reference to the clinical-pathological aspect is dominant. This is also true of Hécaen, who stated in the congress speech already cited: ". . . elle est base sur l'étude des comportements secondaires à l'attainte des ces structures par la maladie (neuropsychologie humaine) ou a leur modification experimentale (neuropsychologie animale)" (ibid). Undoubtedly this restriction of the research subject of neuropsychology in the sense of a predominantly clinical-pathological discipline still has its justification today, since investigations with cerebrally damaged persons, and animals with experimentally induced cerebral change have hitherto been the most important source of neuropsychological knowledge. We believe, however, that confining this discipline to the purely pathological aspect would be inadequate and a restriction for the future, since it would mean that research into the general systematic relations and study of the genesis of these relations – to which we shall refer below – would not be given due weight.

The first definitions of neuropsychology quoted above indicate that one of its main areas must be general basic research in the sense of a *general systematic neuropsychology,* that is to say the study of the relations between the brain and the psychic functions under normal conditions, particularly since the lessons to be learned from a damaged or 'stimulated' brain permit generalisations only with certain reservations [see 63, p. 20 f.].

Although general neuropsychology has not yet established itself as a special branch of neuropsychology, there are already indications of a development in this direction (cf. inter al. the works of Luria and his co-workers with regard to the importance of the prefrontal portions of the cortex and the tertiary cortical fields for programming, regulating, and controlling cognitive processes).

Investigation of the mutual interconnection between the phylogenesis and ontogenesis of the brain on the one hand, and the psychic functions, psychic behavior, on the other, form the basic research subject for a *genetic neuropsychology*. Many questions still await solution, such as the cortical conditionality of the age-connected features of the child, the occurrence of 'optimal phases' (for instance with regard to storage capability), and many other problems of this sort; but this only indicates that neuropsychology still stands at the beginning of its specific tasks.

It is only relatively recently that a discipline called neuro-linguistics or neuro-psycho-linguistics has crystallised as the result of increasingly close and intensive contact between medical and psychological brain research on the one hand, and linguistics or psycho-linguistics on the other. There is a fruitful mutual flow of information between these research fields, which serves the solution of specific specialist problems; but beyond this there is, as one of the main tasks of this interdisciplinary cooperation, the question of the cerebral representation of human speech behavior. Since this problem involves the study of the cerebral prerequisites for speech, which is one of the most important human psychic functions, neuro-linguistics or neuro-psycho-linguistics can be regarded as part of general neuropsychology (e.g., cortical conditions of speech competence and speech utilisation); of genetic neuropsychology (speech acquisition); and clinical-pathological neuropsychology (aphasia in the strict sense).

"It has recently become the habit in natural science circles" (Pick wrote in 1913) " to treat philological studies with a contempt which the present writer certainly cannot share. The fact is completely overlooked that as a natural scientist one can gain greatly from the results of these sciences, if one only adopts the correct standpoint towards their material; and the correct standpoint can only be that we are dealing here with products which in their origin and function prove themselves natural, like every other function of the brain" [135, p. 32 f.].

In the more recent period it was mainly Jakobson [74, 71] who took the initiative in interdisciplinary cooperation between aphasia research and modern linguistics. Jakobson explains the relatively late date of the inclusion of linguistics in brain research by the fact the investigation of aphasia called for a structural analysis of language, something only worked out in the later phases of development of linguistics.

To round off the picture of the future structure of neuropsychology as I see it, it is necessary to emphasize its close links with therapeutic, pedagogic, and work-psychological practice.

Clinical-pathological neuropsychology is not directly a participant in the practice of diagnosis and rehabilitation of the psychic results of brain damage, but it can supply important guiding principles in this respect. This applies both to the construction of test batteries, and also to the construction of programmed rehabilitation methods, etc. (cf. in this connection Luria [113]).

These relations with clinical practice have been in existence and fruitful for a longer period; but for the time being the information flow from genetic neuropsychology to pedagogy is a desideratum. This can undoubtedly be explained by the fact that genetic neuropsychology is itself in the early stages of development. It can be foreseen, however, that the findings on the cerebral prerequisites of the psychic behavior pattern – taking full account of the role of social influence – will allow us to draw important conclusions for the optimalisation of educational and training processes, ranging from motor dexterity to the cognitive process of problem solution.

Recently scientists active in the field of work psychology have drawn attention to the "surprisingly multifold practicable consequences (for instance for requirement analyses, qualification measures, work assessments or analyses of actions in error" [60, p. 17] which result from the utilisation of neuropsychological research results and concepts. Here too a broad field of prospects opens up for "applied neuropsychology".

In accordance with the considerations detailed above, the future structure of neuropsycholgy presents itself as follows. The investigation of the relations between brain and psychic behaviour:

1. under normal conditions: *general systematic neuropsychology* as basic research.
2. under development conditions: *genetic* neuropsychology.
3. under pathological conditions: *clinical-pathological* neuropsychology.
4. under practical conditions: *applied* neuropsychology.

As stated above, observations on the position, structure, and prospects of a scientific discipline must certainly not be banished to the field of theoretical schematic speculation. It is well known that the content of the modern science of science is the study of the system of science with regard to its historic development, to changes in its overall structure, to the processes of 'disintegrative and integrative differentiation' of the individual sciences at interdisciplinary level, to the constant creation of new special fields of an independent character, in particular with reference to the multiplicity of their conditions of existence (communication area) [34, 138, 209].

Neuropsychology can serve as an instructive example for the form and manner in which new branches of science crystallise from their mother sciences and are themselves subject to the process of internal differentiation and structuration.

I believe that the future of neuropsychology should be assessed from this viewpoint.

Notes

1. In this respect Lenneberg's work, *Biological Foundations of Language* [98], for instance, represents a contribution to genetic neuropsychology.
2. At the beginning of the present century important brain researchers such as Pick, Binswanger, Goldstein, Isserlin, Lotmar, and others, already strongly supported the view that proper linguistic knowledge was indispensable for the understanding of aphasically caused speech disturbance.

⟨2⟩

E. WEIGL

Contributions to Neuropsychological Basic Research

1. Introduction

Neuropsychology has its starting point in the achievements of the brain pathology created in the second half of the previous century and the beginning of this century by the classical figures in neurology and psychiatry from Broca, Jackson, Bastian, and Wernicke to Pierre Marie, von Monakow, Head, Goldstein, Kleist, Bonhoeffer, and others. For a long period, brain pathology remained the monopoly of the neurologists and psychiatrists who, with regard to the psychological sequelae of cerebral damage, either borrowed from contemporary psychology or constructed psychological theories for themselves. The psychologists only began to participate in this branch of research relatively late, in the early 1920s. This was the starting period for the neuropsychology of today.

In 1918 the "Institute for Research into the Sequelae of Brain Damage" was founded, and here the outstanding neurologist Goldstein, who died a short while ago, and the outstanding experimental psychologist Gelb worked together to provide the ideal pattern for that direction of research which we now call neuropsychology. In 1926 Gelb wrote that the behavior of brain-damaged persons "appears as the special expression of an all-inclusive law which governs the differing modes of behavior of both the healthy and the sick under differing conditions" [44, p. 26].

At about the same time the great Soviet psychologist Vygotsky began his examination of brain-damaged persons in the Moscow clinic of Rossolimo. He soon developed his basic theses on "Psychology and Localisation of Functions" which arose in the course of a critical discussion of 'localisationism' on one hand and 'equipotentialism' on the other. Six weeks before his early death, Vygotsky, who is regarded by Soviet neuropsychology as its founder, wrote: "It seems to me that the problem of localisation as a general rule includes all that is connected with the study of higher psychological functions and with the study of their disintegration" [109, p. 387].

One of Vygotsky's pupils, the Soviet psychologist and physician Luria, played a leading part in the further development of neuropsychology as a science. Luria's book "Higher Cortical Functions in Man, and Their Disturbance Due to Focal Damage of the Brain" [112] can be regarded as a standard work of neuropsychology.

In the following decades close cooperation between representatives of various branches of neurology (neuroanatomy, neurophysiology, neurosurgery, etc.) and psychology proved increasingly necessary and fruitful in the study of cortically conditioned disturbances of higher cortical functions. At the same time there was a growing tendency to draw in specialists from other neighbouring disciplines to clarifiy all sorts of overlapping problems; this applied in particular to specialists in linguistics [see 71; 72]. In the past decade there have been many international symposia and colloquia, e.g., in 1958 in Boston [132], 1960 in Bucharest [87], 1962 in London, 1964 in Varenna, Italy[1]. These meetings were attended by notable representatives of neurology, neurophysiology, neurosurgery, psychology, linguistics, phonetics, information theory, philosophy, etc. In this respect a high point was reached by the XVIII International Congress for Psychology in Moscow in 1966, at which basic problems of neuropsychology were discussed, particularly in the symposium *Psychopathology and Psychological Processes* in the papers of Pichot, Teuber, Luria, Hécaen, etc.

In recent years international periodicals devoted to neuropsychology have appeared (*Neuropsychologia* and *Cortex*), published by representatives of neuropsychology and its tangential fields in the natural and social sciences. In addition an "International Society for Neuropsychology" has been etablished under the chairmanship of the well-known neurophysiologist Pribram (the psychological side is represented on the executive committee by Luria and Yates). In several countries chairs of neuropsychology have been established, and many neurological and neurosurgical clinics now have neuropsychological departments.

There is a visible increase in the number of neuropsychological centres with specialised thematics, some of them headed by psychologists, and some by neurologists or neurosurgeons. There are such centres in the USSR (Luria, Traugott, Beyn, Kogan, Kryshova, etc.), Roumania (Kreindler), Poland (Stepien, Konorski, Maruszewski), the USA (Teuber, Benton, Wepman, etc.), Britain (Critchley, Zangwill), France (Ajuriaguerra, Hécaen, Barbizet, Lhermitte, etc.), Italy (De Renzi), Austria (Hoff), the Federal Republic of Germany (Bay, Leischner), and elsewhere.

The number of neuropsychological themes is so great that a paper could be devoted to their classification alone. We believe that the importance of the many publications in this field is centred in the fact that to a growing degree the attempt is made to carry out *comparative experiments* – partly correlation-statistical – with regard to affectivity, behavior, perception, memory, speech, etc. This is undertaken on one hand with brain-damaged persons with or without aphasia, with lesions of the dominant or nondominant hemispheres and with ectomised or disconnected hemispheres; and on the other hand with normal children and adults, with the deaf and blind, with morons and psychotics, and finally with animals with experimentally caused brain lesions. In this way our knowledge has been deepened with regard to the dependence of the normal course of various psychic processes on certain brain structures and their interrelationships, and also with regard to the nature of these processes themselves, the 'general factors' (Luria) on which they are based, and the laws governing them [27].

Particular importance attaches to the results of neuropsychological research in view of the dialectical-materialist foundation of modern science. The damaging of various structures of the human brain produces pathological changes of a gnosic, praxic, cognitive, and particularly of a speech nature; and these changes show unusually clearly the dependence of these social functions upon their material substrate. Like many other newer branches of research, neuropsychology may be regarded as a paradigm of the simultaneous specialisation and integration of modern science.

The present work is not designed as a compilation on the problems and results of neuropsychology. It is an attempt to illustrate, from the activities of our own research centre, the neuropsychological treatment of basic questions which affect interdisciplinary themes going beyond our narrow branch of science. For the sake of brevity we must omit here the reproduction of our test results, achieved by experiments and where possible supported by statistics [see 19]. For the same reason we must to a large degree refrain from a discussion of the dependence which we have ascertained of the neuropsychological facts upon the brain structures.

The direction of neuropsychological research we suggest is based on the modern view of the higher cortical functions in man as a verified dynamic system[2] of ontogenetically created polyfunctional re-afferent connections. These links give, in the case of brain-pathological psychic disturbance ('blockings'), many possibilities for utilisation of *experimental 'deblocking'*, particularly of impaired speech functions.

Since in the following discussion will be mainly based on the use of the *deblocking methods* which we have developed, we shall, for the sake of better comprehension, first describe these methods [see ⟨9⟩, 179].

2. Explanatory remarks on the deblocking method as a neuropsychological procedure for the study of aphasic disturbances

2.1. The deblocking phenomenon (d-phenomenon)
The disturbance occurring in brain-damaged persons of higher cortical performances of individual or several functions (syndromes), e.g., of the speech function, can be deblocked under certain experimental conditions to a greater or lesser degree and for a longer or shorter period.[3]

There are patients unable to understand or repeat certain spoken words or sentences, to read them silently or aloud, to copy them or write them to dictation, to name objects or pictures either orally or in writing, etc. Under suitable experimental conditions it is possible to bring such patients to perform correctly these otherwise blocked tasks – that is, to understand, to repeat, to read, to write, to name, etc.

2.2. Basic conditions for the experimental production of the deblocking effect (d-effect)
2.2.1. One or more intact 'approach pathways' must be found to the disturbed performances of a certain function, that is to say that the performances of the patient which one wishes to deblock may not be cancelled or impaired 'on all channels'. For instance, a patient who is not able to understand auditorily words or sentences asa result of his sensory-aphasic disturbance should be able to grasp the meaning of these words or sentences when he reads them, to copy them, to name a picture corresponding to the word, etc.; the patient must have intact functions which make it possible for him to implement the performances otherwise cancelled.
2.2.2. The performance of the intact function must precede in time that of the disturbed function: to deblock the disturbance of a certain speech skill, the patient must first produce this performance over an intact 'channel' (or several intact channels), and then solve the problem of producing the result over the blocked channel, a performance not otherwise possible.
2.2.3. Whether a function is suitable as a deblocking agent depends upon a total or considerable state of intactness, not, however, upon its kind of function, its linguistic level, a certain analyser, etc. for instance, the performances of the intact tactile analyser (recognising by touch a certain object), can deblock the disturbed skills of the acoustic analyser (recognising a sound which identifies the relevant touched object), and vice versa. A quasi-verbal deblockant (e.g., picture recognition) can deblock corresponding disturbed verbal performances (e.g., repetition of the word corresponding to the picture), and vice versa. The intact performances of verbo-receptive functions (e.g., auditory word com-

prehension) can lead to the deblocking of the corresponding performances, of verbo-expressive functions (e.g., reading aloud), and vice versa. Intact performances on the graphemic level (e.g., visual word comprehension) can deblock corresponding performances on the phonetic level (e.g., auditory word comprehension), and vice versa.

2.2.4. The skills of the intact and disturbed functions must stand in a certain degree of relationship: The simplest case in this respect is present when the intact performance of reading a certain word *(table)* leads to deblocking of the disturbed performance of the written naming of the corresponding picture of a table (identity). However, such d-effects can be produced under considerably more complicated conditions. For instance, the correct reading of the words *sharp – tears – biting – cut – fry* can deblock the otherwise disturbed naming of the picture of an onion. In the same way the offering of a certain verb *(button up)* can deblock its antonym *(unbutton)* and the offering of a generic name *(furniture)* can deblock a specific name *(chair)*, etc. This condition of relationship applies not only to the deblocking of individual words of the most various categories (nouns, verbs, concreta and abstracta, etc.) but also for sentences of varying structure (declarative, interrogative, imperative, subordinate sentences, etc.).

2.2.5. Chain deblocking [see ⟨10⟩]: Through the performance of one or more intact functions it is possible to deblock one after the other, not simply the corresponding performances of a single disturbed function, but a whole 'chain' of impaired functions. Take for example a patient whose reading comprehension and copying are intact, but whose oral and written naming, repetition, writing to dictation, and reading aloud are disturbed; after he has read silently a certain word and then copied it, he is subsequently capable of naming correctly the corresponding picture both orally and in writing, to repeat the word, to write it on dictation, and read it aloud.

2.2.6. Effectiveness and stability of the d-effect: The *effectiveness* of the d-effect, that is, the number of successful deblockings expressed as a proportion of the total of d-tests, reaches in optimal cases nearly 100%.

The *stability* of the d-effect, which can be determined by subsequent control tests immediately after the conclusion of the d-tests, and later at longer intervals without 'exercise', can, in our experience, still be demonstrated more than two years later with various patients.

2.3. The technique of the deblocking method

2.3.1. General aphasiological examination of the patients to determine intact and disturbed functions as a preliminary to deblocking.

2.3.2. Statistically significant precontrol: First the degree to which the individual functions of the patient are intact or impaired is determined by quantitative controls of performance (up to 100 items).

Following this, pictures, words, sentences, etc. are chosen from the great number used previously and two groups are formed: (a) items which can serve as 'deblockants' (intact functions); (b) those items which are identical with or semantically related to those named under (a) and with regard to which the patient had completely failed in the precontrol despite repeated tests (disturbed functions).

2.3.3. Deblocking: First input: from the items *of intact* individual function determined in the precontrol a critical item is selected and offered to the patient embedded in a series of 'neutral' items.

Second input: from the complex of disturbed individual performances the corresponding critical item to be deblocked is offered via the particular blocked channel

D-effect: if deblocking is successful, the blocked individual performance will be carried out correctly.

2.3.4. Postcontrols: After the experimental series is completed, but on the same day, all deblocked individual performances are tested once again, and the deblocking rate, that is to say the number of retained deblockings, is registered. To study the post-d-effect the same deblocked individual performances are rechecked for stability at varying intervals.

2.3.5. Prevention of pseudo-deblocking (round-about-way performance). Obviously an alexic patient who has correctly repeated a certain word in the first input can, in the second input, apparently read the identical written word correctly, though in fact he is simply reiterating the word he had previously repeated. In this and similar cases there has not been a re-actualisation of a disturbed function, but a *substitution* on an intact channel. To exclude such round-about-way performances, in our deblocking tests we present the critical word (sentence or picture) in the first input together with a series of other 'neutral' words, so that the patient cannot know in advance which will be the critical word. As a result of their impaired short-term memory, most patients are not able to memorise all items (three or five) offered in the first input.

Another safeguard against pseudo-deblocking is that the position of the critical item in the series is varied from test to test. In addition, 'neutral' series are inserted between the actual deblocking series. In these neutral series, the items offered in the first input have no relationship to those offered in the second input (in such a case the patient naturally fails); in this manner, a possible tendency to memorise the items is weakened or eliminated.

2.3.6. As we have learned from many remarks made by patients, the processes connected with deblocking proceed on an *unconscious, stereotyped, automated* level. Patients are repeatedly astonished at their success when a performance is deblocked.

2.4. Examples of deblocking experiments (excerpts from the experiment reports)

2.4.1. Simple deblocking

Experiment report: Woman patient Be. Sensory aphasia, restituted to a considerable degree, with expressive paraphasic and amnestic disturbances.

Precontrols:

a) auditory word comprehension: completely intact (with concreta); repetition: completely intact.
b) picture naming: in 70% of the cases severely disturbed (total word-dumbness, verbal paraphasia or circumlocution.

   Deblocking:

   First input: *prestimulation* of the speech system by word hearing and repetition.

   Repetition: *Geier – Bäcker – Löwenzahn – Kröte – Weißkohl* [vulture – baker – dandelion – toad – cabbage]; the patient understands and repeats the words correctly.

   Second input: the *deblocking* of the semantically identical performance: naming.

   Presentation of the picture of a dandelion which the patient had recognised in the precontrol, but been unable to name ("Yes, they are small . . . yes, what is the . . . what are they called . . .").

   The patient names the picture correctly, though she is not able to name other, nondeblocked, pictures.

   D-effect: *positive* with regard to the naming of the picture in question.

2.4.2. Chain deblocking

Experiment report: Patient Ha. Motor aphasia.

Precontrols:

a) the following functions prove to be fully intact: auditory word comprehension, repetition, visual word comprehension, copying.
b) the following functions prove to be largely or completely disturbed: reading aloud (60%), oral naming (80%), written naming (100%), writing to dictation (100%), reading aloud what he has written (100%).

Chain deblocking:

First input series: *prestimulation* of the speech system by identical performances of the intact functions.

Coyping: *Lunge – Kuchen – Maurer* [lung – cake – mason] (correct).

Visual word comprehension: presentation of the words *Bank* – *Wolf* – *Rosinen* – *Kuchen* [bank – wolf – raisins – cake]. The patient is requested to match *Kuchen*; he correctly matches it with *Rosinen*.
Oral repetition: *Kuchen* (correct)

Second input series: the *deblocking* of the semantically identical performances of the disturbed functions. In the precontrol the patient had not understood the word *Kuchen* [cake]; he was also unable to read it aloud, write it to dictation, grasp the meaning of the word which he had correctly copied, or name orally or in writing the corresponding picture.

Deblocking:	Performance
written naming of a picture showing a cake	correct
reading *Kuchen* [cake] aloud	correct
oral naming of a picture showing a cake	correct
reading aloud *Kuchen* [cake] written himself	correct

D-effect: *positive* with regard to all performances of the disturbed functions in question.

3. On the problem of the liability to disturbance; the dynamic and structure of the speech-functional system

3.1. Liability of the system to disturbance

From the standpoint of the socially conditioned speech communication process, aphasia is seen as a total or partial impairment of the reception or transmission of speech signals. From the neuropsychological standpoint the speech process is based upon a comprehensive complex system – [211] speaks of a ‘mechanism’ – of analysers, levels, functions, components, subcomponents, etc., with its own structure and dynamic.

One of the questions which arises is this: in a case of aphasia, is the ‘ system’ affected as a whole, and are partial functions which possibly still exist to be regarded as ‘remnants’? Or is it possible to prove that in cases of aphasia there is generally not a ‘total loss’ of the speech system as a whole, and that in fact only certain ‘limbs’ are affected to a greater or lesser degree?

A number of arguments from neuropsychological research can be cited to show that the ‘total loss’ concept may be rejected. As we know, each individual speech system comes into existence ontogenetically as a comprehensive, very complex, and complicated whole based on social, affective, gnosic, cognitive, etc., conditions. This means that this system must be founded on a comprehensive 'construction plan', the 'loss' of which is only conceivable as the result of a breakdown of the higher cortical functions as a whole, a breakdown going far beyond the sphere of speech.

There are frequent cases of spontaneous restitution, even after a period of total aphasia, and these cases speak against the probability of a destruction of the 'construction plan' mentioned above.

In addition, most patients retain whole fields, either in spoken speech (e.g., repetition or auditory word comprehension) or in written speech (reading or writing); and these are fields which developed in childhood in connection with the overall function of the system, not in isolation.

A particular experimental contribution to the solution of the problem is presented by our discovery that even in severe cases of aphasia there is a possibility of re-actualising 'blocked' speech performances and speech functions. Such deblockings depend upon the existence of a wide-spread speech functional system, often corresponding to brain areas far apart from each other. The fact that deblockings can, in practise, take place over the most different channels (analysers), levels, and functions also gives support to this assumption. We draw the conclusion that aphasia basically consists in the 'blocking' of particular portions of a system, but not in the destruction of the system as a whole (see ⟨8⟩).

The results of our deblocking experiments also affect the problem of the 'loss' of individual speech functions. The possibility of deblocking performances of various impaired single functions in speaking and writing (e.g. including picture agnosia) [see 178], excludes the assumption of a total destruction and favours the view that such 'losses' are blocking phenomena.

3.2. The dynamic of the system

In our experiments we set ourselves the aim of finding the answer to the question of the *reaction of the entire system of speech functions to single or combined verbal stimuli.* In normal persons this is not easy, since the cooperation inside the system between 'factors' (Luria), analysers, linguistic levels, components, etc., is almost limitless. However, nature has provided us, in the special conditions presented by pathological cases, with much more favorable prerequisites for experimental investigation of the dynamic of the system.

In this regard use of the deblocking method gives us insights difficult to obtain in any other manner. From our many results we offer an example which appears to us to be of importance for clarifying the character of the dynamic of the speech system.

As we have shown above with several examples, we are able under certain experimental conditions to deblock not simply a single performance in a patient, but successively to deblock a whole 'chain' of performances in his disturbed functions. This finding means more than the simple notification of a 'phenomenon'. What it demonstrates is that the prestimulation produced via the intact input does not simply work in the direction of a certain output, but that it simultaneously continues in the other receptive and expressive channels of spoken and written language, that it sets these channels "in a state of readiness" (⟨10⟩). This is the only explanation for the fact that, as shown above, intact reading comprehension of a certain word and its copying are capable of deblocking the otherwise blocked performances of naming the picture of the object orally and in writing, of writing it to dictation, of its repetition and auditory comprehension. As the result of such experimental findings we believe we are entitled to claim *that the stimuli emanating from a certain intact speech or semispeech complex stimulus have an irradiating effect on the entire the speech-functional system and are capable of setting simultaneously in a state of readiness the manifold functions of this system over the various channels (inputs).*

We were able to confirm such *polyfunctional irradiation effects* in an impressive manner with the aid of a specially developed utilisation of the method of chain deblocking. The process is that individual functions are excluded from the chain of the performances of various disturbed functions which should be deblocked (e.g., naming, repetition, reading aloud). After the chain deblocking has been successfully accomplished, the corresponding performances of this function which has not been directly deblocked are tested (e.g., writing to dictation, spontaneous reproduction, etc.). It then appears that these performances were 'co-deblocked', or in other words that the stimuli experimentally provided by us had affected the speech-functional system *as a whole.*

The validity of this finding can obviously not be simply confined to pathological conditions. It must be a characteristic of the speech-functional system per se, including the normal speech system, though this has not yet been proved experimentally.

3.3. Structure of the system

Despite the comprehensive dynamic of the speech-functional system, the structure of this system displays on one hand the picture of extraordinary complexity, and on the other an astonishingly far-reaching autonomy of its many parts.

3.3.1. Complexity: When, as a neuropsychologist, you are confronted with the overwhelming complexity of disturbances of the speech communication process on the most various levels and channels, connected with the most various functions and their components and subcomponents, with disturbances along the most various 'seams', then you begin to recognise the enormous task of drawing a full picture of the systematic structure of speech.

One of the main activities of our research department is the study of the structures of speech processes and their disturbances. Here is just one example. In order to analyse the disturbance of auditory word comprehension, we have to compile an 'inventory' of the individual components and accompanying components of this function. The process of word comprehension normally begins with adequate reception of the acoustic signal and ends with semantic decoding of the speech information. Along the pathway between these two poles it is necessary to take into consideration a series of re-afferent processes which make the final effect possible.

Linguistically speaking, in the case of a single word, it passes through a phonematic, morphologic, and semantic analysis. To carry out these analyses, inner hearing, inner latent speech movements (verbo-kinaesthesia), and outer articulation in the form of co-articulation, whispering or repetition, may all be drawn into the process. In addition, there are sometimes labiolexic processes (lipreading), particularly when there exist difficulties in phonematic analysis.

This short and simplified presentation of the way in which word comprehension performance comes about already shows the great number of more or less independent functions and components of a receptive and expressive nature, which can play a part in this process. It can be seen that various parts and connections of this system may be disturbed, that various 'factors' can be impaired.

Our neuropsychological analyses of the manifold disturbances of various speech functions encountered in aphasics convinced us that such performances are based upon the participation of a number of more or less independent functions, accompanying functions, components, and subcomponents of a receptive and expressive nature; at present we are a long way from knowing the number. In order to study the isolated effectiveness of certain functions, components, etc., we developed various *elimination methods* [19; 176; 179]. Above all we investigated in aphasics the role of the *verbo-kinaesthetic* accompanying components of receptive reading, word hearing, and labiolexia with regard to visual and auditory word comprehension, lipreading, and subsequent repetition and reading aloud.

A further method for studying the functions and components is successively coupling intact and disturbed functions *(deblocking method)*, with the help of which we can analyse and measure the relations between individual functions and their components – particularly when we simultaneously apply our elimination procedure.

Some provisional results of such experiments may be found in the reports of Böttcher et al. [19].

3.3.2. Autonomy: Apart from the interfunctional connections of the speech system noted above, neuropsychological research has revealed many facts which indicate a far-reaching autonomy of the various speech levels, functions, components, etc. There are very few cases, for instance, of a 'pure' transmission or reception disturbance. In most cases the patient is able to name orally, but not to read aloud, or to understand what he reads, but not what is said to him. There are cases of serious motor aphasia in which all functions of spoken language are affected, while encoding and decoding in written speech are intact. Even in the case of one and the same function, it is not in every case possible to say that it has been affected 'as a whole'. For instance it is possible for the receptive-semantic component of reading to be present (reading comprehension), but for reading aloud, the expressive component, to be impaired. Vice versa, there are cases in which the patient can read aloud correctly, but without understanding what he is reading. In this latter case it is not even possible to say that the 'afference' is disturbed, while the 'efference' is intact. In reality, put in linguistic terms, the graphemic analysis of the writing symbols and their transcoding in the corresponding phonetic-verbo-articulatory schemata are preserved, but the semantic level is blocked. This means that in the same information flow certain functions, levels, etc., may be intact while others are disturbed.

Our own investigations confirm completely the fact that the individual parts of the speech system have relative autonomy. With the aid of various elimination methods which we developed [176; 179] or with the deblocking method, we can prove experimentally such autonomies. It has been shown, for instance, that in word-deaf patients with disturbed repetition the repetition can be deblocked on its own, without the word-deafness being removed. In such cases, put in linguistic terms, the disturbance of phonemic analysis of verbo-acoustic signals has been removed, while syntactic-semantic decoding remains blocked. In other words the patient is able to repeat (words or sentences) without understanding. In the same way we discovered that in certain patients co-articulation was intact, but repetition disturbed, and in other cases vice versa. The variation in the way in which these two closely connected speech functions are affected shows how far their autonomy may go. We were able to make similar observations with regard to the autonomy of 'concrete' and 'abstract' levels. For instance one of our female patients is able to manipulate algebraic letter-symbols in solving equations, but incapable of constructing the simplest words from the very same symbols. In this case the 'concrete' level is shown to be seriously impaired, while the 'abstract' level functions relatively well.

The relative autonomy is a product of the development of speaking and thinking in the ontogenesis. It occurs in the process of automation (stereotyping) of the various speech functions and contributes to screening in the face of disturbances of other parts of the speech functional system.

We have described above the importance of study of the dynamic and structure of the speech system for neurophysiology ⟨8⟩ and for syndrome research ⟨10⟩.

3.3.3. Organisation of the speech system in the form of 'semantic fields'

As noted above, one of the basic prerequisites for success of the successive coupling method used by us is that the speech performance of the intact and the disturbed function (or functions) should stand in a certain syntactic-semantic 'family relationship'[4], or, in other words, should be related to one and the same area of meaning.

In their investigations, Luria and Vinogradova [118] confirmed the assumption that the processes of spoken and written speech systems are based upon individual 'semantic fields', which came into existence ontogenetically and have been fixed lexically. Deblocking research has produced, in a different manner, proof of the *psychological reality* of these 'fields'.

In this respect, we see the deblocking process as follows: the prestimulation of a certain semantic field (over one or more channels) stimulates this field *as a whole*. The various meaning-complexes of such a field are co-stimulated by irradiation, so that favorable conditions may be created under which the subsequent verbal stimuli can penetrate the channel which is otherwise blocked. This explains how it happens that not only is a certain word capable of deblocking the same word, but that such a deblocking can also take place with regard to words with a related meaning. We were also able to prove that the repeated and systematic deblocking of words belonging to the same category (e.g., words about clothing) can make possible the reactualisation (by themselves) of many additional *non*-deblocked relations in this field. Such spontaneous deblockings can result from the systematic stimulation of certain semantic fields on the basis of semantic irradiation effects. This phenomenon occurs not only with regard to words, but also with sentences.

The study of semantic problems along the path we have taken has already produced rich material, including material of interest for the psychology of concept formation, for semiotics, and for linguistics [183], ⟨15⟩.

4. We regard the preceding paragraphs solely as some indication of the wide field of application of neuropsychological research, and in addition

as suggesting certain possibilities for interdisciplinary cooperation with neighboring branches of science. This is confirmed by the varying relations of teamwork, determined by agreement and by theme, which our research center maintains with a number of neurological and neurosurgical institutes at home and abroad, as well as with institutes dealing with psychology, linguistics, etc., with regard to problems of basic research of interest to both sides.

In this respect, two examples of the implementation of such relations of cooperation may be mentioned.

4.1. The Institute for Neurosurgery of the Polish Academy of Sciences in Warsaw (Director: Professor Dr. L. Stepien), specializing in specific localisatory problems, is interested in working together with our research centre in utilising the deblocking method with patients with focal brain lesions. Researchers Szumska, Pilipowska and Celinski in this Polish clinic have been able to publish their findings[5], which show measurable differences in effectiveness (number of successful deblockings) and the period that the d-effect persists, dependent upon the localisation of the cerebral damage (anterior or posterior speech area). (These were cases of the deblocking of naming and repetition disturbances, amongst others.)

4.2. For a longer period our research centre has maintained relations with the "Arbeitsstelle Strukturelle Grammatik" of the German Academy of Sciences in Berlin; these relations have been devoted to the mutual study of 'neuropsycholinguistic' problems[6]. (see: ⟨3⟩, ⟨15⟩, [16], [19])

5. *The importance of neuropsychology for the practice of rehabilitation of the psychological sequelae of cerebral damage*

Although basic research occupies a central position in neuropsychological science, this science has the obligation to make its results available in therapy in the broadest sense, particularly because of the fact that its research is done mainly with sick persons, principally those with impairments in speech communication. A number of the neuropsychological centres mentioned above already devote part of their activities to this important task, with the help of specially trained doctors, psychologists, and logopedic specialists [27; 29; 89; 97; 162; 167; 171; 206].

In this connection, the tendency in the area of rehabilitation to overcome the former empiric stage is becoming stronger although to work out and apply therapeutic methods on a scientific basis presents particularly difficult problems in the treatment of aphasic disturbances.

So far, only a beginning has been made in the exact determination of the degree of disturbance of the whole system of speech functions and other functions, the effectiveness of the various therapeutic methods, and finally the scientific determination of the therapeutic 'overall success'.[7]

An important prerequisite for rehabilitation based upon neuropsychology thus consists in a careful rethinking of *basic conceptions* upon which the practice of therapeutic measures is based. It cannot be a matter of indifference to the therapist whether he proceeds on the assumption that there exist 'irreversible' disturbances of the speech-functional system and linguistic competence, i.e. the 'loss' and 'cancellation' of certain single functions; or whether he assumes, as we have outlined above, that generally the 'construction plan' of the speech-functional system and the linguistic competence have not been affected in aphasics, and that on the other hand the impairment of individual factors, levels, functions, components, etc., is fundamentally 'deblockable', that is to say re-actualisable. For the therapy, it is naturally of the greatest importance that a decision should be reached on the scientific validity of one or the other hypothesis, since in one case it will be necessary to emphasize *'learning anew'* of the functions, and in the other case 're-actualisation' of the functions must be stressed.

On the basis of the possibilities of polyfunctional and syntactic-semantically irradiative effects which we have determined, we are attempting to encourage therapeutic practice, in working out its methods, to take into account the principle of stimulation of the speech-functional system simultaneously 'on all channels' and at the same time systematically in the framework of certain semantic fields (paradigmatic and syntagmatic).

According to our preliminary experience, the reciprocal relations between intact and disturbed functions of the speech functional system, which we have analysed with the aid of the deblocking method in the framework of syndrome research, provide fruitful ground for the working out of recovery methods.

With regard to the diagnosis and treatment of aphasic disturbances, it appears to us that new prospects are opened up if use is made of the knowledge we have won in our study of the complexity and autonomy of the manifold components of the speech system.

The possibilities sketched here for practical use of the results of our neuropsychological experiments naturally represent only extracts from the wide range of application of neuropsychological research.

Notes

1. Founding of the Problem Commission for Aphasia Research within the World Federation of Neurology.
2. In the sense of Vygotsky, Leontyev, Luria, Zhinkin, etc.
3. Dependent upon the brain damage and the consequent syndromatic sequelae, not only the performance of disturbed speech functions, but also *gnosic* functions (e.g., visual, auditory, tactile agnosia) can be deblocked (Weigl [177] and [178]). The possibility of deblocking apraxia, acalculia, and other syndromes has not yet been examined.
   The deblocking process is basically possible in all types of aphasia, without regard to the aetiology (circulatory disturbances, traumata, tumours); difficulties arise mainly in the stage of total aphasia.
4. For reasons of conciseness we speak here only of 'semantic-syntactic' deblocking, but it should be noted that the d-effect can take place on a purely 'phonological' level (e.g., by deblocking the disturbed repetition of unknown or nonsense words).
5. J. Szumska and M. Celinski [161]. Deblocking of the disturbed speech function in focal brain lesions.
6. We introduce here the rather long-winded term 'neuropsycholinguistic' in order to underline the fact that even outside the realm of psycholingustics there are many problems affecting the neuropsychological aspects of linguistic questions.
7. In this connection, attention should be drawn to the classifications of success which are still often used today, though they have little claim to a scientific basis: 'unchanged', 'slight improvement', 'largely recovered', etc.

⟨3⟩

E. WEIGL and M. BIERWISCH

Neuropsychology and Linguistics: Topics of Common Research

1. Introductory remarks

The rapid evolution of psycholinguistics as a particular branch of science[1] has led to an increasing cooperation between psychologists and linguists. A particular set of problems within this branch are those connected with disorders in the use of spoken or written language resulting from cortical lesions. The investigation of these problems calls for intensive collaboaration between neuropsychologists and linguists. Until now, however, this collaboration in general has not gone beyond taking over scattered linguistic concepts by aphasiologists and a linguistic reinterpretation of certain data established and interpreted by aphasiologists. Actual teamwork between representatives of both disciplines, starting with the confrontation of certain hypotheses, continuing with common observations and experiments, and ending with the interpretation and generalization of results, is only just beginning. It seems to us that this latter form of cooperation should be extended according to the requirements of both sciences.[2] This means in particular that sufficiently specific assumptions emerging from modern linguistic theory should be related to equally specific tenets of aphasiology, and that both should be tested against suitable arranged experiments. Below we illustrate, by means of certain preliminary results gained by members of the "Arbeitsgruppe Sprachpathologie" and of the "Arbeitsstelle Strukturelle Grammatik", both at the German Academy of Sciences (DDR), how such " neuropsycholinguistic" research might be devised.

A careful investigation of particular problems of aphasia, if related to the pertinent linguistic framework, provides insights not only into the aphasic phenomena and the normal performance from which aphasia is a specific, highly instructive, deviation, but also into the manner in which the implicit knowledge of a language as described by linguists is put to work. Such insights in turn may indicate something about the psychological reality of certain theoretical assumptions according to which linguistic descriptions, i.e., grammars, of a particular language are constructed.

In this connection, questions of the following type may be raised: given the linguistically motivated set of levels for the representation of linguistic structure and the components of grammars, i.e., the semantic, syntactic, morphological, and phonological rules, how are these levels of representation and components of grammars motivated from the point of view of their accessibility under pathological conditions? To what extent are they connected to relatively autonomous aspects of speech functions or performance strategies? What can be inferred from observations made with respect to the psychological status of linguistic competence as described by linguists? Are linguistic assumptions further justified by such neuropsychological evidence because they are able to provide explanations for particular types of disorders? Might pathological evidence reveal particular gaps in the scope of competence as described by linguists? Examination of questions of this type might complement the kind of research proposed in Miller [126] to study the psychological reality of linguistic concepts.

2. Methodological Remarks

The general line of reasoning along which our investigations are organized is as follows. Underlying all speech behavior or performance[3] is the tacit knowledge of or competence in a given language. This competence in speaking and understanding a particular language is described by linguists in terms of a generative grammar of that language. (Such a description is, of course, idealized in certain ways.) Speech performance, on the other hand, is a rather complex system of components which complement each other, such as auditive perception and lipreading in the processing of spoken language signals; or alternatively, such as auditory perception, reading, speaking spontaneously, etc. Each of these components is presumably made up of a set of steps or loops, e.g., preliminary auditory analysis, identification of the underlying phonemic pattern, actualiziation of the connected meaning, and organization according to syntactic rules, in the component or strategy of auditory perception. All these components and their subcomponents, steps, and loops are connected in a specific way to the underlying competence. (We will discuss this assumption in some detail below.) In normal speech performance there is a complex interaction of these components and subcomponents, to a large extent preventing direct investigation of the detailed structure of the components of speech performance and of their dependence on the structure of competence. If it can now be shown with sufficient clarity that in a given pathological case one (or several) of these components or subcomponents is disturbed in a way in which others are not, then these (sub)components must be considered as relatively autonomous functional units even in normal performance.[4] Otherwise they could not be subject to separate interference in pathological cases. A detailed analysis of different aphasic syndromes along these lines may lead us step by step to a deeper understanding of the complex system of functions of normal speech performance. Because of the dependence of performance on linguistic competence, it may also provide, in certain cases, arguments for or against the psychological reality of particular linguistic hypotheses. And finally it provides a framework for a more detailed interpretation and perhaps explanation of the great variety of aphasic and related syndromes. Notice that for this kind of investigation the enormous variation of syndromes is not a drawback, but rather an advantage: even one particular case, exhibiting a quite special disintegration of certain functions, may enable us to establish the autonomy of a particular subcomponent or the manner of the interaction of subcomponents. It goes without saying that it is the functional, not the physiological, structure of speech performance and speech disturbance that can be approached in this way.

The data on which our conclusions and generalizations are based are essentially of two types. The first type is taken from observation of the spontaneous performance of patients under controlled conditions. The second type is obtained by the application of certain methods of influencing the patient's capabilities in certain types of performance. Here two methods, developed by E. Weigl, are of primary importance: First, the mechanical blocking of the component of latent articulation [179], and second, the successive linking of intact and disturbed performance components, resulting in a *deblocking* of particular sets of performance in the disturbed component, the so-called *deblocking method* (⟨2⟩, ⟨9⟩, ⟨10⟩, ⟨15⟩). For experimental details we refer to the articles quoted.

3. Competence, Performance, and Aphasia

We assumed that linguistic competence, i.e., tacit knowledge of a given language, underlies – or perhaps better, governs as one of several factors – the complex system of performance strategies. Implicit in our research program, moreover, is the hypothesis that aphasic syndromes in general are to be understood as disturbances of complexes of components or subcomponents of the system of performance, while the underlying competence remains intact. (Two particular problems deserving a certain qualification of this tenet will be discussed below.) If this hypothesis is correct, as it seems to be, then obviously competence and performance must be psychologically different aspects of the general phenomenon of speech behavior. In other words: the distinction between competence and performance is not merely a heuristic or methodological assumption, but reflects a fact that can be stablished neuropsychologically. Since the claim that competence and performance are psychologically distinct and the even stronger claim that in aphasia only performance is disturbed are certainly of general interest, we will discuss them in rather more detail.

Some of the earlier linguistic treatments of aphasic phenonema might give the impression that aphasia consists of a partial loss of linguistic competence, i.e., in a reduction of the long term storage of language. Instead of this, we would like to consider aphasia a disturbance of the access to the knowledge of language, which, we would argue, is intact. Since this is not merely tacitly presupposed by our analyses, we will briefly present some arguments which seem to make this assumption unavoidable:

(i) It is usual in a wide variety of aphasic syndromes that one or several components of speech performance are disturbed, while others are not. If aphasic disturbance were a loss of underlying competence, then each performance component that might be disturbed separately would have to be connected to its own competence. We would be forced then to the conclusion that there is a separate competence not only for expressive and receptive performance, but more specific competences for speaking spontaneously, repetition, receptive reading, expressive reading, writing spontaneously, writing dictated messages, etc. This is clearly absurd, if one considers the close interaction of these components and the essential isomorphism of the competence underlying them.

(ii) In many cases, there is a very high fluctuation of performance even within one and the same component: an object that can be named one day cannot be named the next, etc. If competence were lost, such a fluctuation would not occur: a particular performance is possible only if the corresponding part of competence is still intact; it would be impossible if the relevant competence were lost.

(iii) The phenomenon of deblocking, which consists roughly in a transference of one particular act of performance from a still intact component of performance to a disturbed one, would be unexplainable if the underlying competence were destroyed. How could a patient with intact capability of repetition and disturbed capability of naming succeed in naming an object, e.g., a ball, after previous repetition among other things of the word "ball", if the underlying competence of this performance were lost? Notice that even the possibility of his relearning the particular competence of naming a ball is excluded, since there is evidence of the strongest kind that this process cannot be interpreted as some type of reproduction or learning. For details we refer to Weigl (⟨2⟩, ⟨9⟩, ⟨10⟩).

Thus it seems clear to us that competence must be essentially different from performance and that aphasia consists in the interference of different components of the system of performance capabilities. The same view has been emphasized by Lenneberg [98, p. 206 ff.]. This claim does not mean, however, that aphasic disturbance of performance cannot be bound to particular components or aspects of competence. Rather, we will illustrate below very strong connections between aphasic phenomena and quite special aspects or components of competence. It is for this reason that certain aphasic phenomena can be classified and described in terms of the structure of competence, i.e., in terms of grammatical and lexial structure. (This, then, seems to be the rationale behind treatments which deal with aphasia in terms of competence.)

There are two problems with respect to our claim that must be discussed separately. The first is presented by cases of total aphasia. In these cases, obviously, our arguments do not apply: there is no evidence for or against preserved competence. But though the disturbance in these cases goes far beyond the whole system of speech functions, involving also the gnosic functions etc., in general, total aphasia develops after a certain time into other forms of aphasia with partial intactness of different speech functions. At least in these cases the underlying competence cannot have been erased.

The other problem is somewhat more intricate. It concerns cases where all speech behavior suffers from receptive and expressive agrammatism, i.e., cases involving patients whose speaking and comprehension of speech is reduced to only single words. Here it might be argued that a certain part of the competence, viz., the syntactic rules, has been lost. (This argument does not hold, of course, as long as at least one performance component is not affected by agrammatism.) Though this phenomenon does not prove that the syntactic aspect of competence has been destroyed, it does make this assumption possible. The whole situation is rather obscure here. Nevertheless, the following considerations seem to the point. Assume that there are certain very general strategies underlying all types of encoding, decoding, recoding, and serial ordering and that the "efferent motor aphasia" which Luria [108, p. 154] describes as being characterized by a marked disturbance of serial organization of the "kinetic melody" may be a particular instance of serial organization of the " kinetic melody" may be a particular instance of interference with this strategy on the level of phonemic organization. Then agrammatism of the type discussed here might be understood as a very general disturbance of these strategies, which would, obviously, be a precondition for syntactic processes to be put to work. However, the particular syntactic rules which make up the syntactic component of a particular grammar are not to be identified with these general principles necessary for their use in particular acts of performance. This then would mean that the tacit knowledge of syntactic rules, though completely inaccessible because of the interfered principles of coding, would not have to have been lost.[5]

We are not forced, however, to decide on the questions involved in the two problems discussed so far. It is sufficient for our present purpose that for the vast majority of cases there is clear evidence that aphasia does not consist in the loss of competence.

We will not be concerned here, incidentally, with the separate problem whether aphasia is a destruction of or only an interference with particular performance components and whether rehabilitation consequently consists in a substitution of newly acquired skills instead of the destroyed ones or rather in a restitution of the former capabilities. Though we claim that the latter is the case, we will discuss this topic elsewhere. We must also ignore here the large set of interesting problems connected with aphasia in polyglots. They seem not to affect the basic claim of this section.

We will now discuss a set of particular problems of performance, firstly with respect to phonemic and graphemic structure, and secondly with respect to semantic and syntactic phenomena.

4. Intermediate Storage in Speech Perception

Primarily in connection with the problem of the relation between comprehension and speech production in aphasia, the following observations have been made by aphasiologists. Patients suffering from 'sensory aphasia' very often pronounce spontaneously words and sentences correctly without understanding them. Many patients with sensory transcortical aphasia repeat or copronounce (together with the experimenter) words or sentences, but are not able to grasp their meaning. Alexic patients often cannot read words and sentences even if they have previously copied them correctly. (These facts, by the way, have a certain analogy in normal speech behavior: we are able to repeat, to read, and to write meaningless or unknown words.)

Besides the problem of classification of types of aphasia, phenomena of this kind offer certain problems of speech perception from the linguistic point of view. First of all, it follows that a correct phonemic or graphemic identification of given signals does not necessarily presuppose a syntactic and semantic analysis. It can be achieved "below" the semantic and syntactic level, though normally these levels are involved even in the identification of phonemic or graphemic structures, as we will demonstrate below. Secondly, the actualiziation of the external articulation patterns also can proceed without any participation of semantic and syntactic processes. Identification of the relevant phonemic or graphemic cues may be sufficient to evoke them. And finally, short-term storage of these identified cues is necessarily involved in the identification of the perceived phonemic or graphemic patterns. R. Böttcher obtained an interesting confirmation of this latter hypothesis in examining an alexic patient. She gave him several written words which he was unable to read, either receptively (silently) or expressively (aloud). Then she pronounced one of these words, and the patient, whose auditory understanding was intact, immediately decoded its meaning. But in addition to this, he suddenly remembered that he had seen this word previously among the others, and he was able to indicate even the place of this word in the series shown him before. We must emphasize, however, that such results were possible only in fairly simple cases. If we gave to the patient words with too many letters or syllables or more than three words at a time, then the effect just described did not appear. The storage capacity of the patient had then obviously been exceeded. (Similar phenomena have been observed also with other patients by Weigl and Böttcher.) These observations lead to certain conclusions. First of all, the process of understanding written or spoken words must consist of (at least) two subcomponents: identification of the graphemic (or phonemic) structure and actualization of the corresponding meaning, the second of which may be disturbed separately in a given component. Furthermore, and this is less obvious, both subcomponents have outputs stored in the short-term memory, where the first output is an intermediate result on which the second step of the procedure is based. This intermediate step in general remains subliminal or unconscious. These conclusions shed some light on the internal structure of the performance component of receptive reading (and of auditory perception too). We will return to them below in connection with a more complicated phenomenon in disturbed reading.

5. *On the Independence of Graphemic Structure*

In discussing cases such as the one mentioned in the previous section, and in many other problems where both graphic and phonic communication are involved, one is forced to face the question of how the corresponding performance components are related. And this in turn calls for a linguistic investigation of the relation between phonemic and graphemic structure as one of the preconditions for a solution. Given the theory of generative phonology, which assigns to each possible utterance an abstract phonemic and a more concrete phonetic representation, the latter being connected to articulatory and auditory patterns and derived by phonological rules from the former, which in turn provides the abstract form of storage for dictionary entries, the following questions arise:

(i) Is the concrete graphic structure assigned to written utterances derived by graphemic rules from the already established phonemic structure *P*, or is there a separate underlying graphemic structure *G*?

(ii) Assume that there is an autonomous graphemic structure *G*. Is this *G* then derived by certain orthographic rules from the phonemic structure *P* based on the dictionary entries, or is there a particular storage of the graphemic structure for each individual dictionary entry?

These questions pertain, of course, only to languages with alphabetic writing. They have not yet been raised in principle in linguistic theory, let alone answered. Although we know from recent phonological studies that orthography and sound structure are less different than it might seem if the underlying phonemic structure is ignored, this does not prove that graphemic structure in general can be derived from the phonemic representation without separate storage of additional graphemic structures. With respect to the system of performance components this leads to the question of whether dictionary entries are accessible by means of independent phonemic and graphemic structures, or whether their identification converges at an earlier stage. Certain observations made by the "Arbeitsgruppe Sprachpathologie" provide evidence in favor of the latter possibility. In a large variety of cases it has been possible to deblock graphemic structures by means of phonemic ones and vice versa, even in the case of nonsense syllables and words. Since in this case the possibility of lexical storage and hence of separately stored phonemic and graphemic patterns is to be excluded, the existence of one underlying level of abstract internal representation or at least of correspondence rules mediating between two forms of representation seems plausible. If this assumption is correct, then the well-known fact that both receptive and expressive performance in aphasia are often rather dissociated with respect to written and spoken language must be ascribed only to the interference of different performance components, and cannot be ascribed to different aspects of competence. However, further investigation, both linguistic and neuropsychological, is necessary here.

6. The Problem of Labiolexic Structure

Connected with the foregoing question, but still more complicated in a sense, is the following problem. Investigating a patient with word deafness, E. Metze found that the patient understood only 20% of the words pronounced to him. But if he could see at the same time the articulation movements of the examiner, he was able to understand up to 50% of the words pronounced. In this case, therefore, labiolexia (speech- or lipreading) was a very effective support for the understanding of words. This function of lipreading is well known from normal communication under bad acoustic conditions and from the experience of deaf mutes (see, [11; 128]). How does this subsidiary component of labiolexia interact with the component of auditory perception? The assumption which suggests itself, that visual perception somehow directly controls the verbal-kinaesthetic processes, must be ruled out for the following reason.

Using the method of temporary exclusion of latent articulation, which was developed by Weigl ⟨7⟩, it was shown that facilitation by means of lipreading can appear also under the condition of blocked speech movements [19]. Since the dynamic picture perceived in lipreading increases the analysis of the corresponding phonetic event and since it does not rely on latent articulation, the question arises: How are the visual articulation patterns related to phonemic structures? Is there something like a partially autonomous labiolexic structure, connected to the phonemic structure by means of certain rules? If this were the case the preliminary results of auditory and labiolexic analysis could be connected at a rather high stage of neural integration. Or is there only a scattered influence of certain visual images on some of the elements occurring somewhere in the process of auditory perception? At which stage and by what type of linking would this influence be possible?

The problem of phonemic-labiolexic correspondence is still less familiar to linguistic theory than that of the phonemic-graphemic correspondence. It is by no means an irrelevant problem, however, since the communication of deaf mutes is to a large extent based on it.

7. The Role of Latent Articulation in Speech Perception

The influence of lipreading on auditory perception even in blocked coarticulation raises a further problem, connected with the motor theory of speech perception, viz., that of the dependence of auditory speech perception on the verbal-kinaesthetic component. We were forced to put this question not only because of the case of word deafness and word blindness, which have been investigated by the "Arbeitsgruppe Sprachpathologie", do not depend on the presence or absence of latent verbal motions. Moreover, it was demonstrated that even the deblocking of such comprehension impairments is possible also without the participation of reafferent verbal-kinaesthetic impulses. For example: a patient with word deafness and intact receptive word reading was exposed to several written words, the micromovements having been eliminated. Subsequently he was able to understand the critical word which he could not understand before and which he perceived also under the condition of eliminated latent articulation. Therefore, the word must have been deblocked by means of verbo-visual understanding without any articulation. Analogous phenomena have been demonstrated in deblocking receptive alexia through intact auditory comprehension [19].

This shows quite clearly that latent articulation, though doubtlessly functioning in normal speech perception, cannot be a conditio sine qua non either for auditory or for visual perception. This in turn has important consequences for the motor theory of speech perception as developed by Liberman *et al.* [102]. If speech perception is based on an internal production of the utterance to be perceived, then this production need not necessarily be bound to a latent actualization of the internal articulation pattern. Rather, a more abstract level of representation, probably the phonemic one, seems to be the decisive stage to which the auditory pattern must be related in any case. Thus, the latent articulation may be a supporting, but not a necessary component.[6] This assumption is well in line with the analysis-by-synthesis model as developed by Stevens and Halle [160]. It requires, however, a certain modification of the tenets of the motor theory of speech perception: the internal generation of the structure assigned to the perceived signal need not be mediated by the articulation patterns.

8. Problems in Disturbances of Word Reading

During the last year we examined in the "Arbeitsgruppe Sprachpathologie" a very interesting case of receptive alexia. Studying the troubles of patient M., a 62-year old woman with rapidly restituted aphasia, suffering only from alexia, agraphia, and acalculia, we observed that the usual aphasiological classifications in "literal", "verbal", and "propositional alexia" were not adequate for this case. The errors in reading were neither total nor connected exclusively to letters, to words, or to sentences. We became aware of rather intricate relations of particular difficulties and impairments in reading to certain aspects of grammatical structure. In order to clarify these phenomena and the related linguistic problems, a large number of reading experiments were conducted and analyzed from a neuropsychological and linguistic point of view. The results, which will be presented in detail elsewhere by Weigl, Bierwisch, and Böttcher, allow various rather interesting conclusions, not only with respect to alexia, but also with respect to linguistic problems. We found, e.g., that our patient had far greater difficulties in reading abstract than concrete nouns. This result at first glance seems to support the well-known thesis that aphasia reduces primarily the availability of abstract categories. A more detailed analysis, however, revealed a rather different factor. A splitting of nouns into those with prefixes and those without shows clearly (see Table I) that this distinction is much more important than that between concrete and abstract nouns: the rate of success for abstract nouns in general is 46%, but it reduces to 30% for those with prefixes, and increases to 83% for nouns without prefixes. Similarly, the success rate of 94% for concrete nouns in general reduces to 86% for those with prefix, and increases by 1% for those without. This phenomenon holds also for verbs: the overall rate of 47% splits into 38% for prefixed verbs and 57% for prefixless ones. The first impression of the important differences between concrete and abstract nouns (94% vs. 46%) is due to the fact that in the German language, among the abstract nouns, there are a great number of action nouns derived from verbs with a prefix. Instead of, or at least as well as, the concrete/abstract distinction, two other factors must be considered: the internal complexity of prefixed words and the particular difficulties connected with the special character of prefixes. These are characterized, in addition to their particular syntactic status, by minimal semantic specification. Prefixes share this property with other grammatical elements, such as pronouns, auxiliaries, etc. And in fact, not surprisingly, pronouns presented still greater difficulties to our patient. It seems then, that the phenomena related to prefixed words, though the particular role of prefixes is in part idiosyncratic for German, pertain to the more general problem of the distinction of lexical and grammatical morphemes.

Ignoring the concrete/abstract distinction, we had a proportion of 90% vs. 35% for nouns without and with prefix. For pronouns the rate of success was only 29%. A typical situation in this respect was the following: We presented *Es* [it] to the patient, and, unable to read it, she said "one of these horrible little words again", whereas she read the little

Table 1 *Correct reading of isolated words by patient M*

	nouns			
	concrete 94%	abstract 46%	without prefix 90%	with prefix 35%
without prefix	95%	83%		
with prefix	86%	30%		

word *Ei* [egg] without any hesitation. This behavior shows quite clearly an additional, very interesting phenomenon, viz., that the patient, in spite of her failure to read it, has somehow grasped that the presented word *Es* is a pronoun. The same phenomenon is brought up by the striking fact that the high percentage of misreadings (66% vs. 7% failure) in the case of pronouns remains to a very high extent within the category of pronouns. Thus she reads *unser* [our] instead of *euer* [your] and vice versa. In general, 77% of the misreadings were pronouns, 12% were the copula *ist* (which she seemed to use as a kind of "category indicator"), 8% other grammatical elements (auxiliaries and prepositions), and only 2% major lexical categories. Attempting an explanation of these observations forces one to recognize a series of rather complicated steps in the process of understanding written words, beginning with a preliminary subliminal identification of the underlying graphemic pattern (or phonemic – see above, Section 5) which must be stored for further processing, as mentioned in Section 4. The result of this preliminary analysis subsequently leads to an internal generation of the item to be understood by means of information stored in the lexicon. Here an irradiation within a particular class or field of lexical items takes place in disturbed cases, as the one discussed here. Finally an erroneous matching of the stored result of the preliminary analysis and the internally generated item leads to the significant misreading. The details of this process, their motivation and further conclusion, pertaining not only to the case discussed here, will be given elsewhere. It might be noted, however, that this type of misreading seems to give strong support to the analysis-by-synthesis conception of Stevens and Halle [160], since otherwise the fact could not be explained that the misreading is by no means a random phenomenon. And furthermore, it leads to an extension of the idea that even phonemic (or graphemic) analysis might involve the semantic and/or syntactic aspect of the items in question, since the deviation obviously is determined not by their phonemic, but by their semantic (or syntactic) properties.

9. The Role of Semantic Fields in Word Reading

The type of misreading just described is by no means unique. Although it was restricted for our patient M. roughly to grammatical words – only occasionally did we observe misreadings of the same type with major categories, e.g., *verbieten* [prohibit] instead of *erlauben* [allow] etc. – in other cases it occurs mainly with common nouns. Thus the patient W., investigated by I. Weigl (Arbeitsgruppe Sprachpathologie), a much stronger case of alexia, produced among others the following misreadings: *Hose* [trousers] instead of *Bluse* [blouse], *Krawatte* [tie] instead of *Manschette* [cuff], *Mieder* [bodice] instead of *Strickjacke* [cardigan], *Sandalen* [sandals] instead of *Socken* [socks], or *Pfirsiche* [peaches] instead of *Apfelsinen* [oranges], *Bananen* [bananas] instead of *Ananas* [pineapple], *Datteln* [dates] instead of *Feigen* [figs], *Kartoffeln* [potatoes] instead of *Gemüse* [vegetables], *Radieschen* [radish] instead of *Petersilie* [parsley], etc. It is obvious that these misreadings are controlled by particular semantic fields (viz., that of clothing and of vegetables and fruit) and organized according to strong semantic correspondences. Phenomena of this kind show clearly the importance of the internal structure of lexical knowledge in terms of semantic fields and grammatical categories (of which the former are by no means sufficiently accounted for by current linguistic theory) and the reduced preciseness of access to this knowledge in certain cases of alexia (and certainly aphasia too).

The overwhelming importance of semantic fields for the explanation of particular types of disorder – not restricted to alexia only – and for deblocking phenomena has long been emphasized by E. Weigl. In particular, deblocking has been studied by him and his collaborators for several years.[7] In this connection he has developed a method which permits experimental control of the deviation within and across semantic fields and which leads in pathological cases to results similar to those obtained by Luria and Vinogradova [118], with normal subjects. Some of these results have already been published, e.g., by Weigl (⟨2⟩, ⟨10⟩, ⟨15⟩) and Böttcher *et al.* [19]. Thus we may restrict ourselves for the moment to a sketch of some further perspectives both from the neuropsychological and the linguistic point of view.

First of all, a lot of evidence has been gathered for the psychological reality of the fact that the lexical structure of a language is organized according to semantic fields. It remains to be shown how these fields are organized in detail, how the items of the fields are connected to each other, and whether these relations can be expressed in terms of the semantic features developed so far in linguistic theory. Secondly, the different role of semantic and syntactic properties of lexical entries might be studied by means of their different effects in aphasic disturbances. Thus, if a language possesses the difference between verbs and adjectives, though this is rather superficial from a purely semantic point of view, its consequences in aphasia might be rather deep. Questions of this type cover a large set of problems of enormous complexity. Many of them have not even been formulated. Both linguistic and aphasiological investigations will contribute to their solution.

10. Syntactic Problems in Aphasia

We now turn to a particular problem of syntactic performance. In examining Mrs. V., a patient with a rather severe expressive aphasia, alexia, and agraphia, I. Weigl observed a set of very interesting phenomena [19]. V. is able to copy written sentences given to her, but she cannot write without such a visual model, either spontaneously or in dictation. We therefore used this capability of copying to deblock several other components of performance, among others writing dictated sentences. It then turned out that this deblocking was possible not only for single words, but also for whole simple sentences, such as

(1) *Die Mutter bügelt die Wäsche.*
[(The) mother irons the linen.]

Moreover, if a sentence was deblocked, the substitution of nouns was possible without a special new deblocking. Thus in addition to (1) the patient was able to write *Die Mutter bügelt das Kleid* [the dress], *Die Mutter bügelt die Hose* [the trousers], *Die Frau* [the woman] *bügelt das Kleid,* etc., the substituted nouns being the result of an *irradiation of the deblocking effect.* This irradiation, observed for the first time by I. Weigl, is directly bound to particular lexical domains or semantic fields. But while the substitution of nouns occurs rather freely, the substitution of verbs is almost impossible and requires for the most part a deblocking of the new resulting sentence. This shows clearly that the disturbed performance and its deblocking is bound not only to semantic, but also to syntactic aspects of competence. The phenomena mentioned so far may be explained, however, by referring to the syntactic surface structure. We therefore put the question whether there is also evidence for the role of the transformational relations between sentences and the deep structure underlying them according to the theory of generative grammar as presented in Chomsky [28].

To establish this assumption, we started experiments of the following type: Beginning with a deblocked sentence like (1) we dictated to the patient transformationally related sentences such as

(2) *Bügelt die Mutter die Wäsche?*
[Does mother iron the linen?]
(3) *Die Wäsche bügelt die Mutter.*
[The linen mother irons.]
(4) *Die Wäsche wird von der Mutter gebügelt.*
[The linen is ironed by mother.]
(5) *Wer bügelt die Wäsche?*
[Who irons the linen?]

(6) *Was bügelt die Mutter?*
[What does mother iron?]
(7) *Ich weiß, daß die Mutter die Wäsche bügelt.*
[I know that mother irons the linen.]

without previously deblocking them. It turned out that the patient was able to write them, though with some hesitation. Even these hesitations and trials, however, show in a very impressive way how the process is governed by the transformational network relating these sentences to the common underlying structure. The details of these experiments, which are still in progress, and their detailed interpretation will be published elsewhere [16]. It is obvious that these experiments provide evidence of the strongest kind for the psychological reality of the transformational structure postulated for completely independent reasons in linguistic theory, e.g., in Chomsky [28]. Furthermore, it shows that this aspect of linguistic competence may be accessible for a particular component of performance, even if other aspects of the competence are not available for this performance component. Thus the very abstract type of performance controlled by the transformational structure of language can be retained, even if more concrete or peripheral parts of performance are interfered with. Finally, we have evidence from another patient with a syndrome similar in relevant aspects that this retention by no means appears necessarily. For the above-mentioned patient W., the transference from writing a deblocked sentence to the writing of separately deblocked transformationally related sentences was impossible, even in the simplest cases. In other words, transformationally controlled operations constitute a separate subcomponent of performance that may or may not be retained if connected subcomponents are disturbed.

It might be noted in passing that the observations reported on here differ in essential respects from those made by Luria and Tsvetkova [116] with regard to the syntactic performance of so-called dynamic aphasiacs. Luria and Tsvetkova were able to demonstrate that the strategy of syntactic organization can essentially be facilitated in the case of dynamic aphasia, if the patient is provided with a purely linear model of the sentence to be produced – e.g., in the form of a sequence of charts – relating exclusively to the simplest aspect of surface structure. Thus the interference of syntactic behavior in this case must be not only of a different degree, but of an essentially different character compared to the patients we have been investigating. A careful comparison of such different types of interfered syntactic strategies might finally lead to important insights into the different aspects of the complex procedure of organizing the syntactic structure of a sentence according to the underlying grammatical rules.

Conclusions

We have sketched a set of topics calling for linguistic and neuropsychological cooperation and outlined certain assumptions on which in our opinion a common research program could be based. Starting with the assumption that there is an underlying system of linguistic competence and a rather complex set of components of performance, we presented arguments that aphasia must be considered in general as interference of these components and their subcomponents. (Possible exceptions to this assumption might be, but probably are not, cases of total aphasia and total, i.e., receptive and expressive, agrammatism.) Then we illustrated the fact that this interference of performance must be connected in several ways to particular parts of the underlying competence. And we gave examples for the interrelation and separate disturbance of several components and subcomponents of performance.

Investigations of this type might provide evidence for the psychological reality of the structure of competence hypothesized for purely linguistic reasons. And they can lead to a detailed conception of the system of performance components functioning in the normal use of language.

Notes

1. See Osgood and Sebeok [133] for a comprehensive survey.
2. There have been, of course, important efforts in this direction, exemplified in *Disorders of Language* [33a], Osgood and Miron [132], Kreindler and Fradis [88], Carterette [24]; similar attempts have been made in recent time by a number of research groups in various countries.
3. 'Speech behavior or performance' is to be understood in the broadest sense, including writing, reading comprehension, reading aloud, naming of objects and situations, etc. We would include, in particular, all types of written communication because of the highly interesting evidence provided by several types of alexia and agraphia. – Notice, incidentally, that the concept of performance as we use it is by no means to be identified with Goldstein's notion of 'instrumentalities of language'. Goldstein [55, p. 42] distinguishes "two different forms of language: the language proper in which the words have the character of symbols; and the language consisting of learned motor and sensory performances that we call instrumentalities of language". In spite of some superficial similarity to the distinction of competence and performance, Goldstein's distinction is of quite a different type, which we will not discuss here any further. – For some discussion of the competence-performance distinction in modern linguistics as followed here see Chomsky and Miller [29], Chomsky [28] and Bierwisch [13].
4. The assumption of such "functional units" forms the basis of the conception of the Soviet psychological school: Vygotski [170], Luria [109], Leont'ev [101], and others.

5. It seems to us, incidentally, that the disturbance of a general strategy of serial ordering in the sense just mentioned is precisely what Jakobson [71; 72] has in mind in speaking of contiguity disorder. Following Jakobson one might hypothesize a second general strategy, viz., selection from a set of possible items, whose impairment is referred to as similarity disorder. Such a strategy would consequently have to govern the access to the lexicon. In turn, the strategy involved in the different performance components must not be identified with competence. We cannot here go into the details of these problems and the classification of aphasia based on it. Rather we must leave for further discussion the question as to whether and how our particular findings and assumptions relate to these general notions.
6. For details of the problem of latent articulations see. Sokolov [157], Žinkin [211], and Weigl [84]. What has been said with respect to the motor theory of speech perception applies also to the work of Koževnikov and Čistovič ⟨7⟩ as far as this is concerned with speech perception.
7. It may be noted, by the way, that the deblocking effect was originally thought of as being bound to connections within semantic fields, since it was most easily observed in this domain. Only later on, and in part due to neuropsycholinguistic cooperation, it turned out that this phenomenon is much more general and occurs on all levels of linguistic structure: semantic, syntactic, and phonemic.

PART TWO

Neuropsychological methods

⟨4⟩

E. WEIGL

On the Psychology of So-called Processes of Abstraction

Introduction

In medical literature there are numerous descriptions of patients with cerebral lesions who show peculiar abnormalities in their behavior with regard to color. If these afflicted persons are presented with a certain color sample (for example, a skein of colored wool, a piece of colored paper, etc.), they are not capable of picking out, in a normal way, lighter or darker shades of the same color to go with the sample, although their sensory ability to distinguish colors is perfectly intact. In experiments with the Homgren wools, for example, the patients characteristically sort them differently than do normal persons with normal color vision. But, on the other hand, they never make the mistakes which are peculiar to persons without normal color vision. In addition to this abnormal behavior in sorting colors, the patients show a number of other pathological symptoms: seldom or never are they able to name correctly colors which are presented to them, and, if the name of a color is given them, they cannot pick out the corresponding shades from a rather large group of samples, etc. We have to do here with a complex symptom, which belongs in the narrow sense to the so-called 'amnesia for the names of colors', which in turn is a special case of 'amnestic aphasia'.

Formerly the various symptoms were usually traced back to separate, co-existing abnormalities. Gelb and Goldstein [45], however, came to the conclusion that all the symptoms can be traced to a unitary, basic abnormality. They were led to this conclusion on the basis of a behavioral analysis, which they made by means of experiments on both patients and normal persons, concerning the classification of colors with reference to a given sample. In these experiments the main difference in the behavior of the patients and the normal persons can be stated as follows: "In sorting out colors the *attention* of the normal person is forced in a certain *direction* by the instructions given. He looks at the sample solely from the point of view of the simple color regardless of intensity or purity. The concrete color is not appreciated in its purely individual quality, but rather as a representative of the 'concept' red, yellow, blue, etc.; it is appreciated as a *representative* of redness, yellowness, blueness, etc." The authors designate this behavior of normal persons as 'categorial behavior.' It is only on the basis of this behavior that we can voluntarily select, emphasize, and hold firmly in mind *one* quality in a phenomenon, or in other words, that we an 'abstract'.

The behavior of patients is distinguished from this rational behavior of normal persons by its greater 'primitivity', its 'closeness to reality'. It appears all the more primitive and less rational, since it is very difficult or even impossible to focus the mental operations of the patients in a particular direction, demanded by the experimenter. Their reactions (for example, in putting skeins together) are determined by the sensorially manifest *color organizations*[1] *and color groupings* which thrust themselves upon the patients at the particular moment. Their reaction changes with every change of the color organization and grouping. Consequently, the patients *have no principle of classification,* such as is formed in categorial behavior.

The primitive, concrete behavior of patients was demonstrated in a particularly instructive way in the following experiment. They were given three colors and told to place the two together which were 'most alike'. Whether or not the desired result was apparently obtained depended on the way the colors were combined. Thus, for example, the patient Th., when presented with a dark red, a pink, and a medium brown skein, reacted in the way intended by the experimenter; that is, he put the two reddish skeins together. If, however, he was given a sky blue skein instead of the medium brown one, the patient usually could not decide at all, because, for him, the paleness of the sky blue and of the pink 'cohered' as much as the two variants of the basic color hue: red. Whereas on superficial observation it seems as if the patient, when given the identical task, reacts 'correctly' one time and fails another time, the behavioral analysis shows that in reality he does not understand at all what is demanded of him. Since he is not capable of proceeding according to a definite principle of classification, the 'similarity' or 'dissimilarity' of two colored skeins is determined for him by which two of the three colors are experienced by the patient as belonging together in the most impressive way. Thus in certain presentations the identitiy of the basic color tone may just as well prevail as the similarity in paleness, and so forth; or two different ways of grouping the three colors of the traid (one according to brightness, the other according to quality) may, so to speak, compete with each other and hold each other in abeyance.

The authors were able to find reactions of this kind even in normal persons, although in less pronounced form, when they behaved completely 'passively'.

The behavior of patients in the above-mentioned *experiments in the sorting of colors* was quite analogous to that in the particular experiments just described. Hence we are dealing with a pathological change in these patients which is connected with *the problem of so-called 'isolating abstraction'*. One might also say (according to Gelb and Goldstein),

"The patients did not behave normally with regard to abstraction. To be sure their practical reaction (putting colored skeins together) seems to be determined by particular aspects of the colors presented to them, but this is true only in so far as the practical reaction is determined by definite experiences of coherence,[2] through which and with which certain aspects of color come into prominence. On the other hand, it is impossible or very difficult for such patients to select voluntarily a particular aspect of color, just as it is impossible or difficult to guide their attention in a particular direction. If, in sorting, they put particular colors together, this procedure is forced upon them passively by the experience of coherence at the moment. Furthermore, even when a particular aspect of the sensory impression has forced this procedure upon them, the patients are unable to hold fast to this aspect in their subsequent procedure. They cannot make it into a principle of classification, for the particular aspect of color is fundamentally not present to them at all when isolated in one single skein" [45].

In an appendix Gelb and Goldstein [45] report experiments on the sorting of objects, which they carried out analogously to the color experiments. It thereby became clear "that in amnestic aphasia for objects there is a deep psychic change of the total behavior of the patient, analogous to that in amnesia for the names of colors. The change consists in a descent to a level of behavior which is more primitive and more deeply rooted in living reality" [45]. The authors arrived at this hypothesis chiefly through the observation that the sorting or arrangement of objects, as well as of colors, is psychologically something different in patients than it is in normal persons. The patients sort a number of partly heterogeneous, partly homogeneous common objects on the basis of organizations and groupings which they experience concretely and phenomenally; that is, they arrange the objects in the way in which they belong together for them from a palpable, concrete point of view. Here too the organization and grouping are not superimposed by the patient upon the objects to be sorted; but rather he experiences them from the outset as organized and grouped in a definite way. Similarly the homogeneity of the single objects varies with changing organizations and groupings. Although – as we shall see later – this kind of experience is entirely possible for the normal person also, nevertheless the behavior of the normal person differs from that of the patient in that he is at least capable of a different type of procedure. *He can,* to a certain degree, voluntarily superimpose a certain organization upon the given objects.

The problem of the behavior of patients with cerebral lesions and of normal persons in *'sorting'* requires further thorough investigation. In particular it is important to increase, through behavioral analyses, our knowledge of those processes by means of which "sortig according to *various* points of view" is accomplished in patients and, under certain circumstances, in normal persons. Thereby we shall be able to penetrate from a new angle into the problem of the *'processes of abstraction'*, i.e., those processes to which one usually reduces the reaction to the partial conformity of several objects.

I should like at this point to thank Professor Gelb and Professor Goldstein most cordially for the great interest which they have taken in the development of my work and for their assistance and stimulation on numerous occasions.

Investigations concerning the process of sorting in patients with cerebral lesions, normal adults, and children

The investigations in the first section of this article are predominantly descriptive. We shall choose, from the number of patients with cerebral lesions whom we examined, one with a particularly 'typical' manner of reacting, namely L. R., a patient with a frontal lobe injury [149].

The results gained from the other patients and from normal adults and children will be mentioned only for purposes of comparison.

There is a methodological reason for the fact that we start from a case of brain damage in order to crystallize the specific problems in hand; for patients are capable only of "sorting" in very definite ways. What is more, the responses that they are in a position to give are particularly marked in this case. By establishing the ways of sorting that are, as a matter of principle, closed to, or made difficult for, them, we do not only gain some clue as to the typical features of "normal responses", but also come to a better understanding of those modes of behaviour which are common to the non-patient and the patient, since the responses of the latter are more marked. This prevents us from taking certain findings in non-patients as "too much for granted" or considering them as "too likely to occur".[3]

Sorting of Holmgren wool samples

Patient R. was instructed to pick out from a pile of Holmgren wool samples those which are similar to, or go with, a particular sample. The patient slowly tried out various skeins by holding the given sample next to each one. In most cases, however, he rejected the skeins singled out and finally decided upon very few – namely the identical ones.[4]

The experimenter now takes a series of different greens out of the pile, puts them together in a bunch and asks the patient whether these don't all belong or fit together. The patient denies this emphatically and says, pointing to a dark skein in the bunch, "Green!" Then he indicates by gestures that the other skeins have nothing to do with this one and that the experimenter should lay them aside. Suddenly, however, he catches sight of a bright green skein in the bunch (which had evidently been concealed from him previously by the others), and now he endeavors vehemently to make clear to the experimenter that he had made a mistake before, that the first-mentioned dark green skein was not green at all; only this one (the bright green) was green. At the same time he searches with great effort for a new designation for the dark green skein. The patient indignantly rejects the suggestion of the experimenter that one might say of this skein too that it is green, that perhaps all the skeins in the bunch are green. The patient continues in his endeavors to find a special name for the dark green skein.

The behavior of this patient conforms strikingly to the types of reaction which Gelb and Goldstein [45] found in their investigations concerning amnestic aphasia. This patient too is not really contented with his choice until he has found the completely identical colors. Similarly he is quite at a loss when confronted with the idea of applying a principle of classification (for example, the category "green"). He does not understand at all what is meant by the statement, "They are all green". The word "green" suits him only when applied to a certain quite definite shade (very glaring). The 'mistake' which he believes he has made is characteristic of the primitivity of his behavior. In spite of the fact that he was able to apply the word 'green' to both skeins, this occurred in a way which was quite different from what happens with a normal person. Since for him this word is evidently suitable only for a perfectly *definite* color experience, he is, to be sure, capable of designating related experiences by the same term, but only so long as the true shade is not present. As soon as he has found *his* nuance, the one first designated is no longer to be considered at all. The procedure of this patient then is 'uncategorial' in the highest degree. For him designations fit only a very limited type of experience. How far related impressions can be designated by the same name depends upon how far this type can be strechted. In any case, the patient tends, in so far as possible, to possess a particular expression for each nuance of color tone.

Now that we have seen that the patient is incapable of sorting colors according to conceptually established points of view, it will be of interest to become acquainted with his reaction to objects which the normal person can arrange both according to color and according to form.

Sorting of cardboard figures of different color and form

Experiment 1. The patient was presented with 12 unarranged cardboard figures of different color and form: *four equilateral triangles* (red, green, yellow, blue), *four squares* (red, green, yellow, blue), *four circles* (red, green, yellow, blue). He was told to sort them. The patient carried out the task as follows: First he put together a *red* triangle, a *red* circle, and a *red* square in a vertical row. Similarly he put together the yellow, green, and blue figures, so that as a result a series of rows, one red, one yellow, one green, one blue, lay next to each other a few centimeters apart.

The way the patient followed the instructions is extraordinarily typical for the concreteness of his manner of procedure: he 'built'. Although his procedure was co-determined by the color, he did not form four different irregular piles of color, but he first laid down for himself a pattern out of the red figures, and then copied this in the other colors. The patient could give no explanation of the point of view according to which he undertook the arrangement. When told to sort the figures 'differently', the patient proceeded in the following manner: After long consideration he exchanged the circles and triangles within the rows of like color. This procedure shows that the patient is strongly confined in a very definite attitude from which he cannot free himself deliberately. Further, he is not at all capable of reflecting on his method of procedure. These facts strongly indicate that he did not put the figures of like color together because he started from a conceptually fixed principle of sorting, *but rather that his reaction was forced upon him by the sensorially manifest aspects of the situation,* namely by the element of color and by esthetic factors (symmetry, etc.).

Parallel experiments on normal persons. Let us compare with the above the results obtained from normal adults. The subjects without exception reported that in looking over the given material their first impression was that of 'color variety' in which the colors of similiar quality seemed to join together in 'color spots'. Also usually *one* color (red or yellow) thrust itself particularly upon their attention. When told to sort the figures very quickly, inhibiting reflection in so far as possible, most of the subjects – in charateristic contrast to the patient – formed four irregular piles (corresponding to the number of color tones). Only one subject put the figures of like color together in definite patterns, as did the patient. He too *'built'* – from which one sees that the behavior of normal persons, when reacting without any particular reflection, may conform strikingly to that of the patient. The difference between the normal person and the patient becomes clear, however, as soon as the normal person is asked whether one might also sort the figures 'differently'. The normal subject, without long consideration or delay, then mentions sorting *according to form* as a second possibility.

Experiment 2. In order to attain in the patient as well as in the normal subject an orientation toward form, we presented the figures to him again, unarranged, and repeated the instruction to sort them 'differently'. After about five minutes the patient decided on an arrangement in which the yellow, blue, green, and red circles were placed on top of each other in an overlapping fashion. He supported it by pointing to each circle and saying, "all different" (whereby he wanted to indicate the difference in the colors). The patient answered in the affirmative to the experimenter's question as to whether one could also have arranged them in an overlapping line of a blue circle, yellow triangle, green circle, and red circle, i.e., substituting a yellow triangle for the yellow circle.

After the experimenter himself had arranged them in two configurations, an overlapping row of red, green, blue, and yellow circles and an overlapping row made up of a yellow triangle, blue circle, and red square, and asked the patient which arrangement is 'prettier', the patient said, "I think that one" (pointing to the circles). Experimenter: "Why?" Patient (after long consideration): "Because they are all this way" (making circular motions with his finger).

From Experiment 2 we see how careful one must be in judging overt results. Although at the beginning it seemed certain that the patient had finally 'arrived at the form', this supposition was proved false by his reference to the difference in color of the circles. He obviously wanted to proceed 'quite differently' from the way he did in the preceding experiment; but he remained nevertheless oriented according to 'color'. Whereas at first he had been determined by the *similarity* of color, now he was reacting ('quite differently') to the *difference* of color. The similiarity of form in the circles played a decidedly secondary role. This is proved by the fact that the yellow circle could be replaced by a yellow triangle. Not until the two rows were placed beside each other was the patient thereby enabled to make the 'transition' to the element of form. And even this transition does not take place in the 'conceptual sphere', but remains palpable – "because they are all this way" (makes circular motions). It is extremely characteristic for the behavior of the patient that this 'transition' is so difficult for him. The circumstances must be absolutely 'coercive' in order to bring about the shift: 'color' → 'form'. This is in pronounced contrast to the reaction of normal persons, in whom, as we already mentioned, the shift followed immediately without any change of the original conditions.

Experiment 3. In order to emphasize still more the immediate way in which likeness of form suddenly thrusts itself phenomenally upon the apprehension of the subject, we arranged the following experiment. The patient was given all 12 figures face downward. The backs were all white. He was asked to sort them. The patient observed first: "All white". Then, farily quickly, he put together all those of like form in three separate rows. The experiment confirmed our expectations completely. *Now that a phenomenal organization on the basis of color is no longer possible, the 'element of form' immediately obtrudes;* i.e., 'the sphere of color', which does not permit homogeneous organizations, recedes and a new sphere, highly organized within itself, namely that of forms, becomes the prevailing stimulus.

Parallel experiments on normal persons. This type of reaction is also found in normal persons. As soon as the figures are presented to the subjects, they exclaim: "Oh, everything is white", or "Now everything is dead", etc. Then they immediately add: "Now there is no choice", "The identical figures thrust themselves upon one right away". Thus it also holds true for normal persons that this stimulative constellation is palpably coercive in the same way as it is for patients.

The three figures with which we had worked in our experiments up to this point were all *identical (congruent) in form.* Révész [141] in certain experiments in abstraction on monkeys, succeeded in training his two experimental animals so that they reacted in the desired manner to figures which were identical in form (different in color). However, as soon as Révész gave them only similar instead of identical figures (for example, triangle), the monkeys failed. In order to test the behavior of our patient under this change of experimental conditions, we tried the following experiment.

Experiment 4. The patient is given 8 figures of different color and form: *three triangles* (one red acute-angled, one yellow equilateral, one green obtuse angled), *three quadrangles* (one red oblique-angled parallelogram, one yellow oblong, one green square), *two circles* (red and yellow). *Athough Experiments 3 (on the organization of forms) had preceded this one, the patient immediately put the figures of like color together.*

Experiment 5. When, however, all the figures were shown with the white side up, and no specific directions given, the patient arranged them in a line from left to right with the largest figure on the extreme left and gradually decreasing in size. The figures lay in the following order from left to right: oblong, oblique, square, circle, equilateral, acute circle, and obtuse. When asked what this method of arrangement meant, he made an angle with his hands, signifying *that he had put the figures together according to size, "in the form of a wedge".*

Parallel experiments on normal persons. The results of experiments on normal persons also offer proof for the immediacy of the method of arrangement according to size. One normal subject, when told to sort the figures (white side up) with as little reflection as possible, carried out the task exactly as the patient had done. His behavior too was determined by the size or the wedge-like form, although he had not formed any clear concept beforehand of what he was doing. Then, however – when the experimenter said one could also arrange the figures differently – the subject *immediately* put them together *according to form.* Another subject expressed himself about the experimental arrangement of the figures white side up thus: „This is a very unpleasant situation, actually painful. Really the main impression is that of white. One can put the triangles together too. They have something in common. The two circles are pleasant also. The parallelogram doesn't fit with the two quadrangles." We see that in this case the experience of the 'forms' in palpable material is not at all 'coercive' even for normal persons; on the contrary, it is unpleasant. It is necessary to overcome this first impression in order to arrive at an orientation toward the formal element. But, whereas in the normal person this shift is easily accomplished, in the patient it is extremely difficult.

Experiment 6. Since in Experiment 5 all the insistent urging to sort 'differently' did not help the patient at all, the experimenter took these figures away and put back the original arrangement (see Experiment 3) of figures with identical forms, white side up. *Without hesitation the patient put the figures of like form together.* Then these figures were taken away and the patient was again given those of Experiment 5 (white side up). He was told to sort them 'just as' he did those of a moment ago. The patient hesitated a long time; he constantly tended to arrange them once more according to size, *until he suddenly exclaimed "Ah!" and now he immediately put together the three triangles, two circles, square and oblong.* He held the parallelogram in his hand for some time, then put it with the oblong, with the explanation: "a little crooked" (meaning, just like the oblong, only crooked).

If we compare the result of Experiments 4–6 with the preceding, we can establish the fact that the patient in both cases reacted identically. In these last experiments too he was determined first by the 'element of color' (in spite of the preceding experiments in form). But it was especially difficult this time to bring about a reaction to the formal element. An appropriate experiment with especially coercive conditions was necessary. From the explanation with which he put the parallelogram with the two other quadrangles (it was for him "just like the oblong, only somewhat crooked"), we can conclude that here again he did not proceed with the help of a principle of classification, but that he put the figures together only according to their palpable relatedness with regard to form. We found this same hesitancy in the normal person in placing the parallelogramm only when he was acting with as little reflection as possible. Yet as soon as the figures were sorted according to the general principle, 'form', and to the more specialized principle, "quadrangularity", the parallelogram offered no greater difficulties than the square or the oblong. This kind of reaction, however, was lacking in the patient, who constantly tried to achieve a kind of arrangement which would be natural for him, namely the concretely phenomenal arrangement according to size. As already mentioned, there was no question in this experiment of a *voluntary* transition from color to form in the patient; but rather, the way in which the figures acquired pertinence was *dictated* to him by what was palpably manifest.

Summary of the color-form-sorting experiments. In the introduction we have already formulated the question as to the processes on the basis of which "sortings according to various points of view" are obtained in patients or normal persons. In connection with the experimental results of this paragraph we are now able to state the following. Under our particular experimental conditions the normal persons (in so far as they proceeded conceptually) easily succeeded in sorting the given cardboard figures both according to color and according to form. The transition or, as one might say, the 'point of shift' from one method of sorting to the other offered no particular difficulty.

Although on our patient some kind of arrangement of the figures could always be achieved, the difference between his reaction and that of the normal person consisted in the fact that he could not volitionally give up the kind of arrangement which he had just achieved in favor of another. As we have seen, it was not easy for him to pass from putting together figures of like color to putting together figures of like form. To obtain from the patient as prompt a transition from one way of reacting to another as from the normal person, the purely verbal direction "to sort differently" was not sufficient. In general it was necessary to use particularly coercive factors, rooted in palpable immediacy. Thus, in the patient the impulse to change his method of procedure never started from conceptual considerations, but always lay in factors of a purely palpable kind.

There were *three kinds* of condition which brought the patient from his orientation toward organizations within one particular 'sphere' to organizations within another 'sphere' intended by the experimenter. First, the patient was brought to a 'point of shift' by the *juxtaposition* of figures of different color and like form, or of figures of different color and different form (see Experiment 2) Second, the transition from 'size' to 'form' was achieved by the *after-effect* of a corresponding preliminary experiment (see Experiment 6). Third, the *'homogeneity'*, the *'imposs-iblity of organization'* within an experienced area served as a condition for the appearance of a 'point of shift' (see Experiment 3).

The behavior of the patient in the experiment with the cardboard figures is no more to be considered as a sorting in the ordinary sense of the word than his behavior with the skeins of wool. It is rather a matter of direct reaction to organizations of a palpable kind, the comprehension of which does not presuppose a 'categorial' attitude. The correctness of our interpretation is confirmed especially by the parallel experiments on normal persons. From these it is evident that normal persons behave quite similarly to patients when they act quickly with as little reflection as possible. In such behavior it is always evident that the change in the type of reaction is the expression of a 'point of shift' in the phenomenal realm. The change does not occur through a volitional shifting on the part of the subject.

Herewith the phenomenon of the 'point of shift' becomes the focus of our consideration. The way in which the point of shift appears upon the scene and the conditions of its appearance must give us a hint about the way in which those concrete performances are brought about, hitherto usually considered to be the product of particular processes of abstraction.

The following investigations concerning the sorting of objects seem especially suited to add to the further clarification of this problem.

Sorting of objects

The experimental set-up described and illustrated below differs from those previously mentioned in that it was always used routinely as a standard set-up in the investigation of a great number of subjects. We had to keep the external conditions of our experiment constant throughout in order to be able to compare and correlate the reactions of the various subjects.[5]

The objects were chosen and arranged according to quite definite points of view, which were calculated to facilitate closer investigation of the problem of the point of shift. We were chiefly concerned with choosing numerous experimental objects of such a kind that in certain respects they could be "experienced as fitting together very well", and in others "as fitting together very poorly".[6]

Method and experimental arrangement of objects

In the system of the 30 experimental objects employed we included various kinds of possible organizations. The objects could be sorted according to their *use:* (1) toys, (2) tools, (3) smoking paraphernalia, (4) edibles, (5) eating utensils; or according to their *color* (one object of each of the above 5 groups was bright red); or according to their *elongated form* (in each of the 5 groups there was one longish object); or according to their *double occurence* (in each of the 5 groups one object appeared twice, for example two lumps of sugar, etc.). All of these possibilities of sorting were emphasized by the spatial arrangement of objects on the table.

This emphasis on the possible pertinence of the objects to different groups was, however, weakened by the fact that the objects within the several groups stood in a very 'paradoxical' relationship to each other. (For example, the doll's spoon did not go with the ordinary knife and fork, the child's hammer was much too small for the large nail, etc.)

We can, of course, cite only the main points of view which guided us in the construction of our experimental set-up. Everything else is taken up in the discussion of the protocols.

Instructions. The subjects were first asked to look over the set-up and to make themselves familiar with the individual objects. They were permitted to ask about unknown objects. Then they were instructed to choose any object at all. Children were told to choose 'the prettiest', 'the one they liked best', and to hand it to the experimenter. From now on we shall designate this object as the 'first object of departure'. After this was done, the subjects were to hand to the experimenter those objects which, in their opinion, 'belonged with' the chosen object of departure, or 'went with it', or 'which one could suitably hand over with it.' These expressions were used together in this order, especially at the beginning. Each time an object was given to the experimenter it was removed from the sight of the subject. When the subjects thought that "nothing more belonged with, suited, etc., the object of departure", the "series" was considered closed, and all the objects were returned to their original positions. Next a new object of departure was chosen, not by the subject, but by the experimenter. Again the subjects were to hand the experimenter the proper objects. The forming of 'series' was continued as long as the experimenter deemed it necessary. This phase of the experiment we shall designate in the following as the phase of 'handing'.

At the close of this part of the experiment the original arrangement of objects was reconstructed. The subject was then told to sort all the objects in clearly separated groups in the way in which the objects seemed to him to 'belong' or 'fit together'. For this purpose the subject

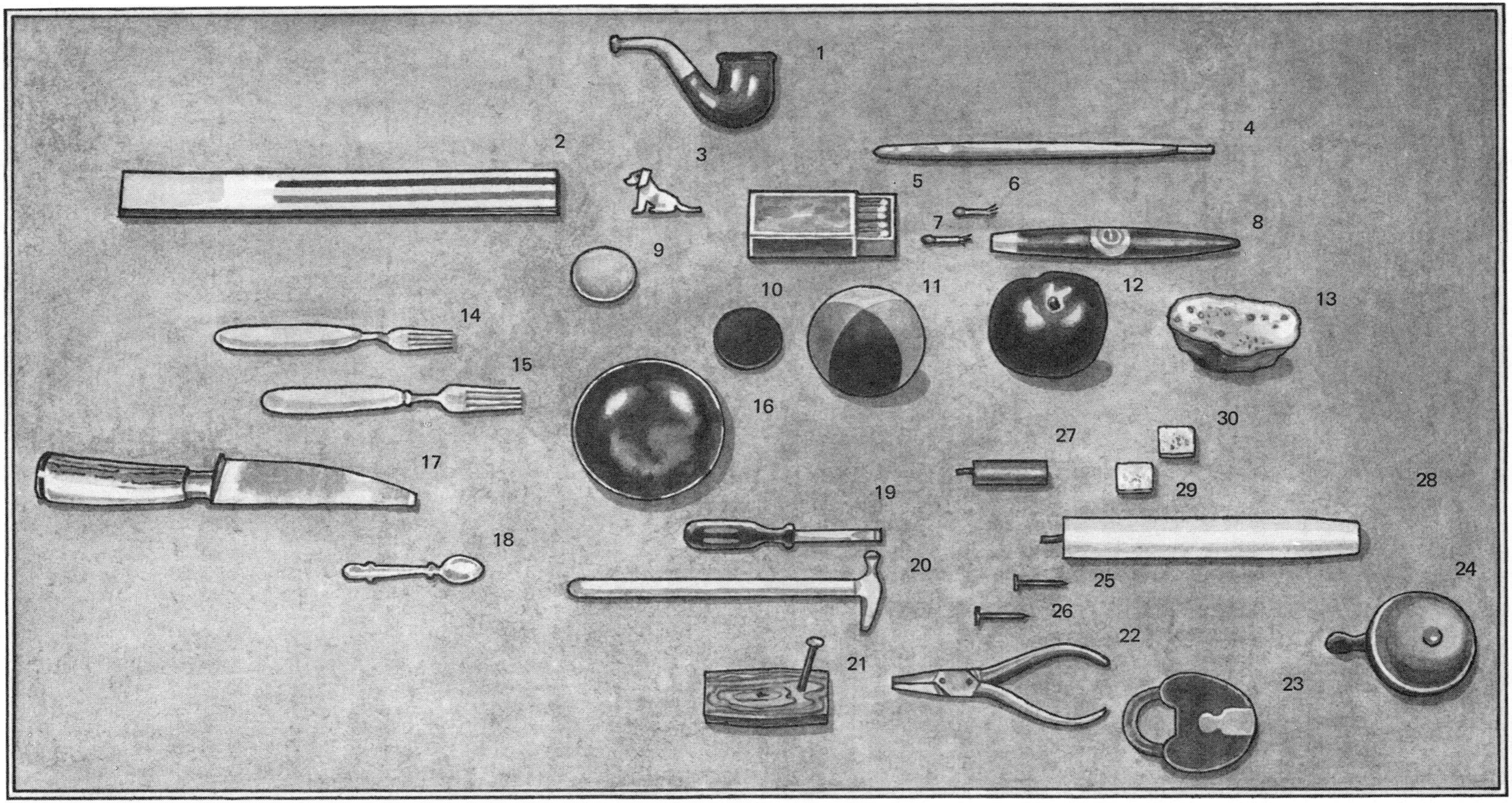

Figure 1 *1 pipe, 2 toy wooden sword, 3 dachshund (made of ivory), 4 Virginia cigar, 5 match box, 6 7 two broken off matches, 8 chocolate cigar, 9 10 red and yellow cardboard discs, 11 ball, 12 red apple, 13 slice of bread, 14 15 two forks, 16 red wooden plate, 17 knife, 18 doll's spoon, 19 screw driver with red handle, 20 child's hammer with white handle, 21 piece of wood (white) with nail in it, 22 pair of pincers, 23 padlock, 24 bicycle bell, 25 26 two nails, 27 28 one red and one white candle, 29 30 two lumps of sugar*

was given a particular place beside the table cloth (on which the objects were set up), where he was to distribute the objects in the aforesaid manner. When this was accomplished, the 'hase of sorting' was finished. This whole experiment we shall designate as the main experiment. After its completion supplementary experiments of various kinds were made, according to whether particular questions presented themselves with regard to the individual subject.

Subjects. Forty kindergarten children (4–6 years old), 30 feeble-minded children of a Frankfurt ungraded school (ca. 3–13), 6 patients with cerebral lesions, and 12 normal adults, most of whom were psychologically trained.

Behavior of Patient R. After the patient, *without saying a word,* had followed the instruction to look at all the objects (he was expressly told he need not name them), he was asked to hand to the experimenter any one of the objects. The patient chose a lump of sugar. Now he was directed to hand over all of the experimental objects which seemed to fit with the object of departure. After minutely examining the array, the patient shook his head and said "nothing" belongs with it. Thereupon the experimenter picked up, one at a time, 20 different objects from the table and each time instructed the patient to hand over whatever objects fit with it. In 12 cases the patient denied emphatically that anything went with the object in question. In 7 cases he handed over one object for each object of departure (for example, the fork for the knife, the match box for the cigar, the pincers for the piece of wood with a nail in it). Once he handed over 2 objects (for the fork, the doll's spoon and the knife). This concluded the phase of 'handing'.

When we consider the pairs of objects which the patient formed several times in this procedure, the type of combination (for example, knife-bread, etc.) seems extremely concrete. The patient usually put the objects together *in a way in which they could actually be used together in the situation of the moment.* Since, by our choice of objects, we had managed that combinations of this kind should be possible only among two or at most three objects, and often not at all, it is not surprising that the patient could not arrive at any real sorting so long as he retained this concrete attitude. Since he was oriented solely toward the manipulative element in the objects, they had in general 'nothing to do with each other' for him.

Among the other patients with cerebral lesions whom we investigated, the reactions of patient B. in [45] particularly resembled those of patient R. He too 'handed over' in general not more than three objects for any one object of departure. The practical utility of the objects was for him too the decisive factor. This led to the result that the patient frequently missed some objects in the array presented to him. For example, with the pipe he handed over the matches and the spoon (for scratching out the pipe) with the words, 'There is no tobacco'. Further, he felt the lack of the key for the padlock, etc. The patient showed this kind of behavior during the whole first phase of the experiment. When, however, the experimenter asked him more and more urgently whether one must always hand over in that way, whether one couldn't do it *differently,* and "what things, for example, one might hand with this [the fork], *which are like it",* then the patient suddenly said, "Oh!" and gave him the second fork. As this still did not seem to satisfy the experimenter, the patient suddenly nodded understandingly at the next object of departure and gave him, one after another, all the objects which were made partly or entirely of metal. From then on this method of sorting determined most of his reactions in handling. In 'sorting' also, he put together in groups the objects made of metal, paper, wood, and the edibles. We shall return later to this method of sorting. It seems to be particularly natural for this patient, since in the Gelb-Goldstein experiments he favoured this type of reaction as well.

The reactions of patient R. in the next phase of the experiment, that of sorting, differ scarcely at all from those just described. When instructed to sort the objects the way they belong together, the patient always picked up from the array one object with both hands, and formed in this way ten pairs (for example: cigar-matchbox, apple-knife, fork-spoon, etc.). The remaining objects he put down separately (for example: bread, pipe, toy dog, etc.). His reaction time was somewhat longer than that of most of our normal adult subjects.

As we have seen, the patient, in sorting, behaves quite similarly to the way he did in "handing". *He persists in his orientation toward the manipulative element.* It is important for our problem that the patient never spontaneously showed even a tendency to actualize other ways of reacting. When asked whether one could put the things together "differently", he answered in the negative, even after long consideration.

Among the normal adult subjects we find certain parallels for this concrete kind of behavior.[7]

Some interpretive observations one of our normal subjects made may contribute especially to our problem of the "point of shift'. As soon as the orientation toward the element of manipulation disappears, this subject experiences the material in a different way. *No longer do objects of common use,* which have more or less to do with each other, lie before him, but now only *„spots of color"* appear to him. We have here, quite unintended by the subject, a spontaneous transition from the "thing sphere" to the "color sphere". It is not the subject who separates, or "abstracts" the colors from the common objects, but the colors suddenly thrust themselves upon him. And this penomenon evidently occurs after a palpably meaningful organization within the context of 'common-use objects' was not able to enforce itself. But this phenomenological experience of the color spots also suddenly yields to another – 'the whole falls apart'; a new organization of another sphere enforces itself: "for grown-ups and for children'. We shall not discuss here to what extent this last distinction is to be considered as more 'concrete' or more 'categorial'. For our purposes it is important that this normal subject, in contrast to the patient R., is able to experience quite a number of transitions between spheres of very different kind.

A comparison of the behavior of this subject and the patient R. brings out especially clearly the *rigidity and monotony* in the patient's behavior as contrasted with the flexibility which is always possible in the normal subject.

This difference can be recognized even more pronouncedly in the reactions of the other *normal adult* subjects. In general, they accomplished both the handing and the sorting on the basis of quite definite principles of classification, i.e., on the basis of categorial behavior. Whereas, in sorting, usually only the point of view of pertinence with regard to use was decisive; in "handing", however, the most varied points of view dominated, one after another in quickly shifting succession (for example, "similarity", "color", etc.). "Points of shift" from one sphere to another appeared, so to speak, constantly. Undoubtedly the external impulse for these changes came in general from the purely phenomenal realm, but the necessary condition for the actualization of such points of shift must usually be sought in the ability of the subject to orient himself to the given material as little concretely and as little practically as possible. In contrast to the results obtained from patient R., we could ascertain in most of the normal subjects a far-reaching *independence of the "real" nature* of the articles presented to them. Frequently their reactions could scarcely have turned out differently *if they had had to deal solely with the names of the experimental objects.* This conceptual method, when applied to our set-up of experimental material, necessarily led to the most varied kinds of arrangement. Thus it actually happend that in the beginning most of these subjects had great difficulties each time with the instruction to hand over or sort what belongs with this or that, or what belongs or fits together. The subjects could scarcely ward off the multiplicity of possibilities of arrangement. Only with difficulty were they able to come to a final decision. When the patient R. likewise hesitated to obey the instruction "to hand over" (or "sort"), it was for just the opposite reason; for him the objects usually did not fit together at all or only very poorly.

Behavior of children. We have, up to this point, become acquainted in the main with two types of reaction: (1) *"sorting in pairs"* (the same in handing) or "segregation" of the objects on the basis of *very concrete* orientation toward *manipulation;* (2) *"sorting in large groups"* (and "handing of long series of objects") on the basis of a more *categorial,* conceptual orientation. Now we have also met with types of reaction which *externally* were identical with this second type in that large groups and long series were formed. But they came about on the basis of a kind of orientation which ist entirely different from the categorial.

To illustrate this last type of reaction we shall cite some extracts from the protocols of kindergarten and ungraded classes.

Four-year-old Mo. tells us, while handing over the bicycle bell, little red candle, etc., to go with the padlock (as object of departure), "You can make a light in the evening when you put on the lock down in the cellar." And when the experimenter asks her what the bell has to do with this, she answers reproachfully, "Why that's upstairs in the apartment!" Similarly, seven-year-old Ste. accompanies his handing of objects to go with the hammer (as object of departure) with the following words: (He hands the sword.) "You can make that with the little hammer." (He hands the white candle.) "You make a light with that when you hammer." (Hands the match box.) "You light the candle with that." (Hands bread.) "You eat that when you're hungry." (Hands pipe.) "And then you smoke the pipe." (Hands dachshund.) "And the doggy must keep watch when the man goes out."

The ungraded school children under ten react in general in a similar way. For example Hö. (eight years, three months) hands over a number of objects to go with the dachshund (as object of departure) and spontaneously gives the following explanations: (Hands plate.) "He drinks out of that." (Hands little red plate.) "He can sit on that." (Hands ball.) " He plays with that." (Hands bread, two lumps of sugar, apple.) "He eats these." (Hands spoon.) "To feed him when he doesn't eat anything." (Hands match box.) "When you want to cook something for the dog."

These few examples are probably sufficient to show that the children frequently handed over most or all of the objects to go with one single object of departure. For the children, "sorting" in the adult sense came into question only in rather rare cases. They understood the instruction in their childlike way. In general, *to belong together* meant to the children "meaningful appurtenance to a situation" and indeed to a situation which from the adult point of view must seem "unreal", "imaginative", "playful". As soon as the attention of the child is attracted by the dachshund, for example, a "story" begins to spin itself about the dog. The main theme is determined by the little dog and the developments are determined by the objects perceived thereafter. It would, of course, be entirely false to maintain that the children "knew", to be sure, that the dachshund was only a "carved bone knickknack", and that they "transformed" it by their fantasy into a "real" animal. This kind of interpretation makes the mistake of identifying the child's world with ours – a mistake which is generally recognized in the child psychology of today. If one observes children in such situations (which from our point of view are "imaginative"), one can no longer harbor any doubts about the vividness, the concreteness of the reaction. The "stories" are not invented, thought up, and then superimposed upon the real world, but rather, *they take place in the real world* – only it is in the world of the child, and not in ours.

We can then assert that on the basis of the childlike orientation the number of objects which belonged together could be increased *ad lib.* The objects, which were perceived as already definitely related to some "story" or other, shifted their functions accordingly. The procedure of the children must be designated as *concrete to the highest degree,* and concrete with reference to the experienced reality of the child. Frequently we were able to observe that with the perception of some previously unnoticed object, the manner of sorting or grouping objects suddenly changed the "story" had evidently taken a new turn through the dominance of a new article.

In one normal, psychologically trained adult we found, under certain conditions, types of reaction which showed a certain relationship to those of the children. The statements of this subject will give us certain hints about the experiences of the children.

Subject He.: The subject repeatedly 'handed' series of as many as 17 objects and sorted 'groups' of as many as eight objects.

As the first object of departure the subject chose the apple and handed over 16 objects to go with it, in the following order: knife, two lumps of sugar, bread, chocolate cigar, Virginia cigar, two forks, doll's spoon, pipe, match box, two matches, two candles, plate. On completing the series she gave us these bits of observation upon herself: "I constantly had a story in mind. By the apple I was led to the situation of eating. This demanded knife, fork, spoon – really a whole cover. In looking for this, I saw these 'impossible' eating utensils and got a real shock. Then I consciously adjusted: 'But they aren't toys'; at this moment the objects were no longer impossible; they fitted the situation of eating; it was as if they were *'changed'*. I went on from one thing to another and could no longer separate. It could have gone on this way for hours – so to speak, a chain of little circles, which hung together."

In another series with the bicycle bell (as object of departure), the subject handed padlock, pincers, hammer, two pegs wood, screw driver, and stated that in handing the lock and pincers she had the idea of a bicycle kit in which these two things belonged. Suddenly – on perceiving the hammer – she was led to the situation of fussing about with gadgets, and this notion caused her to hand two pegs, the wooden board and the screwdriver. It struck her especially that the objects had frequently changed their significance according to the particular object of departure to which they were related. Thus, for example, the plate had functioned as 'eating plate' (objects of departure: apple, dachshund and fork), as 'toy plate' (objects of departure: little plate and ball), and as 'ash tray' (object of departure: Virginia cigar). In 'sorting' she made 'drawers' just as if she had had a "cabinet at home with many things to arrange in it". In doing this she formed the following groups: (1) tools, (2) edibles, (3) toys, (plate, ball, chocolate cigar, 2 little plates, spoon, sword), (4) table silver, (5) match box, 2 matches, 2 candles, (6) Virginia cigar and pipe.

We have to do here with a kind of behavior which is not entirely like any adult behavior yet described. The subject neither lets herself be disturbed by the fact that objects fit together poorly (like patient R.), nor does she feel the objects as very fitting from "conceptual" points of view. The factor which is decisive for her reactions is – as she herself says – the 'situation' in which she finds herself at the moment (usually purely imaginative). Thus, for example, in handing objects to go with the Virginia cigar (as object of departure), a perfectly definite smoking table is present *to her imagination,* on which, so to speak, she puts the object which she hands over. Or another time, with the fork as object of departure, she imagines herself setting the table for dinner. Sometimes a sudden transition from one situation to another occurs (see protocol: bicycle kit – fussing about with gadgets). This transition may be caused by the perception of one or of several objects. But there are always 'stories' present which successively replace one another. Sometimes, however, it also happens that the subject is completely torn away from a situation by the perception of a particular object. She experiences a 'shock'. Then suddenly she realizes the real nature of the various objects; the incongruity of certain objects offends her. A conscious shift is necessary in order to get back to the previous situation. If this transfer is attained, the objects seem as if they were 'changed'; the disharmony no longer exists.

Such reactions to situations differ from the concrete types of behavior (noted particularly in patient R.), especially in the farreaching independence of the real nature of the objects. They differ from the categorial behavior, demonstrated by other normal subjects, in the extraordinary vividness of the procedure, and in their entirely irrational nature. Thus this type of reaction is, on the one hand, *concrete to the highest degree* and, on the other hand, *„highly imaginative"*. We see here the close relationship of this type of reaction to that which we described in children; and at the same time we gain hereby further understanding of the behavior and the experiences of the little ones. One must not, however, overlook the fact that this comparison can be only relative. This is particularly true of the 'experiences of shock', which are expressions of the fact that the world of imagination must remain to a very large extent 'unreal' for us grown-ups. In a little child a transition of such a rude nature is impossible, because his 'actual' reality is by no means so sharply distinguished from the 'reality of imagination'.

We scarcely need mention that the types of behavior here described do not nearly exhaust the material which actually occurs and which we observed. We could set up a whole series of steps of different 'reaction tendencies', rising from the concrete to the more categorial. The selection given from our material, however, will suffice to form a basis for the discussion of our specific problem.

In this context it may be worth-while giving a brief reminder of the studies made by N. Ladîgina-Kots [93] on a chimpanzee, in which a 'shift' of a kind very similar to the one mentioned here is referred to, although no details are supplied. A test is described there in which a bowl of a certain color was held out to a chimpanzee in order to make the animal pick a square piece of the same color as the bowl's from a number of square pieces of different color. N. Ladîgina-Kots, who made the test to find out about the animal's 'capability for abstraction', tells us that in the beginning the animal coped with its task only when another object of identical shape was in the bowl, too – in which case it simply put two identical squares together. It managed to put a square piece of a certain color into a bowl of the same color without any such 'assitance' only "after a large number of continuing systematic tests". While the chimpanzee was being led from putting together identical squares to putting a square into a bowl of the same colour as the square's, something must have happened in the animal that is in a way comparable to the 'shift' in our patient and that suddenly made him see 'colors'.

It is quite plain that there is a radical difference between the first and the second performance of the chimpanzee, which are both the result of training; for seeing a bowl not as a bowl (i.e. as an object that can be handled in a certain manner), but considering only colors as such requires a chimpanzee to adopt a high degree of what might be called 'non-concrete' attitude, which can be brought about only by very specific training, by a constant repetition of 'compelling' circumstances.

Summary of the experiments in the sorting of objects. In looking back over the experiments in sorting which were performed upon the patient, let us ask ourselves what points of view have been furnished for the investigation of our problem of the 'point of shift'. In the main, the answer must be a negative one. Under our experimental conditions, the point of shift occurred not at all or very seldom. This fact is due to the circumstance that in offering the patient (especially patient R.) objects of common use, we forced him from the very beginning into an orientation toward a perfectly definite sphere. The patient concentrates entirely on the practical use of the articles. He tends to "do something with them", to "manipulate" them. Thus it follows that for the patient the objects will fit together not on the basis of any common elements, but on the basis of the way they "can be used together" practically (as palpably experienced). Considering the special nature of our experimental conditions, very narrow limits are set for any change in the patient's type of reaction. And this was actually to be seen in a kind of 'monotony' or 'fixedness' of his behavior.

On the other hand, we found a significantly greater flexibility in the normal adult subjects. Even when they preferred certain definite types of arrangement if they acted unreflectingly, nevertheless a reorientation toward spheres of the most varied kinds was easily possible for them if the experimenter asked whether one could not also sort the things 'differently'. Some subjects even changed their types of sorting solely on the basis of conceptual knowledge, by asking themselves what possibilities of arrangement – purely formally – existed. Here we have to do with 'points of shift' of a purely 'categorial' nature. We also observed in the normal adult subjects (especially when they were acting unreflectingly) transitions from one sphere to another, even within the purely phenomenological realm. And finally a third kind of 'point of shift' should be mentioned, which was caused by definite palpable experiences and which then led to a principle of classification, formulated conceptually (as, for example, when the experience of a red spot of color gave rise to 'sorting according to color' in the categorial sense).

Sorting of objects under particularly 'Coercive' conditions

Up to this point our experiments on patient R., in the sorting of objects, have led only to negative results concerning the 'point of shift.' We should like now to investigate whether there are conditions – and if so of what kind they may be – under which the patient can be led to shift to other types of behavior with regard to objects of common use.

Experiments in threes. Just as we previously presented the patient with three colored skeins, we now present him with three objects, for example: Virginia cigar – match box – pipe. The patient is to put together those two objects which 'fit togehter best'. He decides, in this case, on the Virginia cigar and match box. He refuses to put the pipe with the match box, offering as explanation: 'because there is no tobacco in it'.

The following statements of the patient show how strongly he is still oriented in these experiments toward practical usableness, realizable in the situation of the moment: the knife belongs with the apple rather than with the fork; the bread goes with the knife, but not with the sugar (whereas numerous other subjects felt immediately that bread and sugar belonged together as 'edibles'). In contrast to most of the other subjects, he does not even consider putting the chocolate cigar and the match box together. Of the two possible combinations, only the one 'close to life' is coercive for him. Thus, this sort of experimental condition brought us no further with the patient with regard to the 'point of shift'.

Sorting of objects according to 'material'. The patient is presented with two piles of objects. In the one are only objects made of wood (stethoscope, two pen holders, handle of a hammer, pencil, two spatulas); in the other pile are only objects made of metal (padlock, doll's spoon, bicycle bell, razor, two nails, pair of pincers). The patient is to say whether he finds 'any sense in this arrangement', whether it 'is right this way'. *For a long time he looks at the set-up completely puzzled.* Even the assurance of the experimenter that there are quite definite common elements among the objects in each pile does not add anything to the comprehension of the patient.

Experiment 1. The experimenter takes a nail out of the one pile and the handle of a hammer out of the other, and asks the patient to put these objects where they belong among the other objects. He puts the nail with the wood and the handle with the metal. When asked why he did it this way, he says, "Well, Doctor, you, that way too". (He means to say that the experimenter took the objects from these positions.) The experimenter repeats the experiment with the same object, but in such a way that the patient has no idea where they were taken from. Uncertain and hesitating, the patient glances back and forth from the objects in his hands to the two piles. Finally he decides (still very uncertain), and puts the nail with the wood. Immediately thereupon he evidently intends to put the hammer handle with the metal, but suddenly stops, and cries out animatedly, "Oh, now I know." Absolutely certain and clearly conscious of his purpose, he now puts the two objects on their proper piles and says, 'wood–iron'.

This experiment teaches us that there is another kind of reaction possible for the patient, besides that already mentioned, but that it is realizable only under quite definite, very 'coercive' conditions. The entire lack of voluntary action here is very interesting. *The patient does not come by himself to the point of: 'wood–iron', but this pair forces itself upon him phenomenally; he is completely surprised by it. The abruptness expresses itself unmistakably in the whole behavior of the patient. His features suddenly change; he strikes his head with his palm; he has an absolute need to explain his experience to the experimenter (which is made difficult by his aphasia).*

Experiment 2. In order to ascertain whether this comprehension of the connection 'wood–iron' actually made it possible for the patient to sort according to 'wood' and 'iron', we mix up the objects of the two piles, present them unarranged to the patient, and instruct him to sort them. Without hesitation he obeys the instruction and puts the two piles together again quite correctly. In doing so he proceeds very carefully and pedantically, examining every object very exactly to see of what material it is made.

On first glance the result of this experiment does not seem to agree with our assertion that it is impossible for the patient to sort objects according to a principle of classification. *It looks as though he had actually sorted according to 'material' like a normal person.* If the patient had really succeeded in doing so, if he had finally arrived at the principle, then it would make no difference to him if he were given other materials to sort, besides wood and iron.

Experiment 3. The following objects are added to those already used: a rubber ball, a blotter, a clean piece of paper, a full ink well. All the objects are mixed up and presented to the patient unarranged; the instructions are the same as in Experiment 2. The patient looks at the set-up for a long time and then hesitatingly takes the ink well and puts it in the left hand corner of the table; then he puts the other objects in a horizontal row along the edge of the table at intervals of several centimeters (ink well – stethoscope, standing up – two pencils, together – rubber ball – handle of hammer – two pen holders – bicycle bell – pincers – padlock – paper).

We were extremely surprised by this kind of arrangement. Our efforts to obtain from the patient a clear explanation of his motives for it were unsuccessful. Evidently it was for him only a question of "putting the things in order". The sequence of the objects, as such, had no special significance. This impression was confirmed when the experimenter changed the order of some of the objects and asked the patient "whether one could do it that way too". The patient immediately agreed to this exchange of position.

Since the patient had seemingly forgotten his reaction of Experiment 2, the experimenter mixed up these same objects, presented them to him again, and instructed him to sort them just as he had done before (in Experiment 2). These hints, however, were unsuccessful. The patient again took the ink well and started a new series with it, similar to the one in Experiment 3. He did not get the idea of sorting according to 'material'.

Experiment 4. After the four new objects are removed, the patient looks over the set-up for a short time, then suddenly says, 'Oh', with an understanding smile, and promptly arranges two piles: wood – iron. The experimenter now takes the nail out of the iron pile and puts it with the wood. Then he asks the patient whether one could do it that way too. The patient shakes his head and puts the nail back with the iron.

The result of this experiment teaches us that the changed reaction in Experiment 3 cannot simply be attributed to the patient's *'forgetting'* a principle of classification (material), which he had once grasped. *Rather, the addition of the 4 objects had evidently modified the set-up for the patient in such a way that the distinction: wood – iron, was phenomenologically no longer present for him.*

Experiment 5. The circumstance that the patient in Experiment 3 continually streched out his hand toward the ink well, led us to suspect that his changed behavior was caused by the large size and conspicuousness of this object. The experimenter, therefore, mixes up the objects of Experiment 4, adds only the ink well, and presents them to the patient. Looking over the set-up, the patient suddenly sees the ink well and reacts just as in Experiment 3. He starts a series of objects beginning with the ink well. Nor do the repeated instructions of the experimenter to sort just as before (Experiment 4) distract him from this type of reaction.

The experimenter again presents the original set-up (Experiment 5) and expressly instructs the patient to pay no attention to the ink well. But the patient does not succeed in so doing until the experimenter covers it with his hand. *Now the patient again arranges two piles.* After he is finished, the experimenter uncovers the ink well and points to it with a questioning gesture. At first the patient is stuck; then, however, he says quite suddenly, *'Oh, glass', and places the ink well by itself.*

Having finally got the patient, on the basis of appropriate changes of the objective experimental conditions to put together objects of common use which were made of the same material, we might now expect that the patient, under analogously 'coercive conditions', would also put together objects of the same 'color'.

Sorting of objects according to 'color'. Actually we did succeed in effecting this reaction in the patient in the following way. We gave the patient two piles of objects of common use. The one pile consisted of red objects, the other of white. The patient was to state whether this kind of arrangement made any sense to him. At first he answered in the negative (even after we had had him name the color of each separate object). Not until, as in the wood-iron experiment, he had to decide where to put a red object and a white object, did he suddenly cry out, *"Oh, because it's white", and put the two objects on the corresponding piles.*

These experiments too we performed on normal persons, and were able to establish that there are sometimes even normal people for whom this type of 'sorting' does not immediately appear obvious. With these persons, however, the mere mention of the word 'color' is sufficient to cause the 'point of shift' to occur immediately.

The patient's great difficulty in shifting easily manifested itself also in the test with the well-known Rubin figures [145]. A quick shift (of the vase and of the faces or of the black and white crosses) was quite impossible for the patient. Here too the change of figure and background was achieved only under especially 'coercive' experimental conditions, and only after a disproportionately long reaction time.

Summary of the experiments in the sorting of objects under particularly 'coercive' conditions. From the point of view of external results, we had got patient R. – by the special kind of experimental conditions used – to 'sort' according to 'material' and 'color', disregarding other connections of the objects. The closer analysis of the experiments, however, showed that it was impossible for the patient to classify the single objects with one or the other pile as representatives of corresponding categories ('material' or 'color'). We were, on the contrary, able to establish that the same concrete, palpable factors which had at first influenced him toward 'manipulative' groupings, later – under changed conditions – caused him to form "a wooden and an iron" or "a red and a white" pile. In both cases the mere juxtaposition of wood – iron (or red – white) was not sufficient to make the patient shift from the sphere of 'things' which one 'manipulates' to the sphere of material or color. Whereas the majority of the normal adults whom we investigated felt such juxtaposition to be especially 'obtrusive' and 'obvious', the patient, on the other hand, needed a more forceful foundation. With him the 'point of shift' did not appear until he was about to put a single wooden object with the metal pile (or a red with a white).

Only under these conditions did a new *phenomenal* kind of organization force itself upon the patient. The experiment in which the patient suddenly, so to speak, 'discovered' a third category of material (glass), is likewise typical of a change within the purely palpable realm. After the wooden and iron piles were finally put together by the patient, the ink well, when suddenly added, lost its character as a utilitarian object – it became 'glass'.

One might ask at this point whether and in what way the 'points of shift' are experienced by the patient. Since one can scarcely get any statements from the patient himself on this subject, one is forced to depend on observation of his behavior at the moment when his type of reaction changes. One can certainly conclude from the lighting up in his facial expression, frequently observable on such occasions, and from his joyful exclamations that something happens in the patient. It may, nevertheless, be something quite different from that which happens in the normal person in the same situation. A clue in this direction is perhaps to be found in the fact that the patient, after the point of shift, usually remembers nothing of his previous reaction; even reminders on the part of the experimenter do not help. *For the patient, the organizations within one sphere evidently have nothing to do with those of the other spheres.* His joy on the occasion of a new reaction does not, then, arise – as in the normal person – from the experience of having 'grasped' a new connection; it seems rather to be the expression of the experience of a new situation closer to the performance demanded of him.

Summary of the results concerning sorting

We found in our various experiments that the results of the Gelb-Goldstein work, described in the introduction, were confirmed. Under our experimental conditions, the reactions of the patients whom we investigated (especially patient R.), were determined only by organizations and groupings which forced themselves upon the patients phenomenally. This fact was shown (a) in the experiment with the Homgren wool samples, in which only the identical skeins 'fitted together', and (b) in the different experiments with the cardboard figures; in the latter the instruction 'to sort', was first understood by the patient in the sense of 'to build, to make patterns', and only through appropriate 'coercive' conditions did the quality of 'color' or of 'form' or of 'size' become effective. Finally it was also shown (c) in the experiments with objects, which at first produced in the patient only one and the same reaction (namely, the possibility of using the objects together), and in which again only under especially 'coercive' conditions a grouping of objects of like material and like color was attained.

Again and again we were able to convince ourselves of the lack of real principles of sorting in the patient – first by numerous control experiments, and second by comparison with the reactions of normal adult subjects. Although for the normal adult subjects too there were palpable kinds of organization which were so 'pregnant', so coercive, that the subjects, when left to themselves, reacted to them with only one type of sorting; nevertheless, even in these cases a slight hint on the part of the experimenter was sufficient to occasion in the subjects other types of reaction. In contrast to this behavior, the patient could make nothing of such aids on the part of the experimenter, since it was impossible for him to change a phenomenal organization, once experienced, i.e., to arrive at a 'point of shift' by means of the conceptual realm.

In general, our normal adult subjects behaved 'categorially' in sorting objects. With a little effortless consideration they discovered among the experimental objects a more or less large number of common qualities, which then served them as principles of classification. Frequently they proceeded as if only the names of the objects to be sorted were at their disposal; i.e., the experimental objects were for them only representatives of certain categories. We were sometimes even able to observe that the subjects, when asked "how one might sort differently", no longer paid any attention to the set-up, but simply enumerated in a formal, logical way: "according to color, form, etc." As Gelb and Goldstein [45] have already found, normal subjects are relatively independent of the 'real' nature of objects. On the basis of conceptual knowledge they can, so to speak, superimpose a type of arrangement upon objects.

This type of behavior of the normal adult subjects varied, however, according to the degree to which they succeeded in attaining a naïve, unreflecting attitude toward the experiment. This circumstance was evidenced both by the result and by the experience of the subjects. Sorting according to definite points of view was neglected in favor of 'immediate' reactions to elements of a concrete sort.

The results obtained from the experiments on children cast a new light on the contrast between concrete and categorial behavior. The concrete nature of patient R. (under our experimental conditions) expressed itself in great 'monotony' of behavior and in a "lack of facility in shifting"; the concrete nature of the children expressed itself quite differently. The single objects were constantly new stimuli for the children in working out and giving detail to the 'stories' experienced at the moment. Thereby their reactions took on a constantly changing, lively character.

The conditions necessary for the occurrence of the 'points of shift' in patient R. varied, corresponding to the context in which he experienced the phenomenal organization in question. Thus in one of the experiments with the cardboard figures, the *juxtaposition* of two differently organized 'constellations' was sufficient to cause a shift from the 'sphere of color' to the 'sphere of form'. In another experiment the point of shift from the sphere of 'size' to the sphere of 'form' was achieved by the *after-effect* of a previous experiment with especially coercive conditions. As a further very important necessary condition for the shift, we became acquainted with the *lack of possibility of organization within the sphere just experienced.* Our experiments with objects of common use showed that the shift from one palpable organization to another depends to a high degree on the *nature of the experimental material.* The patient needed stronger support than in the experiments just described in order to shift from 'co-usability' to 'likeness of material' or 'likeness of color'.

In the reactions of the normal adult subjects we were able to distinguish *three kinds of 'points of shift':* first, a change within the purely *phenomenal realm* (analogous to the points of shift in the patient); further, *a shift from the sensory, palpable* realm (for example, 'coloredness') to the *conceptual* (for example, 'category of color'); finally, *'points of shift' within the categorial realm* (for example, from 'color' to 'form'). When the shift took place within the phenomenal realm, it was always a matter of *experiences "of immediate and unreflective nature"* – as statements of numerous subjects confirmed – of certain organizations forcing themselves on the subject. The special conditions for the occurrence of these different kinds of points of shift are extremely varied. We must be contented here with the statement that in the main *two kinds of factor* come into question: first *phenomenal* (of a kind similiar to those which we discussed with regard to the patient), and further *elements grounded in the conceptual knowledge of the individual.*

With the children the turning points remained on the whole *within concrete spheres.* They were usually caused by the 'discovery' of a new, 'especially interesting' object, which then of itself gave a new turn to the story already begun.

From our results up to this point certain conclusions concerning the 'problem of abstraction' may already be drawn. The usual theories of abstraction – although they differ from each other more or less in detail – all have this *basic point of view* in common: the reaction to "partial conformities of several objects of perception (so-called common partial contents)" must be preceded by a stage in which these 'percepts' are experientially present as definite objects with a number of well-defined given properties. And the actual 'feat of abstraction' consists in *either voluntarily or involuntarily singling out, i.e. 'abstracting the common partial content', from all the de facto given contents* (so-called 'distinctio rationis').

But this sort of interpretation does not correspond at all to the psychological facts which we have ascertained, in so far as *concrete kinds of response* are concerned. With respect to the concrete responses, such a 'distinctio rationis' as implied in the theories just mentioned is out of the question. Here neither the behavior nor the statements of our subjects gave evidence for the presence of this sort of abstraction.[8] The concrete behavior, therefore, does not involve 'any voluntary abstraction' nor is there any cogent reason for postulating so-called 'involuntary processes of abstraction' as having any part. If we keep to the factual findings of our behavioral analysis, we see that the subjects – whenever they behave concretely – responded each time to a definite organization within a given unreflectively experienced sphere. When this sphere changed for the subject, there were also changes both as to the experience of the contents and as to the experience of the congruencies among the contents of the sphere. So long as we are responding concretely to a stimulus configuration within a definite unreflectively experienced sphere, we can react only to organizations of *this sphere* and not to organizations of any other sphere. Thus it is impossible, for example, to experience the congruency between an apple and a wooden plate "as to color linkeness" so long as one is experiencing an apple, a wooden plate as 'these things' in a *concrete* manner or situation. While behaving concretely we actually experience a living reality, two definite things – an apple, a wooden plate; if, however, we experience the colors on a concrete basis, then the phenomenal sphere has become changed and we no longer experience an apple, a wooden plate as just 'these things', but as a homogeneous color sphere; that is, in concrete behavior we respond either to things or to colors, but we do not respond to two different spheres simultaneously. Each sphere has its special structural (configurational) laws according to which it organizes itself. The concrete experience of these unmediated spheres is of an unreflected nature (phenomenality), thus not derivable from processes of abstraction. *When, however, we speak of having an experience of an object as "experiencing the object with reference to something" then we use a conceptual formulation which in no way can be indentified with the actual facts of concrete behavior.* Why we use and how we are able to use such formulation and behave conceptually, is a question which can be clarified only in connection with the problem of abstract or categorical behavior. This problem does not fall within the framework of the present paper.[9]

As long as we experience a constellation of stimuli in a certain sphere, we can respond to structures only of this and not of any other sphere. But every sphere has its particular structural laws, which determine its organization. The experience we have of this sphere is of *immediate* nature – i.e. it is no longer derivable from processes of abstraction.[10]

Notes

1. Translator's note: The German word here is *Gliederung,* which means the organization of a unit consisting of articulated members, as, for example, the body. *Gliederung* will be translated throughout as 'organization' (and *gliedern* as 'to organize').
2. Author's note: When in this connection the words 'Coherence' or 'cohering' are used, it does not mean that the particular experience of linking together is "Secondary to the qualities of color", in the sense that it is added to certain already existing qualities of color. On the contrary, Gelb and Goldstein [45] are of the opinion that the experience

of certain color organizations and groupings is decidedly primary. Similarly Volkelt [168] points out that for children the two figures of like color in the Katz experiments do not 'cohere', but rather 'form one single configuration, the two members of which are essentially determined by this comprehensive configuration". The "common element, for instance the green, is not selected by the child from two entirely separate objects (the two green figures by 'attention to only a part of their content', but it is experienced in the comprehensive configuration, which includes the two members, as the leading, sustaining, and essential aspect."

3. Cf. what is said about the applicability of pathological findings in studies of normal psychology in: A. Gelb: "Report on the Ninth Congress for Experimental Psychology", Jena 1926, pp. 24 ff. [see 44]
4. The color sense of his patient was ascertained to be entirely normal by examination with the Nagel anomaloscope.
5. With the help of a checked table cloth it was possible for us to arrange the experimental objects in the same way in every experiment.
6. Quite some time after the completion of the present study, which – as has already been said – is based on Gelb's and Goldstein's joint investigations [45] in terms of both subject and method, Richard Meili published his paper "Experimental Studies of the Sorting of Objects". The main theme of this study, which had been made in complete independence of Gelb's and Goldstein's joint paper published a year earlier, is only a partial aspect of our investigations, an aspect that we have studied only to the extent to which it is directly related to the issue of abstraction. We are happy to say that a number of partial results presented in Meili's study are remarkably close to ours.
7. Editors' note: protocol omitted for lack of space.
8. In order to avoid misinterpretation the Editors have in a few instances altered the original wording of this paragraph.
9. The same view – i.e. that responses of this kind are 'unmediated', 'primitve' processes – is, as we stated in the introduction, also held by Gelb and Goldstein. A similar view was expressed by Révész [139]. The acts of 'abstraction' performed by the apes he used in his experiments seem to Révész to be of quite 'immediate' nature as well and to lend themselves to explanation without reference to higher voluntary processes. Even Volkelt [168] tries to explain the 'acts of abstraction' by children – which have been examined by Katz and others – in new terms, which deviate from the theories upheld so far.
10. After this study had gone to press, volume 100 of the journal appeared, carrying a study by O. Kroh and R. Scholl. Subsequent to Révész's ape experiments and as a result of a large number of experiments of their own, the authors of these studies arrive at conclusions with regard to the immediacy of "partially content-related perception" that are very similar to ours.

⟨5⟩

E. WEIGL

On the Construction of Standard Psychological Tests in Cases of Brain Damage

Attempts to compile aphasic test batteries date back to the last century, both for practical and research purposes. Handbooks of neurology and works by reputed authors often refer to methods for the examination of specialized functions, elaborated according to the individual concepts and interests of the authors. The claim that every large clinic uses its own particular aphasia questionnaire is probably justified.

Everyone working with cases of brain disease, the number of which is rapidly increasing, will agree that the results accruing from the various methods of the different authors are scarcely comparable. This is disturbing, if statistical results are being planned with a view to the precise assessment of the various cerebral syndromes and their localization.

I would like to repeat here the proposal I made at the *Bucharest Symposium upon Aphasia,* 1960 [87], that in addition to the continued employment of individual methods devised by different experts, one should internationally agree to compile a series of standards for general use in published cases.

The elaboration of the basic principles of construction of such standards is an essential prerequisite for such work[1].

We wish to present here suggestions as to the creation of standard methods for working with cases of cerebral disorder, while describing a model of a standard which we suggest for use. This model was devised particularly for the analysis of aphasic and agnosic syndromes.

Basic principles

The necessity for a systematic construction of standards proceeds from the fact that the total number of neuro-physiological methods in use, constitutes a sum of isolated methods, rather than a series of tests which correspond and permit correlation and quantitative assessment of results. The collection of tests for aphasia published by Osgood and Miron [132] illustrates convincingly this state of affairs. Irrespective of their basic theoretical and empirical aspects, some of the methods comprise as many as 25 different tasks, without however forming a coherent system. Without minimizing the value of every one of these tests, we believe that there is justification in questioning the particular criteria which have determined the number of tests applied by the respective authors.

Some 30 years ago Chesher [25], following Head, made quite a remarkable attempt to construct a short systematic Aphasia-Standard. Kreindler and Fradis have recently used this scheme with some slight modifications. Upon the basis of Chesher's techniques, Fradis and I [195; 197] have jointly attempted within the last few years a standard examination of alexic patients.

This standard analysis of aphasic and agnosic syndromes constitutes a considerable extension while applying principles of systematic construction.

One of the reasons why so many experimental methods do not allow ready comparison of results is that entirely different material is used for different tests. As a rule, the objects used for testing visual recognition have nothing in common with those used for tactile-gnosic examinations; there is also no relation between the sounds used for testing auditory agnosics and the tests mentioned before. Again, completely different material is used for testing auditory and visual comprehension of words. There is no doubt that every examination of a particular function has its own particular specificity, requiring therefore its specific testing material. Chesher's principle of testing different functions with identical contents as regards their semantic aspect deserves earnest consideration. Direct comparison of the results obtained by different examinations of function is possible when these refer to one and the same object, its particular sounds, and the particular noun describing it. Even though the practical application of this principle is somewhat limited through the relatively small number of objects with characteristic features as regards touch and sound, it is nevertheless possible to supply at least 10 to 20 items required for a standard (examples: watch, whistle, bunch of keys, small bell).

The usual methods of examination show yet another difficulty: individual functions are tested with the help of *other* functions. Consequently it is not always clear, which of the two functions determines the result. This difficulty has been overcome in our model. The particular function to be examined (*e.g.*, comprehension of words read) is not only tested with one, but with several other functions (Table 1).

The integrity or impairment of each of these responses can, on the other hand, again be assessed via several 'inputs' (Table 1).

In this way, the different possibilities offered through our model allow relatively valid conclusions as to the specificity of the defects found.

For the analysis of a particular defect of function, it is often important to know whether it appears in the input or output, on the afferent or efferent side, in the process of coding or decoding. Lexic understanding of words, can, for example, be totally or severely impaired, as when an alexic patient is asked to select from several objects the appropriate one belonging to a word offered in writing. On the other hand, he may be capable of choosing from several words the one which belongs to the same object, despite his former alexic reaction. (Numerous cases of the sort were observed in hitherto unpublished experiments conducted with Fradis and Mihăilescu.) Our model takes into account, as far as possible, the *reversibility* of afferent and efferent stimuli, of input-output which are to be coded and decoded.

The principle of specificity demands that precision and distinction of the *functional levels* are to be examined. In our model this principle is consequently adhered to in connection with performances of the First

Table 1 *Standard-minimun for the examination of aphasic and agnosic disturbances (syndromes)*

Input				*Output*			
	verbal examination			*non-verbal examination*			
	oral	*graphic*	*gnoso-practic*	*through selection of sounds, objects or words from several offered*			
Recognition of objects							
Visual	Naming	Spontaneous writing	Description through gestures	Sounds	Objects (for tactile perception)	Words (written)	Words (spoken by examiner)
Tactile	Naming	Spontaneous writing	Description through gestures	Sounds	Objects (for visual perception)	Words (written)	Words (spoken by examiner)
Auditory	Naming	Spontaneous writing	Description through gestures	Objects (for tactile perception)	Words (written)	words (spoken by examiner)	
Understanding of words							
Visual (reading)	Reading aloud	Copying	Description through gestures	Sounds	Objects (for tactile perception)	Objects (for visual perception)	Words (spoken by examiner)
Auditory (hearing)	Repeating	Writing from dictation	Description through gestures	Sounds	Objects (for tactile perception)	Objects (for visual perception)	Words (offered in writing)

and Second Signal System (Pavlov), gnosic and cognitive functions: recognition of objects and sounds and their corresponding names are examined separately and in view of their mutual relations. Here, too, the reversibility of input-output positions is of importance. Functions of the First Signal System can in this way be examined through those of the Second Signal System, and vice versa (as for instance, the examination of visual, auditory and tactile recognition through auditory and lexic comprehension of names and vice versa.

The structure of the model allows functions of one and the same analyser as well as of different analysers to be tested separately and the results interpreted accordingly (for example, examination of the visual recognition of objects through optical-lexic understanding of words or through recognition of objects by touch, etc.).

Our standard includes methods for testing verbal and nonverbal performances (Table 1). For the examination of aphasic patients, it is especially important to be able to test different gnosic and cognitive functions without the necessity of using speech (i.e., through matching or pointing to objects). Moreover, direct comparison of verbal and nonverbal reactions concerning the same material is useful in determining specific defects of both types of reaction.

As mentioned before, one of the basic principles of the standard consists in its being suitable for testing various functions, while using one and the same item. To facilitate this, objects are included in the standard which can be identified by healthy subjects not only visually, but by touch and by hearing (i.e., through sounds characteristic of the object). They can also be named, and the denomination can as a rule be easily understood, repeated, read, or written.

In constructing such a model, certain initial difficulties have to be overcome. Above all, there exists only a limited number of objects which meet the required semantic identity in the above sense: many sounds are not specific of particular objects, many objects have no auditory properties, and the range of objects easily recognizable by touch is not very wide. This leads to an unfortunate restriction in the choice of items, both quantitatively and qualitatively.

For that reason, we extend the 'core' of the standard which is composed of semantically identical items by a certain number of objects, sounds, and words. These additional items may be varied and graded in the usual way, according to the degree of difficulty typical of the particular function to be tested (naming, tactile recognition, understanding of the meaning of the word, reading, etc.). Every series of objects, sounds, and words will thus consist of two parts:

(1) items identical with all other series under the semantic aspect (for example, 'watch', 'bell', 'whistle' as objects which can be seen and

handled, as sounds, as words spoken by the subjects and offered to them in writing);

(2) items showing no connection with all remaining series, i.e., of objects which are not at the same time 'audible' (for example, 'pencil'), of sounds, typical neither of visible nor of touchable objects (for example the blowing of the wind), of words naming none of the objects or sounds contained in the standard.

A further advantage of this extension of the 'core' of the standard is that effects of training are avoided, which otherwise might be produced through one and the same semantic content being offered repeatedly.

The *number* of items to be included in the standard depends on statistical requirements for attaining significant values. Moreover, the number of items must allow their continuous, alternative use. One and the same material cannot be used successively for all seven tests, since recognition- and training-effects must be excluded. We recommend, therefore, the 'vertical' use of the methods (Table 1).

Time factor. Reaction times are to be evaluated for every single examination. Comparisons are to be based on reaction times of normal subjects.

Objections may, of course, be raised against our proposed model and its basic principles of construction. Its use as a routine method, to be statistically evaluated only, may of course, as with tests in general, lead easily to a superficial and merely formal analysis of defects and consequently to very doubtful generalizations. Certainly, standard methods can never replace individual methods based on detailed observation of patients and modified accordingly, sometimes even during examination. They can and must be regarded merely as valuable working instruments for the creative scientist. Nevertheless, we consider the introduction of standards necessary, in order to satisfy the justified demand for results allowing statistical comparison and correlation. The use of this kind of standard would not, of course, prevent authors from interpreting and verifying results according to their particular individual theoretical concepts.

Notes

1. Similar discussions took also place at the *Interdisciplinary Conference on Aphasia,* Boston, 1958 (see Osgood and Miron [132]).

⟨6⟩

E. Weigl, R. Böttcher, H.-J. Lander, and E. Metze

Neuropsychological Methods for Analysing the Functions and Components of Speech-Functional Partial Systems.[1]

I. Introduction and Statement of Problems

Certain limits are known to exist in the study of the generally frictionless and hardly comprehensible coordination of the functions and components of the speech-functional system in the fully developed human. However, investigations of this system in the state of ontogenesis, or particularly under the conditions of brain-pathological disturbance, give the advantage that it is often only in such cases that the special nature of the individual functions and components and their interconnection become visible and can be exactly allocated.

In the present work we take the latter neuropsychological path with the aim of demonstrating, on the basis of specially developed experimental methods, a particular manner of analysing the functions and components of the speech-functional system. It should be demonstrated that in this manner it is possible to determine not only qualitative but also quantitative data with regard to the extent of the participation of individual functions and components in the occurrence of certain spoken speech and written speech[1] performances.

In the experiments reported below on the structure and dynamics of the speech-functional system under brain-pathological conditions, we based ourselves upon the selection of two comparable functional constellations, i.e., language comprehension and language reproduction,[2] at the level of spoken language: auditory word comprehension and repetition, and (2) at the level of written language: visual-lexic word comprehension (receptive reading) and expressive reading.

In this connection we studied:

1. The mutual relationship between speech comprehension and speech reproduction, on the one hand at the spoken language level and on the other hand at the written language level. Following this: (1.1) performance in the auditory comprehension of dictated words was compared with performance in the repetition of these words; (1.2) performance in the lexic comprehension of visually-presented words (receptive reading)

was compared with performance in reading these words aloud (expressive reading).

2. The mutual relationship between the spoken language level and the written language level, that is to say: (2.1) we compared the lexic comprehension of visually offered words with the subsequent auditory comprehension of the relevant words offered aloud; and (2.2) vice versa.

For the quantitative determination of the part played by the functions under investigation and their components in bringing about the language achievements demanded, we based ourselves upon special methodical principles:

(1) Successive elimination or release of individual functions and components,

(2) Successive linking of the performances of certain spoken- and written-language functions and components.

For the statistical assessment of the results achieved by these methods we utilised a special process (see pp. 105 and 117).

In the comparative study of the two functional constellations mentioned we used a methodical artifice by chosing two differing aphasic syndromes 'of inverse order'. One syndrome was a case of the disturbance of auditory speech comprehension with intact receptive reading, and the other syndrome concerned an impairment of receptive reading with intact auditory speech comprehension. Additionally, in the first case not only was comprehension of the spoken word disturbed, but also repetition; in the second case not only was comprehension of words read affected, but also reading aloud (see Tab. 1).

Table 1. *Intact and disturbed speech functions in Case 1 and Case 2*

	intact	disturbed	
Functions	word comprehension	word comprehension	word reproduction
Case 1	visual-lexic (receptive reading)	auditory	repetition
Case 2	auditory	visual-lexic (receptive reading)	reading aloud (expressive reading)

In order to attain the function analysis and component analysis described above, we selected two aphasics from the patients who fulfilled these conditions. What we wished to do was to demonstrate in these two model cases the usefulness of our methods. The total of 1200 individual tests, no small number, permitted us to carry out statistically significant interindividual and intraindividual evaluations of the results.

In Case 1 we made the additional observation that auditory word comprehension performances changed significantly depending on the aid given by labiolexia. For this reason we included in his case this auxiliary function in our investigations.

II. Case Reports

Case 1 (Patient M. J.): former office worker, pensioned, born 1910, first hospitalised 1965 because of myocardiac infarction, followed by a cortical embolism and diabetes mellitus, apractic, visual-agnosic, and sensoric-aphasic disturbances. Received three months later at our request in the neurological clinic of the Humboldt University, Berlin (Charité). Neurological report: elementary functions without elementary findings EEG: irregular to slightly altered brain-current picture, left temporobasal to occipital, mainly subcortical. Aphasiological examination: (1) Speech: (1.1) Speech perception and comprehension. (1.1.1) spoken speech: clear-tone audiogram normal; severe impairment of the reception and semantic decoding of auditorily perceived speech signals, which could, however, be compensated to a certain degree by following the visible articulation of the speaker (labiolexia). Without this compensation both the perception of individual sounds and combinations of sounds, particularly consonants, was severely impaired, as was also the perception of sound structures (words and sentences). Similar phonemes were confused with each other, as were sound structures which the patient mainly mistook, comparing only the vowels (which led to the mistakes *Schwanz – Wand, Brust – Wurst, Propf – Kropf – Kopf, Rennen – retten,* etc., or, to quote nonsense word structures: *Tirkel – Tiste, Roof – Hoor,* etc.); sentence comprehension was also seriously disturbed (receptive auditory agrammatism), though the grasping of sentence structures under the conditions of labiolexia was retained to a considerable extent. – (1.1.2) written speech: recognition of letters, understanding of words and sentences intact. – (1.2) speech reproduction: (1.2.1) spoken speech: repetition (without labiolexia) and naming cancelled, or literal- and verbal-paraphasic. – (1.2.2) written speech: expressive reading impossible; copying: intact (but only in segments); writing on dictation: cancelled or severely paragraphic (though word deafness can partially be compensated for by labiolexia). – (1.3) speech production: (1.3.1) spoken speech: spontaneous, dialogised and speech series cancelled or paraphasic, in addition disturbance in finding words. – Other functions: gnosia: visually, auditorily and tactily fully restituted.

– Praxia: slight facial and pantomimic apraxia. – Spatial and temporal orientation: intact. – Script: taking dictation and copying intact. – Mental operations: arithmetic: counting and simple operations intact (with sticks) as well as the written solution of simple problems; mental arithmetic: not possible owing to verbo-receptive and verbo-expressive disturbance; recognition of operational signs partially disturbed. Abstraction greatly reduced in matching colours and forms, otherwise logic intact as far as possible to test. – Memory: immediate retention badly disturbed; long-term memory intact (as far as possible to test). –

Diagnosis: partially restituted sensory aphasia with expressive alexia, total agraphia in dictation writing and spontaneous writing; disturbance in abstract performances and short-term memory.

Case 2 (Patient G. P.): Furrier by trade, later electrotechnician, born 1942. Following mitralstenosis II.–IV. with mitral insufficiency, suffered in 1964 a brain embolism with subsequent spastic hemiparesis on the right and severe motor aphasia, alexia, and agraphia. After first hospitalisation 1964/1965, transferred to the First Medical Clinic of the Humboldt University, Berlin (Charité) and temporary (stationary) treatment in the Neurological Clinic of the Humboldt University, Berlin (Charité) until the death of the patient in 1968. – Neurological: spastic hemiparesis on the right, increase in muscle and tendon reflexes of the right arm, Trömner and Knips reflex positive on the right, the abdominal reflexes not releasable on the right; lower extremities: patellar and Achilles tendon reflexes more lively right than left, Babinski, Oppenheim, Rossolimo, Mendel, and Bechterew reflexes positive on the right. EEG: left-hemisphere damage, particularly temporo-basal. – Necrological report[3]: macroscopically apparent tissue changes in the form of a widespread softening area left frontally (Broca) and parietal-inferior, less temporal. Aphasiological examination: (1) Speech: (1.1) speech perception and comprehension. (1.1.1) spoken speech: reception, differentiation and recognition of single sounds and combinations of sounds intact, as well as intact perception and the semantic decoding of simple sound structures (words and sentences); understanding disturbance and receptive agrammatism with complicated words and syntactical combinations. – (1.1.2) written speech: slight receptive literal alexia and severe verbal and sentence alexia. Single letters were correctly identified visually (matching of identical as well as differing written letters) with the exception of *x, y, z,* and several similarly shaped graphic symbols; on the display of these letters occasional confusion (for instance *D* for *E,* I for *L, V* for *Y*). The visual perception, recognition, and differentiation between visually similar graphemic structures (nonense words) possible in the case of one and two syllable words (no mainly visual-gnostic impairment), but beyond this disturbed or cancelled. The receptive reading of words making sense was seriously disturbed, i.e., the patient in most cases failed completely or mixed up words of similar appearance (i.e., *Schilf – Schiff, Dose – Rose, Linoleum – Limonade*); in the receptive reading of sentences the patient endeavoured, generally unsuccessfully, to grasp the meaning of single words, and thereby to reach the meaning of the whole (receptive lexic agrammatism). – (1.2) Speech reproduction: (1.2.1) spoken speech: (patient did not utilise reading the lip movements of the speaker) repetition of individual phonemes almost intact, repetition partially possible with words but only those with one to three syllable sound structures (literal paraphasia: *Schul* instead of *Flur, Rauch* instead of *Strauch*); in addition amnestic difficulties, particularly with complicated composita (*Haushaltsgerät – Haushaltsge . . ., Molkereierzeugnis – Molkerei, Schneiderartikel – Schneiderab . . .*) and with sentences. Naming of objects and activities partially affected, naming of colours completely cancelled. – (1.2.2.) written speech: expressive reading: naming of letters almost cancelled; reproduction in spoken form of the offered written words seriously disturbed; in the relatively small number of cases in which a word was understood, there was seldom a correct case of reading aloud; the patient generally failed completely or read paralexically, either phonetic-paraphasic (*Akabei* instead of *Papagei, Karozel* instead of *Drossel, Etefan* instead of *Elefant*), or semantic-verbal-paraphasic because of confusing words of similar appearance (i.e., *Fliege* instead of *Filz, Wurst* instead of *Wurzel, Flasche* instead of *Flachs, Silber* instead of *Sirene*), or in the form of semantic deviations (paralexic failures in the same semantic field) such as *stocking* instead of *nylon, boat* instead of *harbour, tree* instead of *pine, horns* instead of *bull*). Expressive sentence reading totally cancelled. – Copying of letters and words intact, also copying with single letter cards. Writing on dictation not possible. – (1.3) Speech production: (1.3.1) spoken speech: spontaneous speech and speech in dialogue: telegraphic style with phonetic paraphasia. – (1.3.2) written speech: spontaneous writing: not possible. – Other functions: gnosia: visually, tactily, and acoustically intact. – Praxia: intact with exception of slight uncertainty in reproducing mimed movements (slight facial apraxia). – Spatial and temporal orientation: intact. – Drawing: intact. – Mental operations: no acalculia. Limitation of classification and ordering. – Memory: long-term memory intact as far as testable; short-term retention sharply reduced both verbo-acoustically and also verbo-visually and visual-objectively. –

Diagnosis: severe efferent motor (innervatoric) aphasia with afferent motor (ideokinetic) elements[4], also alexia (receptive and expressive) and agraphia (spontaneous writing and on dictation); disturbance in abstract performance and short-term memory.

III. Methodology: Test Planning: Results[5]

A. Variant Series I

1. Statement of Purpose

Quantitative measurement of the verbo-receptive and verbo-expressive performances of both patients examined by us under varying test conditions should make it possible to ascertain the share played in bringing about this performance by individual components of the disturbed function participating either effectively or potentially.

2. Components of the Functions of Disturbed Word Comprehension and Word Reproduction

2.1 *Pre-articulatory*[6] *verbo-receptive main components*
In the process of perceiving and understanding words offered either auditorily or visually we distinguish between the 'main components' and the 'accompanying components'. We describe as main components those inner speech processes which ensure the grasping of a word which has been heard or read, and its matching with the corresponding word meaning. These main components – in contrast to their latent-articulatory accompanying components (see 2.2) – implement the spoken speech and written speech perception and its semantic decoding at the pre-articulatory level, that is to say without direct use of the speech apparatus itself.

With regard to auditory word comprehension we speak of the 'verbo-auditory' main component (A) in hearing words spoken, and with regard to visual word comprehension we speak of the 'verbo-visual' main component (R) in the receptive (silent) reading of words offered in written form.

In Case 1 we are dealing not only with the function of understanding spoken words, but also with the auxiliary function, important for this patient, of reading the visible articulation movements of the examiner. The process of the visual grasping of these articulation movements we call the 'labiolexic' main component (L).

Thus the investigations in Variant Series I apply to the following main and auxiliary components (see Tab. 2)
- verbo-auditory main component A of word hearing (Case 1)
- labiolexic auxiliary component L of lipreading (Case 1)
- verbo-visual main component R of receptive word reading (Case 2).

Table 2. *Function and component analysis of Variant Series I*

		auditory word comprehension		
Case 1	function	word hearing	labiolexia*	repetition
	main or auxiliary components	verbo-auditory (A)	visual-lexic (L)*	manifest-
	accompanying components	latent-articulatory (a)$^{+}$	latent-articulatory (l)$^{+}$	articulatory (N)
		lexic word comprehension (receptive reading)		expressive word reading
Case 2	main components	verbo-visual-lexic (R)		manifest-
	accompanying components	latent-articulatory (r)		articulatory (E)

* excludable by covering the mouth movements of the examiner
$^{+}$ excludable by blowing

To determine the share of the main components listed in bringing about the correct comprehension of the heard word (Case 1) or read word (Case 2), procedures were utilised in this examination which will be described later (see pp. 101 ff.).

2.2 Latent-articulatory accompanying components

Many authors have demonstrated objectively, in particular with the aid of electromyographic methods (see the relevant literature in Sokolov [157], 1968), that perception of spoken speech and written speech can be accompanied under certain circumstances by latent speech movements, the verbo-kinestetic feedback of which plays a certain role in grasping verbo-auditory and verbo-visual (lexic) messages. We call these micromovements latent-articulatory inner-speech accompanying components.

The various latent-articulatory components which can accompany word hearing and receptive reading possess their own characteristics: in the perception of spoken speech the transcoding into latent speech movements takes place at the phonetic level, but in receptive reading graphemic patterns are transcoded into latent-articulatory patterns.

The reading of visible articulation movements on the part of the speaker can trigger latent co-articulatory sympathetic movements in the listener. We therefore distinguish between a visual labiolexic main component (L) and a latent-articulatory accompanying component (1).

Our investigations thus have as their subject the following latent-articulatory accompanying components (see Tab. 2):

word hearing a (Case 1)

reading the visible articulation movements of speaker 1 (Case 1)

receptive word reading r (Case 2).

The determination of the specific role of each of these accompanying components in bringing about auditory and lexic word comprehension and of the role of lipreading is undertaken with the help of the elimination method described in 3.

2.3 Verbo-expressive manifest-articulatory components

Following the tests of verbo-receptive functions of word-hearing and receptive word-reading, we tested the likewise disturbed verbo-expressive functions of repetition and reading aloud. In this manner we had the opportunity to assess quantitatively in the case of the two patients the relationship between spoken- and written-language perception and reproduction. In Case 1 we could also investigate the influence upon repetition of the visual perception of visible articulation movements.

With the help of the procedure described below, aimed at ascertaining the part played by the different latent-articulatory accompanying components, we were able to establish the relationship between these components and the corresponding manifest-articulatory components.

3. Procedure for the investigation of the individual components

Tables 3 and 5 show that on the one hand we set ourselves the task of checking the main components named (A in Case 1, R in Case 2), as well as the visual component L of labiolexia (in Case 1) in their separate forms of operation, that is to say with the exclusion of their latent-articulatory accompanying components; on the other hand, by releasing these accompanying components (a and 1 in Case 1, r in Case 2), we gained by comparison information about their form of operation. In addition we asked whether performances in manifest articulation change in repetition (Case 1) and reading aloud (Case 2) when, at the commencement of speech perception the latent articulation is eliminated or released. Under these conditions, what part is played by the main and accompanying components in the genesis of the relevant manifest-articulatory performances?

Table 3. *Survey of the test plan for variant series I; Case 1*

Individual components of word hearing to be tested Test variant		Elimination and lip-reading picture	Relase Latent articulation	Repetition Test variant
I–1.4	main component of word hearing	(A) covered	elimated by blowing	I–2.4 (N)/(A)
I–1.3	latent-articulatory accompanying components	(a) covered	released	I–2.3 (N)/(a)
I–1.2	visual component labiolexia	(L) visible	eliminated by blowing	I–2.2 (N)/(L)
I–1.1	latent-articulatory accompanying components of labiolexia	(l) visible	released	I–2.1 (N)/(l)

3.1 Method for mechanically eliminating the latent-articulatory accompanying components of word hearing (Case 1) and receptive word reading (Case 2)

Weigl ⟨7⟩ reported in his work. *The importance of the afferent verbo-kinaesthetic excitation of the speech apparatus for the expressive and receptive speech process in normal persons and those with speech disturbances* on various procedures for eliminating latent speech movements[7]. A direct mechanical method was used to hinder or prevent such movements either by holding the tongue firmly between the teeth or by holding the mouth open with the tongue slightly extended; this method was used by Sokolov [157] (1968) with normal adults and children, by Nasarova [129] (1952) and Kadochkin [76] (1955) with normal schoolchildren, by Luria [106; 107] (1950, 1963), Blinkov [17] (1948), and Weigl and Fradis [196] (1959) with aphasics.

Weigl [176; ⟨7⟩] developed a second mechanical elimination method and used it with normal adults, aphasics, and in cases of congenital deafness. This method, which was also used in the present tests in order to eliminate latent speech movements, consists of the test person, while listening to or reading speech communication, blowing strongly into a glass tube with constantly puffed cheeks, thus holding a column of liquid at a given height for a given period. In this manner the latent speech-muscle and breathing movements are 'blocked'. Although this method does not exclude the efferent speech impulses from the cortex, as a result of the blocking of the latent speech movements, the test person cannot be exposed to a re-afferent verbo-kinaesthetic feedback, that is to say an implementation of the intended articulatory movements.

Weigl [180] see also ⟨7⟩ summarised thus the results of the utilisation of this method:

"The question was whether, under the condition of such a radical temporary blocking of the verbo-kinaesthetic re-afferent excitations transmitted by the speech apparatus in normal subjects and those with speech disturbances (aphasics and deaf), receptive speech and thought processes were possible at all; this question was answered positively in a series of experiments. In other words the normal subjects were able to understand words and sentences heard and read whilst blowing, and to repeat them later. The same is true for aphasics who – within the bounds imposed by those receptive and expressive speech functions which are still intact in their cases – also showed positive results despite the temporary elimination of the verbo-kinaesthetic analyser which is of particular importance for them." (p. 87)

In the present tests the aim of the elimination method described was the experimental function- and component-analysis of certain disturbed speech use forms.

3.2 Method for investigating the labiolexic auxiliary function

In Case 1, as already noted, we had the opportunity to include in our function- and component-analysis the reading of the visible articulation movements of the speaker during the process of word hearing. It was important for us (see Tab. 3) to allot on the one hand the influence of the visual labiolexic auxiliary component (L), and on the other hand its latent articulatory accompanying component (1) upon performance in auditory word comprehension (A) and repetition (N). The analysis of the functioning of these components appears to us to be all the more important since hitherto very little has been known on the subject, particularly with regard to aphasics.[8]

To assess the role of the labiolexic components we, for our part, utilised the principle of elimination and release. To this end, the spoken words were presented to the patient from behind a cardboard screen, so that he was solely dependent upon acoustic perception; in a test variant the patient was able to note visually the articulation movements of the examiner while the word was being spoken[9].

To assess the special share of the latent-articulatory accompanying component (1) of labiolexia we used the blowing method described above. In one variant (see Tab. 3) we eliminated by blowing the latent-articulatory accompanying component (1) during the lipreading, and in another variant we released it, that is to say the patient did not have to blow while listening to words and lipreading. The comparison of the results of these two variants formed the basis for the separate assessment of the mode of effectiveness of components L and 1. In addition we tested the patients' performances in repetition under the two conditions described above; in this way we were able to discover the influence of the auxiliary and accompanying components of labiolexia upon the manifest-articulatory performances of the patients.

4. Performing the Tests. Methods of Statistical Evaluation of the Tests. Results

4.1 Performing the tests in Case 1

Word material amounting to about 190 nouns (one- to five-syllable concrete nouns) was used to test auditory word comprehension and repetition[10]. For word hearing and subsequent repetition the tests were always conducted with the same words. The absolute number of individual tests upon which the calculations are based vary in the different test variants between 189 and 88 words.

In each case a word was spoken to the patient; he had to make sure whether he understood it; then he had to repeat this word, and finally explain its meaning.

Since spontaneous speech of this patient – apart from frequent paraphasia and difficulty in finding words – was intact to the degree that he could make himself understood, we were able to assess precisely his grasp of the meaning of each individual word offered. In those cases in which the patient had the difficulties mentioned in word explanation, he helped himself either by circumlocution (e.g., with the word 'lottery': 'If I could get money . . .'; 'bridal pair': 'When two people go together.') or by using descriptive gestures (e.g., with the word 'cook' the patient indicated a typical high cook's hat; with the word 'brilliantine' he pointed to his hair). He also indicated regularly when he did not understand the meaning of a word, or only understood it inexactly. In this respect he was very conscientious and self-critical.

Variants I–1.4 and I–2.4: with mouth movements covered and with blowing: while the word was spoken behind the cardboard screen, the patient had to blow; after putting down the blowing tube he had to repeat the word and give its meaning.

These variants served to determine the share of the main component of auditory word comprehension (A), and its influence on the subsequent repetition (N). Eliminated here is the whole of labiolexia (L and 1) as well as the latent-articulatory accompanying component of word hearing (a).

Variant I–1.3 and I–2.3: with mouth movements covered, without blowing: the examiner spoke single words to the patient behind the cardboard screen, and the patient had to repeat the word and give its meaning.

The aim was to ascertain the share of the latent-articulatory accompanying component of word hearing (a) and its influence on the following repetition (N). In this case labiolexia (L and 1) was excluded.

Variant I–1.2 and I–2.2: with mouth movements visible, with blowing: while the words were being said to the patient, he had to use the blowing apparatus, and then, after putting down the tube, to repeat the word he had heard and explain its meaning.

The tests made under these conditions were aimed at finding the share of the visual component of labiolexia (L) in word comprehension and repetition. Both the latent articulatory accompanying components of word hearing (a) and of lipreading (1) were excluded.

Variants I–1.1 and I–2.1: with mouth movements visible, without blowing, i.e., no form of exclusion was practised; the patient could perceive the visible articulation movements of the examiner, and himself perform inner-speech articulation movements during the word hearing and lipreading.

A comparison of the variants I–1.1 and I–2.1 with the variants I–1.2 and I–2.2 made it possible, through extrapolation, to determine the share of the latent-articulatory accompanying component of lipreading (1) with regard to word comprehension and repetition.

4.2 Methods of statistical evaluation of results in Case 1 and Case 2

For the comparison of the results obtained with the methods described above, we applied a special procedure which made possible a statistical evaluation of the efficiency of the components and component complexes investigated within the individual variants.

The comparison was undertaken from the efficiency side, i.e., the behavioural side. An analysis was made of the partial efficiency of individual components in reaching the performance. The statistical comparison is only intended to show whether the efficiency of partial components is statistically significant.

The principle of this procedure is based on the comparison of two differing component complexes (variants), one of which contains more components than the other. In each variant the percentage of correct answer frequency is determined. From the differences derived from a comparison of the variants it is possible to determine the percentage of correct answer frequency arising from the additional effect of the relevant individual components or component complexes. The efficiency of certain accompanying components which is not immediately visible from these differences is extrapolated (see Tables 4 R_{4a} and R_{5a} and also R_{4b} and R_{5b}).

Table 4. *Test results of variant series I; Case 1*

auditory word comprehension performance Rubric	Variants	Component complex	%	χ^2	Rubric	Variants	repetition performance (N) Component complex	%	χ^2
R_{1a}	I–1.1	<[(a)→(A)], [(1) → (L)]>	66		R_{1b}	I–2.1	(N)/[<(a)→(A)], [(1) → (L)]>	30	
	I–1.2	[(A), (L)]	50			I–2.2	(N)/[(A), (L)]	15	
	I–1.3	[(a) → (A)]	25			I–2.3	(N)/[(a) → (A)]	7	
	I–1.4	(A)	23			I–2.4	(N)/(A)	2	
R_{2a}	I–1.3	[(a) → (A)]	25	0.07	R_{2b}	I–2.3	(N)/[(a) → (A)]	7	3.3
	I–1.4	(A)	23			I–2.4	(N)/(A)	2	
		(a)	2				(N)/(a)		
R_{3a}	I–1.2	[(A), (L)]	50	16.1	R_{3b}	I–2.2	(N)/[(A), (L)]	15	11.5
	I–1.4	(A)	23			I–2.4	(N)/(A)	2	
		(L)	27				(N)/(L)	13	
R_{4a}	I–1.1	<[(a) → (A)], [(l) → (L)]>	66	6.7	R_{4b}	I–2.1	(N)/<[(a)→(A)],[(l)→(L)]>	30	7.3
	I–1.2	[(A), (L)]	50			I–2.2	(N)/[(A), (L)]	15	
		(a), (l)	16				(N)/(a), (l)	15	
		(l)	14				(N)/1	10	
R_{5a}	I–1.1	<[(a) → (A)], [(l) → (L)]>	66	48.0	R_{5b}	I–2.1	(N)/<[(a) → (A)], [(l) → (L)]>	30	21.5
	I–1.3	[(a) → (A)]	25			I–2.3	(N)/(a) → (A)	7	
		(L), (l)	41				(N)/(L), (l)	23	
		(I)	14				(N)/(l)	10	

$$\chi^2 (\frac{a}{2} = 2.5\%, Fg = 1) = 3.87$$

* Legend
1. If two components or component complexes are separated by a comma, this means that both occur simultaneously.
2. The arrow is intended to show that the efficiency of the main component is the prerequiste for the accompanying component.
3. The diagonal stroke indicates the temporal order of the various functions.
4. The brackets [ ] and <> symbolise the relevant function complexes, the round brackets symbolise the relevant component complexes.

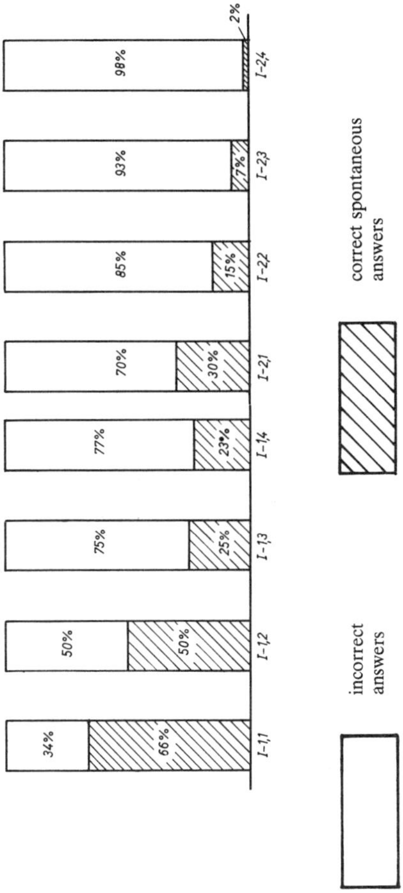

Diagrams 1a, 1b, Percentual portion of spontaneous correct answers in understanding and repetition of words (Case 1)

The percentages quoted represent in each case the percentage of correct spontaneous answers in the various variants in both function fields (auditory or lexic word comprehension, and repetition or reading aloud).

The difference between the test results of each two variants was tested in both function fields in accordance with a nonparametric statistical procedure for the comparison of two relative frequencies described by van der Waerden [165]. The values of the corresponding statistical test function χ^2 are entered in column 5. The corresponding point of significance of the test function was unilaterally fixed at a significance level of $\frac{\alpha}{2} = 2.5\%$ and amounts throughout to $\chi^2 = 3.87$.

4.3 Test results in Case 1

The percentage of correct spontaneous answers on the part of the patient quoted in rubrics R_{1a} and R_{1b} (see Table 4) are in addition given for each variant in the form of histodiagrams for better comprehension (see 1a and 1b). These diagrams give a picture of the effect of use of the methodological principle explained above, for successively eliminating and releasing certain functions and components. Proceeding from the variants I–1.2 and I–2.1, in which all components are actually or potentially released, a *certain performance decline* makes itself evident, dependent upon the elimination conditions.

The rubrics R_{1a} and R_{1b} show first that in the four variants, as a result of the test conditions we created, the differences in the performance in auditory word comprehension and repetition are affected *nearly proportionally*.

Determination of the percentage effect of components in the establishment of word comprehension and repetition performance (see Table 4):

Verbo-auditory main component of word hearing (A) (see Table 4 R_{1a}): The value A:23% ascertained for the isolated effect of this componentshows that when all other components are excluded, auditory word comprehension of the patient is severely impaired.

Latent-articulatory accompanying components of word hearing (a) (see Table 4 R_{2a}): The additional release of this component does not exercise any significant influence on the auditory word comprehension of the patient. The value for these components is about a:2%.

Accordingly, the comprehension of words, insofar as this is possible for this patient, lies exclusively in the activity of the verbo-auditory main component, and not in the latent-articulatory accompanying component.

Labiolexia (L,1) (see Tab. 4 R_{1a}): the correct word comprehension performance of the patient is considerably increased by simultaneous lipreading, and this by 50% to 66%.

The efficiency of the two components of labiolexia in this improvement is composed as follows:

Visual auxiliary component (L) (See Table 4 R_{3a}):

When apart from the A-component only the L-component is effective (and all other components are excluded), that is to say when the patient hears the word uttered, uses the blowing apparatus, and at the same time has the opportunity for lipreading, a significant increase in his word comprehension performance can be observed; L:27%.

Latent-articulatory accompanying component (1) (see Table 4 R_{4a} and R_{5a}): With the help of the extrapolation undertaken in this column we receive for this component, with reagard to the improvement in correct word comprehension performance, the significant value 1:14%.

In other words, the patient understands spoken words to a considerably greater extent when, at the time of the speech perception, he can read the visible articulation movements of the examiner. This facilitation is mainly due to the visual perception of these movements; however, the latent co-articulation during lipreading also contributes to the improvement of the performance of the verbo-receptive function which we are investigating.

Manifest-articulatory components of repetition (N) (see Table 4 R_{1b}–R_{5b}): The test results show that the verbo-expressive functions of the repetition of words are nearly blocked in this patient; in contrast the verbo-receptive function of understanding words has been retained to about 20%.

Influence of the verbo-auditory main-component (A) on repetition (N) (see Table 4 R_{1b}): The value of (N)/(A):2% shows that under the conditions of ‘pure’ word hearing the subsequent repetition is almost cancelled.

Influence of latent-articulatory accompanying components (a) on repetition (N) (see Table 4 R_{2b}): The release of these components leads to no significant change in manifest articulation (N)/(a):5%, i.e., the patient’s repetition is neither better nor worse when he is allowed to co-articulate when hearing words.

Influence of labiolexic auxiliary function on repetition (see Table 4 R_{1b}): Perception of the visible articulation movements of the examiner when offering the words improves significantly correct performance in repetition from 15% to 30%.

With regard to the components of labiolexia we can determine the following induction on repetition:

Visual auxiliary components (L) (see Table 4 R_{3b}):

Visual perception of the visible articulation movements of the examiner significantly improves the repetition performance of the patient (N)/(L):13%.

Latent-articulatory accompanying components (1) (see Table 4 R_{4b} and R_{5b}): If the patient had the opportunity for co-articulation while lipreading, there was an additional significant increase in the repetition performance: (N)/(1):10%.

The results so far obtained show that the high degree of cancellation of word repetition by this patient is independent of the form of verbo-auditory reception, i.e., independent of the presence or absence of latent articulation during the process of word listening.

In addition it is shown that the labiolexic auxiliary function can cancel to a certain degree the total blockage of repetition; on the one hand simple visual lipreading aids repetition of manifest articulation and on the other hand latent co-articulation while lipreading can have a positive effect on manifest articulation.

4.4 Performing the Tests in Case 2 (see Table 5)

In connection with another theme, we had already tried out with this patient before our tests began, a word list of 365 nouns (one- to five-syllable concrete nouns) for word reading comprehension (I–1.1) and expressive word reading (I–2.1). In the variants applied in connection with the use of the blowing apparatus (I–1.2 and I–2.2), we had to be content with a considerably lesser number of individual tests (85), in order not to impose too much strain on the patient, who had a serious heart condition.

Owing to the fact that patient's spontaneous speech was considerably affected motorically, he was only able in rare cases to explain orally the meaning of a word read. On the other hand he drew very cleverly and used very lively gestures, so that he was able in this way to give information about the relevant words, all of which were concrete, insofar as he understood them. Like the first patient, he knew very well when he

Table 5. *Survey of the best plan for variant series I; Case 2*

Test variant	individual components to be tested	elimination and release of latent articulation	expressive reading
I–1.2 and I–2.2	main component of visual-lexic word comprehension (receptive reading)	eliminated	(E)/(R)
I–1.1 and I–2.1	latent-articulatory accompanying component of receptive reading	released	(E)/(r)

did not understand a word, or understood it only vaguely, and he conscientiously expressed such difficulties in comprehension.

The variant I–1.1 was conducted without blowing, but in the variant I–1.2 the patient had to blow during receptive word reading; after interrupting the blowing he had to read the word aloud and finally define its meaning (see Table 5).

4.5 Test results in Case 2 (the statistical evaluation of the results is presented in the manner described, see 4.2)

The graph (see illustrations 2a and 2b) of the patient's correct performance in lexic word comprehension and reading aloud shows the measure of his partial receptive alexia and his even more pronounced expressive alexia. In addition it can be seen that the exclusion of the articulatory accompanying component of receptive word reading [r] does not significantly affect the proportion of correct performances in both disturbed functions.

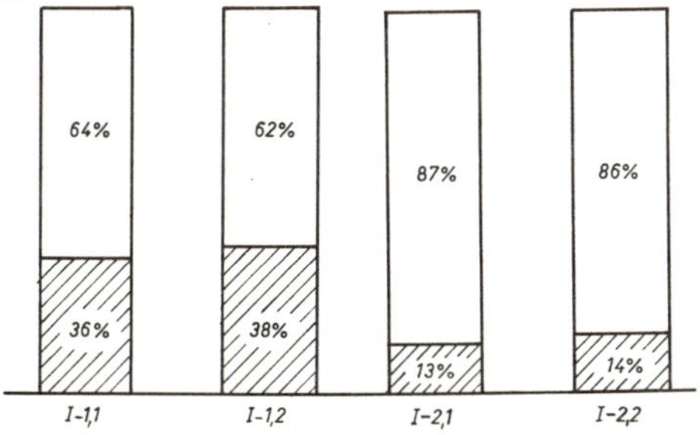

Diagrams 2a, 2b. Percentage of spontaneous correct answers in understanding and reading aloud of words offered in writing (Case 2).

Determining the percentage of efficiency of the individual components in producing receptive and expressive reading (see Table 6):

Verbo-visual main component of receptive word reading (R) (see Table 6 R_{2a}): The separate counting of this component produces the value R:38% for lexic word comprehension. This value demonstrates that this patient suffers from a considerable disturbance in the comprehension of words offered in writing.

Latent-articulatory accompanying component of receptive word reading (r) (see Table 6 R_{1a} and R_{2a}): The latent articulation of receptive word reading, released under these test conditions (without blowing), remains without effect, i.e., there is no change in the result with regard to the lexic word comprehension. In other words, the decisive factor in Case 2 for achievement of word reading comprehension is the verbo-visual main component, the 'pure reading'.

Manifest-articulatory components of expressive word reading (E): The influence of the verbo-visual main component (R) on expressive

Table 6. *Test results in variant series I; Case 2**

Lexic word comprehension performance (receptive reading)					Performance in reading aloud (expressive reading)				
Rubric	Variants	Component complexes	%	$\hat{\chi}^2$	Rubric	Variants	Component Complexes	%	$\hat{\chi}^2$
R_{1a}	I–1.1	[(r) → (R)]	36		R_{1b}	I–2.1	(E)/[(r) → (R)]	13	
R_{2a}	I–1.2	(R)	38	0.26	R_{2b}	I–2.2	(E)/(R)	14	0.09
		(r)	– 2				(E)/(r)	– 1	

$$\hat{\chi}^2\left(\frac{a}{2} = 2.5\%, Fg = 1\right) = 3.87$$

* Legend

1. Where 2 components or component complexes are divided by a *comma,* this means that both appear simultaneously.
2. The *arrow* symbolises the fact that the accompanying component is dependent upon the efficiency of the main component.
3. The *diagonal* indicates the order in time of the relevant functions.
4. The *square* brackets symbolise the corresponding function complexes, the *round* brackets the corresponding component complexes.

word reading (E) (see Table 6 R_{1b} and R_{2b}): Under the conditions of 'pure' word reading, i.e., with the exclusion of the latent-articulatory accompanying component (r), reading aloud is largely cancelled: (E)/(R):14%; in other words expressive word reading is severely disturbed.

The influence of the latent-articulatory accompanying component of receptive word reading (r) on expressive word reading (E) (see Table 6 R_{2b}): With regard to reading aloud, the result remains unchanged, whether the latent-articulatory accompanying component of receptive word reading (r) be eliminated or relased. This means that the verbo-expressive manifest-articulatory disturbance of this patient cannot be proved to be influenced by the latent articulatory speech movements (see however p. 130 ff.).

B. Variant Series II

1. Statement of Purposes

In variant series I, we determined quantitatively the share of the functions and components of various disturbed partial systems in spoken and written language in bringing about verbo-receptive and verbo-expressive performances in our two patients. In variant series II, these affected partial systems are brought into contact experimentally with corresponding intact partial sytems in spoken and written language, they are 'deblocked'. The resultant changes in performance, and the part played in these changes by the components of the intact functions, should be quantitatively determined.

2. Components of the intact functions of visual-lexic and auditory word comprehension

As we have noted, Case 1 has intact visual-lexic comprehension, and Case 2 intact auditory comprehension. With regard to the components of these nondisturbed functions, we make a distinction between main components and accompanying components. In Case 1 we have to do with the verbo-visual main component of receptive word reading (R) and its latent-articulatory accompanying component (r); in Case 2 we are dealing with the verbo-auditory main component of word hearing (A) and its latent-articulatory accompanying component (a)[11].

3. Method of investigating the share of individual components of the intact functions in bringing about the deblocking of the performance of the disturbed functions

3.1 Method of successive linkage of intact and disturbed speech-functional partial systems

For the study of the mutual relations between the relatively autonomous partial systems in brain-damaged patients, a special method was developed by Weigl ⟨2; 9; 10⟩. He was able to demonstrate that deblocking effects (d-effects) could be obtained by the successive experimental linkage of certain performances of intact partial systems with the relevant performances of disturbed partial system. In its simplest form – which is also used in the present investigation – such an effect is produced when access to a certain 'meaning' or combination of meanings, the road to which over one particular channel (or several) is 'blocked', it can be deblocked. This is achieved when the relevant intact speech performance is premised before the disturbed verbo-receptive or verbo-expressive function. In this manner semantically identical or related performances of intact and 'blocked' functions are successively linked with one another. It is for instance possible, when patients are not capable of comprehending or repeating certain words or sentences offered vocally, to have the patients read them mentally or aloud, to copy them or write them on dictation, to name objects or pictures vocally or in writing, etc.; that is to say, under proper experimental conditions to prevail upon them to achieve correctly these performances which are otherwise 'blocked' – to understand, repeat, read, write, name, etc. We shall illustrate this in detail below.

The Weigl deblocking method is a suitable means of giving insight into the complicated structural network of cerebrally-impaired speech systems and their dynamics.[12]

The utilisation of the deblocking method in the present investigation constitutes a special methodological principle. The sequence of functions and their components described above allow quantitative assessments to be made with regard to the part played in the alterations in performance by the effectively and potentially participating sections.

Since the intact and disturbed partial systems of spoken and written speech in Case 1 are matched in reverse by the intact or impaired partial systems of Case 2, we could make an interindividual comparison between these systems, their functions, and components.

In Case 1 we deblocked the performance of the disturbed auditory word comprehension and repetition with the help of the preceding relevant performance of intact receptive word reading (see Table 7).

In Case 2 the deblocking was undertaken by the successive coupling of the intact auditory word comprehension with the semantically-identical performance of the disturbed visual-lexic word comprehension and reading aloud (see Table 9).

3.2 Combining the coupling method with the elimination and release method described

We used once again the elimination and release method described above (see Table 7 and Table 9) in order to determine, under the conditions of the use of the deblocking method, the alteration in effect of the main and accompanying components already tested in variant series I on the one hand, and on the other hand the share of the relevant main and accompanying components of the intact functions in bringing about this change in performance. This provided the 'function and component sequences':

– in which only the main components of the deblocking functions and the functions to be deblocked were effective;

– in which at the same time the aid of individual or all accompanying components were released.

The comparison of performance changes in these variants provided the basis for the quantitative assessment both of the share of the main components and accompanying components in the d-effect, and of the

Table 7. *Survey of the test plan for variant series II; Case 1*

Components of the deblocking function: *receptive word reading*		elimination and release conditions: lipreading picture	elimination and release conditions: latent articulation	components of the function to be deblocked: *auditory word comprehension*	test variants		function to be-deblocked: *repetition* test variants
main component of lexic comprehension	(R)	covered visible	eliminated by blowing	disturbed main component of auditory word comprehension and intact auxiliary component of labiolexia	II–1.4 II–1.2 (A), (L)	manifest articulation	II–2.4 II–2.2
latent-articulatory accompanying components of receptive word reading	(r)	visible covered	released	latent-articulatory accompanying component of word hearing and labiolexia	II–1.3 II–1.1 (a), (l)		II–2.3 II–2.1

relationship between the main components and accompanying components of the deblocking functions and the functions to be deblocked;

– directly following the deblocking of auditory or visual-lexic word comprehension we tested performance in the repetition or reading aloud of the relevant words, in order to assess the effect of the coupling functions on the *verbo-expressive* functions. Once again our aim was to obtain, under the changed test conditions, information both about the quantitative relationship between the components of the implicit intact receptive functions and the disturbed expressive functions, and about the quantitative relationship between the latent-articulatory accompanying components of the intact functions and the disturbed manifest-articulatory components.

4. Performing the experiments. Methods of evaluating statistically the test results. The results

4.1 Performing the tests in Case 1

The word material used with this patient in variant series II consisted of about 50 concrete nouns which he was not able to understand or repeat when they were said to him.

The number of words used in the deblocking tests was determined by the results of variant series I; i.e., we selected those words offered in that series which the patient had not been able to comprehend correctly auditorily and had not been able to repeat.

The deblocking experiments were conducted in the following fashion: the patient first had to read silently a series of five words with different meanings; this caused him no trouble since his word reading comprehension was intact. After the word card had been removed, one of these words – the 'critical' one – was spoken by the examiner, and the patient had to repeat it and say what it meant.[13]

To determine the share of individual components of the deblocking function (receptive word reading) in bringing about the d-effect, with regard to the relevant components of the disturbed functions (auditory word comprehension and repetition), we relied upon a test scheme analogous to that used in variant series I – apart from the additional deblocking functions (see also Table 4 and Table 8).

Variants II–1.4 and II–2.4: with mouthmovement covered and with blowing: the patient was required to blow both during receptive word reading and during the time when the critical word was spoken behind the cardboard screen: after this he was required to repeat and explain the word.

With the help of these variants the d-effect should be determined which proceeds from the main component of intact receptive word reading (R) to the main component of the disturbed auditory word comprehension (A), as well as its influence on the subsequent repetition (N). Here labiolexia (L and l) are excluded as well as the latent-articulatory accompanying components of receptive word reading (r) and word hearing (a).

Variants II–1.3 and II–2.3: with mouth movements covered without blowing: the patient read the five words, and the critical word was then read to him behind the cardboard screen; he was required to repeat and explain it.

In this case the aim was to determine the additional influence exerted by the latent-articulatory accompanying components of receptive word reading (r) upon auditory word comprehension (A) and also upon the subsequent repetition (N). Labiolexia (L and l) were excluded.

Variants II–1.2 and II–2.2: with mouth movements visible, with blowing: during the period of receptive word reading of the five words offered, the patient was required to blow; he also had to blow while the critical word was being said by the examiner. After this the blowing was suspended, and the patient was required to repeat and explain the critical word.

The aim was to determine in what manner the visual component of the intact labiolexic function (L) participated in the deblocking effect from the side of the main component of receptive word reading (R) with regard to the disturbed main component of auditory word comprehension (A) and the subsequent repetition (N). All latent-articulatory accompanying components (r, a, l) were excluded.

Variants II–1.1 and II 2.1: with mouth movement visible, without blowing: here all main and accompanying components were released.

By extrapolation (comparison between variants II–1.2, II–1.1 and II–2.2, II–2,1) it is possible to determine the effect of the latent-articulatory accompanying component of labiolexia (1) under the conditions of the deblocking of auditory word comprehension (A) and subsequent repetition (N).

4.2 Methods for the statistical evaluation of the test results in Case I and Case 2 (see Table 8 and Table 10 as well as Ill. 3 and Ill. 4)

The total percentage figures quoted represent the sum of the percentage of correct replies received in variants I and II. The increase in percent of answer frequency compared to the results of variant series I (see Table 4 and Table 8, as well as Table 6 and Table 10, and Ill. 1 and Ill. 3 as well as Ill. 2 and Ill. 4) is then the result of the deblocking process (deblocked correct replies). The values cited in the column ‘total’ are specifically designed to test statistically the d-effect.

Table 8. *Test results of deblocking performances in auditory word comprehension and repetition. Variant series II; Case;*[1]

Deblocking of comprehension Rubric	Variants	of spoken words Component-combination	total d-effect %	%	$\hat{\chi}^2$	Deblocking of the repetition Rubric	Variants	of relevant words Component-combinations	total d-effect %	%	$\hat{\chi}^2$
	II–1.1	⟨[(a)→(A)], [(l)→(L)]⟩ [(r)→(R)]	95	87	50,6		II–2.1	(N)/{⟨[(a)→(A)], [(1)→ (L)]⟩/[(r)→(R)]}	65	50	45.9
R_{1a}	II–1.2	[(A), (L)]/(R)	97	94	52.1	R_{1b}	II–2.2	(N)/⟨[(A), (L)]/(R)⟩	62	55	40.3
	II–1.3	[(a)→(A)]/[(r)→(R)]	86	81	79.9		II–2.3	(N)/⟨[(a)→(A)]/[(r)→(R)]⟩	39	35	32.7
	II–1.4	(A)/(R)	86	81	87.4		II–2.4	(N)/[(A)/6R)]	52	52	75.0
	II–1.3	[(a)→(A)]/[(r)→(R)]		81			II–2.3	(N)/⟨[(a)→(A)]/[(r)→(R)]⟩		35	
R_{2a}					0	R_{2b}					5.5
	II–1.4	(A)/(R)		81				(N)/[(a), (r)]		52	
		(A), (R)		0				(N)/[(a), (r)]		−17	
	II–1.2	[(A), (L)]/(R)		94			II–2.2	(N)/⟨[(A), (L)]/(R)⟩		55	
R_{3a}					3.3	R_{3b}					0.30
	II–1.4	(A)/(R)		81			II–2.4	(N)/[(A)/(R)]		52	
		(L)		13				(N)/(L)		3	
	II–1.1	⟨[(a)→(A)], [(l)→(L)]⟩/ [(r)→(R)]		87	3.3		II–2.1	(N)}⟨[(a)→(A)], [(l)→(L)]⟩/ [(r)→(R)]}		50	0.30
R_{4a}	II–1.3	[(a)→(A)]/[(r)→(R)]		81		R_{4b}	II–2.3	(N)/⟨[(a)→(A)]/[(r)→(R)]⟩		35	

		(l)→(L)	6				(N)/[(l)→(L)]	15	
		(l)	− 7				(N)/(l)	12	
	II–1.1	⟨[(a)→(A)], ([l)→(L)]⟩/ [(r)→(R)]	87	1.5		II–2.1	(N)/{⟨[(a)→(A)], [(l)→(L)}⟩/ [(r)→(R)]}	50	0.50
R_{5a}	II–1.2	[(A), (L)]/(R)	94		R_{5b}	II–2.2	(N)/⟨[(A), (L)l/(R)⟩	55	
		(a), (l), (r)	− 7				(N)/[(a), (l), (r)]	− 5	
		(l)	− 7				(N)/(l)	12	

$\hat{\chi}^2(\frac{a}{2} = 2.5\%, Fg = 1) = 3.87$

[1] Legend
1. If two components or component complexes are divided by a comma, this means that both act simultaneously.
2. The arrow indicates that the accompanying component depends upon the efficiency of the main component.
3. The diagnonal indicates the temporal order of the funktion concerned.
4. The brackets [ ] or ⟨ ⟩ or { } symbolise the relevant function complexes, the *round* brackets symbolise the relevant component complexes.

The following column, 'd-effect-%', shows the percent of frequency of correct replies specifically induced by the deblocking process (deblocked correct replies). These percentage figures – we call them the d-effects – refer here solely to the remaining portion of *non*correct replies in variant series I. The statistical evidence on the d-effect is based upon the statistical test procedure already described in connection with variant series I (see p. . . . et seq). The comparison was based on the percent of replay frequency of variant series I (cf. Table 4 and Table 6). The values for the statistical test function χ^2 are cited in the following column.

The Comparative diagram of the d-effects obtained in variant series II (Case 1) is at the end of this paper p. 138.

In all following columns the d-effects achieved in the two variants are compared to each other. The statistical comparison resembles that in variant series I (see p. 105).

In Case 1 Table 8 is extrapolated with two different comparisons of the percentage share of the relevant accompanying components in the d-effect (in the columns R_{4a} and R_{5a} as well as R_{4b} and R_{5b}); and the same is done with Case 2 (in the columns R_{2a} and R_{2b} of Table 10).

In the column 'component complexes' the variants described in the text (see 4.1 and 4.4) are shown in symbolic form.

4.3 Test results in Case 1

The d-effects cited in rubrics R_{1a} and R_{1b} of Table 8 are given in Ill. 3a and 3b in the form of column histograms. This display method shows that the method of successive coupling used by us leads to highly significant performance improvement of the impaired functions. This is true for auditory word comprehension and for repetition, though the d-effect is considerably higher with regard to the verbo-receptive functions of comprehension than with regard to the verbo-expressive function of repetition.[14]

Evaluation of the percentage share of individual components of the deblocking functions of receptive word reading (see Table 8 R_{1a}):

Verbo-visual main component of receptive word reading (R): Coupling of the intact main component R with the disturbed main component A produces – with the elimination of all other components – a d-effect of (A)/(R):81%. In other words, the patient understood in variant 1–1.4 only 32% of the spoken words (see Table 4), but now in variant II–1.4, after previous receptive reading, he was able to understand correctly 81% of the 77% of words not previously understood.

Latent-articulatory accompanying component of receptive word reading (r) (see Table 8 R_{2a}): Release of this component in variant II–1.3 effects, compared to variant II–1.4 (no release), no alteration of the d-effect with regard to auditory word comprehension.[15]

Labiolexic auxiliary functions (see Table 8 R_{1a}): in variant I we ascertained (see p. 109) that the labiolexic auxiliary function encourages to a high degree the auditory word comprehension of the patient. Here we shall examine (variants I–1.1 and II–1.2) how the influence of this function and its components alter under the conditions of deblocking.

First the results show that the release of this function produces in our patient no change in the achieved d-effect with regard to word comprehension. The d-effects of 94% and 87% attained under these conditions do not differ significantly from the d-effects in the variant without the help of labiolexia (81%).

In order to understand these results, we must analyse separately the components of labiolexia.

Visual components of labiolexia (L) (see Table 8, R_{3a}): On variant II–1.2, in which only this component, simple lipreading, becomes effective while the latent-articulatory accompanying component (l) is excluded, no significant changes in the d-effect with regard to auditory word comprehension can be shown compared to the variant without labiolexia (II–1.4):L = 13% lies just below the border of significance ($\chi^2 = 3.3$). However, it must not be overlooked that the d-effect without the help of labiolexia is already 94%, thus nearly reaching the 100% mark. In this sense an additional favorable effect of this component can not theoretically be excluded.

Latent-articulatory accompanying components of labiolexia (l) (see Table 8 R_{4a} and R_{5a}): the release of these components produces no significant change in the d-effect with regard to auditory word comprehension ($\chi^2 = 1.4$). As we shall show below in connection with the deblocking of subsequent repetition, when one calculates the share of the l-component with regard to deblocking, one must take into account the fact that the relase of this component takes place at the same time as the release of the r-component of receptive reading, which exercises an inhibiting influence on the d-effect (see p. 123).

The above shows that the patient considerably more frequently understands the meaning of the spoken words, which he otherwise had not understood, when he has previously read them receptively. The visual factor of word reading plays the decisive role in connection with this deblocking process. As we shall see below, the latent articulation during receptive word reading, which does not appear to play any part in the deblocking of the auditory word comprehension of the patient, has a negative influence. The favorable influence of the two labiolexic components on the deblocked auditory word comprehension was not expressed in a manner which could be proved, for reasons still to be discussed.

Manifest-articulatory component of repetition (N) (see Table 8 R_{1b}): following the coupling of the intact main element R with the disturbed main component A, the testing of the repetition of the relevant word (variant II–2.4) shows a d-effect of (N)/(A)/(R) = 52%; i.e., the patient who had failed almost completely in variant I–2.4 (see Table 4) was able, thanks to the deblocking, to repeat correctly about half of the words. The improvement of this manifest-articulatory performance is in this case solely due to the effect of the nonarticulatory main component (R) of receptive word reading (we shall return to this subject).

Influence of latent-articulatory accompanying components of receptive word reading (r) on repetition (N) (see Table 8 R_{2b}): Variant II–2.3 shows that the value of the d-effect under the influence of the released component r sinks from 52% to 35%, i.e., (N)/(a)(r): −17%. This tells us that as soon as the patient has the chance for inner articulation – naturally unconsciously – during receptive reading, his repetition deteriorates. Thus the latent-articulatory accompanying component (r) of receptive reading exercises an inhibiting effect on the manifest-articulatory component (N).

Influence of the labiolexic auxiliary function on repetition (see Table 8 R_{1b}): Under the conditions of deblocking, the release of this function produces no significant change in one case (variant II–2.2), but in the other case (variant II–2.1) a signifcant increase of the d-effect from 35% to 50% can be shown. To understand this finding we shall proceed to an analysis of the influence of each of the two components of labiolexia upon the deblocking of repetition.

Influence of the visual component of labiolexia (L) upon repetition (see Table 8 R_{3b}): comparison of variants II–2.2 and II–2.4 shows that with regard to repetition deblocking brings no significant change (N)/(L) = 3%.

Influence of the latent-articulatory accompanying component (l) (see Table 8 R_{4b} and R_{5b}): as noted above, in calculating the share of the l-component in deblocking repetition, the fact has to be taken into account that this component is released simultaneously with the r-component, the inhibiting nature of which has already been shown in connection with variant II–2.3 (see Table 8 R_{2b}), i.e., in the deblocking of repetition with the elimination of labiolexia (see above). The d-effect in variant II–2.1 (see Table 8 R_{4b} and R_{5b}) with regard to repetition should thus be regarded as the product of the inhibiting r-component and the facilitating l-component. This means that the facilitating influence of the l-component is considerably decreased by the effect of the r-component, and that thus the share of the l-component in reality considerably exceeds the d-effect (N)/(l) = 12%. In other words, latent articulation in receptive word reading induces the deblocking of manifest articulation under the conditions of the simultaneous effect of the facilitating latent-articulatory accompanying component of labiolexia (r) in a negative manner.

4.4 Performing the Tests in Case 2

In variant series II, 65 'critical' words (concreta) written on cards were used with the patient; they were words which he could neither understand lexically nor read aloud.

Table 9. *Survey of the test plan for variant series II. Case 2*

Components of the deblocking function: *auditive word comprehension*		Elimination and release conditions	Components of the function to be deblocked: *lexic word comprehension*	Function to be deblocked: *expressive word reading*		
Main component of auditory word comprehension	(A)	Latent articulation Eliminated by blowing	Disturbed main component of lexical word comprehension	test variants (R) II–1.2	manifest articulation	test variants II–2.2
latent articulatory accompanying component of word hearing	(a)	released	latent articulatory accompanying component of receptive word reading	II–1.1 (r)		II–2.1

The variant shown in Table 9 were carried out in the following manner:

Variants II–1.2 and II–2.2: receptive and expressive word reading, with blowing: while hearing the words and the following receptive word reading the patient had to blow; the blowing then ceased, the word card was removed, and the patient should pronounce the word read and explain it.

Removal of the word card was necessary, so that the patient, after interrupting the blowing, could not conduct latent speech movements on the basis of the card before reading aloud. In pronouncing the word read previously, during blowing, we have a case of delayed 'post-expressive' reading aloud, since the word card is no longer visible. Our test results show that for the patient there was no difference between this 'post-expressive' reading and normal direct reading aloud.

The aim was to test the d-effect exerted by the intact main component of auditory word comprehension (A) upon the disturbed main component of receptive word reading (R), and its influence upon subsequent reading aloud (E). The latentarticulatory accompanying component of word hearing (a) and of receptive word reading (r) were eliminated.

Variants II–1.1 and II–2.1: receptive and expressive word reading, without blowing: three words were spoken to the patient (he understood them without difficulty), then the critical word was offered him on a card, he had to read it mentally; after the card had been removed, he had to speak it aloud and explain the meaning of the word.

By extrapolation the additional effect of the a-component, the latent speech movements during the process of hearing the word, upon the d-effect with regard to receptive and expressive word reading could be evaluated. In this case the two latent-articulatory accompanying components (a) and (r) were released.

4.5 Test Results in Case 2

The column diagrams in illustrations 4a and 4b demonstrate the results summarised in Table 10. They show that the successive coupling between intact word hearing and disturbed receptive and expressive word reading leads to significant or highly significant performance improvement of the impaired functions. In the case of the considerably more seriously disturbed reading aloud, the d-effects lie at a lower level than in the case of receptive reading (see footnote 14).

Shown separately, the share in the d-effect of the components of intact word hearing are as in Ill. 4a, 4b, next page.

Verbo-auditory main component of word hearing (A) (see Table X R_{2a}): the significant performance-improving influence of this component can be seen from the size of the d-effect with reference to the disturbed lexic word comprehension: (R)/(A) = 35%. Normally the patient did not understand about 60% of the words read mentally, but with the aid of the preceding intact word hearing, 35% of these nonunderstood words could be deblocked.

Latent-articulatory accompanying components of word hearing (a) (see Table 10 R_{1a} and R_{2a}): The increase of the d-effect from 35% to 41% with the release of the a-component is not significant; i.e., the a-component cannot be proved to have an effect on the deblocking of the lexic word comprehension disturbance. The number of words offered in writing which were correctly understood by the patient did not change significantly when he was given the previous opportunity to co-articulate in inner speech these words uttered by the examiner.

Manifest-articulatory components of expressive reading (E) (see Table 10 R_{1b} and R_{2b}): the coupling of intact word hearing and disturbed receptive word reading produced in our patient highly significant per-

Table 10. *Test results of deblocking lexic word comprehension and expressive word reading. Variant series II; Case 2*[1]

Deblocking
the comprehension of words offered in writing
Variant series II–1

Rubric	Variants	Component combinations	d-effect %	d-effect %	$\hat{\chi}^2$
R_{1a}	II–1.1	[(r)→(R)]/[(a)→(A)]	62	41	52.5
					0.7
R_{2a}	II–1.2	(R)/(A)	59	35	
		(r), (a)		6	
		(a)		6	

Deblocking
the reading aloud of the relevant word
Variant series II–2

Rubric	Variants	Component combinations	d-effect %	d-effect %	$\hat{\chi}^2$
R_{1b}	II–2.1	(E)/⟨[(r)→(R)]/[(a)←(A)]⟩	49	41	115.9
					14.1
R_{2b}	II–2.2	(E)/[(R)/(A)]	30	18	6.5
		(E)/(r), (a)		23	
		(E)/(a)		23	

Legend:
1. If two components or component complexes are divided by a comma, this indicates that they take place simultaneously.
2. The arrow indicates that the accompanying component depends upon the efficiency of the main component.
3. The diagonal indicates the temporal order of the functions in question.
4. The brackets [ ] and ⟨ ⟩ symbolise the relevant function complexes, the round brackets symbolise the relevant component complexes.

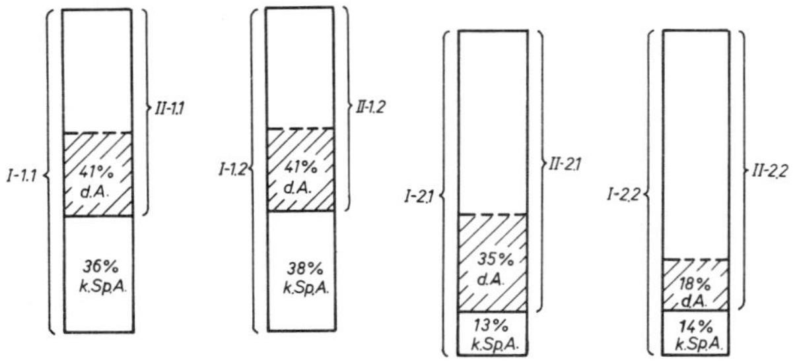

k. Sp. A. = correct spontaneous answers
d. A. = deblocked answers
Ill. 4a, 4b as 3a, 3b (Case 2)

formance improvements with regard to receptive reading, but also with regard to expressive reading.

Influence of verbo-auditory main component (A) on expressive reading (E) (see Table 10 R_{2b}): the significant d-effect resulting from this component for reading aloud amounts to 18%; i.e., the patient, who was not able to read expressively about 90% of the words offered under the conditions of variant I–1.2, was now able to read aloud about 18% of these previously unreadable words. Taking into consideration the seriousness of the expressive alexia of the patient, and the insufficient reinforcement of the d-effect (see footnote 14), this constituted a considerable improvement in performance ($\hat{\chi}^2 = 6.5$).

Influence of the latent-articulatory accompanying component of word hearing (a) on expressive word reading (E) (see Table 10 R_{1b} and R_{2b}): the connection between latent articulation in word hearing and manifest articulation in reading aloud produces a significant reinforcement ($\hat{\chi}^2 = 14.1$) of the latter components (E)/(a):23%; i.e., the patient was able to read correctly a greater number of the words previously heard if he had been able to co-articulate previously when the words were read. The question remains open as to why this positive effect of the a-component does not also make itself apparant in the process of deblocking receptive word reading.

Discussion

With all the caution called for in generalising the results gained with only two patients, this form of comparative examination would appear to be a possible model for further neuro-psychological analyses of functions and components.

Despite the differing aetiology and localisation of the syndromatic forms of disturbance in our two aphasics, there are displayed – leaving aside divergent results – a series of common features with regard to the speech behavior of the patients which allow the conclusion that there exist certain basic regularities behind verbo-receptive and verbo-expressive performances.

As was noted at the start, the basic aim of our examination was to reach valid results with regard to certain structural and dynamic peculiarities of the disturbed speech-functional system by means of special neuro-psychological methods.

For this purpose we extract from the multiplicity of this whole system certain partial systems, those which were inversely disturbed and intact in the patients we examined.

Table 11. *Schematic presentation of the structure and dynamics of simple and combined speech-functional partial systems*

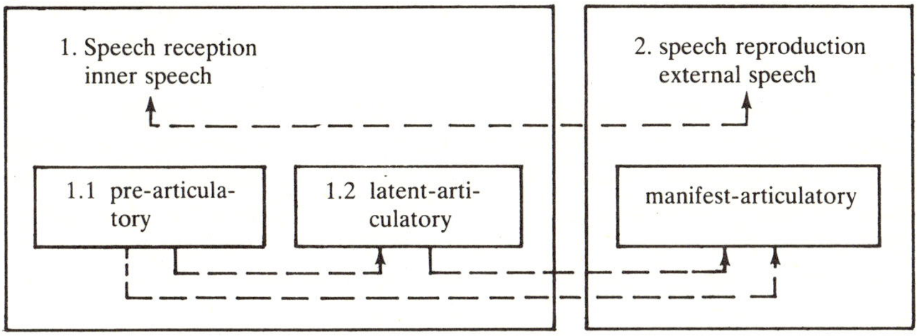

Table 12. *Schematic presentation of the structure and dynamics of experimentally coupled speech-functional partial systems*

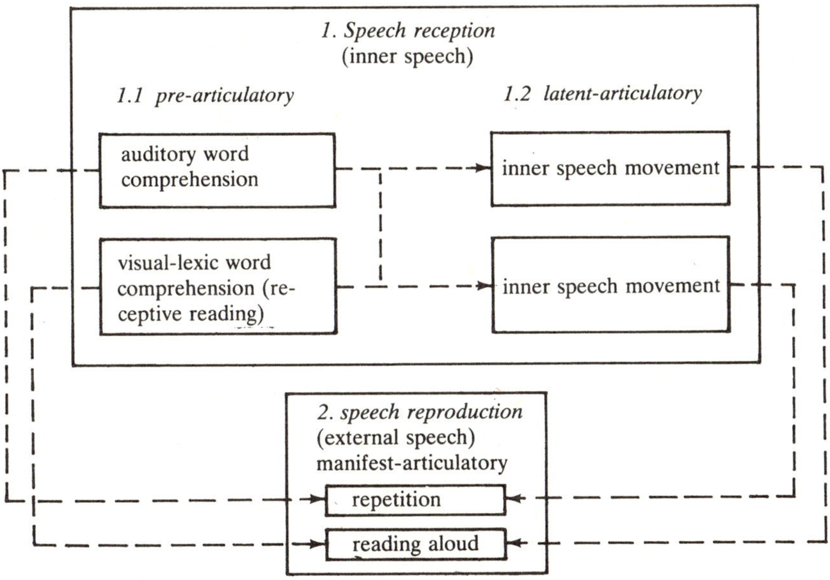

On the basis of the structural-dynamic conception, presented graphically in Tables 11 and 12, regarding the simple, combined, and experimentally coupled speech-functional partial systems investigated, the test results given above allow a number of conclusions to be drawn which can also be of importance for the interpretation of normal function processes.

1. Speech reception: the role of verbo-receptive functions and their components on the inner-speech level in auditory and visual-lexic word comprehension, and particularly:

1.1 the pre-articulatory components, their autonomy against participation in inner speech movements; the relationship between intact and disturbed pre-articulatory components (auditory-lexic) in the framework of experimentally-coupled partial systems (deblocking) (see Table II);

1.2 the latent-articulatory accompanying components of word hearing and receptive word reading; the inner-speech relationship to the relevant pre-articulatory components; the relative independence of liability to disturbance of latent articulation from the function intactness of the pre-articulatory components.

2. Speech reproduction (external speech): special characteristics of the spoken speech reproduction of words offered auditorily or in writing compared to speech reception (speech reception and speech reproduction can to a certain degree be disturbed or intact independently of one another). Relationship between manifest and latent articulation, between pre-articulatory speech reception and speech reproduction (see Table 12).

In the following passages we shall discuss these problems in detail.

1. Speech reception: analysis of the inner speech functions and components of spoken and written speech perceptions and understanding at the word level.

1.1 The pre-articulatory verbo-receptive main components. Seen from the linguistic viewpoint, the speech perception processes dealt with here are processes on the phonetic-phonemic level (auditory speech perception) and on the graphemic level (visual speech perception).

Since word comprehension also presupposes the matching of the phonemic or graphemic structures with the corresponding stored lexical units, the word meanings, we must also take decoding processes at the semantic level into consideration in analysing inner-speech activity.

In this sense the disturbances in word comprehension are phonemic-semantic in Case 1, and graphemic-semantic in Case 2.

On the basis of the prior examination of the two patients (for case reports see p. 96–98), these impairments can be defined even more precisely. In Case 1 the perception of phonemic word structures had already suffered seriously, and the matching of meaning had been secondarily damaged; Case 2 had a relatively intact visual perception of graphemic word structures (in the field of simple words of up to three syllables), but in his case the semantic decoding of these structures was severely limited. Inversely, we could demonstrate in Case 1 the intact nature of the grasping and understanding of graphemic structures, and in Case 2 of phonemic structures.

The parameter which we used in the assessment of our test results with regard to word hearing and receptive reading was the semantic decoding of the relevant word structures offered by us, i.e., word comprehension performance.

The results of those test variants which we carried out in Case 1 and Case 2 with the exclusive participation of the inner-speech pre-articulatory components (main components), show that for these patients the accomplishment of auditory and visual-lexic word comprehension performance depends upon the degree of intactness of these two components (verbo-auditory and verbo-visual), or in other words that the impairment of comprehension of the spoken and written word is due to disturbances at the inner-speech pre-articulatory level.

Relationship between the main components of differing modalities of word comprehension (auditory-lexic):

By successively coupling the disturbed components with the corresponding intact and also pre-articulatory components, significant performance improvements were induced in the word comprehension of the damaged modality. In other words, by means of the successive coupling of intact graphemic-semantic processes (Case 1) and vice versa (Case 2), we were able to create favorable conditions for a far-reaching re-actualisation of the blocked inner speech processes. In Case 1 the provision of a certain graphemic word structure produced the deblocking at the phonemic level and thereby at the semantic level. In Case 2 in which the disturbance of receptive reading particularly affected the matching of word meaning with the corresponding graphemic word structure, the deblocking proceeded directly from the provision of the corresponding sound structures.

By means of the inclusion of labiolexia we were able, in Case 1, to win further information with regard to the inner speech pre-articulatory mechanisms. The results of the test variants in which we utilised the visible articulation movements of the examiner (with the exclusion of latent-articulatory co-movements by the patient) show the highly significant facilitating influence of these visibly observed movements upon the auditory word comprehension of the patient. This means that the impaired grasp of word structures on the phonemic level is greatly improved by visual perception of the articulation movements of the speaker. In this connection it is important to note that these processes take place at the inner-speech pre-articulatory level, i.e., without simultaneous latent speech movements.

1.2 The latent-articulatory accompanying components of speech reception. Like manifest articulation, latent articulation is a verbo-motor process. Damage to the cortical zones primarily responsible for the normal verbo-motor process (premotor, precentral and postcentral sections) must have an effect not only on manifest articulation but also on latent articulation. It therefore appears justifiable, when ascertaining that manifest articulation is intact or subject to certain disturbances, to draw conclusions about the intact nature or impairment of the latent-articulatory processes. If a patient is not capable of repeating correctly words spoken to him, it may be assumed that the inner speech articulatory reproduction of these words is also affected; in the same way it is unlikely that the innervation of latent speech movements during receptive reading could remain intact in the case of damaged reading aloud.

It is assumed that a functional matching, to be more exactly specified, exists between manifest articulation and the latent articulatory processes.

Proceeding first form the directly ascertainable functional capacity of the relevant froms of *manifest* articulation, we receive the following picture (see Table 13):

Case 1

a) the serious disturbance of repetition leads to the conclusion that there is a simultaneous impairment of latent articulation during word hearing (for the time being this applies under the conditions of the elimination of labiolexia);

b) with the release of labiolexia the patient is capable of co-articulating aloud the words spoken to him; in our tests there were not generally such manifest-articulatory utterances, and co-articulation during word hear-

Table 13. *Assumptions about the functional matching between manifest and latent articulation*

	manifest articulation		latent articulation	
	repetition (without labiolexia)	disturbed	in word hearing (without labiolexia)	disturbed
Case 1	co-articulation during word hearing and lipreading	intact	in word hearing and lipreading	intact
	reading aloud	disturbed	in receptive word reading	disturbed
Case 2	repetition	intact	in word hearing	intact
	reading aloud	disturbed	in receptive word reading	disturbed

ing and the simultaneous lipreading of the speech movements took place in latent form. The intact nature of the function of manifest co-articulation justifies the assumption that the latent articulatory accompanying component of labiolexia is also undisturbed;

c) the fact that expressive word reading is almost totally cancelled in this patient makes it likely that latent articulation during receptive word reading is also impaired.

Case 2

a) this patient has intact repetition of simple words, and this leads us to expect corresponding intact latent articulation during word hearing;

b) the serious impairment of expressive word reading gives us the preliminary indication that the corresponding latent articulation during receptive word reading must also be impaired.

Below we shall assess in what way these assumptions were confirmed on the basis of the results achieved in the differing test variants.

As criterion for establishing the intact nature or the damaged nature of the latent-articulatory accompanying components we utilised the effect of the release or elimination of these components on the one hand upon the auditory or lexic word comprehension and on the other hand on the manifest articulation of the subsequent repetition or reading aloud.

The inner-speech relations between latent-articulatory and pre-articulatory components:

The latent-articulatory accompanying components of word hearing and receptive word reading take an intermediate position. 'Inner speech', as well as manifest articulation, represents at the same time a *verbo-motor* process, and, like pre-articulatory speech reception, an *inner-speech* process.

The latent speech movements and the verbo-kinaesthetic feedback proceeding from them, which play a decisive part in acquiring spoken and written speech, are normally 'reduced'[16] as a result of the automation of the process of speech comprehension; i.e., one can grasp the meaning of words spoken or read aloud without utilising inner-articulatory mechanisms. In this sense Weigl [180] concluded as a result of his investigations that despite the important role played by verbo-kinaesthetic stimuli proceeding from the speech organs in learning and developing language and thought, the neuro-muscular re-afferent impulses (verbo-kinaesthetic feedback) are dispensable to a certain degree as soon as the formation and storage of verbo-visual, verbo-acoustic and verbo-motor stereotypes has reached considerable perfection.

On the other hand it is known that in cases of brain-pathological impairment of word comprehension, compensatory latent-articulatory processes may come automatically into action [157]. As a result of this knowledge, we could await, in the case of our patients with serious disturbance of the auditory or word-reading comprehension, recourse to the facilitating effect of latent articulation.

Under our test conditions, this would have meant that the release of the relevant accompanying component would lead to a performance improvement in speech perception. Analogously, the additional release of the latent-articulatory accompanying components of the intact functions should bring about, with the aid of the process of successive coupling, an increase in the performance rate of the disturbed functions.

Expectations of this sort tacitly assume that latent articulation is itself intact. We attempted to demonstrate in the preceding section that with our patients this is not in general the case. There we postulated that firstly the latent-articulatory accompanying components of receptive word reading are disturbed in both patients; that secondly the accompanying components of word hearing are disturbed in Case 1; that thirdly, on the contrary, the accompanying components of labiolexia in Case 1 and of word hearing in Case 2 are intact (see Table 13).

Our test results demonstrate that the performance of the disturbed word comprehension (auditory or lexic) was not changed in either patient by the release of latent articulation.

This result permits of two possible interpretations: either the two patients, despite their receptive impairment, made 'no use' of the possibility of inner articulation (in this case the process of release and elimination could have no effect), or the mechanism of latent speech movement as such is wholely or partially disturbed, so that it cannot be utilised.

The first explanation can be countered by the experience cited that if verbo-receptive processes are hindered, there is generally a certain compensation through inner-speech articulation. The second explanation receives support from the opinion which we developed that verbomotor disturbances prevent such compensation. In other words, the 'inactivity' of the latent-articulatory accompanying components with regard to disturbed word comprehension performance must be evaluated as an expression of damage to this component.

If this interpretation is correct, this means that in both Case 1 and Case 2 not simply certain pre-articulatory components are affected, but also the corresponding latent-articulatory accompanying components.

This does not, however, mean that in our patients the entire field of inner speech is functionally disturbed, but only certain channels. It must also be emphasised that there is a relationship of relative autonomy between the pre-articulatory components and latent articulation at inner speech level [⟨2⟩]; i.e., that these components can be disturbed or intact independent one of the other.

Our statements with regard to the increase in performance in auditory word comprehension by labiolexia in Case 1 can be used as an argument that in those cases in which one latent-articulatory accompanying component is intact, its facilitating effect can be utilised to overcome disturbances in word comprehension performance. With this patient the release of the latent-articulatory accompanying component of lipreading produced a significant improvement in word comprehension performance.

2. Speech reproduction: analysis of verbo-motor functions and components of speech reproduction. Manifest-articulatory components.

In the preceding section we already had an opportunity to discuss a series of essential facts in connection with the speech motor functions of our patients.

The statements in the patients' case reports, detailed above, make it obvious that the disturbances of the verbo-expressive functions which we investigated stem, in a brain-pathologic sense, from completely differing damage. In Case 1 we have a typical sensory-aphasic syndrome – presumably with preponderant lesions in the area of the temporal lobe – which finds expression in serious paraphasic slip; in Case 2 we have a typical Broca-aphasia with afferent-motor elements (fronto-parietal damage), and expressive speech displays telegraphic style.

Despite these differences we could observe a series of common regularities in the speech-motor mechanism in both cases: relative autonomy of speech reception compared to speech reproduction, deblockability of speech reproduction, etc.

In these patients the reproductive speech functions of repetition and reading aloud are more seriously damaged than the receptive functions of auditory or lexic speech comprehension; and this fact shows that these disturbances of the expressive functions are not simply a result of the impairment of speech perception. Indeed, additional factors must be made responsible for the difficulties in word reproduction (see above). In fact, in cases of aphasia there is no general interdependence between receptive and expressive speech functions. Cases are well known of patients who show no difficulty in understanding spoken words, but who are unable to speak normally. The same is true for reading: there can be receptive alexia accompanied by intact reading aloud; and expressive reading may be disturbed independently of reading comprehension. In our patient (Case 1), for instance, word reading comprehension is intact, but he fails in expressive word reading.

On the other hand, speech reproduction can be intact, even if speech reception is damaged with regard to semantic decoding (actual speech comprehension); e.g., there can be repetition or reading aloud with no understanding of the meaning.

Relationship between latent-articulatory and manifest-articulatory components:

In section 1.2 of the discussion we debated the relationship between the inner speech pre-articulatory and latent-articulatory components. It remains for us to analyse in what way the relations present themselves under our test conditions between latent-articulatory and manifest-articulatory components.

The release of the latent-articulatory accompanying components of disturbed word hearing (Case 1) or receptive word reading (Case 2) has no demonstrable influence on the impaired manifest articulation in repetition or reading aloud, and we attributed this to the fact that in these cases the speech motor function (both latent and manifest articulation on the channel concerned) has suffered.

The situation is different when there is a case of one disturbed manifest-articulatory modality being influenced by the intact latent-articulatory accompanying component of another modality. For instance in Case 1, intact latent articulation while reading the lip movements of the examiner at the time of word hearing eases the disturbed manifest articulation performance in subsequent repetition. In Case 2 latent articulation during word hearing was intact, but manifest articulation in reading aloud was damaged. After coupling the two forms of articulation there was a significant increase in performance in reading aloud the relevant words.

The preceding remarks about the influence of latent-articulatory components on manifest-articulatory components concern in the first place results in which there was either no effect or a positive effect. In Case 1 we could also show that the release of latent articulation during intact receptive word reading significantly *reduced* the d-effect with regard to disturbed repetition. The explanation of this inhibition effect appears to us to lie in the fact that in Case 1 the transcoding of the visual perception of written words into the corresponding speech-motor innervation pattern (both manifest articulation in expressive word reading and latent articulation in receptive word reading) is disturbed.

These conclusions show that impairment of the latent-articulatory accompanying components does not take only the form of 'inactivity', but can also be expressed as a negative induction. Further investigations will be necessary to discover the conditions behind each of these forms.

Relationships between pre-articulatory speech reception and manifest-articulatory speech reproduction.

Little is known to date about the mechanism of the transcoding of spoken-speech or written-speech patterns in manifest-articulatory structures (repetition or reading aloud). To us, it appears important that with automated verbal reproduction the triggering of the relevant articulatory innervation pattern can take place direct, i.e., without the cooperation of inner speech articulation in grasping word structures. Like other authors (e.g., Sokolov [156], Weigl [⟨7⟩] shows that in normal cases repetition or reading aloud are accomplished correctly even under conditions of the experimental blocking of latent speech movements during word hearing or voiceless reading. The same is true of aphasics who – within the bounds of those expressive speech functions still intact – are able to repeat and read aloud even if latent articulation is temporarily cancelled during auditory or lexic speech perception.

We were able to confirm these test results in the present work, particularly in connection with the relevant deblocking experiments. We have seen that both performances in disturbed repetition and also in impaired redding aloud can be considerably improved with the aid of previous intact receptive word reading (Case 1) or the retained word hearing (Case 2). This tells us, first, that the disturbances in transcoding in the corresponding manifest articulation pattern can be removed to a certain degree by the intact verbo-receptive modalities of the deblocking functions. The intact grasped graphemic word structures favor the implementation of corresponding articulation patterns in repetition (Case 1), while the correctly perceived phonetic word structures favour the transcoding in the corresponding articulatory structures in reading aloud.

The triggering of the *manifest-articulatory* impulse proceeds in both cases from *inner-speech pre-articulatory* instances.

This last assumption, which will certainly need confirmation by further tests on aphasics and normal subjects, should be of particular importance for the development of adequate models of the structure and dynamics of the speech-functional system. Under the conditions of highly-automated processes at the level of speech reproduction (and probably also at the level of speech production), the path between verbo-receptive or cognitive input and verbo-expressive output appears to be greatly shortened (see footnote 16). In this manner the 'instructions' proceeding from the perception of phonetic or graphemic structures are already able to bring about the evocation of corresponding verbo-motor manifest-articulatory sterotypes (without the deviation by way of an inner-speech-articulatory 'analysis-by-synthesis'.

The aim of the present paper, to reach conclusions about the structure and dynamics of various partial systems of the speech-functional system with the help of experimental neuropsychological methods, appears to us to have been satisfied to the degree that pathological processes basically allow us to draw conclusions about normal occurrences. In this sense we believe that our function analysis and component analysis of verbo-receptive, inner-speech, and verbo-expressive (external speech) processes are suitable to close a series of 'gaps' in the present psychological and linguistic models of speech reception and speech production. We hope to have made also a certain contribution to the problem of the relationship between the levels of spoken speech and written speech (on this see also Weigl [187]).

Notes

1. 'Spoken speech' (understanding and reproducing spoken speech, and voluntary speech) is to be differentiated from 'written speech', which we utilise here in the sense of receptive reading (reading understanding), of expressive reading (aloud), and the various modes of writing (copying, writing on dictation, voluntary writing, etc.).
2. The term 'speech-functional system' is used here in the sense of the Soviet psychologists Vygotsky [169], Leontyev [101], Luria [109; 112], and others, who regard the higher psychical functions as the result of the activity of complicated intracerebral interconnected ontogentically conditioned connections of often widely separated and highly differentiated cortical zones. On the basis of these connections, various sections of the cortex are linked together to become effective as *functional brain systems* – Pavlov spoke of 'functionally combined centres'. These brain systems constitute complete self-regulating servomechanisms which are composed, for their part, of autonomous partial systems (see Weigl ⟨2⟩). The achievements of human language with its manifold use forms are also based on the activities of such functional brain systems.
3. We thank Dr H. Schulze, Neurological Clinic of the Humboldt University, Berlin (Charité), for making the examination and informing us of his findings.
4. We use the classification of efferent and afferent motor (innervatoric and ideokinetic) aphasia in the manner of Luria [112], Leonhard [99], and Schulze [151].
5. Part of the tests and results presented at length here were communicated in another connection in: Böttcher, Metze, and I. Weigl [19] and E. Weigl ⟨2⟩.
6. We group together under the term 'pre-articulatory' those inner-speech processes which are already clearly structured in phonological or graphemic respect (e.g., the inner hearing or inner reading of speech occurrences, the conept of speech communications, etc.), without the innervation of demonstrable specific speech movements (see pp. 101–102). We call these perceptual and conceptual occurrences 'pre-articulatory' since, in contrast to cognitive processes which contain no sound or written structures, these represent a potential pre-stage to latent or manifest articulation.
7. Procedures of registering latent speech movements electromyographically have been developed by Jussewitsch [75], Bassin and Bein [8], Kryshova and Shtayngart [92], Hermann and Krolikova [60], and others. Measurements of verbo-kinaesthetic feedback processes were made by Chésni [26].
8. Luria [107] discovered that in cases of sensory aphasia the understanding of spoken words could be increased by up to 100% when the visible articulation movements of the speaker could be perceived; we could confirm to a considerable degree these findings in our Case 1 (see p. 460). Beltyukov [11] also draws attention to the necessity

for labiolexic investigations in cases of sensory aphasia, in order to answer more precisely questions about the interaction between the visual, acoustic, and verbo-motor analysers. Weigl and Bierwisch ⟨3⟩ posed the question of the relationship between the visually perceived articulatory movements and the acoustically perceived phonemic structures. They believe that two different assumptions are possible in this respect. Either the observable articulation movements form 'autonomous kinemic structures' (the term 'kineme' was used by Alich [6] for those visually observable articulatory movement pictures taking place in a certain order and corresponding to spoken-speech segments), or they were simply discontinuously effective visual cues which can compensate for certain disturbances at the verbo-acoustic level in close connection with co-movements occuring simultaneously in the listener (see p. 9).

9. The word spoken behind the cardboard screen was naturally offered at a volume which made normal acoustic perception possible for the patient.

10. Although the auditory or lexic word comprehension of both patients was considerably more strongly disturbed on the abstract level than on the concrete level, and therefore the abstract level would have been more suitable for proof of our experimentally obtained alteration in performance in speech comprehension, we nevertheless confined ourselves to the exclusive use of concrete terms, since control of comprehension is easier and more reliable. With regard to these concrete nouns, our preliminary tests showed that the auditory and lexic word comprehension and the repetition and reading aloud of both patients was largely independent of word content and word frequency.

    The variations in the number of individual experiments (words) have technical explanations. For instance, the number of tests had to be greatly reduced when using the blowing method, so that the patient should not be overburdened physically.

11. As noted, Case 1 also has intact the labiolexic auxiliary function; since, however, in distinction to receptive reading, this has no function independent of auditory comprehension, we shall deal separately with its part in deblocking the verbo-auditory perception of this patient (see p. 121–122).

12. The nature of the deblocking phenomenon is much more complicated than is shown here. On the one hand we were able to show that not only spoken- and written-language disturbances of word comprehension and word reproduction, but also impairment at the syntactical level (receptive and expressive agramatism), can be deblocked [19; ⟨15⟩; ⟨2⟩; ⟨3⟩].

    In the present investigations we always deblocked only one particular word by the same word accessible over another channel. As shown elsewhere [19; 185], other methods are also possible; for instance a certain word can be deblocked by a related word (synonym, antonym, inclusive term, etc.).

13. In the deblocking tests, 5 words were always provided on word cards; these words were made up of 4 'neutral' ones of different meanings and one 'critical' word, which the patient had been unable to understand or repeat in variant series I (without deblocking). (The word material which had given the patient no difficulties in comprehension or repetition in variant I was not used again in variant II.) The additional four 'neutral' words made it impossible for the patient to predict which of the words offered in the preliminary stage was the 'critical' one, that is to say the word later offered to him auditorily which he had to repeat. This prevented a conscious carry-over of the lexic word comprehension to the subsequent auditory word comprehension and repetition (for the technique of deblocking, see Weigl [⟨2⟩; [19] et seq.)

The quantitative results reported below naturally refer only to the 'critical' and not to the 'neutral' words.

14. In the present work we cannot go more closely into the question of why under certain circumstances the d-effect apporaches the 100% mark, but in other cases, particularly with badly disturbed repetition (Case 1) or reading aloud (Case 2), it lies well under this mark. Our experience shows that this is connected with the fact that one single deblockant is not sufficient to deblock such seriously impaired performances. In such cases we use with success on the one hand the method of combining the functions of several intact functions, and on the other hand 'chain-deblocking' ⟨2⟩].
15. It would have been more advantageous to have carried out a special variant in which only the r-component was released; for technical reasons (overburdening the patient), this was not possible.
16. With regard to the reduction of certain inner-articulatory verbo-kinaesthetic processes in thought and speech reception, Luria [112] stated: "This fact was thoroughly discussed in the psychological investigations of Vygotsky (1934, 1956) and Galperin (1959), in the special tests of Sokolov (1959) and Weigl (1964) and in the electrophysiological tests of Novikova (1955), Bassin and Bein (1957), which demonstrated that adequately fixed thought and speech operations are carried out at a certain level without ascertainable kinaesthesia, and obviously gain a certain independence of the developed processes of articulated speech, to which the subject only returns in case of complicated discursive operations" (p. 157). Reduction processes of this sort have been investigated by Soviet psychology, particularly by A. N. Leontyev, Galperin, Elkonin, Zaporoshets, Luria, etc., in the most differing fields of voluntary acts, thought, speech, etc. (see also Hiebsch et al. (Eds.), 'Results of Soviet Psychology' [67], particularly the papers of Kostyuk, Galperin and Luria). Important contributions to the problem of the various levels of inner speech have been made in the works of Žinkin [211] and A. A. Leontiev [100].

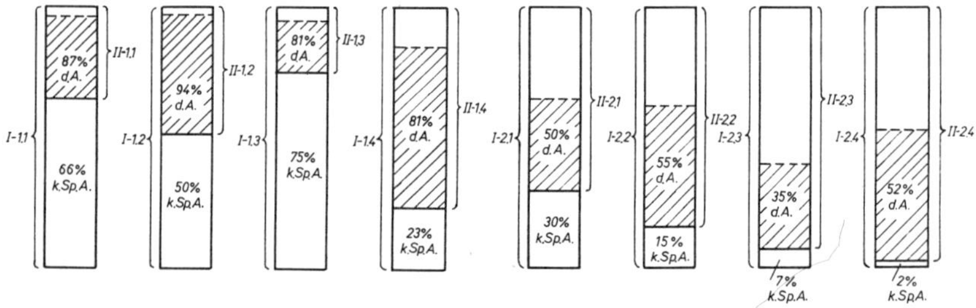

Ill. 3a, 3b. *Comparative diagram of the d-effects in variant series II (Case 1).*
k. Sp. A. = correct spontaneous answers
d. A. = deblocked answers

⟨7⟩

E. WEIGL

The Importance of Afferent, Verbo-Kinaesthetic Excitation of the Speech Apparatus for Expressive and Receptive Speech in Normal Subjects and Subjects with Speech Disturbances

The role of latent speech movements (micromovements) for speaking and thinking has occupied the attention of many researchers since the end of the nineteenth century. R. Schilling's [146] compilation *On Inner Speech* provides us with a comprehensive, though not quite complete, survey of work in this fields up to 1929, together with a series of test methods for examination of the movements, during thought and inner speech, of the muscles controlling breath, larynx, and tongue and of other speech muscles. In the meantime the development of electromyographic and other methods for the registration of neuromuscular processes in the speech organs have greatly enriched our knowledge in this field [8; 40; 66; 75; 130].

I. P. Pavlov and his pupils, basing themselves on the fundamental theses of I. M. Sechenov, have made an outstanding contribution to clarifying the importance of the verbo-motor, verbo-kinaesthetic analysers for the structure and development of the entire verbal and cognitive activity of man, of his *second signal system.* The results of the multifold experimental work of this school with regard to the problem of the verbo-motor analyser are recorded in Zhinkins [210] *Verbal Mechanisms.*

Earlier authors [35; 78; 146 and others] already knew and utilised sporadically the method of temporarily eliminating or disturbing to a greater or lesser degree the latent speech movements (micromovements) in order to investigate the function of the verbo-kinaesthetic analyser.

The elimination method, mainly initiated by the works of A. N. Sokolov [154], and later continued by him, by S. M. Blinkov [17], A. R. Luria [105, 106], L. K. Nasarova [129], L. Kadotchkin [76], and recently by the present author together with A. Fradis [196], consists in general of the following points:

1. Indirect methods of blocking the verbo-motor or verbo-acoustic analysers during the exercise of various mental activities: A. N. Sokolov

[156] and his collaborators require their subjects either to recite syllables ('lalala'), or words, or familiar pieces of poetry, or to listen to texts read by the examiner while they are perceiving pictures, reading words, solving mathematical problems, or translating foreign texts. This inhibits the possibility of performing latent speech movements in accordance with the mental task set, or the acoustic control of their own 'inner speech' (auditory feedback).

2. Direct methods of mechanically inhibiting the verbo-motor analyser: A. N. Sokolov (with normal adults and children), L. K. Nasarova and L. K. Kadotchkin (with normal school children), S. M. Blinkov, A. R. Luria, E. Weigl and A. Fradis (with aphasics) have impeded or blocked latent speech movements partly by holding the lips and the tongue between the teeth and partly by holding the mouth open with slightly protruding tongue.

The results of the works cited allow the following conclusions to be drawn:

1. The elimination of latent speech movement in schoolbeginners leads to considerable disturbance of reading and writing; this fact confirms the correctness of the fundamental importance, as demonstrated in particular by I. P. Pavlov and his pupils, of afferent verbo-kinaesthetic excitations for the stage of development of the various verbal functions, including reading and writing.

2. Since – at least in the early stage of the experiments – the elimination or disturbance of latent speech movements in normal subjects leads to a remarkable disorganisation of inner speech and thought activity, of silent reading, writing, calculation, etc., we can recognise that there is a certain necessity for the factor of verbo-kinaesthetic impulses, even in verbally developed and intellectually developed adults, with regard to these functions.

3. The results of the experiments conducted by Blinkov, Luria, Weigl, and Fradis with aphasic patients with a view to the exclusion of latent speech movements show that under certain circumstances deprival of the afferent verbo-kinaesthetic excitations, which form a prop for the aphasic, can produce an impediment to his verbal and intellectual performance.

It would be a mistake, however, to assume a permanent participation of verbo-kinaesthetic impulses in the process of speech and thought. The experiments referred to demonstrate that both normal subjects and aphasics are also capable of many verbal and cognitive performances even when latent speech movements are excluded or made difficult.

As further proof, we submit below a series of results which we have achieved with the help of a mechanical method which we developed with the aim of excluding latent speech movements.[1]

Description of the elimination procedure

As we have described in [176] the apparatus we constructed consists of a support holding a glass capillary tube bent like a *U* at the bottom. This is extended in a nether direction by a rubber tube, ending in a glass mouthpiece. The glass tube is filled with a coloured liquid. A small writing desk for the text which has to be read or for writing paper may be placed next to the support.

The subject seated in front of the apparatus must, when requested by the examiner, take the glass mouthpiece in his mouth, hold it above his tongue with his teeth, and enclose it hermetically with his lips. At the moment indicated by the examiner, the subject, after breathing in deeply, has to blow lightly into the mouthpiece keeping his cheeks expanded, in this way raising the liquid in the capillary tube to a marked spot on the tube. By constant supervision of the height of the liquid, very exact observation may be maintained that the subject is blowing during the entire test. This supervision is also necessary to prevent the subject from closing the hole in the mouthpiece with his tongue, either consciously or unconsciously, thus annulling the whole test. Normally, if the instructions are strictly adhered to, the liquid is raised to the marked spot, and a slight oscillation caused by the stream of breath is observable; if, however, the mouthpiece is sealed, the level suddenly becomes stable, which cannot evade detection. The examiner must see to it that during the entire experiment the subject keeps his cheeks as extended as possible, that is to say in a state of tension, which helps to eliminate certain speech movements. Another important part of the instructions is that the subject should begin to blow shortly before the beginning of the experiment itself, thus making it impossible for the subject to carry out before this point certain, though very slight, latent speech movements (micromovements). In the same way the blowing may not be ended before the conclusion of the process under investigation, neither may it be interrupted; otherwise this period may be filled with more or less 'secret' speech movements. If the subject becomes tired during the experiment it should be interrupted and conducted later. It is recommended, that this blowing should be practiced with the subject before the first experiments, so that he may become to some degree accustomed to the unusual situation.

The method recommended by us offers, with regard to the elimination of articulation movements, a series of advantages compared to other elimination methods: during the blowing a large portion of the speech apparatus, particularly the lips, jaws, cheeks, and tongue are fixed in a position which almost completely inhibits the participation of these organs in the specific speech movements which are absolutely necessary for the creation of the speech sounds. The constant stream of air used to raise the level of the fluid loses its role as carrier of speech sounds, as we have shown with the aid of pneumograms in the cited work [176]. The blocking of latent speech movements by our method has a separate effect on each of the various articulation areas. The position of the lips, which enclose hermetically the glass mouthpiece, does not permit any specific speech movement in the articulation area between the two lips, or between the lower lips and the upper incisors. Movement of the jaw is prevented by the mouthpiece held between the teeth; the mouth and throat area ends at the mouthpiece, that is to say it is practically closed, and this prevents the formation of a series of other sounds. The tongue, which in accordance with instructions lies under the mouthpiece, loses its freedom of movement, and can no longer form, together with the gums, the channel for a speech stream of air; in the same way the tip of the tongue is incapable of touching the incisors or the front portion of the hard palate, which puts a stop to those sounds which arise in this articulation area. Finally, the mouthpiece prevents contact between the back of the tongue and the gums, which leads to a blocking of the third articulation area. Taken together, the blowing method therefore provides a far-reaching guarantee that all latent speech movements will be inhibited.

Like all other methods of this sort, the one described above has certain disadvantages. Keeping the lips closed and the tongue between the teeth, and also the keeping open of the mouth can, in the long term, lead to certain signs of tiring in some healthy subjects and in many sick subjects; in addition there may be certain negative induction effects arising, at least temporarily, from the creation of special excitation foci. A. N. Sokolov [156] and others have shown that such disturbing effects can be greatly reduced or completely removed by use and practice, and by careful dosage of the use of the method. In our experiments we were able to note such signs of habituation; they were confirmed to us by the subjects themselves and also objectively by the test results which, after early failures, generally improved rapidly.

Experimental Investigations

I. *Tests with normal subjects:* In tests with various normal subjects we were able to note that without exception words and sentences read or heard (read aloud by examiner) during blowing were adequately perceived and understood; in the same way the subjects were able with ease to repeat correctly, after blowing had ceased, words and sentences spoken to them during this activity.

Conclusion: The results gained with the aid of our elimination method confirm the observation made by other authors that for normal adults the impulses arising from latent speech movements are by no means indispensable for the normal course of various expressive (repetition), receptive, inner speech and cognitive performances.

II. *Tests with aphasics:* We carried out the tests with five aphasics. In three of these patients (A. L., I. A., M. P.) predominantly the expressive verbal functions were impaired; in the two others both the expressive and the receptive functions were impaired.

1. *Testing receptive reading (reading comprehension): method:* during blowing the patient is presented a certain sentence which he has to read. The blowing is then interrupted, and the patient must select, from three written sentences offered, that sentence which is *synonymous* with that which he had read.[2]

Results: Patient I. A. (predominantly expressive speech impairment, *no alexia*): the patient understands all sentences correctly, i.e., he selects without difficulty the synonymous sentence.

2. *Testing auditory speech comprehension*

a) word comprehension: method: during the blowing the examiner says one word to the subject; after blowing has been interrupted, five pictures are submitted to the subject, who has to indicate the picture corresponding to the word spoken.

Results: Patient L. A. (slight motor aphasia, mainly disturbance of spontaneous speech; *no disturbance of speech comprehension*): this patient understands correctly all words spoken and promptly indicates the corresponding picture.

b) sentence comprehension: method: during the blowing a sentence is spoken to the patient; after blowing has been interrupted three written sentences are submitted to the patient, including one sentence synonymous with one previously heard, which the patient must select (the test principle is also based upon the 'synonym method').

Results: Patient L. A. (see above: *no disturbance of speech comprehension, no alexia:* this patient promptly finds the sentences synonymous to those spoken. Patient I. A. (see above; *no alexia, but a slight auditory agramatism*): the patient immediately understands correctly four of the eight sentences offered, in the other cases he displays certain differentiation disturbances; he at first wrongly chooses sentences which are verbally similar, instead of synonymous (e.g., after hearing the sentence 'Quarrels between people can have serious results', he selects the sentence 'Quarrels between children can have no serious results', and only finds the correct synonymous sentence, 'When people argue the results can be bad', after the test has been repeated).

3. *Testing repetition: method:* during blowing the examiner speaks

a word or a sentence to the patient, then tells the patient to cease blowing and to repeat.

Results: Patient L. A. (see above; *no repetition disturbance*): the patient reacts completely positively both to words and to sentences. – Patient M. P. (predominantly expressive speech disturbances with simultaneous high degree of peripheral deafness/effective amplification with deaf aid/ *partial paraphasic repetition disturbances*): of seven words spoken to the patient during blowing he is able to repeat five correctly; with the others he fails, although he understood them.

– Patient P. M. (expressive and also receptive speech disturbances; *partial repetition disturbances*): under normal conditions this patient repeated, of 55 words spoken, 45 paraphasically and only 10 correctly; however, when the same 55 words were spoken to her during blowing she answered 25 correctly (20 paraphasically).

Conclusions: (1) It is shown that in the aphasics we examined, the verbal reactions, which have been retained by them under normal conditions, proceed undisturbed despite the fact that latent speech movements have been eliminated by blowing. (2) In the case of the partially-impaired verbal reactions there is no noticeable worsening of performance under the conditions of blowing, and in one case (P. M.) there was even a certain diminution of incorrect reactions.

The elimination of latent speech movements in certain cases of aphasia appears capable of exerting a favourable influence on repetition; if this observation of ours should be confirmed, this would allow certain conclusions to be drawn about the relation between the receptive and expressive components of the auditory analyser. In our case it might be assumed that in aphasic disturbances which predominantly affect the afferent motor-proprioceptive speech processes the 'auditory feedback' [20; 83; and others] in repetition is more or less severly damaged, since the information transmitted over the afferent routes of the cortex resembles 'jumbled telegrams'. If the entire articulatory speech apparatus is inhibited (by mechanical means) during the offering of words by the examiner, then the auditory analyser receives an 'unjumbled', relatively adequate audio-verbal model (Brain [20] speaks of 'schema'), which can then guide the disturbed verbo-motor analyser under more favourable conditions and obviously with better results. However, this is for the time being only a hypothesis, which must await experimental confirmation.

4. *'Deblocking' disturbed verbal reactions in aphasics:* We developed above a hypothesis on the relative independence in aphasics of receptive and expressive speech processes from the activity of the verbo-kinaesthetic excitations of the speech organs; and we found a confirmation of this hypothesis in the results achieved with the temporary

deblocking of certain aphasic disturbances under the conditions of the mechanical elimination of latent speech movements ⟨9⟩.

With the help of our blowing apparatus we have eliminated latent speech movements during deblocking experiments of many different kinds, experiments carried out with three aphasics (M. P., P. M., M. M.). We shall confine ourselves here to a report on the results of these experiments. With the help of the deblocking method which we have developed we temporarily rehabilitated certain disturbed verbal reactions (picture naming and repetition disturbances, expressive alexia, agraphia to dictation, and others) through intact speech performances (e.g., word hearing, receptive reading, copying), and this rehabilitation also remained effective under the conditions of the elimination of verbo-kinaesthetic excitations. This result appears to us worthy of note for two reasons. Firstly, it supports our assumption that fully-developed receptive or expressive speech stereotypes can ensure certain speech and intellectual performances even without an auditory feedback. Secondly, it contributes to the solution of the phenomenon of deblocking by showing that these processes take place at the level of pre-formed visual, acoustic, etc., stereotypes, without necessarily relying upon the cooperation of the verbo-motor kinaesthetic analyser.

III. *Tests with a congenitally deaf subject:* It is obvious that verbo-kinaesthetic excitation plays a decisive role in learning to speak and developing thought in cases of congenital deafness. We asked ourselves what would happen if such a person was temporarily robbed of this function. For this purpose we used our elimination method in an experiment with a deaf girl of 25 (dental technician in a municipal laboratory) who can understand people fairly well by lipreading, and who herself speaks quite understandably.

a) Word comprehension

lexic: the subject reads a written word while she blows; then she must select from a number of pictures the one corresponding to this word.

result: in all cases she is able to select the corresponding picture, promptly and correctly.

labiolexic: the examiner speaks a word, and the subject lip-reads it while she blows. A number of words are then submitted in writing, and she must select the word spoken.

result: the subject selects promptly and correctly from the written list the words, both concrete and abstract, although she had not understood the meaning of some of the (abstract) words.

b) repetition: the examiner speaks a word, the subject reads it labiolexically while she blows and then repeats it.

result: the subject understands all the words spoken and is able to repeat them correctly and promptly.

Conclusion: Sokolov, Zhinkin and others, on the basis of experimental observations, ascribe an important 'compensating' role to the acoustic analyser in the absence or disturbance of verbo-kinaesthetic excitations. Here we have another aspect of the problem. In the case of our subject with congenital deafness, nature has completely excluded this acoustic analyser, and with the help of our test method we temporarily eliminated completely the function of the verbo-kinaesthetic analyser. Despite this she was able to understand, to retain, to repeat and to read what was said to her. It is thus shown that in this case, despite the great importance of the 'auditory feedback', various speech manifestations such as speech comprehension (labiolexic), repetition (labiolexic), and reading, are also possible to a certain degree without the participation of the acoustic analyser. The reason for this would appear to us to lie in the presence of pre-formed visual *perception stereotypes* ('models', 'schemata') which are able to ensure the normal process of the function in question, without the aid of the acoustic analyser, and in our case even without the participation of the verb-kinaesthetic analyser.

Thus the inferences drawn above from the results of the tests eliminating the verbo-kinaesthetic analyser must be supplemented by the following conclusion: despite the undeniable part played by the afferent neuromuscular impulses emanating from the latent speech movements (micromovements) – which have recently been emphasised particularly by Hrbek [68], basing himself upon I. P. Pavlov – it is clear that these excitations are to a certain degree dispensable, as soon as the development, storage and automation of verbal stereotypes has reached a certain degree of perfection. This is also true for those with speech disturbances, both for the congenitally deaf and for aphasics, in as far as these aphasics have retained at least partially the relevant verbal stereotypes.

Notes

1. The experiments reported upon below were conducted in the 'I. P. Pavlov' Neurological Institute of the Academy of the Roumanian People's Republic in Bucharest (Director: Prof. Dr. A. Kreindler) in 1959–1960.
2. This 'synonym method' described by us and A. Fradis [196] has the advantage that it can test, by a nonverbal method, the reading and auditory comprehension of expressively-disturbed aphasics.

PART THREE

Experimental Studies on Neuropsychological Mechanisms of Aphasic Disturbances of Speech Perception and Production

⟨8⟩

E. WEIGL and A. KREINDLER

Contributions to the Interpretation of Certain Aphasic Disturbances as Blocking Phenomena

Temporary Deblocking of Motor-speech Reactions through Word Reading in Cases of Motor Aphasia

Cases of motor aphasia are known in which the patient cannot speak spontaneously at all or only very incorrectly, cannot repeat dictated words, cannot name objects, but despite all this is capable of reading aloud fairly correctly. Proceeding from the noteworthy fact that in these cases of general motor speech defects only expressive reading is notably well preserved, we have in the present study examined the relationship between this intact function and the various disturbed speech reactions (naming objects, repetition and reproduction of words).

The patient Marin Paraschiv with whom we carried out the majority of our experiments, displays aphasic disturbances of a mainly motor type: speech hindrance and paraphasia producing almost incomprehensible spontaneous speech, severe disturbance in naming objects and pictures and repeating offered words or sentences, but at the same time well preserved reading aloud and word-reading comprehension[1].

M. P., 56 years of age, pensioner, former sales-clerk, became sick in April 1952: there was a motor weakness of the dexter extremities which lasted for several hours, and a transitory aphasia. Two days later, as the result of great excitement, there was a recurrence of aphasic disturbances, which lasted for several hours. After five days, incidence of a transitory dexter hemiphlegia, and speech disturbances, at first motor, and later also speech comprehension disturbances. Anamnesis: syphilis (?), overindulgence in beer, deafness. Heightened blood pressure (17/9), hyperglycaemia (1.52 gr. ‰). – Neurological findings: only a slight central hemiparesis of the right nervus facialis. Otological findings: high degree of deafness on both sides of a mixed type, advanced otosclerosis; right ear fully deaf, left ear weak hearing remnants. Psychically normal.

The basic phenomenon established by our investigation is as follows: the extremely severe disturbances of the patient with regard to the naming of visually perceived objects or pictures, as well as repetition and the spontaneous reproduction of words, could be temporarily cancelled, more or less completely, by giving the patient the opportunity to read the relevant words aloud. That is to say, an object or a picture, which the patient is not capable of naming although he recognises it properly, can be named by him correctly as soon as he has read the relevant words in advance. In the same way he only can repeat a word spoken by the examiner and transmitted over a deaf aid after he has read it. And finally the patient, who can scarcely produce an understandable word spontaneously, can reproduce any word clearly from memory when he has previously read it.

The experimental investigations reported upon below deal with the favorable results produced by word reading upon the impaired motor-speech reaction of our patient to objects.

I. Deblocking the Naming of Visually Perceived Pictures of Objects

Before dealing with the problem of deblocking object naming, it must be stated that with reference to our patient it was not a case of word-finding disturbance, such as we encounter in the case of amnesic aphasics, but mainly of motor-effectorically induced disturbances. As many authors have emphasised, a distinction must be made between the inability to find a certain word and the impossibility or the difficulty of uttering it. K. Goldstein [54] speaks very correctly of the necessity of regarding this latter expressive-effectoric impairment as the disturbance of "an acquired motor process, directly associatively induced by the sight of the object" and continues ". . . it is not the use of the speech sounds as symbols, but the word production itself" which is damaged . . . "the acquired word automatisms which play such a great role in normal speech". [52]

As we mentioned, our patient, despite his sometimes desperate efforts, is not capable of naming a visually perceived object, with only a few exceptions; but he can promptly do this if the word is written down for him and he is encouraged to read it aloud. In the experiments reported upon below we used, for technical reasons, pictures of objects instead of the objects themselves. Basically, the results noted were the same in both cases.

First we were interested in the *length of time* over which naming remained favorably affected by reading the word. For this purpose we made the following experiments: The patient is presented with a picture which he should name; after it has been ascertained that he is not able to do this, the picture is removed and instead the relevant written word is shown, which the patient should read in a loud voice; after the word has been removed the picture is presented again and he is asked to name it; if he is able to do this, there is an interval of 30 seconds before he is shown and asked to name the picture; if he succeeds here, too, an interval of ten minutes follows, after which the patient is asked again to name the picture, which is shown to him for the fourth time. This experiment was carried out with a series of 13 different pictures, which the patient was able to name correctly after first reading the corresponding word; after 30 seconds he was still able to name 11 pictures; after 10 minutes, on the other hand, only four pictures (see Table 1, test series 1).

Our results hitherto show that the facilitating effects of word reading do not disappear again immediately, but remain for a period and then disappear slowly, though in some cases they can still be noted even after an interval of ten minutes.

To ascertain the strength of this facilitating effect, we varied our experiment: first, we varied the period between the reading of the word and the second presentation of the corresponding picture, by which we delayed the realisation of the facilitating effect. It became apparent that after the reading of the word we could extend the following delay up to at least 30 seconds without affecting in the least the positive effect (see Table 1, test series 2). In two further series of tests we filled the interval following the reading of the word with non-verbal stimuli: in one series of tests these were acoustic stimuli, provided by a gramophone playing music; in another series these were visual stimuli, in which we provided the patient with magazine pictures (without text) to be looked at silently. Despite such acoustic and visual distractive stimuli, the patient was capable, with a few exceptions, of naming correctly the 'deblocked' pictures (see Table 1, test series 3 and 4).

The *facilitating effect* is thus maintained even when the naming does not take place immediately after reading the corresponding word, but is requested after *a longer span of time* and also when this interval is filled with acoustic or visual distractive stimuli. These results are a clear proof of the *considerable power* of the deblocking effect attained as a result of word reading.

We have carried out parallel experiments of a similar nature with regard to *deblocking disturbed repetition* in our patient. Since this experiment was considerably complicated by his high degree of deafness, we confined ourselves to only a few tests, which produced basically the same results as the deblocking of naming[2]. When we had the patient read a word which he had not been able to repeat, *he was able in most cases to repeat it promptly and correctly, even after an interval of some minutes.*

In the course of our experiments we asked ourselves the obvious question as to the *nature* of the effect we had noted. Could this perhaps simply be a case of 'perseveration' which is so frequent amongst aphasics? Or that the patient, when he is supposed to name the picture, simply 'reproduces' the word he read earlier? Is this simply a case of 'pseudonaming'?

To settle this question we analysed the *behavior of the patient* during the naming and word reading. Generally when he should name an object or a picture he becomes extremely restless, utters inarticulate sounds, blushes, makes despairing hand movements, attempts to describe the object with gestures. As soon as he is then presented with the corresponding word, he reads it promptly aloud, sighs with relief, and clearly shows his joy that he has 'finally found' the desired word, saying in confirmation: "Yes, yes, steamer!", "Yes, yes, skier!" etc. But when he once again confronts the corresponding picture, his behavior changes perceptibly, independently of whether the naming is successful or not. His reading takes place more or less automatically, fluently and with understanding; on the contrary, the naming demands in all cases a particular effort on the part of the patient. He looks very attentively at the picture, as though he could learn the word from it. In contrast to the naming, we noted, in the reproduction experiments reported upon below (second basic test), that in the effort to recall a word read previously the patient closes his eyes, and 'reflects' as though he wants the word to come to him. This shows that the 'deblocking' of naming really is a genuine naming, and not a reproduction of the word read previously.

In order to limit strictly the possibility of reproducing mechanically the word read, we worked out the following 'basic test', which we carried out with 100 differing pictures.

After we have made sure that the patient is not capable of naming a certain picture, the corresponding word, the 'initial word' is presented to him. The reading of this word is followed by a series of other written words, which have no connection with the initial word; the patient reads these intercalated words aloud; finally he is presented again with the *picture* to be named. The patient naturally knew that the reading of the intercalated neutral words would be followed by the picture, and that he would have to name it. In this manner the reading of the 'initial word' has a special import. By inserting the intercalated neutral words we achieved, as we ascertained in many tests, a considerable 'inhibitory effect'. One single intervening word had scarcely any effect on the positive result, but the deblocking effect of the initial word decreased steadily as the number of neutral words increased. Four intercalated words already created considerable difficulty in naming for patient M. P. However, the results achieved in the basic experiment showed that even under such aggravated conditions the facilitating effect could still have considerable influence.

The results of the first basic experiment. After reading the corresponding word and four following intercalated words, the patient was capable of *naming correctly 17 out of 100 pictures.*

For comparison purposes we carried out the same basic test with another patient, who also displayed motor aphasic disturbances together with well-preserved expressive reading. With this patient, Alexandru Ivănescu, we carried out the tests with 48 pictures from the same series as used with M. P., and the facilitating effect of the initial word proved even stronger than in the case of patient M. P. After the initial word and four neutral words had been read he was able to *name the picture correctly in 58% of the cases.*

Another proof that we are dealing in these tests with genuine 'deblocking phenomena' is given by the following finding: although the reading of the initial word is followed by the reading of several intercalated words, the process of naming is in most cases not influenced by these neutral words but only by the initial word which corresponds to the name of the picture. For example, after the patient has read the initial word 'tulip', and the following neutral words 'duck', 'pig', 'grapes' and 'hammer', he names the picture of a tulip correctly as 'tulip', without mentioning a single one of the intercalated words. This means that the deblocking effect, the facilitating effect proceeding from the initial word, is of an *elective* nature, that it only deblocks one particular verbo-motor reaction corresponding to one particular object. In the hundreds of tests we carried out, the cases in which 'inductions' were caused by intercalated words were extremely rare. The unsuccessful attempts at naming are generally marked either by complete suspension of speech or by paraphasia, which have nothing to do with the intercalated words but which remain within the framework of the usual paraphasia in cases of motor aphasia.

Despite their rarity, the 'inductions' are nevertheless extremely interesting. Here are some examples where the patient uttered one of the neutral words instead of the initial word. The initial word is *biliard* (billiards), the neutral words are *mahala* (suburb), *fierăstrău* (saw), *calorifer* (central heating), *răstignive* (crucifixion); the patient names: *calorfer-calorfire* (paraphasic). Another example: the initial word *tenis* (tennis), neutral words: *fotbal* (football), *motocicletă* (motorcycle), *topor* (axe), *gîscă* (goose); the patient names *mot-moto-mox*. In other cases, fragments of the intercalated words appeared transitorily during the naming: initial word *nicovală* (anvil), neutral words: *ciocan* (hammer), *iepure* (have); the patient names *nic-nico-nicolele-nicovole-cioc-nico-nicobală*. The following example displays a paraphasic blending of the initial word with one of the neutral words: initial word *conductă* (piping), neutral words: *cocotat* (risen), *patrafir* (surplice), *protopop* (senior priest), *orthodox* (orthodox): the patient names *conduc-contrafir-conductor.* The following example, in which there is a blending of several of the intercalated words and a synonym of the initial word, is interesting: initial word 'tractor', neutral words: *cleşte* (pliers), *nucă* (nut), *topor* (axe): the patient names *masî-top-cresti-toporî-motorî-mot;* the paraphasic fragments *top-topor* derive from *topor* and *cresti* is a paraphasic distortion of *cleşte,* but the fragment *masî* is connected with *maşină* (car) and *motorî-mot* with 'motor', both of these terms related to the initial word. There were also cases in which the patient, instead of naming the correct initial word, named the initial word of the preceding test: initial word *butoaie* (barrel), neutral words *şosea* (highway), *recomandabil* (recommendable), *memorabil* (memorable), *căluşei* (roundabout); the patient names *pe-pe-pelican-peli.* The word 'pelican' had been the initial word in the previous test.

It has already been stated that the patient is aware that it is the initial word, and not the intercalated words, which corresponds to the picture shown. This *task awareness* explains the elective effect of the initial word, its 'superiority' to the neutral words. The following variant of our basic test may be regarded as the *experimentum crucis* proving the elective character of the deblocking process: after reading to the patient the initial word and the intercalated words, we 'swindled' him by showing him, instead of the picture corresponding to the initial word, a completely different one. Neither patient M. P. or patient A. I. ever named the initial word in such cases. Without exception, the patient tried to name the new picture, but nearly always without success. This shows that the deblocking brought about by the initial word is really 'specific', and that it only leads to a correct naming of the object when the picture corresponding to the initial word is shown, and not another.

In investigating the deblocking effect we were further interested as to whether the facilitating effect was restricted to one single initial word, or whether several initial words, offered simultaneously, could deblock the naming of several corresponding pictures. With this aim we presented two or three pictures simultaneously to the patient M. P., which he could not name; we then presented simultaneously the corresponding two or three initial words, which he read aloud; and finally we presented the pictures again. After the first few tests it became clear that this procedure made the patient completely 'confused'. The creation of several simultaneous stimuli did not facilitate the naming process, but rather inhibited it. Only once was the patient able, after reading two initial words, to name correctly two simultaneously presented pictures. In all the other tests there was either no naming after the reading of the two or three initial words, or at the most there was one correct naming.

II. Deblocking of the Reproduction from Memory of Words Read

After we had made sure that under the conditions of our tests the naming of objects and repetition of words was a genuine deblocking process and not a mechanical reproduction, we proceeded to investigate the possibility of deblocking verbal reproduction itself.

As we ascertained with the help of special tests, which we cannot describe more fully here, the direct retention ability of patient M. P. is severely affected. In comparison to other aphasics whom we tested in this respect, the number of objects, pictures, words, letters and numerals which he is able to memorise visually or tactually is extremely small (he was not tested acoustically because of deafness).[3] This fact must be taken into account with regard to the test results published below.

We worked out the following *second basic test* in order to study the *basic phenomenon* which we had noted with regard to memorised reproduction of words read:

The patient is presented with a certain initial word; he reads it aloud; then four neutral words are intercalated, which he also has to read aloud; and finally he has to reproduce, to utter, the initial word from memory. This second basic test varies from the first in that, instead of the naming of the corresponding picture, the memorised reproduction of the initial word is demanded. In order to draw conclusions from a comparison of the two basic tests, we utilised for the second basic test the same initial words and also the same intercalated words.

The results of the second basic test show that reading the initial word *considerably facilitates the process of spontaneous reproduction of memorised words in an elective manner.* The patient M. P. was capable of *reproducing from memory, verbally and correctly, 33% of the initial words presented.* The achievements of the other patient, A. I., were even better: he was able to reproduce, *verbally and correctly, 81% of the 48 initial words.*

In comparing the two basic tests with regard to the quantitative results, we have to take the following circumstance into consideration: the initial word, read aloud, excites the afferent channels in both tests in the same manner, and in just the same way the four intercalated words work as distracting stimuli. Thus the main difference in the conditions for uttering the corresponding word lies in the fact that in the naming test there is a direct stimulus from a pictured object, a visual nonverbal stimulus which under normal circumstances would not suffice to produce an adequate verbal-motor reaction in the patient; in the second basic test, word reproduction, on the other hand, there is no direct outward stimulus, the impulse arising from the task awareness of the patient and being a conscious voluntary act of reproduction[4], which, however, leads to no positive result under normal conditions. In this sense it became clear that the voluntary impulse to reproduce the initial word is superior to the visual nonverbal stimulus supplied by the picture; in other words *that the deblocking produced by word-reading in the second basic test is more effective than that produced by a pictured object in the first.* With patient M. P.: 33% instead of 17%; with patient A. I.: 81% instead of 58%.

It may appear curious that under the conditions of our test an object-naming based upon a direct external nonverbal stimulus proves to be more difficult than the voluntary reproduction of the initial word, with no direct reinforcing external stimulus. This suggests that the external visual nonverbal stimulus exerts, to some extent, an inhibitory tendency on the verbo-motor reaction of our patients.

To check this hypothesis, we introduced the following variant into our second basic test: if the patient was not able to reproduce the initial word, we showed him the corresponding picture. That is to say, we investigated, when the deblocking of the initial word did not occur in the voluntary manner, whether showing the corresponding picture had a facilitative or inhibitory effect. Only in one out of eight such tests did the display of the corresponding picture help patient M. P. to reproduce the 'blocked' word correctly, or to be more precise, to name the picture correctly. In the other cases the display of the picture did not help the patient to say the initial word; on the contrary, we were able to observe an *inhibitory* effect emanating from the picture: immediately after the patient had succeeded in reproducing the initial word, if we displayed the corresponding picture he was not capable of repeating the word correctly once more, but got stuck in futile paraphasic efforts. For instance he reproduced correctly the initial word *mușețel* (camomile); but as soon as we showed him the corresponding picture (which he certainly recognised as such), he was not able to do more than utter a few unarticulated sounds *(t-t-tău)*.[5] This can be taken as further proof that under our test conditions the naming of objects and word reproduction are two separate processes.

III. Reinforcement of the Deblocking Effect

The quantitative results of the two basic experiments show that under our more stringent conditions, deblocking was only successful in a relative small proportion of the tests in the case of patient M. P., and that even with patient A. I. a considerable number of non-deblocked pictures and departure words remained. In order to reinforce the deblocking effect in these unsuccessful cases, we utilised the following method in the two basic tests: if the patient was not capable of naming or reproducing the initial word despite its being read, we *repeated the test,* that is to say we submitted the initial word to the patient once again, and had him name it or repeat it after four neutral words had been interposed. If the patient was still unable to perform the task after this repetition, we returned again to the initial word, and did this up to four times if necessary. In this way we reinforced the deblocking effect.

A glance at Table 2 shows that *in a considerable number of cases the repetition of the test resulted in a notable reinforcement of the deblocking effect.*

In the case of patient M. P., the first repetition heightened the number of deblockings in both the first and second basic test by about 50%, and in the case of A. I. by more than 95%. We were able to deblock the remaining words in the case of A. I. by further repetitions (up to three); in the case of M. P. about 20% of the pictures or initial words remained un-deblocked even after four repetitions. With M. P. it was particularly clear that those pictures and initial words which could not be deblocked initially needed a differing number of reinforcements before they could be named or reproduced.

In this connection we are naturally confronted with the question as to the degree to which the positive and negative results in the two basic tests and the number of necessary reinforcements depend upon the *meaning-content* of the pictures or initial words. Our analysis in this connection produced no clear correlation between deblocking effect and meaning-content. An initial word which belonged to a meaning-group, for instance the word 'lamp', could not be deblocked at all in the naming test, but was immediately in repetition. Vice versa, the picture 'painting' could be named on its first display, but could not be reproduced even after four repeats.

The results are clearer with regard to the *phonetic structure* of the initial words. When these words were grouped according to the number of yllables it was seen that in both basic tests the deblocking of the multisyllable words was more difficult (patient M. P., for example, named or reproduced 10 of 11 one-syllable words, but only 9 of 22 four-syllable to six-syllable words). We must however emphasise that this is not an absolute rule. For instance in both basic tests patient M. P. was able after deblocking to name or to repeat phonetically relatively complicated initial words such as *bibliotecă* (library); *libelulă* (dragonf-ly), *cununie* (wedding), *brutărie* (bakery) etc.; but he was not able to do this with much simpler initial words, such as *dans* (dance), *placă* (disc), etc.

The phenomenon which we have described thus consists of the fact that in certain aphasics the speech-motor apparatus cannot be spontaneously triggered, but that achievement is only possible for a short period, generally not exceeding ten minutes, as the result of stimuli resulting from word reading. The act of reading thus 'deblocks' the speech-motor apparatus. The visual stimulus alone – visual perception of the object or its picture – is, on the contrary, not sufficient to trigger the speech-motor reaction. Letter symbols are a more effective stimulus than perception of the object or its picture. This means, in Pavlov's sense, that a stimulus of the first signal system – the perception of the object or its picture – does not trigger the function of the apparatus; this can, however, be accomplished by a stimulus of the second signal system, the visual word structure.

We must now consider the question of the level at which deblocking takes place from the neurophysiological point of view. One might think that it occurs in the visual analyser; but we have already seen that the visually perceived object is not sufficient to trigger functioning of the verbo-motor apparatus. The visual stimulus cannot produce in the verbo-motor apparatus a sufficiently heightened state of excitation; however the stimulus proceeding from visual word structure can place the visual analyser in a state of excitation which can bring about the functioning of the speech-motor apparatus, and this heightened state can last for some minutes.

We have observed the same basic phenomenon, the phenomenon of 'deblocking', with regard to the repetition of words and the reproduction of read words from memory.

We shall preface with some remarks our attempt to find a neurophysiological explanation for this basic phenomenon.

Every function develops upon a morphological substrate. In the framework of the central nervous system, however, only the less differentiated functions are always linked with the same morphological substrate, for instance the afferent motor tract with the pyramidal tract. The more complicated the functions, the more they can utilise various morphological substrates. This is the explanation for the origin of the temporary connections, the basis of conditioned nervous activity, that strictly determined and always changing signalling activity connected with the continuous changes in the environment. A temporary connection which links two formations with one another can come about for a certain period between two centers in the framework of a certain structure; it can then dissolve again, and another connection can come about inside another structure, for instance between one of the previously connected centres and a third centre. The old structure which served the first connection now becomes free, and a different structure is placed at the disposal of the new connection. Seen from this viewpoint the cortex appears like a large network, a 'carpet' as Pavlov described it, consisting of nerve fibres which link the milliards of cells of the cortex with one another. This 'carpet' carries a large number of morpho-functional units. The more primitive, older, and deeply rooted one of these units is, and the longer and more firmly the traces have been imprinted, the more stable this unit is, the more strongly it is linked to the substrate, and the more difficult it is to untie the knots which have once become stabilised. Vice versa, the younger a link is, the more labile the morpho-functional structure, and the easier it is to untie. The unusual mobility and lability of the morpho-functional cortical structures explain the fact that one certain anatomic formation, one special unit, can belong at one certain instant to one morpho-functional structure, and at another instant to another structure, according to the way in which it links or unlinks itself with others. The localisation is thus dynamic, mobile, and steadily changing, according to the demands of the environment and the organism. In the cortex there is a constant creation and dissolution of functional connections between various structural formations, and in this way new morpho-functional units are constantly being created, while others vanish.

Although the possibilities for the formation of morpho-functional units are extremely numerous, a certain limit is set by the special nature of the substrate itself. The entire cortex possesses great association possibilities, but clinical experience shows us that certain types of associations are linked with certain areas of the cortex, and others with other areas with a differing structure and localisation. Language, which from the physiological viewpoint is certainly based upon a broad association net and in Pavlov's sense represents the second signal system, is the result of far-reaching connections which occur between very different points of the cortex. These connections must, however, necessarily pass a certain zone of the brain, the zone of the gyrus angularis of the anterior portions of the first and second temporal convolutions, all situated in the left hemisphere. Other connections could have at the most an indirect effect on the actual speech function. The syndrome of the right parietal lobe, recently described, also shows that for the construction of our body scheme, which has certainly developed in the course of phylogenesis on the basis of many new links, structures of the level of this lobe and not of other lobes are necessary.

Neurological clinical work supplies a growing quantity of factual material confirming the assumption that structural junctions exist in our brains, zones where varying functions and structures meet and integrate, in the process of which they mutually influence each other into something qualitatively new. Such junctions are the language zone in the so-called dominant hemisphere, and also the right parietal lobe and both prefrontal areas.

Now we can perhaps go further in our neurophysiological analysis of the phenomenon which we have ascertained. The speech function is based upon morpho-functional formations of junctions in the cortex. Such formations include for instance the Broca region of the third anterior frontal convolution, the gyrus angularis, and others. At these levels, at these junctions or crossings, many very different afferences of all analysers and other cortical areas meet or intersect. There are morpho-functional structures for the various components of language. Reading, for example, is dependent upon an extremely complicated structure, the visual analyser, which links parts of the acoustic, speech-motor analyser in a chain of its afferent, kinaesthetic, and efferent-motor components. Such a structure demands an incredible number of synapses which, as the result of their increasingly frequent use, grow increasingly 'imprinted' and manage to bind together in one functional unit a large group of the neurons and pathways included in the same function.

The verbo-motor component of speech has a similar structure, though here the 'junction' of the structure is situated nearer to the motor analyser, Operculum Rolandi. In the case of patient M. P. a series of the synapses of this morpho-functional verbo-motor structure are *blocked,* so that the spontaneous reproduction of a word is not possible. It does not even happen when the visual excitation (pictures of objects, etc.) reaches this level. As soon, however, as the visual analyser is set in a state of particular excitation by the reading aloud of the word, this achieves the deblocking at the level of the morpho-functional, verbo-motor structure, in part by stimulating the kinaesthetic afferences at the level of this structure. The morpho-functional structure of the act of reading exerts a facilitating influence upon the speech-motor structure. Such supporting influences are known within the central nervous system, for instance the facilitating influence of the morpho-functional structure of the reticular system upon other structures.

The introduction of other stimuli between the moment of perception of the word (word reading) and the speech-motor deblocking in our patient, for instance the exposition of acoustic or visual stimuli (music, magazine illustrations, intercalated words, etc.) does not inhibit the basic phenomenon; that is to say, the trace left by the act of reading is longer-lasting and cannot be so easily erased by other stimuli. This may be explained by the fact that the trace is connected with the motor peripherally elaborated model, with what A. R. Luria calls 'the articulatory inner scheme'. At the moment when the word is read this scheme is induced, and the trace left by reading, together with this scheme, forms a functional whole, the trace of which is more difficult to remove. That is to say, in the process of competition between the traces – the trace left in the neuron network by the reading of the initial word, and the trace left by reading the intercalated words – the trace left by the initial word proves itself more constant. The traces left in the neuron network by reading the intercalated words are weaker and can therefore not conceal the more strongly defined trace of the initial word.

In all these considerations with regard to the neuronal level, we have certainly and intentionally neglected the fact that the act of reading is also connected with the second signal system, and that the act of spontaneous utterance of a word is a complicated process, with important semantic components, which takes place in the same system. But these processes too take place at the level of the neuronal network of the cortex, and the elementary laws which govern the function of this network must also be applicable to this complicated process.

Apart from the theoretical interest which may be claimed by our findings on the verbal deblocking processes in cases of motor aphasia, we believe that we are right to assume that this opens up certain pathways in the clinical-therapeutic field for the *speech-treatment* of certain types of aphasia.

This appears to be confirmed by a series of provisional experiments which we have carried out in this field. The patient A. I., mentioned above, displays mainly disturbances of a motor-aphasic nature, disturbance of spontaneous speech, of repetition (particularly of sentences), of naming objects, etc., though at the same time his reading comprehension and reading aloud are well maintained. With him we conducted the following experiments. Basing ourselves on the excellent visual memory of this patient (a chemical engineer), we prevailed upon him to mark visually simple short sentences which we had written down. We asked him to read these sentences aloud, demanded that he should memorise them 'photographically', copy them from memory according to the visual word picture (copying is well preserved in his case), and finally, when he was sure of himself after he had tested himself several times, we requested him to read aloud, with his eyes shut, the sentence pictures he could visualise. Without dealing at length at present with this preliminary experiment we may claim that we have achieved extraordinary results with patient A. I. by use of this method. He is able to read sentences from memory so correctly that listeners have the impression that a normal person is speaking. In this manner we were able to get the patient to the 'spontaneous speaking' of two, three, or sometimes even four short sentences with a completely normal expression. We have also made parallel experiments in the deblocking of the repetition of sentences in this manner, by asking the patient, when he could not repeat a sentence, to memorise it visually and then to repeat it. The result was just as positive as with the simple spontaneous 'reading' of sentences from memory.

A continuation of these experiments with this patient and others of this type will show how far it is possible to extend the area of deblocked sentences, and above all whether and to what degree the temporary deblocking of the speech-motor reaction of the patient can be converted into a permanent deblocking, and finally whether it can lead to a deblocking of the verbal effectors in general. The question further arises as to whether there are not also other deblocking possibilities, for instance in aphasics with alexic disturbances in whom the connection between verbo-acoustic stimuli and verbo-motoric reaction is well maintained. We have, for instance, attained certain successes in deblocking the badly disturbed naming of articles through utilising the retained facility of repetition in a case of transcortical motor aphasia with alexia.

From the clinical-therapeutic viewpoint we are thus faced with the problem, in applying the deblocking method, of choosing the best-maintained function in order to deblock the disturbed function.

Summary

1. This work is based upon the conception that certain aphasic disturbances are 'blocking phenomena' which can be temporarily 'deblocked' with the aid of speech functions which have remained intact.

2. Experiments with two patients with motor aphasia, who suffer from a disturbance in naming objects, repetition, and spontaneous reproduction of words, but whose *expressive word reading is intact,* lead to the following basic phenomenon: the speech-motor deficiencies mentioned could be temporarily suspended or 'deblocked' by having the patient previously read aloud the relevant words.

3. The deblocking effect proceeding from the read word is effective for a certain *time span;* that is to say that even when a longer or shorter interval is interposed between the reading of the word and the request to name the picture, repeat the word, or spontaneously produce the word, the patient is nevertheless able to accomplish the task correctly. There also occurs a certain *resistance* of the deblocking effect with regard to various diversion stimuli offered during the time interval (music, looking at magazine pictures, reading a number of written words). In the case of the written words there was a decline in performance dependent upon the number of words intercalated. In cases in which the deblocking effect did not come into effect after the first word reading, it was possible to *reinforce* it by having the patient read the relevant word repeatedly.

4. In the neurophysiological interpretation of the deblocking phenomena we based ourselves upon the concept that the speech function depends upon morpho-functional formations of 'junctions' in

the cortex in which there cross very differing afferences of all analysers and other cortical areas.

Table 1. *First Test Series: Repeated Picture Naming after Deblocking at Varying Intervals*

Picture Word	Time span between reading the word and naming the picture seconds																
	0	5	10	15	20	25	30	35	40	45	50	55	60	120	180	300	600
1. Steamer	+						+										+
2. Tram	+						+										+
3. Football	+						−										−
4. Poppy	+						+										−
5. Strawberry	+						+										−
6. Saw	+						−										−
7. Axe	+						+										−
8. Motorcycle	+						+										−
9. Locomotive	+						+										−
10. Plums	+						+										+
11. Boxer	+						+									+	−
12. Skier	+						−								−		−
13. Plane	+						+								+		+

Second Test Series: Picture Naming, Each Picture after differing Interval

Picture Word	Time span between reading the word and naming the picture seconds																
	0	5	10	15	20	25	30	35	40	45	50	55	60	120	180	300	600
1. Swimmer		+															
2. Lily			+														
3. Raspberry				+													
4. Anvil					+												
5. Drill						+											
6. Tulip							+										
7. Carnation								+									
8. Skaters									+								
9. Tractor										+							
10. Watering-can											+						
11. Comb												+					
12. Airplane													+				

Third Test Series: In the time span imposed between the reading of the word and the naming of the picture the patient is shown magazine pictures

Picture Word	Time span between reading the word and naming the picture seconds																
	0	5	10	15	20	25	30	35	40	45	50	55	60	120	180	300	600
1. Swimmer		−															
2. Lily			+														
3. Raspberry				−													
4. Anvil					+												
5. Drill						+											
6. Tulip							+										
7. Carnation								+									
8. Skaters									−								
9. Tractor										+							
10. Watering-can											+						
11. Comb												+					
12. Airplane													+				

Fourth Test Series: In the time span imposed between the reading of the word and the naming of the picture gramophone music is played to the patient

Picture Word	Time span between reading the word and naming the picture seconds																
	0	5	10	15	20	25	30	35	40	45	50	55	60	120	180	300	600
1. Rake		+															
2. Toothbrush			+														
3. Cherries				+													
4. Poppy					+												
5. Clothesbrush						+											
6. Nailfile							+										
7. Handbag								+									
8. Vegetables									+								

Table 2. *Patient M. P.*

	First basic test Picture naming No. of correctly named pictures	absolute	percent	Second basic test Word reproduction No. of correctly reproduced initial words	absolute	percent
first presentation	100	17	17	100	33	33
1. repetition	83	29	35	67	14	20
2. repetition	54	15	28	38	15	28
3. repetition	39	11	28	29	9	23
4. repetition	28	7	25	29	6	20
			Patient A. I.			
first presentation	48	28	58	48	39	81
1. repetition	20	17	85	9	7	
2. repetition	3	2		2	2	
3. repetition	1	1				

Notes

1. This patient was examined in 1953 by E. Facon and N. Wertheim, who reported on it in 1957 [38]. They emphasised mainly the fact that the patient, despite the other severe motor-aphasic disturbances, is able to read aloud almost normally. In this paper we are not able to give details of the speech and reading comprehension of the patient. It should however be stated that he displays, with completely intact visual and acoustic word comprehension, far-reaching disturbance of sentence comprehension and comprehension of the whole (impressive agrammatism). The ability of the patient to discover and correct to a certain extent word errors was examined by E. Weigl and A. Fradis [196] in a work on the role of the kinaesthetic-motor analyser in compensating for reading disturbances.
2. These and all other main tests have been tape-recorded.
3. It should be added that the patient M. P., just because of his very greatly reduced direct retention ability, is a really 'ideal' subject for our tests; with him we could repeat the same test an unlimited number of times without any fear of falsifying the results because of the training effects.
4. In a certain manner we have, at least in the case of M. P., the deaf patient, reinforced the task awareness by a direct external stimulus: at the moment when the patient should repeat the initial word, we presented him with the piece of card on which this word was written, but with the white side upwards. The visual perception of the card acted to some extent as an instruction.
5. In amnestic-aphasic patients – as A. Pick and R. Thiele point out – display of the corresponding picture often has a positive effect, helping them to find the words.

⟨9⟩

E. WEIGL

The Phenomenon of Temporary Deblocking in Aphasia[1]

I. Data in literature concerning the temporary, spontaneous or induced appearance of certain adequate verbal reactions in aphasics

Adequate verbal reactions are sometimes observed in aphasics having more or less severe receptive or expressive troubles. This phenomenon has for a long time been a subject of interest to many investigators in this field. But although numerous valuable observations have been gathered by many authors in the past, there are no works of synthesis on the subject. One of the few works offering a somewhat more detailed study of this problem (among others) is the book *L'aphasie et la desintégration fonctionelle du langage* by Alajouanine and Mozziconacci [5].

By analysing the phenomena referred to by these authors and relating them to other facts found by various investigators, we reached the conclusion that a thorough study of these verbal performances in aphasics requires in the first place a clear distinction between the following two groups of phenomena. The first comprises reactions appearing spontaneously, occasionally, sparsely, and automatically in certain affective conditions (indignation, impatience, tenderness, etc.) or situative ones (certain stereotypies, polite formulae, etc.). In a recent work entitled *Principle of Baillarger-Jackson,* Alajouanine [2] emphasizes that as far back as 1865 the French physician M. Baillarger had inferred from his observations on aphasics that: "Il est bien évident qu'ici l'incitation motrice volontaire était abolie et que l'incitation motrice spontanée persistait." The special importance of this conclusion has been readily recognized by the great neurologist Jackson who called it *Baillarger's Principle.* A thorough analysis of this principle induced Jackson [70] to write: "Under the excitement the patient may swear . . . the patient cannot repeat it, he cannot 'say' what he has just 'uttered'. Sometimes, however, a patient, ordinarily speechless, may get out a phrase appropriate to some simple circumstance, such as 'good-bye' when a friend is leaving . . . he cannot repeat it when entreated" (p. 163). Broca [22] already showed that one of his patients with total aphasia was sometimes able to profer perfectly pronounced invectives. The example given by Gowers of an aphasic stating "I cannot say no!" is well known.

Examples of such 'occasional utterances', as Jackson calls them, are extremely frequent in literature concerning aphasia. Alajouanine and Mozziconacci cite very characteristic examples to this effect. An aphasic patient, coming to consultation accompanied by her small daughter, when questioned about the latter's name, cries out in deep sorrow: "Ah! ma pauvre petite Jacqueline, je ne sais même plus ton nom!", while another patient asked about her son's name, desperately turns to him and entreats him: "Mais aide-moi donc, Raymond!" [2; p. 47]

All these phenomena have the fact in common that their spontaneous, occasional appearance depends on very complex stimuli, in contrast to a second group of adequate receptive and expressive verbal reactions also to be observed in aphasics but only as a result of deliberately created circumstances. Pick [134] finds that aphasics with verbal deafness, after correctly repeating a word pronounced by the examiner, succeed in understanding it; other patients immediately understand the word pronounced by the examiner if the corresponding object is simultaneously presented. Luria [105] also demonstrates that in expressive aphasics with partial receptive verbo-auditory troubles these can be compensated by simultaneously presenting corresponding objects or by inducing the patient to follow the movements of the examiner's lips while he pronounces the respective word. Révész [143] observed with respect to astereognosic patients: "It is surprising how sure patients are in their search for requested objects with closed eyes, even if they were previously unable to recognise any of these objects" (p. 81).

As for the temporary removal of certain expressive troubles during examination of aphasics, many authors use the method of the 'first links' [53], by pronouncing the first letter or syllable in order to make the patient complete the 'forgotten' word (especially in cases of amnestic aphasia) or by uttering the beginning of an expression, a proverb, etc. to be completed by the patient. In this respect Alajouanine and Mozziconacci cite the following example: a patient incapable of naming the image of a zebra is told: "Courir comme une . . .?" and the patient promptly continues: "comme une zèbre." Besides this associative assistance in evoking a word or sentence, the procedure of 'helping' the amnestic aphasic by automatic speech is also known. Patients unable to recall, either spontaneously or at request, a certain isolated day of the week, a month, letter, or figure, are able to find and correctly pronounce them when they enumerate the days of the week, the months of the year, the alphabet, numbers, etc., or when they read them among other words in a written sentence, etc. For the temporary removal of certain anomic amnestic troubles Chromov [30] uses the presentation of corresponding images. For instance, a patient unable to find the word 'to bark', remembers it as soon as he sees the image of a dog and pronounces it correctly; the same patient cannot name the color of the gooseberry, but on seeing red color promptly finds its name. Besides the adjuvant part played by automatisms, Meier and Müller-Hegemann [122] point out that of praxis in troubles of naming of amnestic type. By handling certain objects (putting on a shoe, locking the door with a key, cutting with a knife, stamping a sheet of paper, combing his hair, etc.) the patient often finds the name of the respective verb. Weisenburg and McBride remark, in their book on aphasia [205], that a patient incapable of pronouncing the word 'scissors' had 'learned' it by writing it down, always looking at a pair of scissors and handling this object (p. 288); obviously, the occurence of the adequate expressive verbal performance is due in this case to simultaneous application of several combined stimuli (writing, looking at an object, and handling it). Head [61], Chesher [25], Schuell [150], Leischner [95], as well as the author in collaboration with Fradis et al. [197], used simultaneous stimulation by adjuvant agents in their examinations of various receptive and expressive verbal troubles. For instance, if it is found that the patient is incapable of receptive reading of a certain word, he is made to look at a series of images comprising the correspondent of the written word; in spite of their receptive alexia, certain patients find the corresponding image when they are thus helped; or, the examiner pronounces a word and the patient must select it from a series of written words. Leischner [95] remarks that agraphic troubles concerning the writing of a word on dictation can sometimes disappear by simultaneously pointing out the corresponding object (p. 87), etc.

II. The phenomenon of temporary deblocking

Although literature concerning aphasia offers a rich material covering the most varied possibilities of eliciting adequate verbal reactions, these phenomena were nevertheless sparsely investigated and that only during the pursuit of other problems (e.g. in order to establish the extent to which certain analysers are involved in various aphasic troubles as compared to other analysers, etc.). Besides, most authors refer to methods aimed at the temporary removal of verbal troubles of amnestic type, troubles in evocation, naming, etc., by means of the so-called facilitation[2] in an associative way, by automatisms, etc. [see 5; p. 47]. In the literature we meet very rarely the attempt to investigate the motives of the origin of the 'facilitations'. In this regard, the remark of K.

Heilbronner [65] is significant, who observed that a patient with total verbal alexia was able to point out among a series of written words that which was asked: "It seems hardly possible to me to give a satisfactory explication for that behaviour . . ." (p. 481).

The purpose of the present work was to make the possibility of inducing adequate verbal reactions in aphasics the object of *a systematic study using original methods of investigation.* We detected such a 'deblocking' phenomenon (as we called it) while investigating the relationships between intact and disturbed verbal functions in aphasics. Starting from the fact that reading aloud is perfectly intact in some of these patients in spite of severe expressive troubles, we remarked that in certain circumstances this undisturbed function is able to exert a positive, though temporary, influence on the performances of various other disturbed verbal functions. The first results of our investigations were reported with Kreindler in the work *Beiträge zur Auffassung gewisser aphasischer Störungen als Blockierungserscheinungen. Temporäre Deblockierung sprachmotorischer Reaktionen durch Wortlesen bei motorischer Aphasie* [200].

In continuing these investigations we endeavoured to include in our study not only amnestic troubles, but also a wide field of pathological verbal performances, viz. various expressive troubles (aphasic, alexic, agraphic, etc.) as well as receptive ones (e.g. verbal deafness, receptive alexia), concerning visual, auditory, verbo-motor, and other analysers.

The choice of the term 'deblocking' for the studied phenomenon was rooted in the conception that the neurophysiological process on which the phenomenon is based consists in the temporary removal of a functional 'blocking' due to lesions at the level of the cerebral cortex. The simple fact that a trouble appearing in a patient in ordinary circumstances may disappear in other circumstances does not sufficiently justify us in considering the phenomenon as the effect of a deblocking. As shown by Goldstein [53; p. 123] and others, patients often discover such 'round-about-ways' themselves, i.e., they find other ways by which to achieve, at least apparently, adequate performances, *Ersatzleistungen,* without even provisionally removing the trouble in question. A blind man learning to read by means of his touch circumvenes the use of the optico-lexic function, but this function still remains injured. Likewise, the reading of an alexic able to read only by means of the kinaestheticmotor analyser by movements of the head or the finger actually represents a 'pseudolexia' (Goldstein). Our method of deblocking endeavours to exclude the use of such 'round-about-ways'. For instance, if an alexic patient (with no troubles of repetition) is able to read a word after previously repeating the same word uttered by the examiner, we cannot be sure that he actually 'reads'; he may very well 'memorize' the word after repeating it and, seeing it written, say it 'by heart' without reading it in fact. One of our own patients with expressive alexia, after having repeated the word 'guitar', looked at the written word and said: "I know this is 'guitar', but I cannot read it", i.e., he was conscious that in this case the ability of correctly pronouncing the written word was only due to the renewed loud reproduction of the previously repeated word and not to actual reading (he might have correctly rendered this word without even looking at the written one). Conversely, if a patient with troubles of repetition, but intact expressive reading, is able to repeat correctly a word after reading it, the possibility of an *Ersatzleistung* is still present, i.e., of a pseudo-deblocking, since patients with a well developed visual memory can visually 'memorize' the word (after reading it) and then, instead of repeating it, they read it aloud according to the previously recorded optical image.

Our work does not pursue the various *Ersatzleistungen* but only phenomena truly representing a temporary deliverance of blocked pathways, i.e., the provisional recuperation of troubles of verbal performance in aphasics. The phenomenon of temporary deblocking in aphasics consists in the temporary disappearance of total or partial troubles of various verbal performances when the disturbed, 'blocked', verbal reaction is preceded by an unblocked adequate reaction, provided that both performances refer to the same word. We have thus obtained deblocking in troubles like anomia, arepetition, alexia, agraphia, verbal deafness, etc. A patient with troubles of naming can temporarily acquire the ability of naming a certain picture provided he has previously read the corresponding word, an alexic patient succeeds in correctly reading a word after hearing this word uttered by the examiner, a patient with word deafness understands the spoken word after previously copying it, etc. During our experimental investigations the phenomenon of deblocking we also found that in certain cases the effect of deblocking is not limited to the performance obtained for a single blocked verbal function. It may simultaneously extend to other impaired verbal functions but, again, provided that these refer to one and the same word. For instance, the troubles of a patient who is unable to name a certain image, to repeat the corresponding word uttered by the examiner and to write it on dictation, can be simultaneously removed if the patient is previously given the opportunity to read the word, provided he is not affected by alexic troubles. The patient is thus simultaneously enabled to name the image, repeat its name uttered by the examiner and write it on dictation.

III. Methods of deblocking

In elaborating experimental methods of deblocking we had in mind the 'purest', most specific form of studying the phenomenon. We have therefore endeavoured to eliminate other factors able to create the appearance of deblocking, actually constituting 'round-about-ways'. We were thus led by the following principles in elaborating our methods. The patient is to be kept ignorant of the object of deblocking, as well as of the deblocking stimulus; the process must, to a certain degree, develop 'automatically'. We intend, e. g., to deblock troubles of naming in a patient by means of reading. In a previous test we must first establish a number of pictures which the patient cannot name at all, or can only paraphasically do so. Besides written names of these pictures, a group of other written, 'neutral' words must also be prepared. In order to deblock the naming of, e. g., a picture showing slippers, a group of words including 'slippers' is shown to the patient, who can read them without knowing which one corresponds to the picture constituting the object of the deblocking experiment. After reading these words the patient is confronted by several different pictures, only one of which – 'slippers', in our case – corresponds to the previously read word. The patient was therefore unable to 'prepare' himself beforehand by memorizing the word. At the same time the real effect of deblocking can be assessed by comparing the naming of 'nondeblocked' images (i. e., those not read previously) to that of the 'deblocked' one.

This is, therefore, the experimental pattern for deblocking: the deblocking stimulus, as well as the corresponding exciting agent to be deblocked are presented among other stimuli of the same kind (written or spoken words, pictures etc.) in order to prevent patients from using undisturbed functions instead of the disturbed one.

This 'ideal' pattern was varied according to deblocking pathways, form of aphasia, state of the patient, his intellectual level, etc. On some patients, for instance, the application of too many stimuli exerts an inhibitory effect reducing the deblocking effect; in such cases, of course, the pattern must to a certain extent be simplified, the number of 'neutral' stimuli be reduced, etc.

Each patient was subjected, to a preparatory standard test [197] in order to establish the disturbed verbal functions and the extent of the trouble, the functional level of the lesion, as well as the more or less preserved verbal functions. For instance, in patient P. I. (see case 3), suffering from motor transcortical aphasia, we found a 100% performance of word repetition, in contrast to his partially troubled (33%)[3] expressive word reading. Naturally, repetition was used for this patient in order to deblock his expressive reading. Conversely, for the patient

T. J. (case 1), with mixed aphasia exhibiting zero performance for repetition and 70% for expressive word reading, we tried to deblock repetition by expressive word reading. The results obtained by means of the standard test thus pointed out the direction in which deblocking was to be carried out in each individual patient. In order to prepare adequate experimental material for the patient under study, the 'blocked' images, words, etc. and the deblocking stimuli to be used were all established beforehand. As to the selection of patients, we chose cases in a relatively stable state as far as the aphasic snydrome was concerned, in order to be able to prolong our experiments over the longest possible period in the most stable conditions. We chose patients with widely differing forms of aphasia, allowing us to gain additional knowledge on the sphere of these phenomena; we examined cases of predominantly expressive aphasia as well as motor transcortical ones, cases of receptive aphasia, mixed aphasia, amnestic aphasia, cases of alexia with discrete aphasic troubles.

The most important clinical data[4] are given below with respect to the seven patients on which the present work was concentrated:

Case 1: T. J., aged 64, pensioned (formerly a worker), admitted to the hospital on the 12th of May 1960. Exhibits an ictus on the 7th of May 1960, followed by troubles of speech. High arterial blood pressure with left ventricular hypertrophy. Marked tendon reflexes in upper limbs, especially on the right side. Right homonimous haemianopsia; bilateral hypoacusia. EEG: 15. XII. 1960: bilateral temporal foci. Diagnosis at leaving: left temporo-posterior cerebral thrombosis, aphasia. *Aphasiologic examination:* appreciably disturbed spontaneous speech and dialogue, literal and verbal paraphasia, frequent perseveration, diminished vocabulary. Partially preserved automatic speech. Appreciably deteriorated sentence reading and auditory receptive verbal functions (does not obey spoken or written words). Word repetition also completely abolished (paraphasia), as well as the naming of objects, pictures, and partly of colours. A relatively well preserved function is expressive reading for letters and usual concrete words, as well as copied writing. Total agraphia on dictation. Total acalculia. Receptive alexic troubles can be temporarily removed by means of auditory adjuvant stimuli (a word, corresponding to the written one, is uttered by the examiner) or visual ones (exhibiting an image corresponding to the written word). Conclusion: mixed aphasia.

Case 2: I. A.[5], aged 53, pensioned (formerly chemical engineer), admitted on the 2nd of September 1957. Myocardic infarct on the 2nd of November 1956; following an effort on the 12th of November, he suddenly suffers a right haemiplegia with aphasia by embolia; motor deficiency much improved recently, aphasia less improved. EEG: 1. XII. 1958: left temporal focus. Diagnosis at leaving: right haemiparesis, aphasia. *Aphasiologic examination:* spontaneous speech and dialogue: telegraphic style. Intact automatic speech. Auditory and reading receptive verbal functions almost completely preserved (slight difficulties in auditory understanding of some abstract words and sentences). No agraphia (except slight sparse paragraphia); sometimes, errors of mental and written computation. Excepting expressive reading, which is completely intact, all other expressive verbal functions, such as naming and, to a certain extent, word repetition ,are disturbed. Conclusion: *predominantly expressive aphasia.*

Case 3: P. I., aged 60, pensioned (formerly diver), admitted on the 9th of April 1959. Ictus on the 30th of September 1958, followed by coma; right haemiparesis and aphasia following the ictus; after one month of treatment, motor deficiency partially (especially brachially) improved. High arterial blood pressure for the last four years (14/8 during hospitalization). Diagnosis at leaving: hypertonal disease, brain hemorrhage, aphasia, slight right haemiparesis. *Aphasiologic examination:* spontaneous speech and dialogue exhibit long and frequent intervals of amnestic and paraphasic type; when answering, automatically repeats the question and then adds his answer. Intact automatic speech and repetition, as well as reading and auditory receptive verbal functions (obeys verbal and written orders). Partially impaired naming (objects, images, colours) and expressive reading (letters and, especially, less usual words and more complicated sentences). Partial mental and written acalculia. Conclusion: transcortical expressive aphasia.

Case 4: L. D., aged 37, shop assistent, admitted on the 23rd of March 1960. Skull trauma in February 1960 (from accident) in the frontal and occipital areas, loss of consciousness and state of coma lasting 3 weeks, otorrhage; after recovery: complete amnesia of all facts related to the accident; at home, he does not remember his children's names; he forgets everything concerning his profession. Radiological examination: numerous lines of parieto-temporal fractures on the right side, marked diploic vascularization. EEG: 29, VI. 1960: left lesional focus with slight irritative signs. Psychic examination: diminution of self-criticism concerning verbal amnesia; childish behaviour, tendency to puns, but absence of severe psychic troubles. Diagnosis at leaving: post-traumatic encephalopatia, amnestic aphasia. *Aphasiologic examination:* spontaneous speech and dialogue: frequently intermittent owing to amnestic troubles, abundance of periphrase and verbal stereotypy, sparse verbal paraphasia. Intact automatic speech and repetition. Absence of either agraphia, alexia, or acalculia. Partially impaired naming of objects, pictures, and colours (he is even unable to recognize and name various kinds of cloth, well-known to the patient from his previous professional activity). Marked word deafness only for abstract unusual words and for more complicated sentences (but he correctly performs verbal and written orders). Conclusion: post-traumatic amnestic aphasia.

Case 5: V. M.[6], aged 62, worker, admitted on the 27th of October 1960. Antecedents: high blood pressure, lues in 1916, incompletely treated. Onset: 4–5 weeks prior to admission, paresthetic fits in right upper limb, lasting 5–10 minutes, subsequent sudden appearance of total alexia and narrowing of right visual field; slight anomic troubles in current speech. Right homonymous haemianopsia; eye bottom: marked arteriosclerosis of retinal vessels, normal papillae. Intensely positive WBR and Citochol in the blood. C. S. F. examination: positive globulines, negative colloidal gold reactions, elements 4,6/mm. c. c., albumine 0.38‰. EEG: flat desynchronized pattern on all leads; hyperpnoea does not change the pattern. Diagnosis at leaving: hypertonal disease with slight right haemiparesis, right sensory Jacksonian seizures, alexia. *Aphasiologic examination:* excepting frequent intermittences and hesitations due to amnestic troubles, spontaneous speech and dialogue is intact, as well as automatic speech and repetition. Fixing and evoking memory for recent events is impaired. Preserved auditory verbal understanding (correctly performs verbal orders). Sparsely and slightly troubled naming of objects and pictures (amnesia). Partial agraphia only when copying. Total alexia excepting expressive and receptive literal reading, which is partly intact. Receptive and expressive verbal and sentence-alexic troubles can be temporarily removed by means of auditory stimuli (word uttered by examiner, corresponding to written word) or visual ones (image corresponding to written word). Severe troubles concerning identification, naming and sorting of colors. Conclusion: total alexia (excepting the partly intact literal one), slight aphasic troubles of naming (amnesia) as well as agnosia and amnesia for colors.

Case 6: T. M., aged 65, pensioned (formerly teacher), admitted on the 13th of April 1960. Sudden onset of disease on the 5th of April 1960, without loss of consciousness, with left frontoparietally localized headaches; at first, jargon-aphasia; max. blood pressure 19. Eye bottom: vascular sclerosis. Perceives sounds and tuning fork and identifies sound pitch. EEG: 26. VI. 1960 – electrogenesis troubles of centrencephalic origin. Diagnosis at leaving: cerebral vascular insufficiency, aphasia, high blood pressure. *Aphasiologic examination:* relatively well preserved spontaneous speech in Russian (maternal language), as well as in Roumanian; the patient is rather silent, talks in short, but correct sentences. Intact automatic speech. Partial auditory agnosia for noise and sound, partial word deafness (in both languages). Intact letter repetition, partly preserved word repetition, completely abolished sentence repetition. Partly disturbed naming (amnesia). Almost preserved expressive reading, partly disturbed receptive reading (only for unusual words and complicated sentences), performs written orders. Agraphia only on dictation. No acalculia. Conclusion: predominantly receptive aphasia with partial word deafness.

Case 7: M. M., aged 57, pensioned (formerly employee in textile commerce), first admitted on the 11th of May 1953. Speech troubles had suddenly appeared two weeks previously. Slight signs of right haemiparesis. Diagnosis at leaving: hypertonal disease and cerebral arteriosclerosis; sensory aphasia (the patient was hospitalized several times in the years 1957, 1959, 1960). *Aphasiologic examination:* spontaneous speech and dialogue: frequent verbal stereotypy (polite formulae, etc.), telegraphic style with long intermittences, literal and verbal paraphasia, perseveration, small vocabulary. Automatic speech and repetition, as well as naming completely, resp. almost completely impaired. Total word deafness for abstract and unusual words, as well as for sentences (obeys only simple orders), partly intact one for concrete words and simple sentences. Total receptive alexia for abstract words and simple sentences, much less marked for letters and usual words; total expressive alexia for sentences, only partial one for words (no literal alexia). Total agraphia for words and sentences on dictation, in contrast to intact writing when copying. Almost complete acalculia. It must be noted that word deafness as well as verbal receptive alexia are considerably diminished by means of visual stimuli (images) or auditory ones (word uttered by the examiner). Conclusion: mixed aphasia.

IV. Results obtained by deblocking receptive and expressive verbal troubles in aphasics

Deblocking troubles of word repetition by expressive reading

Case 1: *patient T. J.*

disturbed function	*better preserved function*
word repetition	*expressive word reading*
0%	70%

Repetition (words and sentences) is completely abolished in patient T. J. (dumbness or paraphasia) while expressive word reading is preserved for the greater part (excepting some sparse paraphasia).

Experiment: We previously established the words which the patient was able to repeat only paraphasically or not at all. During the test, each of these words was separately presented to the patient in writing; the patient correctly read them aloud. The examiner then successively uttered three different words, only one out of which was identical to that previously read by the patient, and the latter had to repeat each word separately. For instance, the examiner said *cerb* (hart), the patient, unable to repeat it, answered: "I get confused in this . . . I do not understand". Then the word *cerb* (hart) was presented in writing, the patient correctly read it aloud and understood it. The examiner then uttered the word *bărci* (boats), *the patient this time correctly repeated 'cerb',* the examiner: *papuci* (slippers), the patient: "I do not understand". In the next test the word 'slippers' is deblocked. After the patient read this word, the examiner again uttered three words, viz: *scrimă* (fencing), the patient paraphasically repeated *crimă* (crime), *spălat* (washed), the patient: "I do not understand", and, finally, *papuci* again, *this time the patient correctly repeated: 'papuci'*. The patient similarly succeeded in correctly repeating, by means of deblocking other words, too, e. g., *acoperis* (roof – prior to deblocking: 'rope . . . fa . . .'), *alergători* (runners – previously: 'verbo . . .'), *sarpe* (snake – previously: 'ciarp'), *combinat* (factory – previously: 'copil . . . copilas'), *statuie* (statue – previously 'aviu . . .'), etc.

Out of 12 words uttered by the examiner we succeeded in deblocking the repetition of a total of 10 words previously read by the patient, in contrast to the other 24 undeblocked (unread) words, that the patient could repeat only paraphysically or not at all. A control immediately following the end of the experiment showed that the patient was unable to repeat any of the previously deblocked words; the aftereffect of deblocking had in the meanwhile been extinguished.

Case 2: Patient I. A., also exhibiting troubles of repeated speech (words and sentences), but with intact expressive and receptive reading; we successfully attempted to deblock by lexical means not only troubles in word repetition but also those in repeating *sentences* previously uttered by the examiner. For instance after the sentence *Controlez starea utilajului* (I check the state of tools) was uttered by the examiner, the patient repeated, prior to deblocking: 'contr . . . contro . . . zice . . . covor'; then the same sentence was presented to him in writing, the patient correctly read it aloud and understood it. Then the examiner again uttered the same sentence (after removal of the card on which the sentence had been written), this time *the patient succeeded in correctly repeating the sentence.* The same positive result was also obtained for another sentence *Sedinta de productie s-a amînat* (the production meeting was put off), before deblocking, the patient repeated it as follows: 'şedinţa . . . şed . . .', *by means of deblocking he repeated it without any mistake.*

Deblocking troubles of picture naming

A. By repetition

Case 3: *patient P. I.*

disturbed function	*better preserved function*
naming	*repetition*
60%	100%

Patient P. I. exhibits paraphasia to picture naming, whereas repetition is completely unimpaired (characteristic feature for transcortical aphasia).

Experiment: The pictures which are not correctly named by the patient are previously established. During the test the examiner successively utters words – each corresponding to one of these pictures – and the patient has to repeat each one in turn. Then, in order to eliminate the purely mnestic effect of the repetition, the examiner asks the patient various questions, which the latter has to answer, then he is shown the picture he has to name. For instance, the patient is made to look at the picture of a bag before deblocking, and he says: 'this is . . . has . . . taken in the hand'. To achieve deblocking, he is asked to repeat the word 'bag' pronounced by the examiner; the patient repeats it accurately. The examiner inserts the question: 'what is your name?' which the patient answers correctly. Finally, the patient is again shown the picture of the bag, which *he promptly recognizes and correctly names.* Another example: before deblocking, when looking at a picture showing a cobbler mending boots, the patient says: 'hammer . . . he strikes with a hammer'. After correctly repeating the word 'cobbler' and answering an irrelevant question asked by the examiner, the patient is again confronted with the picture, which *he correctly names:* 'cobbler'. In another case the patient, seeing the picture of a thigh paraphasically names it a 'strawberry'; by means of deblocking, however, the patient *easily gives the correct naming of the picture.* In this way, the names of a series of other images are also deblocked, e. g., 'typewirter' (before: 'here, I see, is . . .'), 'gramophone record' (before: 'this is also . . .'), 'hairbrush' (before: 'toothbrush . . . comb . . . on the head'), etc.

The patient succeeds in correctly naming, with the aid of deblocking, all of the six pictures he is shown, in spite of inserted irrelevant conversation, although before deblocking he could only paraphasically name the pictures. The effect of deblocking was also preserved after the end of the experiment.

B. By expressive word reading

Case 4: *Patient L. D.*

disturbed function	*better preserved function*
naming	*expressive word reading*
30%	100%

Receptive and expressive word reading are intact in this patient, who exhibits partial anomic troubles of anmestic type in naming pictures.

Experiment: Before beginning the experiment, the pictures which the patient is unable to name are established (either declaring that he does not find the word, or using periphrases). During the test, four written words are shown to him, among these the name of the picture to be deblocked; he is made to read aloud all four words, then three pictures are successively shown to him, only one of which corresponds to the previously read name. The patient has to name these images. For instance, after correctly reading aloud the words: bag, bicycle, *trunks,* fencing, the patient is confronted with the picture of a tractor, which he is unable to name and says: 'a small motor, a specially made installation'; but this time *he names correctly* the picture *trunks* (before deblocking he had used, owing to his anomia, the periphrase "these are made in order to contain objects when one is leaving for some place"). Another example: looking at the picture 'barrels' before deblocking, the worried patient cries out with unusual frankness "By Jove, I forgot, oh, how sorry I am I forgot!". But by means of deblocking (after reading the words: rake, raspberry, warehouse, *barrels*) *he is able to name correctly the corresponding picture,* while he cannot find a name for the next one ('swallows'), saying: 'small birds'. Other pictures could also be deblocked, e. g., the picture of a basket (before: "Something to be carried to the market"), 'typewriter' (before: 'this is a work I do not know'), 'factories' (before: 'here . . .'), 'library' ('an office with some apparatus'), etc.

Out of the 16 pictures that the patient was unable to name before deblocking by reading, he succeeds in naming 13 by means of deblocking, in contrast to the still impaired naming of the other 16 non-deblocked (previously not read) pictures. The control carried out immediately after the end of the experiment shows that only 5 names were retained out of the 13 previously deblocked ones, the patient being unable to name the other pictures.

Deblocking receptive and expressive alexia

A. By verbal auditory means

Case 5: *Patient V. M.*

disturbed function	*better preserved function*
expressive and receptive reading	*verbal auditory comprehension*
0%	100%

The patient is a receptive as well as expressive total alexic, for words as well as for sentences (only partly for letters), in contrast to completely preserved auditory comprehension of words and sentences.

Experiment: groups of three written words are shown to the patient, who is unable to read them, either mentally or aloud; only after the examiner has uttered one of these words can the patient find it, by means of these auditory adjuvant stimuli, among the words on the card; the cards are then removed. Subsequently the patient is again confronted with the three written words and asked to read them aloud. For instance, the following words were simultaneously shown to the patient: skill, property, *intelligence;* the patient was incapable of reading them either aloud or in his mind; but after the examiner had uttered the word 'intelligence', the patient promptly found it; when the words were again exhibited, this time successively, first the word 'property', the patient could not read it, then came the word 'intelligence', *he correctly read it aloud,* finally the word 'skill', the patient was incapable of reading it. In this way we also succeeded in deblocking other words, like 'diligence', 'journey', 'report', 'memorable', 'enmity', etc.

In the course of this experiment, using deblocking by verbal auditory means, the patient managed to read correctly aloud and to understand all eight words previously uttered by the examiner, while he could not read, either receptively or expressively, the other undeblocked 16 words. This performance is the more remarkable as the words used were 'difficult' abstract ones. The effect of every deblocking was extinguished immediately after the end of the experiment.

Deblocking of sentence alexia: we used the same method as for deblocking verbal alexia; e. g., three cards are put before the patient, each with one of the following sentences in cursive writing: (1) "the battalion prepares for the battle", (2) "leaving for holidays is welcome", (3) *"qualifying for a profession is useful"*. The patient proves to be completely alexic for these sentences. The examiner then loudly utters the words of the third sentence, asking the patient to look for it among the three cards exhibited. After carefully looking at each individual sentence, the patient makes a correct decision. The examiner takes the cards and again successively shows them to the patient; although the latter remains alexic for the first and second sentences, *he correctly reads the third one aloud.* The same positive result was obtained on reading other sentences, as, e. g., *"quarrels between men may have serious consequences",* in this case, the patient was even able to distinguish this sentence from the markedly similar one "quarrels between children cannot have serious consequences".

Whereas the patient was unable to read any of the 14 undeblocked sentences, he could correctly read in his mind and aloud four out of the seven sentences deblocked by verbal auditory means; for the other three sentences, he was rather confused at first when asked to point out the sentence uttered by the examiner, so that the experiment had to be repeated. For instance, the patient first confused two sentences differing by a single word, viz, *'learning a profession is useful'* and *'learning a melody is useful';* when the experiment was repeated, however, he corrected his error, realising that the second sentence contained a word he could not read (*melody*). Another confusion was made between two other sentences with identical beginning and ending: *"The basis of marriage is love between husband and wife"* and "The basis of divorce is misunderstanding between husband and wife"; in this case, after the first sentence had been read aloud by the examiner, the patient pointed out the second by mistake; after repeating the experiment, however, he spontaneously corrected his error. These 'confusions' may be explained less by the alexic troubles of the patient then by a certain degree of inattentiveness. As in the case of verbal alexia, the deblocking effect was extinguished immediately after the end of the experiment.

B. By word repetition

Case 3: *Patient P. I.*

disturbed function	*better preserved function*
expressive word reading	*word repetition*
33%	100%

As in the case of deblocking anomic troubles (see page 177) we used for this patient his intact repeated speech in order to deblock expressive alexic troubles (paralexia).

Experiment: We first established the words that the patient was incapable of correctly reading aloud. During the test, the examiners utters groups of five different words, always containing one of the 'blocked' ones. The patient correctly repeats aloud each of these five words, then he is made to read aloud the word in question. For instance, the patient is requested to repeat the following words which he does correctly: bath, *plumper (tinichigiu),* plums, sheep, pig. Then the examiner hands the patient a card on which the word 'plumber' is written. Although he had previously been unable to read this word correctly (he had read it paralexically: 'in . . . in . . . inket'), this time *he promptly and correctly renders it.* Another example: the patient correctly repeats the words: *raspberry,* bath, vegetables, hair-brush, train. When the written word raspberry (*zmeură* in Roumanian) is shown to him, *he promptly and correctly reads it* (before deblocking he had paralexically read it 'ramură' . . . zău . . . ză . . . mea'). By means of deblocking the patient also succeeds in reading aloud correctly a series of other words which he had previously read in a paralexical manner, e. g., *Murfatlar* (before: 'Monfatar . . . mr . . . mr . . . m . . . fa . . .'), *orgoliu* (before: 'oro . . . orl . . . ro . . . rologiu') *proclamare* (before: 'coială . . . coroială'), *împopoțona* (before: 'mpode . . . mpodo . . . podo'), etc.

By means of deblocking, the patient succeeds in reading correctly the 21 words which he had previously read in a paralexical manner; slight paralexia still occurs in a single case ('funculiță', instead of 'furculiță'), while in 4 cases the test had to be repeated in order to enforce the deblocking effect. For instance, the word *protopop* (bevore: 'Cot . . . crot . . . otop') is still more paralexically read after deblocking, 'otropop', and is correctly read only after repeating the test. In order to assess deblocking after-effects we mad the patient read the deblocked words immediately after the end of the experiment, then 24 hours and, finally, 48 hours later. Immediately after the experiment, the patient was able to read aloud correctly all 21 words deblocked during the experiment; out of 13 such words he could still read 10 correctly 24 hours later, and out of another 8 deblocked words he could still read 7 after 48 hours. The deblocking aftereffect was therefore preserved in this case after 24 to 48 hours, with rare exceptions.

The deblocking of expressive *sentence alexia:* we used a simplified method in this case. The examiner utters the sentence that the patient was previously incapable of correctly reading aloud and the latter has to repeat it. Then the written sentence is presented and the patient must read it. For instance, the sentence *Bănuțul de zece copeici* (the ten-penny coin) is read before deblocking as *bănuțul de zece copii* (the ten-children coin), but it is *correctly* read after deblocking. Another example: *De la Copenhaga la București* (from Copenhagen to Bucharest) is first read: 'Cupeică . . . ma . . . cupeică . . . cu . . . a de la cupeică la București'. In this case the patient perseveres in the word *copeici* in the preceding sentence and persists in the paralexic version *cupeică.* After deblocking, however, *he reads the sentences promptly and accurately.* He also succeeds in reading the following sentences expressively and with no paralexia: *in patria noastră înfloreste o viată nouă* (a new life blooms in our country – before: 'în piața noastră însumetiță înflori o viață nouă); *în anii libertății* (in the years of freedom – before :'anii . . . ani . . . elibe . . . anii . . . în anii eliberării'); *pregătiri pentru însămînțările de primăvară* (preparations for spring sowing – before: 'pentru plecarea . . . pentr a însămîn țare de primăvară'), etc.

After the end of the experiment, the patient was able to read perfectly all these sentences.

The deblocking of verbal deafness

By copied writing

Case 6: *Patient T. M.*

disturbed function	*better presserved function*
verbal auditory comprehension	*copied writing*
60%	100%

In addition to partial agnosis for sounds and noise, the patient also exhibits a partial verbal deafness. Most of the time he is only able to understand if the word is repeated several times; he is otherwise either totally incapable of understanding anything (words or sentences) or only capable of guesswork and wrong interpretation, whereas copied writing (as well as reading) is completely preserved.

Experiment: The words for which the patient has no correct auditory comprehension are previously established. The test is carried out as follows: the patient copies out one of the words he is not able to understand by auditory means; then he is given four other words that he must read aloud *(Störreize);* finally the examiner utters the word previously copied by the patient, and the latter must, either verbally or by gesture, convey its significance. For instance, the patient copies the word 'pictures', then reads aloud the words: cupboard, hart, vigorous, inside; then the examiner utters the word 'pictures'; the patient, on hearing this word previously had answered: 'I don't understand', this time, by means of deblocking, *he correctly understands and explains it:* 'on the wall'. Another example: during the preliminary test the patient had not understood the word 'gate' by auditory means; by means of deblocking and after reading aloud another four inserted words, *he understands the word* when uttered by the examiner and correctly explains it: 'in the courtyard'. In this way we also succeeded in deblocking a number of other words, previously not, or wrongly, understood by the patient, e. g., the word 'clown' (the patient: 'at the circus'), the word 'woodchopper' (the patient: 'who cuts wood'), the word 'trunks' (the patient: 'for clothes, for packages'), the word 'typewriter' (the patient performs the corresponding gesture).

By means of deblocking, the patient correctly understands eight words out of the nine he could not previously understand by auditory means; only the word *servietă* (portfolio) was misunderstood in the copying stage, taken for *serviciu* (service) and accordingly explained 'doing good' (in the sense of doing oneself a good turn, a 'service'). The control test carried out immediately after the end of the experiment allowed us to find that the deblocked effect had been entirely preserved.

The deblocking of troubles in auditory comprehension of *sentences:* the following procedure was used to this end: we previously established a series of verbal commands not understood and not carried out by the patient. We confronted him with each one of these written sentences separately, asking him to copy them. Then the examiner uttered each one of the sentences, asking the patient to perform the order. For instance, the patient copies the sentence 'shake hands', then the examiner orally asks him: 'shake hands'; before deblocking, the patient is unable to understand a single word, but on hearing the order by means of deblocking he asks: 'shall I shake hands?' and reaches his hand to the examiner. A similar procedure was used for all other orders, e. g., 'Clap your hands!', 'Look out of the window!', 'Lift your right hand!', 'Stand up from that chair!', 'Go to the door!', 'Sit down!'.

All seven verbal commands were correctly performed by means of deblocking. As in the case of the after-effect of deblocking verbal deafness for words, the one for sentences was not extinguished after the end of the experiment.

The deblocking of agraphia dictation

A. By copied writing

Case 1: *Patient T. J.*

disturbed function	*better preserved function*
writing on dictation	*copied writing*
0%	70%

As compared to the completely abolished writing on dictation, copied writing is much better preserved.

Experiment: the patient has to copy a word. The examiner then removes the written original as well as the word copied by the patient and dictates the same word; if the patient is incapable of correctly copying the word on his first attempt, he may try again; if a series of tests is performed, the word is repeated once more each time that the patient is not able to write it correctly from the first dictation.

Figure 1 shows that prior to deblocking the patient wrote all 12 dictated words in a completely paragraphic manner; he first succeeded in copying only ten words and could only write the remaining two after several repetitions. By means of deblocking, the patient was able to write on dictation six words correctly, or almost correctly (*ţărani* – peasants, *servietă* – bag, *placă* – plate, *biliard, acordeon, bibliotecă* – library), two words with slight literal paragraphie (*Sah* – chess, *sfinc* – Sphinx), while the remaining four were not deblocked at all (larger literal paragraphia, incomparably smaller, however, than before deblocking; the words were: *poartă* – gate, *chitară* – guitar, *acoperiş* – roof, *sandale* – sandals). The deblocking after-effect was extinguished immediately after the end of the experiment.

B. By expressive reading

Case 7: *Patient M. M.*

disturbed function	*better preserved function*
writing on dictation	*expressive verbal reading*
8%	73%

In this patient, expressive reading is incomparably better preserved than writing on dictation, which is almost completely abolished.

Experiment: The patient reads one word aloud, then the examiner removes the written word and dictates it to the patient.

As seen in figure 2, out of 20 words written before deblocking with complete (mostly verbal) paragraphia – 15 words were written correctly by means of deblocking or with incomparably slighter paragraphia. As in the above mentioned case, the deblocking after-effect was completely extinguished immediately after the end of the experiment.

It must be noted that results obtained in these two patients are the more remarkable as both exhibited relatively marked sensory troubles (verbal deafness and receptive verbal alexia).

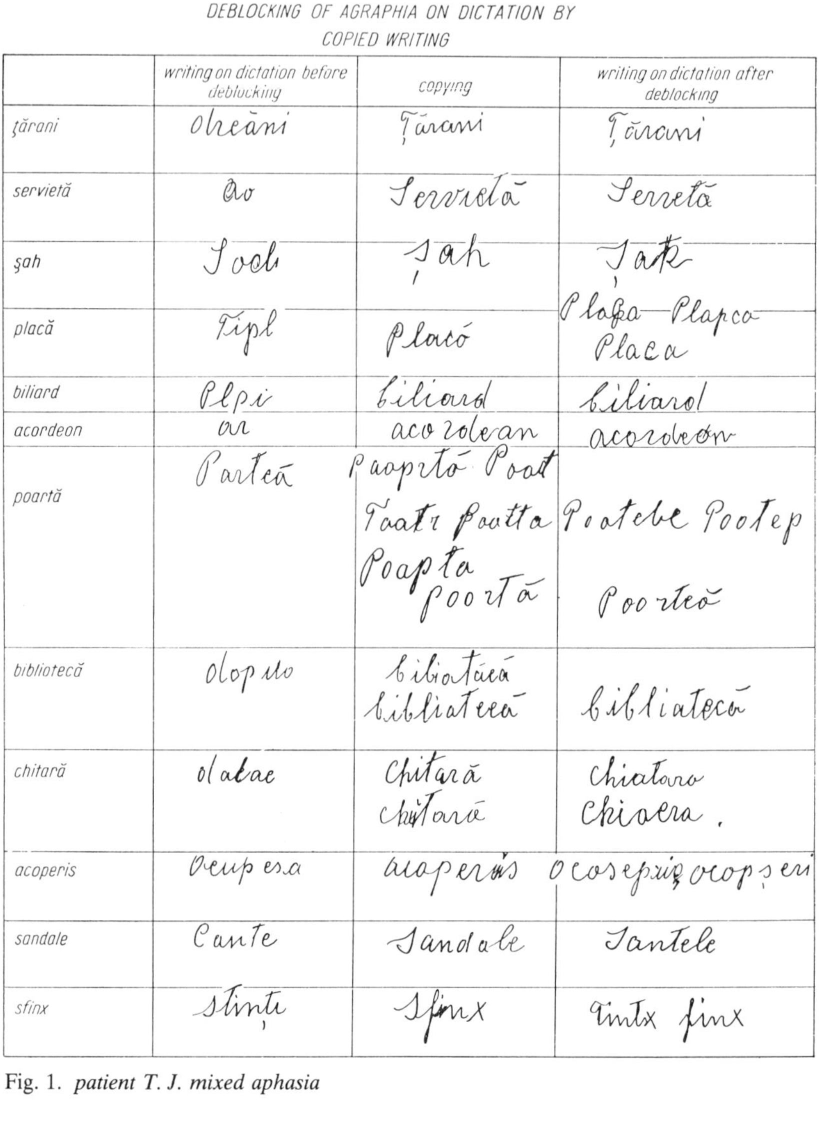

Fig. 1. *patient T. J. mixed aphasia*

Simultaneous deblocking of several disturbed verbal reactions

A. *By a single stimulus*

Case 7: *Patient M. M.*

disturbed functions			*better preserved function*
naming	*writing on dictation*	*repetition*	*expressing reading*
5%	8%	6%	73%

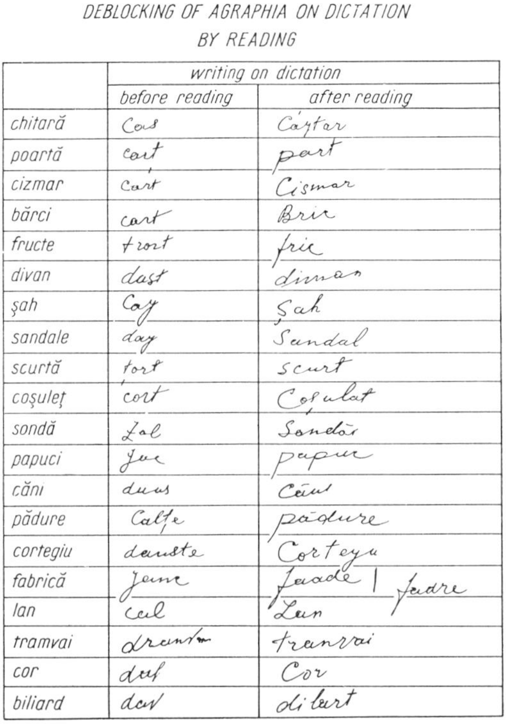

DEBLOCKING OF AGRAPHIA ON DICTATION BY READING

	writing on dictation	
	before reading	after reading
chitară	Cas	Caytar
poartă	cart	part
cizmar	Cart	Cismar
bărci	cart	Brir
fructe	frort	frie
divan	dast	dimar
şah	Cay	Şah
sandale	day	Sandal
scurtă	fort	scurt
coşuleţ	cort	Coşulat
sondă	Lal	Sondăr
papuci	Jur	papur
căni	dus	Căn
pădure	Calfe	pădure
cortegiu	danste	Corteyu
fabrică	Jeme	faade | fadre
lan	Cal	Lan
tramvai	drantm	tranvai
cor	duf	Cor
biliard	dar	dilart

Fig. 2. *patient M. M. mixed aphasia*

This patient exhibits a marked difference between performances concerning the almost completely abolished functions of naming, writing on dictation, and repetition, on one hand, and the relatively well preserved expressive reading, on the other.

Experiment: A series of pictures which the patient is incapable of correctly naming is established: nor can he write the corresponding words on dictation or repeat them. The experiment consists in requesting the patient to name one of the pictures of this series, then dictating the corresponding word, and, finally, in uttering the word in order to make the patient repeat it. Then the word is exhibited in writing and the patient correctly reads it aloud. After this the examiner again utters the word, dictates it to the patient, and finally exhibits the picture to be named.

Figure 3 shows some examples of naming, writing, and repetition troubles before deblocking, as well as their removal after deblocking. Out of 9 deblocking performances carried out in this experiment, 5 succeeded in all 3 functions, 4 only in naming and repeating, which

SUCCESSIVE DEBLOCKING OF NAMING, WRITING ON DICTATION AND REPETITION BY EXPRESSIVE READING

Image Word	before deblocking			after deblocking		
	naming	writing on dictation	repetition	repetition	writing on dictation	naming
tînăr (youngman)	"tovarăsul mic este" (the comrade small is)	Vie	"crii... pro" (paraphasic)	correct	tiner	correct
vultur (eagle)	"nu pot" (I can't)	Viic	"proc" (paraphasic)	correct	Vultur	correct
tobă (drum)	"nu pot, nu stiu" (I can't, I don't know)	fuere	"proc" (paraphasic)	correct	tobă	correct
covor (carpet)	"nu pot să vorbesc" (I can't speak)	[illegible]	"vro... plo" (paraphasic)	correct	Covor	correct

Fig. 3. *patient M. M. mixed aphasia*

proves agraphia on dictation to be more 'resistant' to deblocking. The after-effect of simultaneous deblocking was extinguished immediately after the end of the experiment.

B. By combined stimuli

Case 1: *Patient T. J.*

disturbed functions		*better preserved functions*		
naming	*repetition*	*writing on dictation*	*copied writing*	*expressive reading*
19%	0%	0%	70%	70%

In this patient two verbal functions are completely abolished (repetition and writing on dictation), while the third ins only partly disturbed (naming). Copied writing and expressive reading are, however, better preserved.

Experiment: The method is similar to that used in the previous case, excepting the fact that, instead of one deblocking stimulus, two stimuli are applied, expressive reading and copied writing; i. e. the patient has to copy the respective word and read it aloud. Then he is requested to name the image, to repeat the corresponding word uttered by the examiner, and to write it on dictation.

Figure 4 below shows examples where, in all cases, the originally disturbed functions are deblocked after the performance of copied writing and expressive reading.

Out of the 8 tests, 5 succeeded in all 3 functions, 3 only in naming and repetition; i. e., writing on dictation is more difficult to deblock, as also seen in the previous case. The deblocking after-effect was in this case also extinguished immediately after the end of the experiment.

SUCCESSIVE DEBLOCKING OF NAMING, REPETITION AND WRITING ON DICTATION BY COMBINED STIMULI (COPYING AND READING)

Image Word	before deblocking			Deblocking by copying and reading	after deblocking		
	naming	repetition	writing on dictation		naming	repetition	writing on dictation
pălării (hats)	"par...plu...port" (paraphasic)	"pălăride" (paraphasic)	Palăugle	Pălăreii	correct	correct	Pălărie
divan	"vataite" (paraphasic)	"vecet" (paraphasic)	C	Divan	correct	correct	Divan
scurtă (coat)	"nu pot" (I can't)	"curfe" (paraphasic)	Corte	Scurtă	correct	correct	scurtă
pădure (wood)	"schela" (scaffold)	"nu pot" (I can't)	Pode	Păolure	correct	correct	Părolure Pŏolure

Fig. 4. *patient T. J. mixed aphasia*

Discussion of results

As shown above, we studied in aphasic patients of various types the deblocking of the following verbal dysfunctions: verbal deafness, troubles in repetion and naming, alexia, agraphia. These dysfunctions were deblocked by other verbal performances, where these proved better, or were completely preserved. We thus succeeded in deblocking, e. g., troubles of repetition by reading, in some cases, and alexic troubles by intact repetition, in other cases. For certain disturbed verbal performances we found several ways of deblocking; e. g., alexic troubles were deblocked by verbal auditory means and also, in other cases, by repetition. Troubles in naming were deblocked by verbal auditory means, as well as by reading; we deblocked verbal deafness by reading and copied writing, while agraphia on dictation was removed by reading, as well as by copied writing, i. e., by stimuli belonging to the same graphie function. Of course, these ways of deblocking only constitute a beginning; they could doubtlessly be widened and varied, as could the number of disturbed verbal functions subject to the deblocking method.

Our data shows the phenomenon of deblocking is the result of *experimental conditions,* created with the special aim of achieving certain impaired verbal performances by means of specific stimuli. The deblocking effect presupposes a relation of *time – succession,* i. e., the deblocking stimulus must *precede* the blocked reaction, in contrast to other phenomena mentioned above, where the effect is sometimes conditioned by the simultaneous presence of both stimuli (e. g., finding the picture corresponding to a written word).

One of the main conditions for achievement of the deblocking effect is that the deblocking verbal performance (e. g., reading), as well as the one to be deblocked (e. g., naming), should refer *to one and the same word* (e. g., reading the words 'trunks' and naming the picture of this object). If one or several modes of comprehension or expression are disturbed in a patient (auditory or reading comprehension, repetition, loud reading, writing of a word, the naming of the corresponding picture, etc.), while another or several other modes of comprehending or expressing the same word are better preserved, then, by means of the latter, the receptive or expressive troubles concerning this word can be temporarily removed. Deblocking is therefore a *strictly limited, intransmissible* phenomenon. By deblocking the repetition of a certain word, we do not also deblock by this the repetition of other words, not even of synonyms or of either semantically or phonetically related words.

Our experiments demonstrate *that the performance of a single verbal function may simultaneously deblock the corresponding performances of several other expressive or receptive verbal functions.* We succeeded, for instance, in simultaneously deblocking troubles of naming, repeated speech, and writing on dictation by reading (see case 7, page 184). It must be noted, however, that up to the present such simultaneous deblocking was only obtained in a few cases, while in others deblocking did not affect the performances of other verbal functions. In this respect systematic investigations are still to be carried out on a larger number of patients.

The fact that when deblocking exerts a small effect it always refers to the same word, while, on the other hand, it can simultaneously involve several disturbed verbal modalities of the same word, seems to be extremely important in the attempt at elucidating the pathophysiology of temporary conditioned connections in the brain cortex. During their experiments on conditioned reflexes, Ivanov-Smolenski [69] observed similar phenomena. After elaborating a conditioned reaction by a direct stimulus (e. g., a motor reaction to the appearance of a green light), they were able to obtain the same conditioned reaction immediately, without any previous elaboration, by simply uttering the words 'green light' or by displaying a card on which these words were written[7], whereas no adequate motor conditioned reaction was obtained to any other uttered or written word. In spite of the fact that the phenomena investigated, as well as the methods used in the above mentioned experiments are different from ours, certain conclusions present a close resemblance. The Soviet investigators found that the direct stimulus (green light) can be replaced by the words 'green light' uttered by the examiner or by the same written words, but not by any other words; i. e., only the verbal symbols corresponding to this visual stimulus can lead to the previously elaborated motor reaction.

The effect of deblocking has a *temporary* character. By investigating the duration of the deblocking effect we found that it is extinguisted after a certain period[8]. The interval between applying the deblocking stimulus and inducing the reaction to be deblocked should not exceed, in our opinion, a certain limit (approximately ten minutes), otherwise the deblocking effect disappears, i. e., the adequate reactions fails to occur[9]. On the other hand, the fact that deblocking still occurs even when the deblocking stimulus and the disturbed reaction are separated by a certain interval shows that the effect of deblocking is not a kind of *Kurzschlußreaktion,* but can be maintained without being extinguished for a certain time. Our experiments have further proved that after it has once occurred (in an adequate reaction) the after-effect often acquires a greater 'resistance', is able to persist for a longer time, for hours or even days, without requiring the assistance of a fresh deblocking stimulus. As shown above, the patient P. I. (case 3) with partial expressive alexia, who could correctly read aloud the words previously deblocked by repetition, often preserves this adequate reaction when he is given the same word for the second or third time, without repeating it again, even for a period of 48 hours.

In a previous work ⟨8⟩ we demonstrated the *resistance* of the deblocking effect to spurious stimuli *(Stör- oder Ablenkungsreize),* especially obvious when we 'fill' the intervals between application of the deblocking stimulus and the one to be deblocked by visual stimuli (looking at pictures), auditory ones (listening to music), lexical ones (reading other words, asking questions which have to be answered), etc. Of course, as we have already shown, the deblocking effect is generally diminshed in proportion to the number of these spurious stimuli, their affective contents, etc.

In the above mentioned work, we have also insisted on the fact that if the deblocking effect does not occur after the first deblocking stimulus, the effect can be *enforced* by repeating the stimulus (see p. 156 f. above). For instance, if a patient with agraphia on dictation is unable to write the word correctly after reading it for the first time, a positive result may still be obtained by repeating the test several times. In addition to this reinforcement by repetition of the deblocking stimulus, we also used with some success a reinforcement by simultaneous association of another deblocking stimulus. The method of combined stimuli is especially advisable when the function mediating the deblocking action is in its turn partly disturbed in the patient under investigation. For instance, in patient T. J. (case 1) with completely abolished repetition and writing on dictation, we simultaneously used as deblocking agents two partly disturbed functions, viz., copied writing and expressive reading (p. 175).

In our experiments, the deblocking of the performance of certain verbal functions occurs by the patient's performing other verbal functions which are either completely intact or at least better preserved. *The deblocking effect is usually the greater, the less troubled the deblocking function.* We must, however, make a distinction between functions and performances. For instance, a partly disturbed function may also act as deblocking function, provided the trouble is much smaller than that affecting the function to be deblocked. As shown above, repetition may be deblocked by expressive reading even if the latter is itself partly disturbed (case 1, page 175). In exchange, the verbal performance by means of which deblocking occurs must be completely intact (devoid of any paraphasic, paralexical, or paragraphic troubles). If the repetition of the word 'slippers' is to be deblocked, e. g., by previously making the patient read this word, then we must ascertain by several preceding tests whether the patient exhibits any expressive alexic troubles when reading this word. Any disfunction in the deblocking verbal performance exerts an unfavourable influence on the deblocking process, disturbing or even completely abolishing it.

As for *the extent to which the function to be deblocked is disturbed,* we obtained satisfactory results even when this function was 100% imparied (e. g., repetition in case 1, expressive and receptive reading in case 5, etc.). Nevertheless, the result of deblocking for each separate case can only be conclusive if previous repeated testes have proved that the verbal performance to be deblocked is completely abolished in normal conditions. In other words, if sometimes the patient is also able to repeat a certain word even without any previous deblocking, we cannot be certain whether the patient has repeated the word (in the course of the experiment) as a result of deblocking or only in a spontaneous manner, independent of deblocking.

The ways of deblocking are extremely varied. Deblocking can be performed not only with respect to expressive troubles, but also to receptive ones, not only at the level of the visual analyser, but also of the auditory verbo-motor or tactile one, etc. From a series of experiments to be reported elsewhere, we can conclude that deblocking is possible not only in relation to direct verbal functions (second signaling system), but also to predominantly nonverbal ones, e. g., deblocking of auditory, or visual agnosis, astereognosis, etc. (the first signaling system).[10] The fact that in certain (as yet unpublished) cases we succeeded in deblocking (by reading and copied writing, respectively) troubles of repeated speech and writing on dictation, not only with respect to words having a definite meaning, but also to *senseless and unknown words,* shows that the phenomenon of deblocking is not related exclusively to the semantic sphere, but also comprises verbal performances outside this sphere. It has also been demonstrated that receptive as well as expressive functions (e. g., auditory comprehension or repetition of a word) may serve as deblocking stimuli, and that these may belong to various analysers.

Deblocking may take place between various expressive functions (e. g., repetition by expressive reading), between various receptive ones (e. g., verbal deafness by verbal auditory comprehension), as well as between one receptive function and another expressive one, or conversely (e. g., expressive reading by verbal auditory means, verbal deafness by expressive reading).

Our deblocking experiments were carried out at a *level* situated in the wide field of language, i. e., within the second signaling system, in the words of I. P. Pavlov. Even when we deblock dysfunction in recognising a certain kind of noise or picture, we are still in the same field, since this recognition is closely related to naming. We have deblocked words as well as sentences, their auditory and lexic comprehension, as well as their loud articulation. Nevertheless, the majority of verbal performances involved in these deblocking experiments occur in normal men in a completely, or almost completely, *automatic* way. For instance, the auditory or lexic comprehension of the word 'slippers', its repetition, the act of reading it aloud or writing it down, require, as a rule, no participation of any process of highly developed thought. The experiments performed on patient V. M. (case 5) constitute an exception to this rule; in this case, we deblocked receptive and expressive alexic troubles concerning *abstract words and sentences* and tested the deblocking effect by the method of synonyms (e. g., the word 'dexterity' must be identified with the word 'skill', the sentence "The basis of marriage is love between husband and wife", with the sentence "Marriage is based on reciprocal love"). The success of these experiments proves that deblocking can also be achieved at a higher level of language.

Deblocking can be carried out in *the most different forms of aphasia:* in aphasics with predominantly expressive, receptive, or mixed troubles, amnestic aphasics, alexic patients without marked aphasic disturbances, etc. This fact justifies the belief that *blocking is a general phenomenon of the aphasic syndrome* and that the possibility of temporarily deblocking aphasic troubles is not limited to certain forms of aphasia.

It must be noted, however, that we encountered cases – especially patients with total aphasia or severe sensory troubles – in which we were unable to discover any way of deblocking one or several verbal troubles. We must also remark that we did not meet with success in every case experimented upon, the outcome being to a certain extent dependent on the actual state of the patient. In some cases, when the general condition of the patient was appreciably improved, we could observe one or two years after our initial experiments that certain phenomena of deblocking could no more be obtained, although they had originally been easy to achieve. Conversely, patients in an improved condition proved to be accessible to experiments for which they had previously been totally inappropriate. But even when a way of deblocking is found to be efficient in a patient, this does not signify that all verbal performances of this type can be deblocked. In case 1, for instance (page 184), the deblocking of severe troubles of agraphia on dictation was completely successful in only 6 words out of 12, and could only partly, or not at all, be achieved for the rest. The systematic study of the causes of partial or total insuccess met with in the course of our deblocking experiments, as well as the elaboration of more efficent methods, opens a wide field of investigation.

Kreindler [85] advanced the hypothesis that the region of the brain cortex situated in the so-called 'language area' at the level of the dominant hemisphere plays the part of activating area for all formations involved in the function of language. It keeps under control certain basic physiological phenomena involved in language, such as directing and maintaining attention towards verbal performance, keeping an adequate speed of reaction, maintaining good mobility of excitatory and inhibitory processes in the field of verbal performances, ensuring a sufficiently intense and constant vestigial process in the verbal neuronal network by an adequate verbal stimulus, etc. In aphasia a basic disturbance occurs in these processes; *the phenomenon of blocking* and all its variants constitute a disturbance of this type. The phenomenon of blocking takes place at the level of synapses in the effector or along the pathway leading from afference to efference in the field of language performance.

The phenomenon of *deblocking* studied by us is a physiological process occurring at the level of the neuronal chain. For example, when expressive verbal alexia is deblocked by repeating the blocked word, blocking occurs at the level ot the efference of the reading process; the picture of the word does not lead to adequate performance because the optico-lexical excitatory process remains subliminal owing to blocking and is unable to induce a sufficient central excitation of the verbo-motor apparatus. But as soon as this excitatory process meets on its way the trace of another preexisting excitatory process, a liminal undisturbed process also progressing towards the verbo-motor apparatus, the subliminal process reaches by summation a state of central excitation sufficiently intense (efficient threshold) to succeed in penetrating the blocking present at the level of one or several synapses.

The process of deblocking is therefore one of *summation between a subliminal process and the trace of another process* at the same level. This assumption is also supported by the fact that deblocking is a temporary process, similar to other vestigial processes known in the central nervous system.

The temporary deblocking described above exhibits two different aspects. On one hand, there is the study of the phenomenon in itself, of experimental conditions leading to its achievement, of deblocking pathways, forms of aphasic troubles and types of investigated aphasia, etc. On the other hand, our method may at the same time provide *an objective method of studying verbal functions in aphasics*. We have the conviction that a continued deep and systematic study of this phenomenon may be of use not only to neurophysiologists, psychologists and linguists in their study of pathologic and normal verbal functions, but also a real help for those involved in reeducating aphasics.

Notes

1. This study was carried out in the Neurological Institute 'I. P. Pavlov' of the Academy of the Roumanian People's Republic (Dir. Prof. Dr. A. Kreindler).
2. Besides, the term facilitation has acquired a very precise maning in neurophysiology in the course of the last decades – since Wedensky and Sherrington – a meaning appreciably different from the one assumed by some authors on aphasia.
3. All figures refer to the percentage of correct answers given by patients in various tests of naming, word repetition, writing, reading, etc., where 50–75 images or words were used.
4. We express our gratitude to the physicians M. I. Botez, A. Fradis, V. Ionăsescu, V. Voiculescu, I. Voinescu for their kind permission to use the results of clinic examinations and to Dr. E. Crighel with respect to the results of electroencephalographic examinations.
5. See our previous work ⟨8⟩.
6. See [88].
7. Ivanov-Smolenski explains the phenomenon by a selective irradiation of the excitation process from the first signaling system to the second.
8. It is interesting that some patients realize that (in our experimental conditions) the effect of deblocking is temporary: e. g., patient M. M. (case 7), after succeeding in repeating the word 'Slippers' by means of deblocking, spontaneously cries out, with deep regret: "Slippers – have them now, not tomorrow!", i. e., the patient is able to repeat the word correctly, but he will not be able to do so later, 'tomorrow'".
9. See ⟨8⟩.
10. For example, in patient T. M. (case 6) with partial deafness to noise and sound we succeeded in deblocking these troubles by previously making the patient copy the names of these auditory stimuli. In another case (patient St. Gh.), an aphasic with partial visual agnosis for pictures, we obtained correct recognition of the latter by carrying out deblocking by verbal auditory means, i. e., uttering the names of pictures that the patient had to find among other pictures [19].

E. WEIGL

On the Problem of Cortical Syndromes: Experimental Studies

As one of Kurt Goldstein's oldest students and collaborators, I consider it an honor as well as my duty to make a modest contribution to this volume published in his memory. I welcome the opportunity to express my deep gratitude to this outstanding man at whose home – first in Frankfurt, and later in Berlin – I had the privilege of being warmly received whenever I called.

The seminars for the study of the after-effects of brain lesions, which were held in the nineteen-twenties at the University of Frankfurt by Kurt Goldstein and Adhémar Gelb were an experience never to be forgotten by those privileged to attend them. Here we witnessed the classical investigations of aphasia, agnosia, and apraxia in patients who were to become famous; and we were encouraged to conduct our own experiments under the guidance of these two unique teachers.

The ideal cooperation and severe, mutual criticism practiced in Frankfurt in those days by the eminent experimental psychologist Gelb and the internationally known neurologist and brain expert, Goldstein, continue to serve as a model for neuro-psychological research.

Hitler's disastrous seizure of power put a sudden end to this personally and professionally stimulating contact with Kurt Goldstein, my great friend and teacher. Of Jewish origin, known to be a Democrat, he managed to escape Hitler's bloodthirsty hangmen, almost as if by a miracle, at the very last moment.

While writing these lines, I have in front of me Kurt Goldstein's last letter to me. In this letter he expressed his great satisfaction that his former pupil and collaborator had remained loyal to aphasia research, the field he himself had loved so much. In this letter, written in 1962, he told me that, despite his advanced age, he was incessantly at work, getting 'immer mehr in das Fahrwasser der Philosophie'; and he added, '. . . man hat das Gefühl, es hat alles nicht mehr so sehr viel Sinn in dieser Welt', a remark that sounded somehow like a sigh. Its interpretation must be left to those who had the privilege of being among his close friends during his last years. But of those who know the true value of his contribution to science, none will share his doubts as to the 'use' of his own life.

Kurt Goldstein's work is classic in the field of brain pathology. His work, his deep insight into the intricate mechanisms of the normal and impaired human brain, will remain an inexhaustible source of knowledge for many generations of scientists to come.

Many decades ago, Goldstein made profound contributions to the problem dealt with in this paper, i.e., the problem of higher cortical syndromes. He expressed his far-reaching ideas mainly in his papers *Zur Theorie der Funktion des Nervensystems* [49], *Das Symptom, seine Entstehung und Bedeutung für unsere Auffassung vom Bau und der Funktion des Nervensystems* [50], *Über Aphasie* [51], and finally in his comprehensive work *Language and Language Disturbances* [53]. The method of psychological case analysis which he elaborated jointly with A. Gelb, and his attempt to regard cortical syndromes not as "ein zufälliges Nebeneinander" of single disturbances due to local injury [51, p. 27], but as the result of *disturbances of a system,* in the sense of impairment of certain 'basic functions' [53, p. 3], justify his being regarded as the founder of modern neuro-psychology [cf. 110, 163 et al.].

I have tried to find a new approach to the problem of cortical syndromes to be described in this paper. Proceeding from the examination of patients with different cortical syndromes, we pursue questions concerning the reciprocal structural and dynamic relations between the various disturbances of single functions, their hierarchy, the extent of their impairment, and potential avenues of relief.

The experimental study of syndromes is carried through with the help of the *deblocking method* [⟨9⟩, 179]. In order to facilitate understanding of this paper, a brief description of this method follows.

The deblocking method makes use of the fact that the capacity for decoding, coding, and recoding verbal information [71] is not completely obliterated in most aphasic patients. Though examination of these processes via certain 'channels' may show them to be more or less severely disturbed, an examination utilizing other 'channels' might indicate that the processes are completely – or almost completely – intact; the specific findings depend on the localization of the lesion, i e., on the 'type' of aphasia. The alexic patient, for instance, understands without difficulty the meaning of a certain word when hearing it, yet he fails to do so when reading it, i. e., verbo-visually; conversely, the patient with sensory aphasia remains 'deaf' to the meaning of a word spoken to him, while he is able to understand the same word as soon as it is shown to him in writing.

The conditions underlying disturbances of decoding, illustrated in the foregoing examples, are similar to those that underlie disturbances of coding and recoding. A patient suffering from disturbances in naming of objects may well be able to read a certain word aloud, whereas he fails, when asked, to name the respective object, i. e., in the expressive use of the same word. Patients with expressive-alexic disturbances can react quite normally when requested to name objects, while reading aloud the very same words prove to be an insurmountable difficulty.

In the elaboration of our deblocking method, we proceeded from these relations between intact and disturbed functions of speech which are well known in aphasia research and rehabilitation work. The deblocking effect is attained through use of the intact channel leading to a certain 'meaning', in order to eliminate the 'blocking' when the same meaning cannot be decoded, coded, or recoded via other channels. This is achieved through prompting of the intact speech performance just before we test the disturbed verbo-receptive or verbo-expressive function. If, for example, a patient with word-deafness is requested first to read a given word, he will subsequently be able to understand its meaning upon hearing it. The same applies to patients with disturbances of repetition who can repeat a word which they have previously copied in writing.

The phenomenon of deblocking in aphasic patients consists in removing, for longer or shorter periods, total or partial disturbances of various speech and other performances. The deblocking effect (d-effect) is attained through linking two semantically related performances of a preserved and a 'blocked' function, evoking the unimpaired *prior* to the disturbed performance.

'Simple' Deblocking

Example 1. Deblocking of impairment of auditory word understanding through intact picture naming in a case with predominantly sensory aphasia.

Control experiments. (a) A list of words is drawn up, the meaning of which the patient does not understand when they are spoken to him.[1] (b) It ist ascertained that the patient is capable of naming correctly all pictures used for deblocking later on.

Main experiment. In order to deblock one of the words not understood by the patient, e. g., 'slipper', the patient is first shown a number of pictures, among them one of a slipper (first input). The pictures are then removed, and the examiner pronounces a number of words, among them the word 'slipper' (second input). The d-effect consists in the patient's remaining 'deaf' to all these words, with the exception of the word 'slipper'.

Example 2. Deblocking of disturbances of anomia through preserved auditory word understanding in a case with amnesic aphasia.

Control experiments. (a) A record is made of pictures which the patient cannot name, even though he is able to recognize them. *(b)* Auditory word understanding is checked, mainly of the 'critical' words to be used later.

Main experiment. In order to deblock the naming of those pictures that the patient failed to name in the control experiment, e. g., one showing a slipper, the examiner pronounces several words, among them the critical word 'slipper' (first input). Following this, the patient is shown several pictures (second input), and he is able to name only the one showing the slipper.

In a similar way, we succeeded in eliminating experimentally disturbances of oral repetition, of reading, of writing, etc., in various types of aphasia. It is possible, for example, to deblock disturbances of repetition by means of intact word reading, or, conversely, disturbed word reading by means of intact repetition. We have also obtained the d-effect in disturbances of written naming by means of intact copying; in agraphia on dictation by means of intact reading, etc.; finally, we have been able to deblock nonverbal, gnostic disturbances, such as disturbances of picture recognition, by having the patient read the names of the objects before presenting the pictures of the objects to be named.

As we have shown in detail elsewhere ⟨9⟩, [179], the main difference between the deblocking method described above and the usual facilitation methods (e. g., in cases of word-deafness, the patient is asked to select pictures named by the examiner; or, in cases of alexia, the patient is asked to match words offered in writing with simultaneously presented pictures) consists in the patient's complete lack of insight into the procedure. In our experiments, the patient cannot possibly know which of the items (pictures, words) offered in the control experiments (first input) will prove to be the 'critical' one in the test that follows. Deliberate memorization of all items (five as a rule) is either exceedingly difficult or completely impossible for patients with brain lesions which ordinarily impair short-term memory to some degree. In order to prevent the patient right from the beginning from 'discovering' the principle underlying our method, we usually include 'neutral' series among the actual deblocking series. For example, when deblocking disturbances of anomia through intact oral repetition, we include in the first input some series that contain not one single word corresponding to the pictures to be named later; correct picture naming can, of course, not be expected in these instances. In this way, the majority of our patients do not become aware at all of how we evoke their correct response. When asked how it is that all at once they can understand, write, or read a certain word, the patients usually express their conviction that they 'suddenly remembered it'. Typically they cannot even remember having spoken, heard, read, or copied the very word beforehand, and they reject the idea when it is suggested by the examiner.

It must be stressed that the d-effect is by no means limited, e. g., to deblocking word-understanding in cases of word deafness by means of naming the picture corresponding to the critical noun; or, in cases of anomia, to deblocking the naming of a certain picture by means of hearing the critical noun beforehand. Modifications in our experimental technique made us realize that the critical word need not necessarily be contained in the series offered for the first input. For example, we were able to deblock the auditory understanding of verbs, such as 'to close', when we offered the antonym 'to open' within the first input series. Similarly, we could deblock the name of an onion through having the patient repeat aloud in the first input series 'hot, tears, sharp, frying', etc. This means that the d-effect need not be restricted to the identical object or word, as we had presumed in the beginning [⟨9⟩, p. 184]. Instead, the d-effect is the result of *prestimulation* of a certain 'semantic field'[2] within which certain related concepts, e. g., synonyms, antonyms, generic nouns, are ontogenetically connected. These may lead to deblocking the 'blocked' stimulus – or at least, facilitate its deblocking – much as do the identical concepts.

The above-mentioned fact, that the patients was neither directly nor consciously engaged in this process of deblocking, indicates the automatic, stereotype character of these processes, during which stored connections can be reactivated, connections which the patient, due to his cerebral lesion, is not capable of reactivating on his own.

From the neurophysiological point of view, which we cannot enlarge upon within the scope of this paper, these effects probably must be ascribed to a process of *summation* between a pathologically subliminal and a supraliminal stimulus [⟨8⟩, p. 160 ff.].

'Chain' Deblocking

The investigations described heretofore pertain to certain discrete symptoms of various aphasic or agnostic syndromes. I have previously reported ⟨9⟩ on a method that could serve a more direct study of syndromatic connections. This method consists in having a given deblocker successively deblock a 'chain' of single performances of various impaired functions, instead of deblocking only one particular impaired performance, provided all intact or disturbed performances involve one and the same semantic field. The following examples will illustrate our method.

Example 3.[3] Patient M. M., age 57, retired, formerly employed in the textile trade; first admitted on May 11, 1953. Speech difficulties had appeared suddenly two weeks before admission. Slight signs of right hemiparesis. Diagnosis: hypertensive desease and cerebral arteriosclerosis; sensory aphasia. The patient was hospitalized on repeated occasions in 1957, 1959, and 1960.

Aphasia examination. Spontaneous speech and dialogue: frequent verbal stereotypy, polite formulae, etc.; telegraphic style with long intermittent pauses, literal and verbal paraphasia, perseveration, small vocabulary. Automatic speech and repetition as well as naming, completely or almost completely abolished. Total word deafness for abstract and unusual words, as well as for sentences (obeys only simple orders), only partial word deafness for concrete words and simple sentences. Total receptive alexia for abstract words and simple sentences, much less marked for letters and common words; total expressive alexia for sentences, only partial alexia for single words, no literal alexia. Total agraphia for words and sentences on dictation, in constrast to intact writing when copying. Almost complete acalculia. It must be noted that word deafness as well as verbal receptive alexia are considerably diminished by means of visual stimuli (pictures) or auditory ones (words uttered by the examiner). *Conclusion: mixed aphasia.*

Control experiment (see Figure 1). The patient can neither name correctly the picture of a boy (he tries to circumscribe what he sees), nor write the word 'boy' correctly on dictation (he scribbles some meaningless word consisting of three letters), nor repeat the word 'boy' (he merely articulates in a totally paraphasic manner meaningless sequences of sounds).

Main experiment. Some days later the patient is offered the written word 'boy' which he can read promptly. Silent reading – at least of conrete

picture Word	before deblocking			after deblocking		
	naming	writing on dictation	repetition	repetition	writing on dictation	naming
tînăr (youngman)	"tovarăşul mic este" (the comrade small is)	Vie	"crii... pro" (paraphasic)	correct	tiner	correct
vultur (eagle)	"nu pot" (I can't)	Vrie	"proc" (paraphasic)	correct	Vultur	correct
tobă (drum)	"nu pot, nu stiu" (I can't, I don't know)	[illegible]	"proc" (paraphasic)	correct	tobă	correct
covor (carpet)	"nu pot să vorbesc" (I can't speak)	[illegible]	"vro... plo" (paraphasic)	correct	Covor.	correct

Figure 1. *Patient M. M. Successive deblocking of naming, writing on dictation, and repetition through reading aloud*

words – is still intact. This intact performance now effects the deblocking of the following: He is able to repeat correctly the word spoken to him, to write it correctly on dictation, and to name correctly the corresponding picture when it is shown to him.

The three other control experiments also showed the patient to be completely anomic when requested to name pictures ('I can't', 'I don't know'); to be capable only of producing brief sequences of letters without meaning, when requested to write on dictation (frequent perseverations); and to utter totally paraphasic sequences of sounds (*pro, plo, vro,* etc.) when he was asked to repeat. In the main experiments, however, the earlier reading aloud of the critical word deblocked the whole chain of verbal performances consisting of repetition, writing on dictation and naming.

Example 4. Patient T. J., age 64, retired laborer; admitted to the hospital on May 12, 1960. Apoplexy five days before admission, followed by speech disturbances. High arterial blood pressure with left ventricular hypertrophy. Marked tendon reflexes in upper limbs, especially on the right side. Right homonymous hemianopsia; bilateral hypoacusia. EEG, December 15, 1960: bilateral temporal foci. Diagnosis: left posterior temporal cerebral thrombosis; aphasia.

Aphasia examination: Appreciably disturbed spontaneous speech and dialogue, literal and verbal paraphasia, frequent perseveration, diminished vocabulary. Partially preserved automatic speech. Appreciably deteriorated sentence reading and auditory receptive verbal functions (does not obey spoken or written words). Word repetition also completely abolished (paraphasia), as is naming of real and pictured objects; partial disturbance of color naming. Relatively well preserved are reading aloud of letters and of common concrete words, as well as copied writing. Total agraphia on dictation. Total acalculia. Difficulties of silent reading can be temporarily removed by means of auditory adjuvant stimuli (the written word is spoken aloud by the examiner) or visual ones (exhibiting a picture corresponding to the written word). *Conclusion: mixed aphasia.*

In this case too (Figure 2), we applied the chain deblocking method to impaired picture naming, repetition, and writing on dictation. Here, however, we used a *combined deblocker:* reading aloud and copying. This combination had proved necessary in the control experiments primarily in view of picture naming, which could be deblocked neither through copying alone nor through reading aloud by itself, but only when both these performances were combined. Comparison between the single performances during the control experiments and in the main experiment shows the chain-like effect of deblocking of several discrete performances.

picture Word	before deblocking			Deblocking by copying and reading	after deblocking		
	naming	repetition	writing on dictation		naming	repetition	writing on dictation
pălării (hats)	"par plu port" (paraphasic)	"pălăride" (paraphasic)	Palăngle	Pălăreii	correct	correct	Pălărie
divan	"vataite" (paraphasic)	"vecet" (paraphasic)	C	Divan	correct	correct	Divan
scurtă (coat)	"nu pot" (I can't)	"curfe" (paraphasic)	Corte	Scurtă	correct	correct	scurtă
pădure (wood)	"schela" (scaffold)	"nu pot" (I can't)	Pode	Păolure	correct	correct	Părdure Păolure

Figure 2. *Patient T. J. Successive deblocking of naming, repetition, and writing on dictation by combined stimuli (copying and reading).*

We thus succeeded in both patients in deblocking 'in a chain' the three impaired functions in aphasic syndromes with anomia, agraphia-on-dictation and disturbances of repetition.

Thanks to the chain deblocking experiments carried on subsequently, in collaboration with Erika Metze and Renate Böttcher, we have gathered additional information concerning the significance of this method for aphasic syndrome research.

Example 5. Patient M. J., age 55, retired employee of a trade enterprise, was first admitted to the municipal hospital ('Oskar-Ziethen-Krankenhaus', Berlin) on January 27, 1965, and then to the University Neurological Clinic, Charité, Berlin (Prof. K. Leonhard, Director) on March 31, 1965. A myocardial infarction was followed three weeks later by a cortical embolism and diabetes mellitus with aphasic, apraxic, and visual agnosic disturbances. No other findings on neurological examination. EEG: Irregular, with minor general changes; left temporal-basal focus extending into occipital region, predominantly subcortical in character.

Aphasia examination: Spontaneous speech and dialogue are much better, i. e., more fluent, than reactive speech, yet they show many paraphasic failures, perseveration, and word finding disturbances; other verbal-expressive functions, such as automatic speech, repetition, oral naming, and reading aloud, are severely impaired or even abolished. Among the verbal-receptive functions, auditory understanding of concrete words and simple sentences is relatively intact, but there is word deafness for abstract and unusual words and for more complicated sentences; silent reading is intact. Total agraphia for spontaneous writing, writing on dictation, and written naming. When tested a year later, copying and drawing were found to be intact. Color perception intact, but color naming and understanding of names of colors are disturbed. Visual, auditory, and tactile gnosis intact. Slight facial and pantomimical apraxia. Acalculia: only simple written arithmetical operations can be executed. 'Abstract' thinking as tested by sorting tests is reduced. *Conclusion: mixed aphasia (primarily sensory aphasia).*

The peculiarity of this case lies above all in the fact that 'simple' deblocking, i. e., deblocking of the performances of a particular impaired function through one (or several) preserved functions, was not possible. With patients M. M. and T. J we had succeeded in deblocking disturbances of repetition and naming by means of reading aloud, either alone or in conjunction with copying. In the case of patient M. J. such 'simple' deblocking accomplished but little for repetition and writing on dictation, and failed altogether for oral and written naming and for reading aloud. These performances could only be deblocked within a 'chain.'

Furthermore, we found with this patient, as with others, that the greatest possible d-effects could be guaranteed only if the links of the chain had *a certain sequence.* The sequence is shown in our protocol (Figure 3) and consists of the following order: repetition – writing on dictation – oral naming –written naming – reading aloud. This sequence is based on our observations during several preliminary experiments. We had found that if, for instance, reading aloud was removed from the sixth position in the chain to an earlier position, the d-effect could not be obtained; the same applies to oral naming, which could only be deblocked after writing on dictation. Comparison with other patients shows that this succession varies from case to case, which means that it must be ascertained empirically for each new patient.

In contrast to our procedure with patients M. M. and T. J., we could forego control experiments to check the impaired functions in the case of patient M. J., as he showed complete absence of repetition, agraphia-on-dictation, anomia (orally as well as in writing), and expressive alexia.

One complete protocol of the deblocking experiments carried out with patient M. J. is given in Figure 3.[4] The mistakes can be divided into three main groups: (1) total failures, i. e., the patient is completely unable to repeat, name, write on dictation, etc. (see Figure 3, Papagei, Klammer, Matrosen, Pinsel); (2) in other instances the patient's responses are totally paraphasic ('saleweiniger' instead of 'Matrosen' on repetition), totally paralexic ('ein lebes' instead of 'Globus' when reading aloud), or partially paragraphic ('Pagen' instead of 'Papagei' when writing on dictation); (3) yet, most mistakes are, in fact, true deblocking effects, as they are merely literal-paraphasic or literal-alexic reactions ('Kense' instead of 'Kekse', 'Ladel' instead of 'Nadel', 'Dacke' or 'Dacker' instead of 'Dackel', 'Füchs' instead of 'Fuchs', 'Krägen' instead of 'Kragen', etc.); literal-paragraphic deviations did not occur.

FROM APHASIA TO SCHIZOPHRENIA

	copying	repetition	writing on dictation	oral naming	written naming	reading aloud
I	Wange Jüdel Papagei	"krieg ich nicht"	Per Pagen	legaex	Pagel	nicht möglich
II	Stirn Rumpel Klammer	nicht möglich	a S Klapper	fange	nicht möglict	Kanne
III	Matrosen Tulpe Palme	"saleweinger"	Mali Mali	lege	nicht möglich	trase
IV	Pinsel Wer Sahne	nicht möglich	nicht möglich	lame schekin	S Malen malen Pipe Pinsel	Pinsel
V	n Art Kekse Amsel	Keks	Ax Kekor Kekse	Kekse	Kekse	Kense
VI	Rote hase Decke	Decke	Decke	'ne Decke	Decke	Decke
VII	Sand Nadeln Maus	Nadel	-nadel	Feder..... Stege	nadel	Ladel
VIII	Dackel Bank Falte	'ne Dacke	Dacket	Deckel, Dackel, Deckel	Dackel	Deckel..Dacker
IX	Lilie s Regal Blitz	Dicks	Biltz Blitz	liks	Blitz	Bix
X	globus Rose Buch	Globus	globus globus	der lege..legök	Globus	ein lebes
XI	Stein Schlauch Raupe	'n Strauch..... Strauss	l Schlauch	'n Stauch..... Schlauch	Schlauch	Schlauch
XII	Wolf Fuss nest	Nest	nest	Nest	Nest	Nest
XIII	Krebs Seide gas	Krebs	Krebs Krebs Krebs	'n Krebs	Krebs	Krebs
XIV	Hütte Fuchs Linde	Füchs	Fuchs	Füchs	Fuchs	Füchs
XV	motte Bier kragen	streiger	Kragen Krachen	Krägen	Kragen	Krägen

Figure 3. *Patient M. J. 'Chain' deblocking.*

Results

1. Chain deblocking can be evoked through performances of a variety of preserved receptive or expressive functions.

2. Performances of a single function or, should this be insufficient, of combined functions (e. g., reading and copying) can serve as deblockers.

3. The succession of the performances of impaired functions to be deblocked is not important, as long as the discrete performances can be restored by means of 'simple' deblocking, i. e., not within a 'chain'.

4. In a number of cases, performances of certain impaired functions could not be deblocked except within a 'chain' (for example: oral naming and reading aloud in the case of patient M. J.).

5. In the latter cases the sequence of the links of the chain cannot be interchanged arbitrarily. The d-effect is obtained only if the performance

to be deblocked follows several performances of other functions. The succession of the performances is to be ascertained in each case through preliminary experiments.

Discussion

The study of the deblocking phenomenon appears to be highly suitable for the investigation of the problem of aphasic syndromes. A number of problems concerning the reciprocal relationships between preserved and disturbed speech functions, on the one hand, and relationships between various symptoms of aphasia, on the other hand, can thus be investigated experimentally.

The method of 'simple' deblocking makes use of the fact that verbal decoding, coding, and recoding of the meaning of a given word or sentence may be possible for the aphasic via some 'channels', even though other 'channels' may be 'blocked'. Certain aphasic disturbances can be eliminated for shorter or longer periods through successive experimental linking of intact and impaired functions.

We have shown in detail in earlier papers [175, 179] that the means by which d-effects can be obtained are manifold indeed. It is possible to deblock not only expressive but also receptive impairments via visual as well as auditory, tactile, or verbo-motor analyzers. It was further shown that preserved understanding of words or sentences, naming of objects, repetition, reading, or writing can all serve equally well as deblockers. On the one hand, d-effects can be evoked on the level of receptive functions, (e. g., preserved silent reading can deblock impaired auditory word understanding), while, on the other hand, it is possible to eliminate expressive disturbances through the utilization of preserved performances (e. g., disturbances of repetition through reading aloud). Finally, expressive aphasic disturbances can be deblocked receptively[5], and vice versa (e. g., the inability to read aloud can be deblocked through hearing the words spoken; word deafness may be deblocked through repetition).

Although we carried through our deblocking experiments primarily with verbal performances in the widest sense of this term, deblockers – as well as disturbances to be deblocked – may be nonverbal. It is possible, for example, to deblock disturbances of object naming through perception of corresponding noises (e. g., naming of an animal after having heard the relevant typical animal sounds), or picture-agnosia through hearing the words to be deblocked [177; 178].

These facts comprise a number of important aspects which allow us to draw conclusions regarding the nature of syndromatic disturbances. The numerous interrelations between various discrete functions, functional levels, and analyzers indicate above all – as Goldstein has pointed out repeatedly – that after-effects of brain lesions are disturbances of *systems.*

The qualitative and statistical analysis of data collected from a sufficiently large number of different syndromes would seem a promising approach to the comparative study of the structure of these syndromes.

Going beyond the results that can be attained with the method of 'simple' deblocking, the method of 'chain deblocking' is an instrument for a more comprehensive analysis of the dynamic structure of syndromes. The main feature of the phenomenon of chain deblocking is the fact that single or combined deblocking stimuli can eliminate not only the performance disturbance of one impaired function, as in the case of 'simple' deblocking, but that, in certain cases, the disturbances of several component parts of a given syndrome can be eliminated simultaneously.

Examples of some of our chain deblocking experiments are summarized in Table 1; they illustrate clearly the polyfunctional effect of the deblocking stimuli. In all the cases listed in this table, earlier reading, be it aloud or silent, or hearing the spoken word, in some cases combined with copying, was sufficient to deblock simultaneously the performances of several component parts (up to five) of the respective aphasic syndromes. This is due to the fact that, under certain conditions, the effect of semantic information radiates over the speech-functional system as a whole. This means, for example, that through hearing a word (decod-

Table 1. *Examples of different forms of chain-deblocking.*

Patient	Deblocking functions	Functions to be deblocked →	→	→	→	→
Schw. W.	silent reading and copying	oral naming	written naming			
G. P.	word-hearing and copying	silent reading	reading aloud	oral naming		
M. M.	reading aloud	repetition	writing on dictation	oral naming		
T. J.	reading aloud and copying	oral naming	repetition	writing on dictation		
D. E.	silent reading and copying	repetition	writing on dictation	oral naming		
T. B.	silent reading and copying	writing on dictation	reading aloud	oral naming	written naming	
M. J.	silent reading and copying	repetition	writing on dictation	oral naming	written naming	reading aloud

ing) all other forms of decoding, coding, and recoding of this word – such as receptive understanding, repetition, reading aloud, writing – are simultaneously put into a state of readiness. This process of radiation is to be regarded as a form of simultaneous prestimulation of the 'blocked' channels which favors the deblocking of the impaired speech performances.

The assumption of polyfunctional effects of this kind cannot be restricted to the pathological sphere, but must be regarded as a characteristic feature of the speech-functional system.

In order to understand fully the specificity of this radiation, its *selective* character must be stressed. As indicated above, the verbal deblocking stimuli that we use do not lead to a general functional readiness of the impaired component parts of the speech system. The functional readiness is, in fact, specifically related to the *semantic field* to which the particular verbal deblocking stimulus belongs. The selective character of deblocking or radiating is, therefore, primarily determined by the factor of meaning. These findings seem to confirm Goldstein's thesis of the importance of the problem of meaning in interpretation of disturbances of higher cortical functions. He writes: "Thus, the problem of meaning assumed *central importance* in the interpretation of aphasic symptoms" [53, p. 23]. Using Lotmar's term, Goldstein speaks of a 'sphere of meaning', referring to observations made on patients with amnesic aphasia[6] who produce "other words that belong to the sphere of meaning of the demanded words" [55, p. 47].

In this connection, we must point out that receptive and expressive reactivation of meaning connections by our deblocking method takes place on a level of language behavior that does not permit the use of Goldstein's dichotomy 'concrete-abstract'. Although deblocking enables patients to code, decode, and recode correctly both 'concrete' and 'abstract' meanings, the reactivation of these verbal reactions takes place quasi-automatically, without active and conscious participation of the patient. The verbal behavior of aphasic individuals during the successful deblocking process is similar to that of normal subjects when given the task to understand, repeat, read, or write familiar words or sentences, or to name well-known objects. Goldstein referred to this form of behavior in connection with the 'automatisms' of thinking when he wrote, 'Thereby, not only present events play a role, but also the remnants of previous thinking that were fixed as thoughts in the form of automatisms. They become more or less effective, facilitating the active process of thinking. Thus we have also in thinking to distinguish an active and a passive part. The fixated thoughts often appear in words. That form occurs particularly when the concern is not so much with creation of new concepts but with reproduction of old ones for special purposes . . ." [55, p. 44].

In the case of our deblocking, we are dealing just with this 'reproduction of old ones', i. e., of words or sentences ' in the form of fixed automatisms'.[7] We think we are not mistaken in the assumption that a more profound study of the level of the stored thought and language patterns would lead to a clarification and revision of the problem of so-called concrete and abstract behavior. In such a study the deblocking method might be utilized, along with other methods.[8]

The polyfunctional effects of the speech system also help to explain other penomena of chain deblocking. In our experiments, we found that the *sequence* of the links of the 'chain' plays an important part. Through variation of the sequence of these links we could show that, in certain cases, such as patient M. J., these links cannot be interchanged at will. Only if performances of certain functions are deblocked first can failure in subsequent performances be eliminated. This proves that a positive induction radiates from the disturbed performances as soon as they are deblocked, affects the links that follow, and intensifies the effect of the actual deblocker. It is this *summation* of deblocking effects which is ultimately responsible for the elimination of the impairment of performances of certain severely disturbed functions. At times it is necessary for several pre-deblocked performances to participate in this intensification of the d-effect. In the case of patient M. J., the inability to read a certain word aloud could only be eliminated through his reading the same word first silently, and then copying it (the actual deblocking process), before his inability to write the word on dictation or to use it as the name of an object orally and in writing could be deblocked.

The variety of these phenomena raises a number of questions concerning the structure and dynamics of the speech-functional system, its disturbances, and the possibilities of removing them (deblocking). The interrelations existing within the 'chain' seem to indicate a certain *hierarchy* among the functions involved, a hierarchy which determines for any given disturbance the possibility of its being deblocked and, once deblocked, the likelihood that the regained performance will induce additional positive effects. Without doubt, the final analysis of these interrelations will lead to more definite conclusions concerning relationships within and among syndromes. Statistically significant evidence has yet to be collected and analyzed before the ideas outlined here can be said to contribute comprehensively towards the systematic analysis of the structure and dynamics of these syndromes.

In concluding this paper, written in memory of Kurt Goldstein, I wish to stress once more the sincerity of my feelings for this great man, for whom I cherish a deep love, respect, and gratefulness – the sincerity of which remain unaltered, even though my path in research may deviate from the direction he had shown me many years ago.

Notes

1. In order to avoid 'pseudo-deblocking', one must take into consideration the possible fluctuations of performances. In the control experiments we make sure that disturbances of naming certain pictures do not appear and disappear from one experiment to the next. Thus we carry through quantitative controls in order to assess the extent of the disturbance that is being studied.
2. Only vaguely similar to the use of this term in linguistics, e. g., by Trier, we define 'semantic fields' as ontogenetically developed systems of meaning, comprising not only logical and linguistic but also psychological and social relations, and, therefore, differing from individual to individual.
3. The reports of the Roumanian patients M. M. and T. J., including Fig. 1 and Fig. 2, are taken from ⟨9⟩. These investigations were carried out at the Neurological Institute of the Academy of Science of the Socialist Republic of Roumania (Professor A. Kreindler, Director).
4. These experiments were carried out by my collaborator Erika Metze.
5. In a separate paper ⟨7⟩ we have dealt with the problem of expressive disturbances being deblocked by purely receptive means through the exclusion of even latent speech movements.
6. Nevertheless, it must be stressed that our statements concerning 'semantic fields' are not limited to amnesic aphasia, but apply to all types of aphasia.
7. For the sake of avoiding misunderstandings, it should be pointed out that the abovementioned 'automatisms' are not identical with those showing a complete absence of all meaningful language behavior, e. g., the mere mechanical reproduction of sequences of letters, words or figures, etc., or as Goldstein calls it, 'reproductions of simple associations of sound complexes to a particular object' [55, p. 41].
8. The author in no way excludes his own views of 'concrete' and 'abstract' behavior, published as early as 1927 and 1933 (see ⟨4⟩ and [174]), from this necessity of revision.

⟨11⟩

E. WEIGL

Neuropsychological Approach to the Problem of Transcoding

The fact that we are normally able to change-over, more or less arbitrarily, from one sign-system to another, and to transpose individual sign-units of one into the corresponding units of another code system, often allows us to forget that this is a process of a particular kind. We know that it is not sufficient to acquire and store varying code systems; after this, of decisive importance in processing information is the automation of the ability to switch between these systems, and to match the corresponding sign-units.[1]

In contrast to the neuropsychological study of the processes of *decoding,* that is the recognition and the understanding of the perceived structures, and the *encoding*, that is the implement of structures in the form of certain code-units, the processes of switching and transcoding have, as far as I know, hitherto scarcely been the subject of systematic neuropsychological investigation.

When we speak in this connection of switching, we mean those mechanisms which ensure the correlated change-over from one sign-system to another (and vice versa). Switches of this sort are necessary e. g. when transposing from visual to acoustic systems, from speech systems to nonspeech systems, from spoken to written speech systems, as well as from the systems of a natural language to an artificial language, etc. Our entire life is filled with such permanent processes of change, when we express ourselves in one language and then in another, when we change from spoken address to written record, when we read after a concert the relevant partitura, when we first speak about mathematical facts and then note them in formulae, etc.

The real *transcoding process* only begins when the system-change is linked with the task of creating relations between specific corresponding structures in differing code systems, *of transposing certain prescribed units of one code system into the relevant units of another code system.* This is the case, for instance, when acoustic sign patterns are converted into visual (and vice versa); when certain lexical or syntactical structures of one natural language are converted into another; when one and the same word (sentence) is auditorily perceived and then written down; when a musical phrase is sung or played and observed by ear, and then transcoded in musical notes, etc.

In the present work we shall occupy ourselves primarly with the problem of *transcoding.* In this connection, attention is drawn to certain aspects of these mechanisms, particularly on the level of spoken and written speech, but also marginally in the field of numeral words and figures as well as in the field of tone symbols and musical notes. Our argument in this respect will be based upon clinical neuropsychological evidence.[2]

1. Transcoding on the level of spoken and written speech

The speech-functional system with its varied receptive, reproductive and productive functions, in combination with the differing code systems of spoken and written speech, provide a particularly suitable field for the study of transcoding processes and their disturbance.

Highly-automated processes of system change, of the confrontation between units of spoken speech (lexical and syntactical), etc., may be encountered everywhere in the field of language, for instance in the auditory reception, the stenographic notation and later the typewritten transcription of dictation; in the simultaneous interpretation from one language into one other or several other languages; the transcription in figures of numeral words perceived auditorily or visually; or the transcription in musical notes of tone symbols heard or read. Frequently the standard of professional qualification of a person depends upon the degree of automation of such, and many other, transcoding processes; and in this connection adhesion to a particular code systems (for instance in predominantly acoustically-inclined or visually-inclined persons) and clumsiness in transition, in transposition, etc., can be an obstacle in pursuing various professional activities.

Even the most elementary reproductive speech functions such as repetition and reading aloud, copying and writing on dictation, are based upon more or less complicated transcoding processes.

In reading aloud, receptively perceived verbo-visual structures are converted into the relevant verbo-motoric structures; in writing on dictation the auditorily-perceived structures are converted into the corresponding grapho-motoric innervation patterns. Analogously, in repetition, the perceived verbo-auditory structures are transposed into the relevant verbomotoric ones; and in copying, the verbo-visually perceived structures are transposed into the corresponding grapho-motoric innervation patterns.

Fig. 1 shows schematically the relations which come into question in the speech-functional (and also in the linguistic) respect.

On the basis of one and the same verbo-auditory input, the transcoding can operate in the direction of a corresponding verbo-motoric reproduction (repetition) or a grapho-motoric reproduction (writing on dictation), and analogously can, on the basis of one and the same verbo-visual input bring about a corresponding verbo-motoric reproduction (reading aloud) or a grapho-motoric reproduction (copying). But in these two directions the transcoding can also lead from gnoso-visual input (object, picture) to spoken or written naming, or from an internal input (cognitive, inner speech) to spontaneous speech or writing.

From a linguistic point of view the transcoding processes mentioned here concern the transposition of phonetic or graphemic units into the relevant phonetic-articulatoric or graphemic structures.

The reproductive functions of repetition and copying are, in the linguistic sense, not real transcoding processes, since they both take place at the same level of speech: repetition takes place on the phonetic-articulatoric level, and copying within the graphemic area. The functions of spoken and written naming mean, for the linguist, mainly encoding events in the form of phonetic or graphemic implementation. Linguistics must, in the same way, leave the encoding of mental schemes in verbo-motoric or grapho-motoric structures in spontaneous speech and writing to the field of psychology (neuropsychology, psycholinguistics).

1.1 Methods for Proving Aphasic Transcoding Disturbances

The transcoding processes referred to above demonstrate themselves under normal conditions as typical black-box phenomena. Perception and the understanding of the sense of presented speech patterns are accessible to a certain degree to experimental examination, and the processes of reproducing such structures can be checked to a broad extent on the relevant output performances; but the psychological reality of the transcoding mechanism is as a rule difficult to prove. In this respect, clinical neuropsychological research can make a decisive contribution to clarifying the black box area. The present paper is designed to serve, to some modest degree, this aim.

The basic model from which we proceed is based upon the following considerations. In order to win significant testimony on the status of certain transcoding processes, it must first be ascertained whether, in the cases under consideration, the conditions are even present for using these mechanisms.

Prerequisites of this sort are *not* present, if, when the reproduction of speech structures are abandoned, (a) *input disturbance* is already present, that is if the pattern presented auditorily or visually cannot be

Fig. 1. *Transcoding at the level of spoken and written speech. General schema.*

Input	1	verbo-auditory		verbo-visual	
external	2	phonetic		graphemic	
			word comprehension		
Output	1	verbo-motoric	grapho-motoric	verbo-motoric	grapho-motoric
	2	phon.-artic.	graphemic	phon.-artic.	graphemic
		repetition	writing on dictation	reading aloud	copying
Input external		gnoso-visual		Input internal	
				cognitive-inner speech	
		object recognition		mental schemes	
Output	1	verbo-motoric	grapho-motoric	verbo-motoric	grapho-motoric
		phon.-artic.	graphemic	phon.-artic.	graphemic
		naming		spontaneous speech	spontaneous writing
		oral	written		

Note: 1 functional levels; 2 linguistic levels

adequately grasped, and (b) when the *reproduction process* as such is *generally affected* verbo-motorically or grapho-motorically, that is when these skills are impaired *at all functional levels* (spontaneous speech, repetition, reading aloud, naming, or spontaneous writing, copying, writing on dictation); and it makes no difference whether these are afferent or efferent motoric disturbances (in the sense of Luria and Leonhard). In these cases, in which there is either no suitable input model available for transcoding, or where the verbo-motoric or grapho-motoric damage excludes transposal in general (both forms of disturbance can be simultaneously present), nothing can be said about the status of transcoding itself (see p. 218).

Circumstances can, however, be found in which (1) the *input is intact* and (2) the verbo-motoric or grapho-motoric *output functions are not disturbed at all function levels,* but only with respect to certain channels; that is to say that one and the same offered speech structure can be implemented on one channel (for instance by reading aloud), but not on another channel (for instance by repetition). This means that the relevant transcodings are possible, but only under particular conditions. In this way the transcoding mechanism itself can be made evident with regard to its intactness or disturbance.

In such cases the basic model presents itself thus:

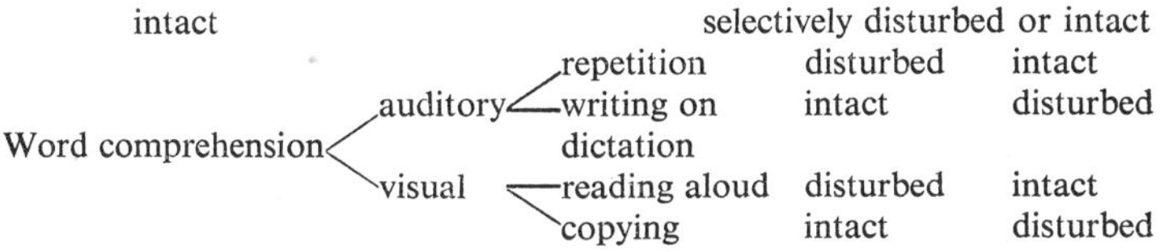

Fig. 2. *Basic model for proving transcoding disturbances.*

Accordingly the first task was to discover patients with the prerequisites (1) and (2). For this purpose I utilised the results of a broadly designed standard examination of about 55 aphasics, based on specially developed testing principles [cf. 197; ⟨5⟩], which I carried out together with my Roumanian friends and colleagues A. Fradis, L. Mihăilescu and N. Gheorghiță [cf. 199].

This test battery, which we created, makes it possible to provide an exact statistical comparison between the various functions participating in receptive and reproductive language processes. These investigations are concerned both with the sound and the literal levels, and also the word and sentence levels. For the problems treated here we refer solely to the lexical level, and here to concrete nouns which allow at the same time the naming of objects.

The fact that each of the speech functions which interests us here was tested separately with the same word material (20 words), provides the advantage that the extent to which one or other of the tested functions is intact or disturbed in each individual patient may be determined quantitatively and comparably. In addition the tests allow us to ascertain whether a particular word can be auditorily or visually understood, repeated, read aloud, copied, written on dictation or used to name an object; and whether, finally, a particular word can be identified in simultaneous auditory and visual presentation.

The results of these tests provide the prerequisites for studying the performances of the patients with regard to the various forms of transcoding auditorily-perceived or visually-perceived word structures into the relevant verbo-motoric or grapho-motoric innervation patterns.

First we selected, on the basis of the results of the standard tests, those patients in whom the input functions, that is auditory or visual word comprehension, were completely or mainly intact (80% to 100% correct responses), while one of the verbo-motoric or grapho-motoric functions was completely or partially impaired (0% to 20%, in a few cases up to 35% correct responses) (cf. Fig. 3). It emerged that a number of patients had intact auditory understanding of a word but could not repeat this word, and other patients could not write it on dictation. In the same way, in one group of patients visual word comprehension was intact, but reading aloud was disturbed. Finally, a few patients under the same conditions were not capable of copying word structures which they had correctly grasped visually.[3]

1.2 Forms of Disturbances in Transcoding

1.2.1 *Input-dependent Disturbances in Transcoding*

The next step in our investigation was to select, from the patients described in Fig. 3 those in which either one of the two verbo-motoric output functions (repetition or reading aloud), or one of the graphomotoric functions (copying or writing on dictation) was disturbed (cf. Fig. 4).

Patient Pa. cannot repeat words spoken to him, although he has no trouble in reading them aloud. Conversely, the patients Ca. C. and Pe. M. can repeat words presented to them, they fail however when they should read the same words aloud. Analogously with the eight patients in the last column: their copying shows little or no disturbance; at the same time their writing on dictation of the same words is completely or seriously affected.

In the cases reported upon here, the transcoding disturbances are thus dependent on the input modality (verbo-auditory or visual), although these functions as such are not generally impaired.

Fig. 3. *Individual correlations between verbo-receptive and verbo-reproductive functions (input intact-output disturbed)*

	input function totally/largely intact word comprehension auditory verbo-receptive	output function disturbed repetition verbo-motoric		input function totally/largely intact word comprehension auditory verbo-receptive	output function disturbed writing on dictation grapho-motoric
patients			patients		
T.E.	100	0	T.E.	100	0
Ma.P.	100	0	Să.V.	100	0
B.U.	100	0	F.A.	100	0
E.D.	100	0	A.V.	100	0
Să.V.	100	5	R.I.	100	0
I.I.	100	5	Si.V.	100	0
M.V.	85	0	Pe.M.	95	0
Pe.M.	85	10	A.St.	100	10
R.I.	100	20	Ca.C.	85	0
			Po.I.	85	0
			M.V.	85	0
			Gü.Gh.	100	20
			J.I.	100	20
			A.C.	100	30

	word comprehension visual	reading aloud		word comprehension visual	copying
T.E.	100	0	F.A.	100	0
B.U.	100	5	A.V.	90	5
Ma.P.	100	5	Pe.M.	85	0
W.M.	100	5			
F.A.	100	20			
J.I.	100	25			
A.V.	90	20			
Pe.M.	85	35			
Ca.C.	80	30			

percentage of correct answers

patients	input function totally/largely intact word comprehension auditory verbo-receptive	output function disturbed repetition verbo-motoric	input function totally/partially intact word comprehension visually verbo-receptive	comparative output function totally/largely intact reading aloud verbo-motoric
Pa.M.	95	10	100	100
	word comprehension visual verbo-receptive	reading aloud verbo-motoric	word-comprehension auditory verbo-receptive	repetition verbo-motoric
Ca.C.	80	30	100	100
Pe.M.	85	35	95	100
	word comprehension auditory verbo-receptive	writing on dictation grapho-motoric	word comprehension visually verbo-receptive	copying grapho-motoric
Sa.V.	100	0	100	100
R.I.	100	0	70	100
Si.V.	100	0	100	90
T.E.	100	0	100	85
Ca.C.	100	15	80	95
Gü.Gh.	100	20	100	95
J.I.	100	20	100	80
A.C.	100	30	100	90
			percentages of correct answers	

Fig. 4. *Selective input-dependent disturbances of transcoding.*

1.2.2 *Output-dependent Disturbances in Transcoding*

Another aspect of selective transcoding disturbance is shown in Fig. 5. This demonstrates that with one and the same intact input (verbo-auditory or verbo-visual), one of the reproductive functions dependent upon this input can be disturbed while the other is intact.

The four patients of the first column perceive spoken words correctly in all cases, and repeat them either completely or mainly correctly; on the other hand their writing on dictation is either completely or seriously disturbed (though copying is largely intact). The three patients of the second column, who show no receptive alexic disturbances in reading words, can copy the words mainly correctly, but fail completely or seriously in reading them aloud (at the same time their repetition is completely intact, or in other cases seriously or completely disturbed).

The results of Fig. 5 demonstrate that the switching from correctly-perceived phonetic word structure to the equivalent phonetic-articulatory word structure (repetition) may be intact; but that it is at the same time disturbed in transcoding into the corresponding graphemic structure (writing on dictation). Analogously the transcoding of the semantically-decoded graphemic structure into the relevant graphemic structure (copying) may be intact, but not into the corresponding phonetic-articulatory structure (reading aloud). In these cases too there is thus a selective impairment in the transposition from a certain receptive function to the reproductive function dependent upon it.[4] The transcoding disturbances of this sort are thus connected with the output modality (verbo-motoric or grapho-motoric), although these modalities themselves are not generally impaired (cf. comparative functions).

1.3 Method of Investigating Direct Transcoding

1.3.1 *From Spoken to Written Speech and vice versa*

In the disturbances in transcoding which we have determined, we are confronted with the question as to the stage of processing between input and output at which this mechanism is interrupted. It might be expected, for instance, that in transcoding disturbances between spoken and written speech the transition from the phonemic to the graphemic level (and vice versa) is affected. The transposal processes of this sort hitherto discussed also demand, however, a system-change from perception to reproduction; they are therefore not suitable for providing an answer to this question. For this purpose we needed the result of a process in which there is a direct transcoding from phonetic to graphemic structures (and vice versa) at the receptive level.

In the framework of the standard test described above, we utilised

Patients	input function totally/largely intact word comprehension auditory verbo-receptive	output function totally/largely intact repetition verbo-motoric	output function disturbed writing on dictation writing on dictation grapho-motoric	comparative output function totally/largely intact copying grapho-motoric
Si.V.	100	85	0	95
Ca.C.	100	100	15	95
Gü.Gh.	100	90	20	95
A.C.	100	95	30	90
	word comprehension visual verbo-receptive	copying grapho-motoric	reading aloud verbo-motoric	totally intact/disturbed repetition verbo-motoric
T.E.	100	85	0	0
J.I.	100	80	25	30
Ca.C.	80	95	30	100
			percentage of correct answers	

Fig. 5. *Selective output-dependent disturbances of transcoding.*

a procedure of this type in the form of audio-visual matching tests [cf. ⟨12⟩; 197]. The procedure is that the patient, after a spoken word has been presented, should select the corresponding visually-offered word from a series of different written words on display. In the reverse test the patient is presented with a word in written form, and a number of words are then spoken, including the word corresponding to that presented; this the patient has to identify.

Fig. 6 shows that patients who fail in the task of reproducing auditorily perceived or visually perceived words at a particular function-level may still be able to carry out correctly audio-visual matching tests. What do these observations tell us about the 'point of fracture' in the processes of transcoding?

Let us take the case of a patient for whom the spoken-written transcoding process is disturbed at a certain function-level between perception and reproduction; if there is a blockage of the transfer from the phonemic to graphemic level then this should show itself in the audio-visual matching tests. It is shown, however, that patients who cannot write on dictation, or can only write to a limited degree, word structures which they have correctly perceived phonetically, as well as patients who completely or largely fail to read aloud the correctly grasped graphemic word structures, are capable of matching correctly these same words after they have been presented audio-visually.

With regard to the 'point of fracture' this result means that it must lie 'beyond' direct audio-visual comparison, and in fact at a point where the task is to implement, on a certain specified channel, the successful transcoding either verbo-motorically or grapho-motorically.

1.4 Dependence of Disturbances in Transcoding upon the Linguistic Levels

Above we spoke in general of intact or disturbed speech functions. We omitted from consideration, however, the fact that these functions can take place at different linguistic levels. Both in speech reception and speech reproduction (and production) at the lexical level the phonologic or graphemic aspect must be distinguished from the semantic aspect. The relative autonomy of phonologic or graphemic word structures compared to their semantic content is shown alone by the observation that normally unknown or senseless word structures (within certain bounds) can be easily repeated, read aloud, copied or written on dictation.

In interpreting transcoding performances in cases of aphasia it is particularly important to take into consideration the two levels mentioned, particularly where there are disturbances of auditory or visual word

patients	input function totally/largely intact Word comprehension auditory verbo-receptive	output function disturbed writing on dictation grapho-motoric	input functions totally/largely intact matching auditory-visual
Să.V.	100	0	100
Si.V.	100	0	100
T.E.	100	0	85
Ca.C.	100	15	90
Pa.M.	85	5	100
Gü.Gh.	100	20	100
J.I.	100	20	100
A.C.	100	30	100
	word comprehension visual verbo-receptive	reading aloud verbo-motoric	matching auditory-visual
B.U.	100	5	100
Ma.P.	100	5	100
J.I.	100	25	100
A.V.	90	20	100
Ca.C.	100	30	90
		percentage of correct answers	

Fig 6. *Immediate verbo-auditory-visual transcoding (input intact-output disturbed).*

comprehension while the patient retains the ability to implement correctly the semantically non-decoded auditory or visual word structures either verbo-motorically (repeating and reading aloud) or grapho-motorically (copying and writing on dictation).

The examples given in Fig. 7 are cases of this sort. In these patients auditory or visual word comprehension is either totally or seriously disturbed, and thus the positive performances of the patients in the corresponding reproduction of these words can only be explained by assuming that solely the phonetic or graphemic aspects of the word structures have been effective [cf. ⟨12⟩].

patients	input function disturbed word comprehension auditory verbo-receptive	output function totally/partially intact repetition verbo-motoric
Tu.V.	5	100
Bo.I.	20	100
Do.M.	25	100
Gh.Gh.	30	80
	word comprehension auditory verbo-receptive	writing on dictation grapho-motoric
Bo.I.	20	90
Tu.V.	0	45
Gh.Gh.	0	40
	word comprehension visual verbo-receptive	reading aloud verbo-motoric
Do.M.	20	100
Gh.Gh.	0	65

patients	input function disturbed word comprehension auditory verbo-receptive	output function totally/partially intact repetition verbo-motoric
	word comprehension visual verbo-receptive	copying grapho-motoric
M.V.	0	100
Gh.Hh.	0	65
Du.M.	0	40
	percentage of correct answers	

Fig. 7. *Non-semantic production at the level of spoken and written language.*

In such cases the patients respond to the meaningful words offered in the same way as normal subjects respond to unknown or meaningless words: in both cases the reproductive process takes place on a non-semantic phonetic or graphemic level. This makes it understandable that a portion of the cases cited in Fig. 7 are able to repeat either mainly or completely correctly, and able to write on dictation either mainly or completely correctly, despite their total or very-limited auditory word comprehension. Other patients, on the other hand, are totally or mainly receptively alexic, but despite this they can read aloud or copy (even transcribing from printed to written script) either correctly or at least partially correctly.

A further confirmation of the findings with regard to transcoding at non-semantic levels can be shown with the aid of audio-visual matching tests mentioned earlier.

The cases shown in Fig. 8 are characterised by the fact that here both auditory and visual word comprehension are simultaneously either totally or seriously disturbed. Even these patients are capable of correctly matching audio-visually the non-understood words; in most cases they could match all words, in two cases the majority.

These positive performances of the patients at the spoken and written level of language depend also upon the working of certain linguistic correspondence relations, described by Gibson *et al.* [48], Bierwisch [14], and others. Here we have a coincidence of neuropsychological and linguistic (psycholinguistic) observations and hypotheses [188; ⟨3⟩].

In establishing a basic model for the proof of transcoding disturbances (see p. 213) we claimed that general impairment in contrast to the selective impairment of verbo-motoric or grapho-motoric reproduction (or both), offered no prerequisites for such proof. This does not, however, exclude the possibility that apart from selective disturbance of

patients	input function disturbed word comprehension auditory	visual	output function totally/largely intact matching auditory-visual
Si.S.	0	0	100
Ta.J.	5	0	100
T.I.	35	35	100
Gh.Gh.	30	0	75
			percentage of correct answers

Note: the values given above (except the pat. Gh. Gh.) refer to experiences at the abstract word level; the differences between the performances of word comprehension and word matching are only evident at this level.

Fig. 8. *Immediate auditory-visual transcoding in cases of disturbed input.*

the transcoding mechanisms there exist also polymodal or even general disturbances. At first sight it might appear that amongst the patients examined by us there are cases of this sort.

Fig. 9 shows cases in which all reproductive performances are completely or largely impaired on the verbo-motoric or grapho-motoric level (with intact auditory and visual word comprehension). In addition, in the case of patient A. V. (also with intact auditory and visual word comprehension), the reproductive performances on all levels are completely or seriously disturbed. Despite this, we are inclined to characterise the disturbances noted in these patients as *secondary impediments* in the transcoding process (in the sense defined above). In all cases we are dealing with the most serious forms of efferent-motoric aphasia and agraphia. In word reproduction the patients get no further than literal-paraphasic sound production; their written expressions are either totally lacking, or are confined to senseless scribbles. Thus in these patients the impairment of output-performances is so strong that it cannot be available for transcoding tasks.

We believe that genuine polymodal or general transcoding disturbances must fulfil the following conditions: it must be proved that verbo-motoric or grapho-motoric reproduction has not been completely suspended. This would, for instance, be the case, if the patients, in transcoding the word structures perceived auditively-intact or visually-intact, had produced only verbal-paraphasic lapses [cf. 3], that is to say they are capable of reproducing sensible words in repetition, reading aloud, naming, or in copying and writing on dictation, but these words do not correspond with the input words. Thus it would be proved that neither the verbo-motoric nor the grapho-motoric as such was affected, but only the selection in the semantic field. Under these circumstances it would have to be investigated whether there were such cases with polymodal or general transcoding disturbances.[5]

2. Transcoding Processes on the Level of numeral Words and Figures

In daily life we use numeral words and figures without it generally being clear to us that this use is dependent upon a complicated interplay of various sign systems. In the same way there is generally little understanding of the complicated relations of systems which has to be grasped by the child in his first years at school in acquiring numeral words and figures – quite apart from their mathematical manipulation. As elements of the spoken and written language the numeral words, both in their spoken and written form, have an analogous status to that of other lexical units within natural languages. This is also true for the transcod-

patients	input functions totally/largely intact word comprehension verbo-receptive: auditory	visual	output functions disturbed verbo-motoric: repetition	reading aloud	naming
T.E.	100	100	0	0	10
Ma.P.	100	100	0	5	5
E.D.	90	85	0	25	20
R.I.	100	70	20	15	5
J.I.	100	100	30	25	0

	word comprehension verbo-receptive: auditory	visual	grapho-motoric: copying	writing on dictation
F.A.	100	100	0	0
Pe.M.	95	85	0	0

	word comprehension verbo-receptive: auditory	visual	repetition	reading aloud	naming	copying	writing on dictation
			verbo-motoric and grapho-motoric				
A.V.	100	100	20	20	25	0	5
					percentage of correct answers		

Fig. 9. *Disturbance of the total verbo-motoric and grapho-motoric reproduction performances (or of both).*

ing processes between the spoken and the written numeral words (see Fig. 10).

The situation is different with reagrd to the conventionally created figure symbols, which, as ideographic signs, form part of another system. In contrast to the signs of the language system they can only be perceived visually, and implemented graphically, without direct connections to spoken or written language. They embody the number system, as individual or combined elements, in their own ideographic manner. Transcoding processes occur at the pure figure level in the form of the matching of figures with equivalent figures (for instance from printed to handwritten, from Roman to Arabic figures, etc.), or in the form of the written transposing of figures (see Fig. 10).

The conversion of numeral words into figures and vice versa entails a considerable complication of the process of transposition. Just as the numeral words, expressed in spoken or written language, can be converted into the corresponding figures, so can the figures be transcoded into the relevant numeral words in spoken or written language. Accordingly, auditorily perceived numeral words can be reproduced as figures, or visually perceived numeral words can be written as figures; conversely, visually presented figures can be read aloud as numeral words, or written as numeral words.[6]

Finally, one and the same discernable quantitiy can be expressed either as a numeral word or as a figure or combination of figures. In the same way auditorily or visually perceived identical numeral words, and visually perceived identical figures can be matched with one another; the matching can also be accomplished between auditorily presented or visually presented numeral words and the corresponding figures.[7]

We have presented the multifold relations between numeral words (auditory and visual) and figures in Fig. 10, in order to draw attention to the wide range of transcoding possibilities which occur in practice in one or the other form. This table shows the degree to which these system-relations become complicated by the addition of the ideographic figure system, compared to the usual spoken-language/written-language relation. It may almost be called a miracle that the brain of a schoolchild can store and automate such a network of transcoding alternatives.

Together with Irina Weigl I have carried out tests on a series of aphasics of various types in order to determine their capacity to perform transcoding between the numeral word system and the figure system.[8]

First it became clear that the patients whom we tested showed no noticeable disturbances in manipulating figures, as long as the tasks set did not demand the simultaneous use of numeral words (auditorily or visually). The patients were able to copy figures correctly, to match quantities of sticks or sums of money (coins and notes) with the

input	1	verbo-auditory		verbo-visual		graphic-visual	
	2	phonetic		graphemic		ideographic	
		numeral word				figure	
output	1	verbo-mot.	grapho-mot.	verbo-mot.	grapho-mot.	grapho-mot.	grapho-mot.
	2	phon.-art.	graphemic	phon.-art.	graphemic	graphic	graphic
	3	repetition	writing on dictation	reading aloud	copying	writing on dictation	copying
		matching					
		numeral word		figure	sets		
		auditory	visual	visual	visual		

Note: 1 and 3: functional levels; 2: linguistic levels.

Fig. 10. *Transcoding at the level of numeral word–figure: general schema.*

corresponding figure cards, or to express them in written figures. Further, they could, in response to questions, even write down in figures a series of personal data, such as age, birthday, house number, telephone number, tram number, shoe size, food prices etc. It should be noted that most of these patients were incapable of understanding or solving the very simplest orally-set calculations.

A particularly impressive example in this connection is patient W., a former teacher: she is able to solve correctly algebraic equations with one unknown, for instance the problems: $a + b = 12$, $a = 2$, $b = ?$; $10 - x = 5$, $x = ?$; $(5 - 2) - (3 - 1) = ?$, etc. When the same problems were set orally the patient failed totally (it should be added that this patient is literal-alexic, that is to say that she does not recognise letters as letters, but does recognise them as algebraic symbols).

Compared to such positive performances in dealing with figures, the patients tested by us showed in some cases severe or complete breakdown of the capacity to understand, repeat, read aloud or write on dictation numeral words presented auditorily or visually, or to match numeral words with sticks or sums of money.

After these preliminary investigations we carried out with the patients the following transcoding experiments:

(1) Matching auditorily presented numeral words with the corresponding figure cards.

(2) Written transposition (writing on dictation) into figures of auditorily presented numeral words.

(3) Written transposition (copying) into figures of visually presented numeral words.

(4) Reading aloud of figures.

(5) Written transposition of figures into numeral words.

Since the breakdown in manipulating numeral words was total in a few cases only (for instance in writing on dictation in numeral words), but otherwise it was partial, the transcoding tests produced total failure in a few cases (for instance the written transposal of figures into numeral words), but otherwise partial failure (between 40% and 80% incorrect responses).

The results summarised here already show that the disturbance of figure/numeral-word transposition in the patients tested by us is aphasically-conditioned; that is to say that the aphasic disturbances have their full effect on the numeral words, while the elements of the ideographic figure system are not affected by these disturbances. This means that the transcoding difficulties noted here are really of secondary nature, compared to the greater or lesser blockage of the access to the numeral word system.

It may be assumed that in the cases of occipitally or parieto-occipitally damaged patients – amongst our patients there were none with such lesions – there would be, in reversal, disturbances in the field of figure symbols, while the use of numeral words remains intact. In such cases too there must be transposition difficulties of a *secondary* nature.

Further research must be undertaken to determine whether there are 'genuine' transcoding disturbances in the field of numeral-word/figure transposition. In such cases the receptive and the reproductive functions should not be affected either on the numeral word level or on the figure level; all that should be affected would be the processes of transcoding the relevant units.

3. Transcoding Processes on the Level of tone Symbols and musical Notes (see Fig. 11)

Tone symbols, like numeral words, are the conventionally-created signs for tones in spoken and written language. The relations shown in Fig. 1 and Fig. 10 apply also to tone symbols with certain exceptions discussed below.

The conventionally-created musical notes are, like the figures, ideographic signs, exclusively visually-perceptible and graphically-implementable, without direct connections in spoken or written language. They form elements or element-combinations of the system of musical notes. The convertibility of tone symbols into musical notes and vice versa has been conventionally determined. Auditorily or visually perceived tone symbols can be written as musical notes, and conversely, visually perceived musical notes can be verbalised or written as tone symbols. Tone symbols presented auditorily or visually can be matched with visually presented musical notes.

Just as it is possible to match auditorily or visually perceived tone symbols with the corresponding tones or sequences of tones, so can the visually perceived musical notes be matched with the corresponding tones or sequences of tones. In the same way tone symbols and musical notes can be interpreted musically (by singing or playing), and tones can be fixed verbally or in writing in the form of tone symbols, or graphically as musical notes.

As the schematic summary of transcoding alternative shows (see Fig. 11), all possible transitions between tone symbols and musical notes are still more complicated than those between numeral words and figures, since here there is added the direct relation between tones and tone symbols, and tones and musical notes.

I myself have conducted no investigations into cortically-caused disturbances of transcoding performances in the field of tone symbols and

input	1 2	verbo-auditory phonetic		verbo-visual graphemic		graphic-visual ideographic	
		tone symbols				musical notes	
output	1 2 3	verbo-mot. phon.-art. repetition	grapho-mot. graphemic writing on dictation	verbo-mot. phon.art. reading aloud	grapho-mot. graphemic copying	grapho-mot. graphic writing on dictation	grapho-mot. graphic copying
		matching					
input	1 3	tone symbols auditory visual naming oral written	tones auditory singing playing	musical notes visual writing of notes			

Note: 1 and 3: functional levels; 2: linguistic levels.

Fig. 11. *Transcoding at the level of tone symbols – musical notes – tones: general schema.*

musical notes. In the literature there can be found only relatively few, and mainly rather incomplete, findings in this respect [cf. 95].[9] I regard as still the most productive the reports by E. Feuchtwanger [39] in his well-known work *Amusie,* in particular the experimental testing of his two patients. In the case of the patient L. H., a pianist with motor aphasia, Feuchtwanger observed that she recognised music notes correctly, matched them correctly into tones, could also find the corresponding keys on the piano, and could play from sheet music; on the other hand she was to a large extent unable to understand tone symbols, to find them on the keyboard (she could only match visually presented tone symbols with the corresponding key), to name tones by their tone symbols or to write tone symbols either spontaneously or on dictation. The matching of tone symbols and musical notes had been impaired, as had reading aloud both from musical notes and tone symbols.
The author ascribes the disturbances of his patient to an impairment of the 'sound-name-function', that is to say solely to the acoustic function and not the visual function. Unfortunately, his material does not show clearly whether the use of the visually presented tone symbols was in fact intact, or less disturbed than the auditorily presented tone symbol. In any case this patient's ability to manipulate musical notes was relatively intact, but the language-based tone symbol had been largely blocked, both receptively and reproductively, by the aphasic disturbance of the subject.

The transcoding disturbances experimentally observed by Feuchtwanger may therefore well be, analogously with the numeral-word/figure disturbances of our patients, of a *secondary* nature, dependent upon the impairment of the speech-functional system.

Systematic investigations in the field of tone-symbol/music-notes relationship would undoubtedly be a suitable way of gaining additional important information with regard to the transcoding problem, information which probably would also be of interest from the music-pedagogic viewpoint.

Discussion

The results communicated above on the examination of aphasic patients can be summed up in the following conclusions (see Fig. 12):

1.1 The uttering of one and the same word can be disturbed after auditory presentation (repetition), but intact after visual presentation (reading aloud) (see Fig. 12:1).

1.2 The writing of one and the same word can be intact after visual presentation (copying), but disturbed after auditory presentation (writing on dictation) (see Fig. 12:2).

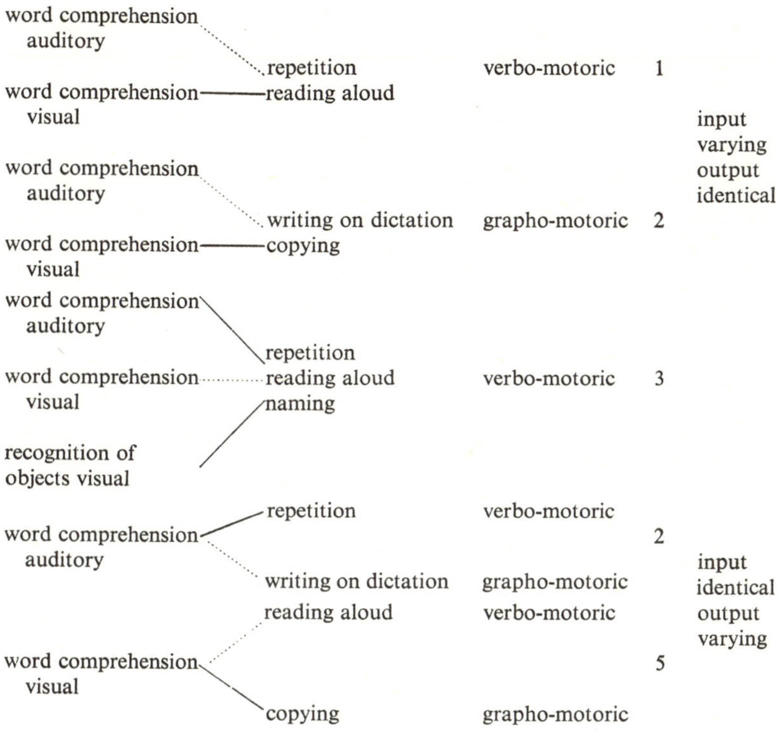

Fig. 12. *Schema of input- or output-dependent transcoding disturbances.*

2.1 After auditory presentation the uttering of a word can be intact (repetition), and writing of the word disturbed (writing on dictation) (see Fig. 12:3).

2.2 After visual presentation the uttering of a word (reading aloud) can be disturbed, but the writing of the same word (copying) intact (see Fig. 12:4).[10]

These conclusions show:

(a) Both the verbo-motoric and grapho-motoric reproduction of words can be selective, that is impaired dependent upon the *input* modus.

(b) With one and the same input (auditory or visual) the verbo-motoric or grapho-motoric reproduction can be selective, that is blocked dependent upon the *output* modus.

The dependent nature of the disturbance is connected in a part of the cases with the input modus (1.1, 1.2 and 1.3),[11] and in other cases with the output modus (2.1 and 2.2), although, as noted, neither of these function levels is the cause for the breakdown of the relevant reproduction performances.

We regarded this finding as a proof that the disturbances referred to are due to *selective impairment of the transcoding processes.*

Taking as examples the cases in which the transposition of phonetic into graphemic structures (writing on dictation) was not successful, we can show that in these patients the failure was not due to the inability to switch from one linguistic level to another. The results of our audiovisual matching tests, in which these patients all had positive performances, show that direct audio-visual transcoding is intact in their cases. This tells us that the disturbance first appears after the transition from one linguistic level to another; this occurs when the correctly perceived word structures, transcoded at the receptive level, must be transformed into the equivalent verbo-motoric or grapho-motoric innervation pattern, a process which we also regard as transcoding.

We have repeatedly shown, however, that transformations of this type are certainly possible on certain function levels. Thus the impairment in the evocation of the corresponding innervation pattern of a verbo-motoric or grapho-motoric nature can only lie in the *disturbed relation between the already transcoded pattern* (for instance phonetic-graphemic) *and the innervation pattern to be triggered.* In certain patients or groups of patients, one or the other of these relations can be selectively impaired.

From the results of our experiments we can conclude that the transcoding processes depend not only upon the function level but also upon the linguistic level. It might have been expected that patients whose word understanding is disturbed both auditorily and visually would not be capable of identifying equivalent spoken and written words presented to them. Experience shows, however, that in a majority of the cases correct matching is nevertheless possible.[12] The word structures are therefore identified exclusively on the basis of their phonemic-graphemic correspondence relations; the transcoding takes place on this level.

In the present investigation we could, however, display only a very limited segment from the relations of dependence between the linguistic levels and transcoding. This may be explained by the particular test circumstances to which we refer:

(1) The functions of repetition, reading aloud, copying and writing on dictation constitute only a relatively elementary reproductive form of language use. The clinical-neuropsychological knowledge gained in connection with these functions is valid for the time being only for this level, and cannot be projected without further ado on other function levels (for instance spontaneous speech and writing).

(2) Although our standard test to which we have referred also includes tests on the literal and sentence levels, and takes in abstract words, we have relied here in our evaluation solely on the results obtained when presenting concrete individual words. This thus represents a limitation to a certain linguistic level, the lexical level, and further to a certain word category (concrete nouns). It is well known that aphasic disturbances of reproductive functions can take differing forms with varying classes of words and in varying syntactical connections. Patients who achieve positive results with nouns on all channels fail in the reproduction of words of the so-called lexical subclasses (conjunctions, prepositions etc.) and also in dependence upon the syntactical and semantic structure of the context [cf. for example 86; 119; ⟨3⟩ 203].

Our remarks on numeral words/figures and tone symbols/musical notes demonstrate, with regard to transcoding problems, certain common factors and on the other hand certain typical differences in comparison with spoken and written speech.

We must admit that our analysis of the test results given above is a description of facts rather than an interpretation. A neuropsychological explanation of these facts would have demanded details of the cortical damage of the various groups of patients in which one or the other form of transcoding disturbance occurs. For this there is not sufficient data on the patients examined by us (mainly vascular patients with predominantly motor or mixed aphasia). It must be left to future experiments to seek, when fixing the groups of patients, how one or the other form of transcoding disturbance has a certain connection with corresponding cortical damage.[13]

It must be emphasized, however, that even when section findings are available for the interpretation of varying transcoding disturbances, which allow conclusions to be drawn with regard to certain localized correlations, this will not be of much help in clarifying the cortical representation of the mechanisms of the sort described here. For the time being we lack properly-founded hypotheses, for instance for the way in which code systems and their alternating relations are 'fixed' in the human brain; how we should picture the long-term cerebral storage of these units which can be transcoded from one sign system to another; how the highly automated retrievability of such units is achieved; and which brainfunctional mechanisms form the basis of the ability to change systems, etc.[14]

The answers to these and innumerable further questions of this sort will undoubtedly be an important field for future inter-disciplinary research, though basic preliminary work has already been done with regard to the problem of system change in the areas of neurophysiology, neurobiochemistry, and also in neuropsychology. An all-round survey of the results of modern brain research in these fields is given in the works of Luria [112; 113] and Pribram [137] and others.

In this connection I would like to draw attention to an area of research with particular prospects, commissurotomy, a field which also deals with certain transcoding processes between the two hemispheres, particularly in the sector of language [153; 158].

A further neuropsychological problem, the solution of which is of decisive importance for the study of transcoding mechanisms, is the ontogenesis of these processes. The acquisition of correlating sign systems and the automated ability to change systems, together with the aimed transcoding of sign patterns, presume extremely complicated learning processes. How, for instance, does a child acquire the ability to switch from one speech function to another, from one linguistic level to another, or to reproduce certain verbal structures, etc.? What mechanisms must be fixed in the long-term storage systems for this?

In the sense of genetic neuropsychological research we are inevitably confronted with the question as to the connections between the facts hitherto known about brain maturation, and the development in childhood of the transcoding mechanisms referred to here, particularly in the speech sector [cf. 98].

Here we must content ourselves with drawing attention to the still scarcely surveyable complex of problems resulting from investigation of the transcoding processes, and to hope that the present work will, in this respect, give the reader certain stimuli and impulses.

Notes

1. The various code terms used in this paper – derived from communication engineering and information theory – have become acclimatised in most branches of modern science. For instance Steinbuch [159, p. 66] defined from the cybernetic standpoint the term 'code-convertor' in the sense of a transformation of information from one code into another with specific mention of translation processes in the language field. From the viewpoint of work psychology Hacker [60, p. 233] speaks of 'transcoding in the true sense'; here he ascribes the transformation performances to an 'independent function' everywhere 'where the task has as its main content the transcoding from one language system (code) into another'. The author adds that these transcoding processes are still 'little known'. Using methods of mathematical linguistics, Chomsky and Miller [29] have undertaken the attempt to prove the justification for transferring the code concept into the field of natural languages (see the chapter 'Some Algebraic Aspects of Coding', 1963: 277 et seq.).

   In our investigation the code concept is given a certain – perhaps not quite unproblematic – broadening, when we proceed on the assumption that differing speech functions (for instance speech reception and speech reproduction), possess varying code systems, and that therefore the transpositions from perceived to reproduced units can be given the status of transcoding processes. Whatever attitude may be taken to this broadening of concept, the fact is undeniable that the conversion of a perceived speech structure into the corresponding verbo-motoric or grapho-motoric innervation pattern is conditional upon system change and transposal processes [cf. 31].

2. Certain aspects of these analyses were already communicated under the title 'Neuropsychological Experiments on Transcoding between Spoken and Written Language Structures' ⟨12⟩.
3. Here and in the following quantitative reports on results we shall not deal in detail with the question as to whether general conclusions can be drawn from the number in each group of patients who fulfil the relevant conditions – for instance disturbance of repetition with concomitant intact word comprehension – along the lines that under these circumstances certain reproductive disturbances occur more often than others (for instance dictatagraphic disturbances more frequently than repetition disturbances). Although the composition of the patients tested by us was not specially selected, it shows certain specific qualities (for instance a relatively small proportion of sensoric-aphasic patients), so that generalisations can only be made with caution. In addition we have cited as examples only those cases in which the correlation appeared particularly obvious.
4. Selective transcoding disturbances can naturally affect simultaneously more than one output function. In two cases (patient A. St. and patient Le. T.) with completely or largely intact word comprehension we found repetition intact, but reading aloud and naming seriously impaired. In another case (patient Pa. M.) repetition and naming were mainly disturbed, though reading aloud was completely intact.
5. Among the patients examined by us there were none who fulfilled these conditions.
6. In practice some of us feel the effect of the complicated nature of this conversion process when we have to fill out a cheque not only in figures but also in words; we are completely accustomed to the verbalisation of figures, but writing them down, a process which is generally little automated, gives us trouble.
7. The order of the figures in figure combinations does not always follow, in all natural languages, the order in which they are verbalised (in German, for instance the figure units 13–99, with the exception of the round tens, are inverted in speech in comparison to the figure combination).
8. This examination has not yet been completed; for this reason only a few provisional results are given here.
9. Wertheim and Botez (1961) have constructed a music test battery consisting of 45 different individual tests, designed for the musical training of patients with amusia. The authors have published the test results attained by two persons with brain damage whom they examined. For our special aim these results are not conclusive, since in one case the patient was a musician without any musical training, and in the other the patient had suffered no noticeable impairment in transcoding performances in the field of note naming, musical notes and tone sequences.
10. Of the variants theoretically possible we found that the following were not represented amongst the patients we examined:

    (a) with intact word-reading capacity: reading aloud intact, copying disturbed;

    (b) with intact auditory word comprehension: writing on dictation intact, repetition disturbed;

(c) with intact auditory and visual word comprehension: writing on dictation intact, copying disturbed. There are cases in which writing on dictation is intact and copying disturbed, but only where there is at the same time disturbance of visual word comprehension, that is to say receptive alexia.

The lack of these variants shows that under our conditions copying-agraphia is coupled with expressive alexia, dictatagraphia with copying-agraphia and with repetition disturbances. A generalisation of these findings does not seem required, since it is not certain whether a broadening of the number of patients (using the same examination method), would not also produce the missing variants [cf. for instance 64].

11. For the sake of completeness we have, in Fig. 12, included in the schema verbomotoric function of oral naming (compared to repetition and reading aloud). The situation characterised in Fig. 12/13 is displayed by patient Ca. C., whose auditory and visual word comprehension and visual picture recognition are mainly or completely intact, as are repetition and oral naming, while reading aloud is severely impaired (20% correct responses). (See also Footnote 4).
12. Amongst all the patients examined we found only 4 cases in which audio-visual matching (with simultaneous breakdown of auditory and visual word comprehension) failed completely (see ⟨12⟩), where transcoding was therefore not possible on the phonemic-graphemic level.
13. Luria [112] shows interesting steps in this direction. In connection with writing on dictation, which he also describes as the result of a transcoding process [112:74], and particularly with regard to dictatagraphia, he describes the brain-dynamic conditions for these conversion mechanisms and their disturbance.
14. In Geschwind's paper 'Neurological Foundations of Language' [46] we can find certain answers concerning the problem of the cerebral representation of transcoding processes, especially with reference to the cortico-cortical connections. In this paper Geschwind writes: "We might almost say that the method of coding changes at each group neurons . . ." [47:190].

⟨12⟩

E. WEIGL

Neuropsychological Experiments on Transcoding between Spoken and Written Language Structures

It is well known that the problem of transcoding, i. e., of converting units in one code system into the corresponding units in another code system, plays a crucial part in the most varying forms of the use of signs, above all in human laugage. One particular aspect of the phenomenon of transcoding are those processes upon which is based the conversion of units from the spoken sign system into the corresponding units of the written sign system and vice versa. For example, when writing to dictation, auditorily perceived units are converted into corresponding graphemic units, and when reading aloud visually perceived graphemic items are converted into equivalent phonetic structures. In these forms of transcoding it is always the case that, for the given pattern in one of the two linguistic sign systems, the pattern corresponding to it in the other system has to be found and realized either verbo-motorically in reading aloud or grapho-motorically in writing to dictation. The fact that finding the corresponding graphemic and phonetic structures is normally more or less automatic to the skilled reader and writer should not induce us to underestimate the complexity of the underlying neuropsychological and psycholinguistic processes. This is shown particularly clearly in the construction of these operations during the school years and their decomposition under cerebral pathological conditions in cases of aphasia, alexia and agraphia.

From the neuropsychological point of view, the acquisition of the ability to convert the auditory or visual perception of linguistic signs into the grapho-motoric or verbo-motoric innervation pattern presupposes the development of complicated functional brain systems [see 117, p. 28 ff.; 188, p. 47 ff.], which in the course of the implied speech functions becoming automatic, are gradually reduced and simplified [188, p. 47 ff.]. in cases of brain damage there may be impairment to a greater or lesser degree of the ability to switch from one functional level to the other, even if both of the levels themselves remain intact. In collaboration with A. Fradis (unpublished) I was able to show this by experimental work on transcoding disorders in cases of agraphia to dictation. The experiments showed that a number of aphasics were unable to write down words to dictation, although both their input function, i. e., their auditory word comprehension, and their output function, i. e., their writing ability (for example in copying) were not impaired. In other words, what failed to function was obviously the transfer mechanism from the verbo-auditory to the grapho-motoric functional level [see 188, p. 94 ff.].

The analysis of the neuropsychological conditions on transcoding between written and spoken language needs to be supplemented by a psycholinguistic study to explain the objective relations between the two linguistic sign systems. The finding of corresponding graphemic and phonemic structures mentioned above presupposes that within the system of every natural language which uses alphabetic writing there are regular correspondences between the graphemes and the phonological segments. Bierwisch [14] has carried out the first analysis, as exemplified by written and spoken German, of the question of which units of the phonetic structure the graphemes are actually related to and what conditions this relation is subject to (p. 22 ff.). He came to the conclusion "that the relation of the phonetic to the graphemic structure, the transcoding of spoken into written language, and vice versa, is mediated by a complex network of relations formulated in terms of GPC rules" (i. e., graphemic-phonological correspondence rules) (p. 14). Bierwisch states a number of important correspondence rules for German, together with exception rules to supplement them.

These linguistic findings on the existence of rules for relating the graphemic and phonological levels are crucial to understandig how the transcoding processes discussed in the present article come about. Graphemic-phonological transcoding processes can only take place at all on the condition of the proper working of such rules. From the neuropsychological point of view this in turn means that these rules must become established in the long-term memory storage of the child during the acquisition of the written language at school and must be gradually made available for all kinds of switching processes between spoken and written language functions [see 188, p. 51 ff.].

The present article is aimed at examining the working of the rules relating graphemic and phonetic structures with the aid of a special method used on brain damaged patients with certain disorders affecting language. The method consists of matching auditorily perceived words with the corresponding written words. Our aim was to study the behaviour of aphasics whose input functions had broken down on the semantic level, i. e., auditory and visual word comprehension (sensory-aphasic word deafness and simultaneous receptive alexia). In other words we asked the question whether aphasics who can neither understand the words spoken by the experimenter nor grasp the meaning of the corresponding written words are able to relate these words to each other correctly. This was intended to enable us to find out whether inability to decode semantically causes a breakdown of transcoding between the spoken and written modes, or whether transfer processes of this kind are possible even under these conditions, i. e., on the graphemic-phonological level only.

In addition, we included in the analysis of our results patients whose auditory or visual word comprehension alone was impaired (word deafness without receptive alexia and vice versa). For these patients the task consisted in assigning a word not understood auditorily to the corresponding word understood visually, and vice versa. The results of the experiments with these patients were intended to lead to conclusions on the transcoding processes between written and spoken language which take place during confrontation between graphemic and phonetic word structures.

The following is based on the quantitative results of a standard examination worked out by me in collaboration with my Rumanian colleagues A. Fradis, L. Mihăilescu and N. Gheorghiţă (see Weigl and Fradis [197]; Weigl, Fradis, Mihăilescu and N. Gheorghiţă [199]; Weigl ⟨5⟩) and tested on more than 50 aphasics. Some of the tests included in this standard examination concern the matching of individual spoken and written words. The standard examination also includes, inter alia, certain methods for the separate testing of auditory and visual word comprehension and of repetition and reading aloud, all tests using the same concrete and/or abstract word material.

The 54 patients tested by this standard examination, according to our general assessment, included the following types of aphasia[1]: motor aphasia – 23 patients; sensory aphasia – 9 patients; mixed aphasia – 13 patients; amnestic aphasia – 4 patients; 'pure' alexia (i. e., alexia with intact auditory word comprehension, repetition and writing to dictation – 5 patients).

Preliminary Examination: Testing of auditory and visual Word Comprehension

Words used

To determine the ability of the aphasics with regard to the task of matching equivalent spoken and written words it was necessary to know to what extent the patients understood auditorily and visually the words they had to match. In a number of cases total or severe word comprehension disorders are to be expected only on the abstract level (e. g., with words such as *enmity, patriotism, sadness, aim,* etc.). We therefore carried out our examination of some of the patients using both concrete and abstract words (see Table 2).

A total of 20 concrete and 20 abstract words were chosen, using the same word material auditorily and visually.

Experimental method

Concrete words: The patient was given a word orally. He had to explain the meaning of this word using the means at his disposal, either verbally or, if he was unable to do this, by gestures or drawings etc.

Abstract words: Since the comprehension of abstract words in cases of aphasia cannot usually be tested directly, i. e., verbally or by gestures, drawings, etc., we were obliged to use a more complicated, indirect method in our examination. The patient had to match a word spoken by the experimenter to a synonym spoken among several words, i. e., by saying 'yes', nodding the head, etc., in order to indicate the matching word. For example, the Rumanian word *duşmanie* ('enmity') was spoken and the patient was asked whether *duşmanie* matches with *cununie* ('wedding'), *vrăşmăşie* (synonym of 'enmity') or *invidie* ('envy'). He had to answer 'yes' when the word *vrăşmăşie* was spoken. In the test of visual word comprehension the same method was used as in the test of auditory word comprehension, except that the words were presented in writing.

Results of the preliminary examination

Apart from a group of patients whose auditory and visual word comprehension was intact, we were able to identify the following groups with total or severe impairment of word comprehension.

Group I. simultaneous, bimodal breakdown of auditory and visual word comprehension, i. e., word deafness with alexia simultaneously (11 patients, including 6 with mixed, 2 with motor and 3 with sensory aphasia).

Group II. Unimodal word comprehension impairment (12 patients).

Group IIa: impairment of visual word comprehension without impairment of auditory word comprehension, i. e., receptive alexia without word deafness (7 patients, including 5 alexics, one patient with sensory and one with motor aphasia).

Group IIb: impairment of auditory word comprehension without impairment of visual word comprehension, i. e., word deafness without receptive alexia (5 patients, including two with sensory, two with amnestic and one with motor aphasia).

Main Experiments: Test of relating Spoken and Written Language on Word Level

Words used

The words used in these experiments are the same as in the word comprehension tests, i. e., the same 20 concrete and 20 abstract words already tested with regard to semantic comprehension were spoken and at the same time shown in writing by the experimenter, and had to be matched with each other by the patients.

Experimental method

From a series of different items in a particular mode (auditory or visual) that item had to be selected which corresponded to a particular item which was presented at the same time but was hetero-modal. We worked on the principle of reversal by interchange of modes.

Variant 1. The word group from which a particular word had to be chosen consisted of three words presented in writing. The patient had to indicate (by pointing out the word in question) which of these three words corresponded to the word spoken by the experimenter.

Variant 2. The word group from which a particular word had to be chosen consisted of three words spoken by the experimenter. The patient had to indicate (by nodding the head on hearing the word in question) which of the words spoken corresponded to the word presented in writing.

Carrying out two variants of the series of tests is on the one hand a form of re-testing method. On the other hand, it takes into account the known fact that in certain patients transcoding may take place in one direction but not – or at least only to a negligible degree – in the other direction. It is thus possible, even with patients whose ability to perform the task in one direction is blocked, to include their more or less correct answers for the other variant in the analysis.

Overall results of the auditory-visual matching experiments

For the aphasic patients we examined the total number of correct matching performances was very high (approx. 85%).

Completely or largely correct matching was achieved by approximately 65% of all patients.

Only 5 patients failed completely in these experiments (see discussion below).

Results of the auditory-visual matching performances of the two groups of patients (see Table 1A)

Group 1. Of the 11 patients in whom both auditory and visual word comprehension on concrete and/or abstract word level had totally or largely broken down (between 0 and 35% correct answers), i. e., in cases of simultaneous word deafness and receptive alexia, nine achieved partially, largely or completely correct matching performances for one or both variants. Only two patients in this group failed completely in both variants of the test, both in the cause of concrete and of abstract words (see discussion).

Table 1. *Group Comparison for (A) Word Comprehension and Auditory-Visual Matching and (B) Repetition and Reading Aloud**

			(A)				(B)		
			Word comprehension		Auditory–visual matching				
	Pat.		auditory–visual		Variant 1	Variant 2	Repe-tition	Reading aloud	c/a
	S.S.	(1)	0	0	100	80	50	15	a
	C.C.	(2)	5	0	100	100	85	40	a
	T.J.	(3)	5	0	45	100	0	25	a
	A.St.	(4)	10	30	75	50	80	10	a
	T.I.	(5)	35	35	100	75	90	65	a
	V.M.	(6)	20	15	60	35	100	65	c
gr.I	Gh.Gh.	(7)	30	0	75	85	80	65	c
	Do.M.	(8)	25	20	50	–	100	100	c
	T.V.	(9)	5	0	0	40	100	25	c
	O.I.	(10)	0	0	0	5	90	5	a
	D.St.	(11)	0	0	0	0	100	0	a
	Di.M.	(12)	100	0	100	100	100	0	a
	Gh.M.	(13)	100	0	85	–	100	0	c
	N.T.	(14)	100	0	55	75	100	45	c
	W.M.	(15)	100	0	50	80	100	0	c
gr.IIa	M.V.	(16)	85	0	70	15	0	0	c
	L.T.	(17)	95	0	5	–	100	5	c
	I.I.	(18)	100	20	15	–	5	0	c
	P.M.	(19)	0	75	95	100	0	95	a
	L.D.	(20)	10	90	65	95	100	100	a
gr.IIb	M.M.	(21)	0	45	100	95	0	70	a
	B.I.	(22)	20	70	100	100	100	95	c
	Z.I.	(23)	0	85	90	0	5	75	c

* Relative frequency of correct responses. Key: a – abstract words; c – concrete words (cf. Table 2); – not tested.

Group II. There were two groups of patients with unimodal word comprehension impairment.

Group IIa. There were seven patients with total breakdown of visual word comprehension and largely or fully intact auditory word comprehension (receptive alexia without word deafness).

In five patients from this group the number of correct matching performances varied between 50% and 95% for Variant 1, and for Variant 2 the figure reached 80% in three cases. Total failure occurred in two patients in this group (see discussion).

Group IIb. In the five patients of this group auditory word comprehension had largely or totally broken down, with partial or largely intact word reading comprehension (word deafness without receptive alexia). The number of correct matching performances of the five patients in this group varied for Variant 1 between 65% and 100%. For Variant 2 the figure reached 90–100% in 4 cases. In three cases the rate of correct matching performances was even higher than for the visual word comprehension performances. In this group no patient failed completely in the matching tests.

The fact that in half the patients of Groups I and II the results for both variants correspond confirms the validity of our statement that the matching of spoken and written words is possible even if there is bimodal and unimodal word comprehension impairment. We may further state that such a possibility depends in certain cases on the 'direction' in which the experiments are carried out. This is seen most clearly in patient Z. I. (23) (see Table 1 A), whose correct matching performances for Variant 1 are 90% but are totally lacking for Variant 2. The explanation of these differences must be the subject of further research.

Table 2 shows that in a number of cases the auditory or visual word comprehension impairment only becomes clearly apparent on the abstract word level, and that the differences between the rate of word comprehension impairment and that of the correct matching performance between spoken and written words can thus only be established on this level. [On the other hand the case of Patient Di. M. (12) shows that there are patients whose performance is the same with concrete as with abstract words.]

Summary of the experimental results

1. In the aphasics examined as a whole (54 patients) the relative frequency of correct auditory-visual matching was very high (approx. 85%). Completely or largely correct matching occurred in 60% to 70% of all cases. Only five patients failed completely.

Table 2. *Comparison of Results Using Concrete and Abstract Words**

	Concrete words				Abstract words			
	Word comprehension		Auditory-visual matching		Word comprehension		Auditory-visual matching	
Pat.	Auditory	Visual	Var. 1	Var. 2	Auditory	Visual	Var. 1	Var. 2
C.C. (2)	100	80	80	90	5	0	100	100
T.I. (5)	85	90	80	55	35	35	100	75
I.I. (19)	85	100	100	75	0	75	95	100
L.T. (20)	95	90	100	100	10	90	65	95
M.M. (21)	70	80	50	75	0	45	100	90
T.J. (3)	55	45	35	55	5	0	45	100
S.S. (1)	5	5	45	50	0	0	100	100
Di.M. (12)	100	0	95	80	100	0	100	100

* Relative frequency of correct responses.

2. All patients without word comprehension impairment (auditory or visual) carried out the matching tasks correctly.

3. Of the 11 patients whose auditory and visual word comprehension had totally or largely broken down (Group I), the rate of correct answers was between 75% and 100% in five cases (Variant 1).

4. Of the 12 patients with unimodal word comprehension impairment (Group II), eight patients succeeded in 70% and 100% of cases in matching the words correctly.

5. The results for the two variants (see Table 1 A) are not entirely comparable, because in some cases only Variant 1 was used; in the case of the other patients the auditory-visual test results of half the patients in Groups I and II correspond fully or largely (differences of between 0 and 20%); in the other cases the differences vary between 25% and 55%, except for one patient (Z. I. (23)) who failed completely with Variant 2. His rate of correct answers with Variant 1 was 90%.

6. It was confirmed that for a series of patients the difference between the rate of word comprehension impairment (auditory or visual) and the rate of correct matching between auditory and visual words was only evident on the abstract word level, so that in these cases the possibility of correct transcoding performance in cases of bimodal and unimodal word comprehension impairment could only be proved on this level.[2]

Discussion

What is of interest first of all is the fact that the task of matching auditory and visual words was carried out correctly by our patients to a surprisingly great extent (on average in 85% of the cases in relation to the total number of items presented). This result seems surprising to us even in those cases of aphasia in which auditory and visual word comprehension is intact, but in which, spontaneous speech and writing are more or less seriously impaired. In view of the serious disorder to the speech functional system in aphasia, the fact that such a relatively complex function as the transcoding of spoken and written language has not suffered in such a large number of patients (approx. 65%), allows us to draw certain conclusions concerning the nature of this function. Above all, this form of transcoding, i. e., not only the interchanging use of phonologic and graphematic units. Only this relation, therefore, can form the basis for the auditory-visual transcoding process in the normal person and in the aphasic with bimodal (and sometimes unimodal) word comprehension impairment under the conditions we have described.[3]

With regard to the matching performances of the aphasics who we examined, this means that, in the case of bimodal word comprehension impairment (Group I) and, in part, also of unimodal word comprehension impairment (Group II), the correspondence rules once acquired by the patients and stored in the long-term memory may remain wholly or largely effective, even if semantic decoding has broken down.

In order to state more precisely the problem of how the transcoding processes take place, it is furthermore crucial to examine the role of the verbo-expressive (verbo-kinaesthetic) components of auditory and visual perception. In our matching experiments the general possibility exists of latently or manifestly articulating, i. e., of speaking, repeating or reading aloud both the word (or words) spoken by the experimenter and the word (or words) presented in writing.

Under these conditions, identification takes place by way of the phonetic-articulatory structures produced by the patients themselves, even if the meaning of the word in question was not correctly understood auditorily or visually. In other words, transcoding can be carried out by means of an identical phonetic-articulatory structure as long as repetiton and reading aloud are equally intact. Another possibility of identification on a phonetic-articulatory basis exists if repetition has broken down and only expressive readings is presented. In this case the patient is able to compare his own articulatory pattern when reading aloud directly with the phonetic pattern spoken by the experimenter.

The results in Table 1 B show that seven patients of Group I (patients 2, 4–9) and two patients of Group IIb (patients 20, 22) were still able to repeat a large proportion of the auditorily perceived words correctly, even if they did not understand the meanings (ignoring the patients who failed the matching tests). Expressive reading without semantic comprehension occured throughout only with one patient from Group I (patient 8) and partilally with one patient from Group IIa (patient 14).

The assumption discussed above of transcoding between spoken and written words on a phonetic-articulatory basis thus applies to those patients whose repetition and reading aloud without semantic comprehension and whose matching of auditorily perceived words to words given of different sign systems but also the identification of equivalent word structures of these two subsystems, turns out to be surprisingly more resistant than semantic decoding to pathologically conditioned impairment of the speech system. Added to this, the solution of the matching task under the conditions created by us makes the identification of the equivalent structures dependent on a choice, i. e., not merely an affirmative or negative answer but the selection of the correct corresponding word from among various alternatives. Where these are auditorily presented individual or word sequences, they must be stored in short-term memory in order to carry out the choice. But, as is well known, both the short-term storage of this kind (because of the amnestic-aphasic disorders) and the selection and retrieval processes in various types of aphasia often presented great difficulties.

If there are nevertheless many patients who succeeded in solving this complicated task, then it can be assumed that we are here faced with highly automatic processes which take place largely independently of a number of other linguistic processes. This assumption is supported by the fact that not only did all the aphasic patients with intact auditory and visual word comprehension (with one single exception) carry out the matching task correctly, but so also do most of the patients with bimodal or unimodal word comprehension impairment.

On the other hand the results of Groups I and II raise additional problems concerning the establishment of transcoding between spoken and written language. The ability of the patients of Group I, in particular, to match spoken and written words correctly, although they did not understand them either auditorily or visually, raises the question of how their performances were possible, since the semantic level was beyond these patients. To answer this question it is necessary to bear in mind similar identification processes in the normal speaker/hearer. It is well known that we are all capable of matching spoken words with the corresponding written words – and vice versa – even if we do not understand their meaning, and even if they are nonsense words.[4] The explanation of how these transcoding performances come about can provide us with the key to understanding the positive results we obtained above all with the patients of Group I. After all, these patients are in a similar position regarding the real words presented to them as a normal person is regarding unknown or nonsense words.

If, in pairing equivalent words presented orally and graphically, we exclude the common semantic relation – regardless of whether they are inaccessible for objective or subjective reasons – then the only *tertium comparations* which remains is the invariant relation between them as in writing, is wholly or largely intact (patients 5–8, 20, 22). In the three cases in Group IIb (patients 19, 21, 22) in which only expressive reading was intact, it is the second of the phonetic-articulatory alternatives we have mentioned (the confrontation of the articulatory pattern produced by himself in reading aloud with the pattern spoken by the experimenter) which is relevant.

Under the conditions of Group II, in which semantic decoding of the words presented is visually intact on one of the channels, a further assumption may be made besides the hypothesis of transcoding on the phonemic-graphemic level. It is conceivable that if a word presented in isolation (e. g., orally) and not semantically understood by the patients is perceived simultaneously with a word understood in another (e. g., visual) mode, then it can be understood under the influence of this semantically correctly decoded word.

I have discussed elsewhere occurrences of this kind in detail in connection with the phenomenon of deblocking (see Weigl, ⟨9⟩, [183], [187]). Numerous experiments of the same kind also deal with deblocking processes on the auditory-visual level. I was able to show unequivocally that in the case of unimodal word comprehension impairment (either auditorily or visually), the succession 'understood word (one mode) – not understood word (other mode)" can lead to the deblocking of modally dependent semantic decoding disorders. Analogous, if not identical, conditions were present in our matching experiments[5] regarding the Group II patients. In these cases too, successful matching performances may be based at least in part on deblocking effects. Under these conditions the transcoding process can – after deblocking – as in the case of patients without word comprehension impairment, take place via the common semantic relation of the phonemic and graphemic structures.

In the preceding discussion (above) our attention was focussed exclusively to those cases in which the required matching took place successfully. However, it was to be expected that there would be cases which would completely or largely fail in tests of this kind. It is first of all striking that only 5 of the 54 patients we examined were not successful in the auditory-visual matching test[6] (see Table 3). This means that, for example, compared with word comprehension impairment this form of

Table 3. *Comparative Test Results for Patients who failed in Auditory-Visual Matching*[a]

Pat.	Word comprehension		Repetition	Reading aloud	Auditory–visual matching	
	Auditory	Visual			Variant 1	c/a
O.I. (10)	0	0	90	5	0	a
D.St. (11)	0	0	100	0	0	a
L.T. (17)	95	0	100	5	5	c
I.I. (18)	100	20	5	0	15	c
R.I. (21)	100	70	20	15	30	c

[a] Relative frequency of correct responses.

impairment of linguistic operations seems to be relatively rare (at least with vascular patients, who formed the majority of our patients). In view of the fact that both the semantic decoding and the transcoding of visual units are highly automatic processes, the resistance of the latter mental activity to the influence of cerebral damage is remarkable.

Among the 'failures', Patient R. I. (24) stands out particularly. Both the input functions of this patient, i. e., auditory and visual word comprehension, were wholly and largely intact, respectively. Nevertheless this patient (with whom only Variant 1 was tested) achieved only very slight positive results (30%). This case would seem to suggest that there is a transcoding impairment which is independent of the input functions. In addition, the verbo-motor functions of repetition and oral reading of this patient were seriously impaired, which also suggests difficulties in transferring from one functional mode to another. In the other four patients special transcoding disorders likewise cannot be excluded. (These patients (cf. also Table 1), who belonged to Group I [Patients D. St. (11) and O. I. (10)] and to Group IIa [Patients L. T. (17 and I. I. (18)] differed from the other patients of the same group only in that they were not capable of carrying out the required matchings (this applies also to their performance in repetition and reading aloud).

The aspects of the transcoding phenomenon examined in the experimental tests described here are only one very limited section of the vast area of those processes on which is based the human faculty of transfering particular units from one sign system to those of another. Although the concept of transcoding continually appears in scientific writing in one connection or another[7], this problem has not, to our knowledge, been systematically examined in the sense used here, taking into special consideration the various components involved. Studies of this nature seem to use not only to be of theoretical but also of practical interest, above all regarding the acquisition of the transcoding faculty, for example in learning the written language, translating from one language into another, etc. In our view, the explanation of the neuropsychological and linguistic preconditions of these learning processes would lead to new insights from the didactic point of view.

Summary

'Trancoding' means the relating of certain units in one sign system to corresponding units of another sign system. The present study examined experimentally the transcoding of word structures of the spoken linguistic sign system into the corresponding patterns of the written linguistic sign system and vice versa. On the basis of a preliminary experiment, it was established, with the help of auditory and visual word comprehension tests, which of the words tested were understood and which were not understood by a group of 54 patients. Apart from those patients who had neither auditory nor visual word comprehension impairments, there was a group of patients who were unable to decode the words either auditorily or visually and another group in whom either visual or auditory word comprehension had broken down. The results of auditory-visual matching tests in these groups were as follows.

1. Of all aphasics examined the frequency of correct matchings was very high throughout (approx. 85%); correct matchings were carried out by approx. 65% of all patients.

2. All patients without word comprehension impairment carried out the matching tasks correctly.

3. Even in most cases of patients with both bimodal and unimodal (either auditory or visual) word comprehension impairment the rate of correct auditory – visual matching was very high (70% and 100%).

The positive results for patients with bimodal and unimodal word comprehension impairment were due to transcoding processes not on the semantic level but on the phonemic-graphemic level. Reference is made here to psycho linguinustic hypotheses on the existence of graphemic-phonemic correspondence and exception rules (Bierwisch). In addition, the possible role of deblocking effects in positive matching in cases of unimodal word comprehension impairment in connection with transcoding is also discussed. These deblocking effects could proceed from word structures understood semantically, having their influence on the blocked word structures in the other mode. In extremely rare cases (5 out of 54 patients) of failure in the matching tests, the existence of a special transcoding impairment is assumed which is independent of the status of the input function (auditory and visual word comprehension). The theoretical and practical, above all didactic, importance of the study of transcoding performance in connection with the acquisition of different sign systems was pointed out.

Notes

1. Classical typology is used for the sake of simplicity.
2. It must be taken into account that seven patients were examined using concrete words only.
3. A particular problem, which we cannot deal with at length here, is whether in nonsemantic transcoding it is whole phonetic or graphemic structures or segments that are being confronted. In this connection it is significant that among the patients with intact auditory – visual matching ability were some who were not – or were hardly – able to identify the correct letters on a letter display having had the letter names spoken to them. This tends to support the notion that the identification of hetero-modal word structures is even possible with patients who fail on the letter level (i. e., in cases of literal alexia).
4. Of course this only applies subject to certain restrictions (above all, the word structures must belong to our language phonologically and graphemically).
5. An exact comparison between the experimental conditions in the matching experiments discussed in the present article and the deblocking experiments would go beyond our present scope. The main difference is that in the matching tests there were conscious selection processes with conscious choice in which the patient already knew the critical word, whereas in the deblocking experiments the auditory – visual confrontation was guided by the experimenter without the patient's knowledge.
6. The failure of these patients was indicated either by their answering 'I can't do that', or 'It's not there', or by their producing totally inadequate reactions such as perseveration of one and the same word, an obviously random choice, etc.
7. Hints in this direction are given, e. g., by Leischner [95], who speaks of 'instability on switching over' in the transfer from 'one graphic symbol category to another', (p. 86 and 87), i. e., from one particular kind of writing to another (e. g., from printing to handwriting), and by Luria [112] who describes the process of transfer from auditorily perceived phonemic patterns to the corresponding graphemic patterns and of these, in turn, to a 'kinaesthetic system' of the succession of grapho-motor innervation as a process of *pereshifrovka* i. e., transcoding (p. 74).

⟨13⟩

E. WEIGL and A. FRADIS

The Transcoding Processes in Patients with Agraphia to Dictation*

Agraphia has been studied with reference to the case material, the localization of brain damage, and the possible correlations among agraphia and aphasia forms or among agraphia and other aphasic disturbances (especially alexia) [64; 95; 106].

Another way of contributing to the neuropsychologic interpretation of the agraphic syndrome consists of analyzing the various functions and components involved in writing which are likely to be affected by cerebral damage. The disturbances in writing to dictation deserve special attention, bearing in mind the fact that this act involves extremely complex mechanisms consisting of multiple links.

Luria [106; 117] has closely studied writing to dictation from the point of view of both the development of this function in children and its deautomation in patients with cerebral damage. Starting from Vygotski's conception of the 'condensation' of higher mental processes during ontogenesis, Luria has shown that writing to dictation, which in its learning period is composed of a set of components (auditory, articulatory, visual, grapho-motor, kineasthetic, etc.), becomes increasingly simple, until it reaches the point of a direct trigger of certain grapho-motor stereotypes by verbo-auditory stimuli. Under pathological conditions, however, *deautomation* of writing results in its decomposition into more or less isolated components, totally or partially disturbed, according to the damaged cortical zones.

Leischner [95] distinguished the following components of the writing process: verbal, auditory, apraxic, visual, and motor. When these components were disturbed, various forms of writing disturbances resulted.

In the present paper an attempt is made to analyze from the neuropsychological point of view the syndrome of *pure word agraphia to dictation*[1] (that is, without word agraphia in copying) with special reference to the *disturbance in the transcoding process.*

* The authors express their thanks to L. Mihăilescu and N. Gheorghiță for their valuable contributions to the investigation of the patients.

Contrary to *decoding,* that is, the recognition and understanding of perceived structures, and encoding, that is, the communication of the structures in the form of certain code-units, we mean, by *transcoding,* the task of creating relations between specific corresponding structures in differing code systems, of *transposing certain prescribed units of one code system into the relevant units of another code system* [⟨11⟩, ⟨12⟩].

The term writing to dictation refers, from the linguistic point of view, to the shift from the verbal sound to the visual-graphic sign system, that is, the shift from the phonetic to the corresponding graphemic structures.

From the neuropsychological point of view, however, this process appears to be more complex. Starting from the receptive function, that is, from the verbo-auditory perception, the writer must shift to the verbo-visual level, that is, to the system of graphic signs, and finally, he must shift to the grapho-motor function to be able to transpose the word from its auditory into its written form.

A beginner learning to write to dictation has to go through several stages in order to attain this ability. The word uttered by the schoolmaster is repeated by the pupil (for self-dictation purposes): then the pupil has to produce the graphemic structure of the word by remembering it from reading: finally, the pupil must reactivate the grapho-motor structures learned and stored beforehand through copied writing which, across the learning, precedes writing to dictation [188, pp. 87-98].

Writing to dictation is then acquired across the learning process through a set of functional components each of which possesses a distinct 'code' [⟨11⟩]. Therefore, from the neuropsychological point of view the shift from one verbal function to another, i. e., the transcoding process, can be considered to be a switching process between different functional systems.

By automation of writing to dictation the learning stages are reduced and condensed. However, even in the skilled writer some of these stages reappear at writing to dictation of unfamiliar words (unusual or foreign words): repetition, self-dictation or intentional visual recalling of the graphemic forms also may be resorted to in such cases.[2]

In cases with word agraphia to dictation the automated process is resolved into its components, revealing, in this way, the complicated chain of shifting from one function to another. As one or more of these functions are disturbed, it is only natural to expect the transcoding process to be interrupted, or at least slowed down, at its 'weak' links.

By examining aphasic patients with partial or total word agraphia to dictation, we have been able to obtain some data on the status of various components necessarily or potentially involved in the process of writing to dictation. Starting with separate comparative testing of verbo-auditory, verbo-motor, verbo-visual, audio-visual, and grapho-motor components in the patients studied, we attempted to analyze the stages of the transcoding process.

Method

By means of a standard examination for aphasia developed by us [⟨5⟩; 197] we studied patients with various forms of aphasia, testing a number of verbal and nonverbal functions (image recognition, oral naming, repetition, auditory and lexical understanding on the letter, word and sentence levels, reading aloud, copied writing and writing to dictation, and so forth).

1. The States of the Process of Writing to Dictation, Its Components, and Its Stages of Transcoding

1.1 The Input Stage: Verbo-Auditory Perception of the Words

This stage involves the receptive process, i. e., the verbo-auditory one, which is evaluated by the *assessment of the auditory understanding of words* enunciated by the examiner. It is ovious that total loss of the ability to perceive the phonetic structure of the word and to understand it will preclude correct writing to dictation. Still, correct writing (within certain linguistic limits) by normal subjects, of unknown or meaningless words, points to the fact that there must be two linguistic levels: the phonetic-graphemic and the semantic. We shall see later that the distinction is valid also for disturbances in writing to dictation.
To examine the perception and understanding of words, we used tests of repetition and of verbo-audio-visual matching (as referenced) in addition to our standard test.

1.2 The Transcoding Stages

These stages are those of the internal processes of selection and matching of phonetic and graphemic structures (first stage) and of activation processes of grapho-motor stereotypes, corresponding to the auditory and visual word structures (second stage).

The analysis of writing-reading acquisition in school children provides information which may help us better understand the transcoding stages, which proved to be impaired in our patients.

1.2.1 The first transcoding stage: the shift from the verbo-auditory (phonetic) to the verbo-visual (graphemic) level. We consider this shift from the sign system of spoken to that of written language to be the *first nodal point* of the transcoding *process* within writing to dictation.

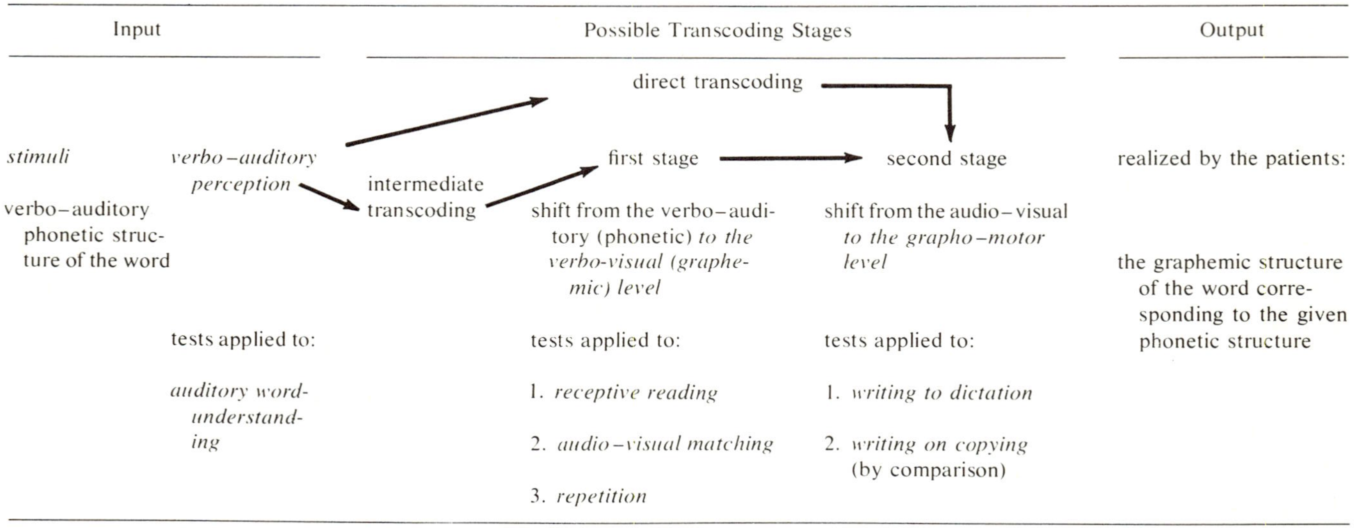

Fig. 1. *The transcoding stages in the process of writing to dictation.*

From experience we know that the school child who is beginning to learn to write has to be trained, an important prerequisite in this connection being, for instance, the previous reinforcement of the reading habit (receptive and expressive) [188]. Still more decisive, however, is the acquisition of the ability to voluntarily shift from one system to another and to find out, on the basis of a given phonetic structure, the corresponding graphemic one.

Also, in cases of disturbed writing to dictation the transcoding processes are likely to play an important role.

With regard to these processes, it then seems important to examine, on the one hand, the patients' receptive reading performances, that is, their ability to perceive and to understand the written words that they have to write to dictation and, on the other hand, their ability to directly turn from the heard phonetic to the read graphemic structures. A list of the tests applied follows (see Fig. 1).

(a) Receptive reading. Like verbo-auditory understanding, lexical (visual) understanding, that is, silent reading, has two levels: the graphemic one, i. e., perception of the graphemic structure of the word, and the semantic one, i. e., comprehension of the meaning of that structure. We are normally able to establish the identity of two corresponding graphemic structures written, for example, one in print and one in cursive writing, even without grasping their sense. That is to say, we can confine ourselves to the graphemic level only; on the other hand, we perform the semantic decoding of some written words frequently without taking notice even of the letters composing it. We shall subsequently show that this distinction is also important in cases with disturbed writing to dictation. Receptive reading (and to a certain degree, expressive also) plays an important role during the learning stage of writing to dictation. In a skilled writer receptive reading may also serve as a guide in writing, by self-verification.

(b) Verbo-audio-visual matching. The matching of a word enunciated by the examiner with those presented in written form enables us to study the phonetic-graphemic transcoding process independently of the grapho-motor-one. This matching necessarily takes place on the phonetic-graphemic level, whether the meaning of the presented words is or is not comprehended. Correct performance on this test shows that the subject is able to correctly perceive the phonetic and graphemic structure of the words presented.

In a paper dealing with transcoding on the phonetic-graphemic level, see ⟨12⟩, we studied the correlations between patients' performances on a verbo-audio-visual matching test and their performances in auditory and visual understanding of words, mostly in cases with total loss of these two functions. We even noted correct performances on the verbo-audio-visual matching test in some patients with word deafness accompanied by receptive alexia, an observation which proved that these patients had retained the perception of phonetic and graphemic structures.

(c) Repetition. We consider this function an auxiliary function belonging, at least potentially, to the first stage of transcoding since many aphasics, as well as children, learning to write, frequently use the verbo-kinaestesic analyzer as a guide both in copying and in writing to dictation because they facilitate their performance by self-dictation (see Nasarowa [129]). Predictably then, the repetition disability had to specifically interfere with writing to dictation.

1.2.2 The second stage of transcoding: the shift from the verbo-audio-visual to the grapho-motor level. From the neuropsychological point of view, within the process of writing to dictation, the shift from the spoken (phonetic) to the written (graphemic) language system must be followed by a further change in system, namely, by a shift from receptive (verbo-audio-visual) verbal functions to the grapho-motor-motor function, i. e., to writing proper, which represents the *second nodal point.*

In order to examine the performance of our patients on this grapho-motor level, we applied the basic test: *writing to dictation.*

As a first step in the acquisition of reading and writing, one seeks to develop copying ability (more particularly the ability to transpose some given graphemic structures into handwriting). In this way an improvement is obtained in grapho-motor performance which is subsequently necessary for writing to dictation, that is, necessary at the stage when the graphemic structure must be produced by the pupil without a model, i. e., solely on the basis of auditory perception of the phonetic structure.

The acquisition of writing requires, then, in addition to the acquisition of a new system of verbal (graphic) signs the development of the new, grapho-motor function. Writing to dictation involves the capacity for a twofold transcoding, namely, the shift from the phonetic to the graphemic and then to the grapho-motor level.

Under automatic conditions, when the writing subject produces the lexical units he has perceived auditorily not letter by letter but as whole units, the process of writing to dictation must supply corresponding grapho-motor patterns which are, at least for familiar words, stored. The existence of such word patterns with automated retrievability is a basic prerequisite of all forms of writing.

We have discussed above the various transcoding stages. Still, we consider the first stage (see Fig. 1) as 'facultative', bearing in mind that in normals having acquired skill in writing to dictation this stage can be absent following automation of this activity. Under such circumstances, one may presume that the verbo-auditory stimulus is able to directly elicit the grapho-motor stereotypes.

Results and Discussion

From our standard examination of aphasia, which constituted the base of the present study, we shall only set forth part of the results obtained (35 of the 54 cases studied), establishing and classifying the number of patients with agraphia to dictation on the basis of the correct-performance percentages (CP) on this test. The quantitative evaluation of performance was expressed by the CP of 20 items (pictures, letters, and words). The number of items (words) and their semantic content for all the functions studied were identical. We considered that patients with a CP under 50% (at the most, 9 performances out of 20 possible ones) had agraphia to dictation. We found 15 such cases[3] (Table 1).

2.1 Verbo-Auditory Perception and Understanding

In order to find out whether the patients had correctly perceived and understood the phonetic structure of the words enunciated, we used three tests within our standard examination: verbo-auditory perception and understanding, repetition, and verbo-audio-visual matching.

When a patient was able to understand, to repeat, or to match the spoken word with the written word, he could be considered to have correctly perceived the given word, or at least its phonetic structure.

It appears from our data that in no case were disturbances noted on all three of the above-mentioned tests, because on at least one of them the performance was correct. Therefore, all the patients with disturbed writing to dictation were able to correctly perceive the phonetic structure of the words (even without understanding their meanings), and poor performance in writing had to be accounted for by impairment on other levels. Therefore, correct writing to dictation requires more than an intact verbo-auditory perception.

In addition to assessing word perception and understanding, the tests for repetition and verbo-audio-visual matching are important in the examination of the transcoding process.

2.2 Repetition

As we have seen, transcoding in the case of writing to dictation may also involve repetition as an auxiliary function.

Aphasic patients frequently try to repeat the word dictated, for self-diction purposes, the same as school children do.

Among the 15 patients with disability to write to dictation, eight showed repetition disturbances. It is possible that their difficulty in repeating was interfering with a correct verbo-auditory-verbo-visual (phonetic-graphemic) transcoding through loss of the supplementary verbokinaesthetic stimulus.

Table 1. *Results of Standard Examination of Patients with Various Forms of Agraphia*[a]

No.	Name of patient	Form of aphasia	Auditory understanding (1)	Repetition	Receptive reading (2)	Audio–visual matching (3)	Expressive reading (4)	Writing to dictation	Writing on copying	Form of agraphia
1.	S. V.	Motor	100	85	100	100	90	0	90	Word agraphia to dictation
2.	C. C.	Motor	100	100	80	20	90	15	90	
3.	T. I.	Mixed	85	100	95	80	85	15	65	
4.	G. G.	Motor	100	90	100	100	90	20	90	
5.	A. G.	Motor	100	90	100	100	100	30	90	
6.	S. E.	Mixed	100	100	95	85	95	45	80	
7.	Z. I.	Sensory	0	5	85	90	0	0	85	
8.	S. V.	Motor	100	5	100	90	65	0	100	
9.	M. M.	Sensory	70	0	80	50	55	0	90	
10.	T. E.	Motor	100	0	100	85	0	0	85	
11.	P. M.	Motor	85	10	100	100	100	5	70	
12.	J. I.	Motor	100	30	100	100	25	20	80	
13.	G. G.	Sensory	30	80	0	75	65	40	85	
14.	R. I.	Motor	100	20	70	30	15	0	90	
15.	M. V.	Sensory	85	0	0	70	0	0	100	
16.	T. J.	Mixed	55	5	45	35	5	0	15	Total word agraphia
17.	O. I.	Sensory	85	100	0	0	85	0	0	
18.	P. M.	Mixed	90	65	85	85	35	0	0	
19.	A. V.	Motor	100	20	90	100	20	0	25	
20.	F. A.	Motor	100	50	100	95	20	10	40	
21.	A. S.	Motor	100	80	55	20	80	10	40	
22.	W. M.	Pure Alexia	100	100	0	50	0	80	35	Word agraphia on copying
23.	N. T.	Pure Alexia	100	100	0	55	45	85	40	
24.	D. M.	Pure Alexia	100	100	0	95	0	100	35	

[a] The figures represent the percentage of correct performances (CP) on the respective tests: (1) expression by gestures, of the meaning of spoken words, (2) expression by gestures, of the meaning of written words, (3) choice of the written word corresponding to the spoken one, and (4) reading aloud.

That disturbed repetition plays an important role in disturbed writing to dictation is also suggested by the fact that repetition was preserved in all our nonagraphic patients.

2.3 Verbo-Audio-Visual Matching

The basic test at the first facultative transcoding stage, from the verbo-auditory (phonetic) to the verbo-visual (graphemic) level, requires the ability to compare *directly* the phonetic word structure with the corresponding graphemic one.

Among the patients with disturbed writing to dictation, two cases (2 and 14) showed marked failures on this test, and it could be presumed that the *first nodal point,* namely, the mechanism of shift from the phonetic to the graphemic level, was impaired. It is remarkable that in both cases the CP to auditory understanding and to receptive reading were superior to those on the matching test; this points to a higher degree of preservation of perception of both the phonetic and the graphemic structure when separately tested than of the ability to transcode from the phonetic to the graphemic structure.

In the remaining 13 patients with disturbed writing to dictation, the verbo-audio-visual matching was rather well preserved, which suggests that the interruption of the transcoding process must be looked for somewhere else, i. e., in the shift to the grapho-motor level.

The fact that all nonagraphic patients retained their verbo-audio-visual matching ability suggests that this stage is necessary, though not sufficient, to achieve a correct writing to dictation performance.

2.4 Receptive Reading

The results of this test are important for ascertaining the extent to which this function is required by the transcoding process on writing to dictation.

Among our patients with agraphia to dictation, only two cases (cases 13 and 15) displayed disturbances on receptive reading. Correlation of results obtained on this test to those of the test for audio-visual matching showed the following: (a) in two cases (13 and 15) with receptive reading disturbances the audio-visual matching was considerably preserved, and (b) in two cases (2 and 14) the audio-visual matching was disturbed but the receptive reading was considerably preserved; in these cases when both verbo-visual (receptive reading) and verbo-auditory understanding were preserved (see Table 1), but the audio-visual matching was impaired, one may admit that a true disturbance in the process of audio-visual transcoding is present.

2.5 The Basic Test: Writing to Dictation[4]

From Table 1 it appears that the 15 patients with *pure agraphia to dictation,* i. e., without agraphia to copying, show a 0 to 45% CP on the writing to dictation test (in seven cases, 0 to 5%) but a 65 to 100% CP (in eight cases, 90 to 100%) on the copied writing test.

Pure agraphia to dictation appears, therefore, to be an *independent, selective* disturbance. This fact seems to be of particular importance since among these cases five patients were free of any disturbances at the input stage as well as the first stage of transcoding, i. e., without disturbances in the tests of verbo-auditory perception, receptive word reading, verbo-audio-visual matching, and repetition. In these cases it seems clear that the break in the transcoding process takes place *after the shift* from the phonological to the graphemic system, beyond the auditory-visual level, that is, at the second, grapho-motor, stage of transcoding. But the fact that copied writing was partially or totally preserved (see Table 1, cases 1–5) demonstrates the *selective* character of the agraphia to dictation.

Fradis [41] showing that in sensory aphasics writing to dictation of certain letters can be severly disturbed even though repetition and copying of letters is correct, has explained the phenomenon by noting the difficulty such patients have in finding the graphic pattern corresponding to the sound heard. Here also, a selective blocking of the second stage of grapho-motor transcoding seems to occur and concern only writing to dictation, for both auditory input (explored by repetition) and graphomotor output (explored by copying) are possible.[5]

Conclusions

On the basis of the results presented we conclude that the transcoding processes on the first and the second level are *mechanisms sui generis.* The proof for this assumption can be found (a) in the result that the verbo-audio-visual matching can be disturbed even when both auditory and visual word understandings are intact (see above), and (b) in comparison of the cases of total agraphia, agraphia to dictation, and agraphia to copying, which demonstrates the existence of a specific mechanism of transcoding by the following:

(1) In cases in which the shift to the grapho-motor level is fully lost (total agraphia), grapho-motor transcoding can be assumed to be not selectively but totally disturbed.

(2) Yet, in those cases in which one and the same word can be correctly copied but not written to dictation, and vice versa, there is a *selective* blocking of the channel to the grapho-motor act: this is particularly conspicuous when the input functions (verbo-auditory of

visual perception) and the transcoding stage from the phonetic to the graphemic level (especially the audio-visual matching) are intact.

(3) To analyze point (2) on the basis of our standard examination, the cases with agraphia on copying and total agraphia must be compared with the cases of agraphia to dictation.

3.1 Transcoding Processes in Pure Agraphia on Copying as Compared with Those in Pure Agraphia to Dictation

'Pure' copied writing disturbances (without agraphic disturbances to dictation) are considered in the literature [12; 96] to be characteristic of 'pure' or 'subcortical' alexia. As a matter of fact, our patients with pure copying disturbances (cases 22, 23 and 24) also had alexia (receptive and expressive).

It is clear that some of the patients cannot copy words which they fail to understand, whereas others can, just as normal subjects, copy words even though they do not understand them. The mere correlation of alexia and pure copying agraphia is not sufficient to explain the complicated processes which underlie these disturbances.

Disturbed receptive reading in cases of pure agraphia on copying might be due to the impossiblity of decoding the graphemic model presented. Still, in D. M. (case 24), who scored 95% on the verbo-audio-visual matching test, therefore proving to have retained the ability to perform on the graphemic (but not on the semantic) level, the copied writing disability cannot be explained by a disturbed verbo-visual perception of words.

Since none of the patients with word-copying disability had letter copying agraphia, their visual perception cannot have been impaired.

Just as writing to dictation is possible even when there is loss of understanding of auditorily presented words, that is, by perception of the phonetic structures alone, copied writing is also possible (within certain linguistic limits) without comprehension of graphemic structure (receptive alexia). Furthermore, a 100% CP for writing to dictation, in the same patient (case 24) with total agraphia on copying, points to a retained ability to write. Accordingly, as with writing to dictation, copied writing may be impaired on the level of transcoding from the visually perceived graphemic structure to the corresponding grapho-motor one. In particular, when the visually perceived word is transposed by transcription (not slavishly) in the respective subject's handwriting, a shift must take place from a graphemic structure to certain corresponding grapho-motor structures produced in the writing subject's own code.

We assume also that in our cases with pure copied writing disability, transcoding is also partly disturbed on the level of the shift from the graphemic structure perceived to the grapho-motor act. Since in these patients the grapho-motor performance on dictation is preserved, the conclusions may be drawn that their copying disturbance is due to a *selective* blocking of grapho-motor transcoding.

3.2 Transcoding Process in Total Agraphia (Writing to Dictation and Copied Writing)

On writing to dictation and copied writing tests, six of our patients displayed 0 to 10% and 0 to 40% CP, respectively. In cases 18 and 20, both the verbo-auditory and verbo-visual input functions (see auditory understanding, receptive reading, and verbo-audio-visual matching) were preserved; also preserved were writing on dictation of letters and/or letter copying, which rules out the total impairment of the grapho-motor act. Therefore, in these two cases of total agraphia it is possible to assume a disturbance of grapho-motor transcoding which this time is not selective (as it is with writing to dictation or copied writing), but *general* in character.

In our standard examination we have not included tests for spontaneous writing. Therefore, we cannot correlate our results concerning the grapho-motor transcoding processes with the disturbances of our patients in spontaneous writing. However, we have observed that all patients with severe agraphia to dictation are incapable of writing spontaneously. We can assume thus that the blocking of the grapho-motor transcoding mechanism in patients with agraphia to dictation, on copying and spontaneous writing is really *general.*

We could not find significant indications in our cases of a correlation between the disturbance of transcoding processes and the different forms of aphasia. The investigation of this problem as well as the question of the neurophysiological background of the transcoding mechanisms should be an important future task.

Notes

1. Word agraphia has been studied here only with reference to concrete nouns. For the sake of brevity we shall refer to it as 'agraphia to dictation' instead of 'pure word agraphia to dictation'.
2. Similarly, when automatic silent reading proves difficult, the reader has recourse to uttering.
3. Almost a third (five cases) of the patients with word agraphia to dictation displayed at the same time *letter* graphia to dictation (0 to 25% CP).
4. In an attempt to explain the role of the grapho-motor function in cases with agraphia we excluded from the outset, as was but natural, those patients who, being hemiplegic, could not (or refused) to write with either the right or the left hand.

5. The term of 'output' is to be understood by the patient's answer on the dictation test, which can be objectively ascertained, no matter whether he refuses to write or whether his writing consists exclusively of illegible (sometimes iterative) signs, isolated letters or syllables, or literal or verbal paragraphias. We had a number of cases with more or less important misspellings, particularly among the patients with a lower educational level. Such mistakes were not considered when estimating the results. The majority of the patients in the present study either could not write at all to dictation or exclusively wrote a letter or a syllable.

⟨14⟩

L. MIHĂILESCU, I. WEIGL, E. WEIGL and A. KREINDLER

Performance in Aphasics at Conceptual and Operational Words used Single or within Syntagms

The problem of classifying the words of the vocabulary has concerned other authors too. Guiraud [59] based on a statistical analysis of the vocabulary, classified the words in 'tool' words ('mots outils' – articles, prepositions, conjunctions, pronouns etc.) and 'strong' words ('mots forts' – nouns, verbs, adjectives, adverbs, etc.). Zipf [212] considered the following classification: conceptual words and articulatory words. Miller [126], in an interpretation according to the informational content, discriminated words more strongly influenced by the verbal context but poorer in informational content (articles, prepositions, conjunctions) from words less dependent in meaning on the context but with a richer informational content (nouns, verbs, adjectives, adverbs). Marshall and Newcombe [119] and Marshall et al. [120] distinguish words belonging to the 'major grammatical classes' (nouns, verbs, adjectives) from 'functional words' (prepositions, conjunctions, adverbs, pronouns, etc.). In this connection, Vendries [166] quoted the example of the Chinese language in which he was distinguishing 'les mots pleins' from 'les mots vides'; the latter, somewhat recalling the conjunctions in Rumanian, do not exist by themselves and do not take meaning unless they get in touch with another linguistic element with which they form a whole, while the former possess meaning independently.

The classification of words in the vocabulary, as conceived by the two teams to which the authors of the present paper are belonging, comprise some common elements. Thus, in the Romanian team's view, the vocabulary comprises *conceptual* and *operational* words. The German team classified the words in two categories, viz. *major lexical categories* and *grammatical words.*

Kreindler, in 1968 [86], distinguished two characteristics of language based on two fundamental processes: the process of representation bound to concrete thinking and the operational processes whereby words are arranged in the logical-grammatical order required by grammar usage. Based on this general concept, Kreindler and Mihăilescu [90] believe that verbal symbolization of reality and its reflection in human consciousness is done by conceptual words (nouns, verbs, adjectives) which are, in turn, subdivided in two mentally representable and abstract words. The constructive function of operating the links, the logical-syntactical connections among words within the syntagmatic process is fulfilled by operational words (auxiliary verbs, prepositions, conjunctions, certain pronouns with relational function, articles). Maybe it is for this very reason that the informational value of operational words is less than that of conceptual ones, the operational words by their very functional role have to be less precise, more flexible in order to be more easily adjustable to the wide diversity of contextual and logical-grammatical requirements, viz. to the numerous variants in which they can virtually appear in order to play their constructive part.

Weigl and Bierwisch ⟨3⟩ start from the concept that in so far as the categories of words are concerned their specific role in verbal comprehension, production and reproduction, the degree of lability of such performances under pathologic conditions, a psycholinguistic analysis is primarily required. In this connection, one might say that any classification of words as isolated units is in a way an artificial procedure as a word belongs to a given grammatical category not by dint of an 'attribute' it possesses, but as the result of the function it is called to serve within grammatical-syntactical structures. This is primarily the case of grammar words which without the context are both semantically and syntactically less determined. The various groups of words of the major lexical category (nouns, verbs, adjectives), in spite of their comparative autonomy, viz. that the can be understood without a conteeyt, receive, however, their definite meaning only within a given context (for example the noun 'board' may be understood both as an object with some given characteristics and figuratively as the meals served). The morphologic form in which nouns, verbs adjectives can be appropriately used (singular, plural, person, tense, article, etc.) also depends very strictly upon the semantical-syntactical category where they are placed. The syntactical character of the group of words of the major category also appears from the fact that such isolated words may often be elliptic sentences (as for instance 'Go!' or 'Beautiful!').

Dealing with word categories in this respect Weigl and Bierwisch [193], in collaboration with Böttcher *et al.* [19] carried out an ample research on dyslexia cases concerning the dependence of verbal lexical understanding upon the degree of grammatical determination of lexical units. The results obtained upon presentation of the same words at first in single unit form and then within a context demonstrated the significant influence exerted by syntactical structures on comprehension of words.

Our joint research was designed to investigate deeper into this problem and supplement the results previously obtained by either team separately. By working out a common methodology and by accumulating experimental material on the same criteria in the Rumanian and German language, it has been possible, on the one hand, to compare among them the various aphasic disorders from the point of view of the mechanisms of language independently of the structure of the language and, on the other, to compare them considering what is specific to either language. The analysis of results was made considering the following aspects:

(1) The 'conceptual' and 'major' (nouns, verbs) and the 'operational' and 'grammatical' (prepositions, conjunctions) lexical categories, respectively.

(2) Usage of lexical categories (nouns, verbs, prepositions, conjunctions) as single units and within syntagms.

(3) The various modalities of speech: expressive reading, repetition and writing to dictation.

The material here reported only refers to our findings in Romanianspeaking aphasics, those in German speakers having been reserved for a separate paper.

Method

As the present research was aimed to assess performance in aphasic patients concerning the way they use conceptual and operational words, the words selected were nouns and verbs, for the first, and prepositions and conjunctions for the second category. The words originally presented as single lexical units were subsequently used to form two- and three-word syntagms.

The nouns used were in the nominative case, singular or plural, and the verbs at the indicative mood, third person singular. In the syntagms they were used in the same form, i. e. same case, number, mood, or person, in order to secure comparability of results. In a few cases, however, this was not possible as three-word syntagms had to be constructed according to correct grammatical usage and current speech. The prepositions and conjunctions being inflexible words were always the same. Abstract nouns were not used, but only nouns standing for mentally representable objects.

First stage. The patients were presented with series of 25 prepositions, 25 conjunctions, 50 nouns and 50 verbs. Nouns and verbs were divided into two categories of 25 each, viz. 'initial' and 'final' nouns and verbs, respectively (to be used in the third stage of the experiment for constructing three-word syntagms). Every isolated word was written on a card, the patient having to read it; the same word series were used for assessing repetition and dictated writing. The order in which the words of each series were repeated was invariable with all the patients, and it was established according to word-frequency in normal Rumanian speakers, on the basis of data previously reported by Kreindler and Mihăilescu [90] and Mihăilescu, Voinescu and Fradis [125]. Each series was arranged in the decreasing order of the frequency-value of the words, as established elsewhere [90; 125].

Table 1. *Series of stimuli used*

Single words		Syntagms	
		two-word	three-word
Prepositions	Nouns	Prep. + Noun	Noun + Prep. + Noun
1) de (of)	rufe (laundry)	de rufe (of laundry)	coş de rufe (laundry basket)
2) la (at, in)	fabrică factory)	la fabrică (at / in the factory)	muncitor la fabrică (worker at the factory)
3) în (in)	grădină (garden)	în grădină (in the garden)	legume în grădină (vegetables in the garden)
4) cu (with)	vînt (wind)	cu vînt (with wind, windy)	vreme cu vînt (windy weather)
5) pe (on, in)	cîmp (field)	pe cîmp (in/on the field)	cartofi pe cîmp (potatoes in the field)
6) din (of, from)	oraş (town)	din oraş (of/from town)	om din oraş (man from/of the town)
7) pentru (for)	lemne (wood)	pentru lemne (for wood)	ladă pentru lemne (wood box)
8) după (behind)	dulap (cupboard)	după dulap (behind the cupboard)	mătura după dulap (broom behind the cupboard)
9) într-o (in a)	sală (hall)	într-o sală (in a hall)	copii într-o sală (children in a hall)
10) pînă (till, until)	seara (night)	pînă seara (until night)	lucrează pînă seara [works until night (comes)]
11) lîngă (near, by)	divan (sofa)	lîngă divan [near (by) the sofa]	scaun lîngă divan [chair near (by) the sofa]
12) prin (through)	pădure (forest)	prin pădure (through the forest)	potecă prin pădure (path through the forest)
13) despre (about)	vînătoare (hunting)	despre vînătoare (about hunting)	poveste despre vînătoare (story about hunting)
14) dintre (among)	şcolari (school-children)	dintre şcolari (among school-children)	premianţi dintre şcolari (prize winners among school-children)

Single words		Syntagms	
		two-word	three-word
Prepositions	Nouns	Prep. + Noun	Noun + Prep. + Noun
15) asupra (on)	satul (village)	asupra satului (on the village)	ploaie asupra satului (rain on the village)
16) spre (to)	lună (moon)	spre lună (to the moon)	zbor spre lună (flight to the moon)
17) printre (among)	flori (flowers)	printre flori (among flowers)	floare printre flori (flower among flowers)
18) între (among)	săteni (villagers)	între săteni (among villagers)	fruntaşi între săteni (frontrankers among the villagers)
19) fără (without)	soare (sun)	fără soare (without sun)	zi fără soare (day without sun)
20) către (to)	popor (the people)	către popor (to the people)	cuvîntarea către popor (speech to the people)
21) peste (over)	munti (mountains)	peste munti (over the mountains)	zăpadă peste munti (snow over the moun-tains)
22) dintr-o (of)	bucată (piece)	dintr-o bucată (of one piece)	bărbat dintr-o bucată (man of one piece; Rumanian idiom = up-right man)
23) sub (under)	masă (table)	sub masă (under the table)	covor sub masă (carpet under the table)
24) decît (only)	carne (meat)	decît carne (only meat)	nu mănîncă decît carne (eats only meat)
25) înaintea (before)	uşa (door)	înaintea uşii (before the door)	prag înaintea uşii (threshold before the door)

Second stage. Each of the 25 prepositions was associated with a noun of the 'final' series, there being formed this way 25 syntagms of two words each, of the type: 'in the garden', 'in the fields', 'at the factory'.

The 25 conjunctions were associated with 25 'final' verbs which had previously been presented isolated, there resulting 25 syntagms of two words each, of the type: 'and treads', 'when (he) searches', 'when (he) writes'.

Each syntagm written on a card was presented to the patient to read. The same syntagms were used also on repetition and dictated-writing tests.

Third stage. At this point of the experiment, the stimuli were syntagms made up of three words. They were formed by adding to two-word syntagms an 'initial' noun and verb, respectively, so that they symmetrically complete it. Our objectives did not require the syntagms to have a typical sentence-construction such as subject, predicate, complement, attribute etc.; they had the following type of construction: initial noun – preposition – final noun; e. g. 'vegetables in the garden, worker at the factory', 'potatoes in the field', or initial verb – conjunction – final verb; e. g. 'washes and irons', 'finds when searches', 'reads or writes', in 25 syntagms for each type of construction.

Thus, though each syntagm as a whole made a single stimulus, the total number of words presented in the experiment was the following: each

Table 2. *Series of stimuli used*

Single words		Syntagms	
		Two-word	Three-word
Conjunctions	Verbs	Conj.+Verb	Verb + Conj. + Verb
1) şi (and)	calcă (irons)	şi calcă (and irons)	spală şi calcă (washes and irons)
2) să (to)	coasă (sew)	să coasă (to sew)	începe să coasă (stars to sew)
3) că (that)	vine (comes)	că vine (that comes)	vede că vine [sees that (it) is coming]
4) cînd (when)	caută (seeks)	cînd caută [when (he) seeks]	găseşte cînd caută [(he) finds when (he) seeks]
5) dar (but)	plăteşte (pays)	dar plăteşte [but (he) pays]	cumpără dar plăteşte [(he) buys but (he) pays]
5) sau (or)	scrie (writes)	sau scrie (or writes)	citeşte sau scrie [(he) reads or writes]
7) dacă (if)	rămîne (stays)	dacă rămîne [if (he) stays]	spune dacă rămîne [(he) says if (he) stays]
8) cum (when)	adoarme (falls asleep)	cum adoarme [when (he) falls asleep]	visează cum adoarme (he dreams when he falls asleep)
9) însă (but)	tace (keeps silent)	însă tace [but keeps silent]	suferă însă tace [(he) suffers but keeps silent]
10) unde (where)	poate (can)	unde poate [where (he) can]	merge unde poate [(he) goes where (he) can]

Single words		Syntagms	
		Two-word	Three-word
Conjunctions	Verbs	Conj.+Verb	Verb + Conj. + Verb
11) ca să (in order to)	învingă (vanquish)	ca să învingă (in order to vanquish)	luptă ca să învingă (he fights in order to vanquish)
12) iar (again)	găteşte (cooks)	iar găteşte (cooks again)	mama iar găteşte (mother cooks again)
13) totuşi (however)	răsare (rises)	totuşi răsare (rises, however)	soare totuşi răsare (the sun rises, however)
14) nici (neither . . . nor)	ninge (snows)	nici ninge (neither snows)	nici plouă, nici ninge [(it) neither rains, nor shows]
15) ori (or)	pierde (loses)	ori pierde (or loses)	cîştigă ori pierde (wins or loses)
16) fiindcă (because)	vrea (wants)	fiindcă vrea [because (he) wants]	stă fiindcă vrea [(he) stays because (he) wants to]
17) desi (although)	are (has)	deşi are [although (he) has]	cere deşi are [(he) begs although (he) has]
18) decît să (rather than)	bea (drinks)	decît să bea (rather than drinks)	rabdă decît să bea [(he) endures rather than drinks]
19) de (so that)	răsună (rings)	de răsună [so that (it) rings]	strigă de răsună [he shouts so that it rings]
20) ci (but)	strănută (sneezes)	ci strănută [but (he) sneezes)	nu tuşeşte ci strănută [(he) does not cough but (he) sneezes]
21) cît (as much as)	învată (learns)	cît învată [as much as (he) learns]	ştie cît învată [(he) knows as much as (he) learns]
22) încît (so that)	oboseşte (gets tired)	încît oboseşte [so that (he) gets tired]	aleargă încît oboseşte [(he) runs so that he gets tired]
23) pînă (until)	răspunde (answers)	pînă răspunde [until (he) answers]	aşteaptă pĭna răspunde [wait until (he) answers]
24) deoarece (because)	pleacă (leaves)	deoarece pleacă [because (he) leaves]	încuie deoarece pleacă [(he) locks because (he) leaves]
25) deci (thus)	culege (reaps)	deci culege [thus (he) reaps]	seamănă deci culege [(he) sows, thus (he) reaps]

preposition and conjunction was a stimulus three times, namely, when presented as a single unit and when comprised in two – and three-word syntagms; each final noun and verb appeared three times and each initial noun and verb two times. This amounted, then, to 400 isolated lexical units per patient and, considering we were studying three speech modalities (reading, repetition, dictated writing), the total number of words over the whole group of patients was 14,000.

Assessment of Performances

I. *Positive performances* were estimated those responses which were correct and given promptly and unhesitatingly.
II. *Negative performances:* total lack of response.
III. *Inadequate performances:*
A. *Unspecific performances* were considered those in which the response was totally incongruous with the stimulus presented. For example, instead of reading or repeating the word presented, the patient told his name, said 'Good day' or 'one', in the last instance also starting automatically to count, for his responses to the next stimuli were successively 'two', 'three' etc. Sometimes these unspecific responses were stereotypies which also appeared in the patient's dialogued speech. This category also included perserverations.
B. *Erroneous performances.* The types of errors found in our material could be classified in the following categories:
1) *Articulatory (phonemic) and writing (graphemic) errors* producing a deformation of the phonematic structure of the word. This category comprised paraphasic and paralexic phonematic errors on repetition and expressive reading tests and litteral paragraphic errors on dictated-writting tests.

2) *Semantical-syntactical* errors altering the semantic content of the word by:

a) *Substitution* of one word for another, both as single lexical units and within syntagms.

b) *Wrong grammatical usage* consisting in wrong case and number, for nouns, and wrong mood, person and number for verbs.

c) *Omission of words* was a peculiar error of the semantico-syntactic type specific to syntagms with one or two words omitted from the response.

Interpretation of wrong performances involved some difficulties, for in some responses the superimposition of semantico-syntactical errors upon articulatory (or writing) paraphasic errors could alter the stimulus word in such a way that it became a different word, with another meaning. The meaning of the new word was asked for when the patient was able to answer. Was he not able to do so, he was rated according to the general trend of his performance, the predominance of one or another type of error.

Also those performances in which the patient had come to the right answer by successive trials were considered erroneous. Whether he did so by giving correctly words other than the given one (two or even three different prepositions which successively preceded the right one) or by forming intermediate meaningless verbal structures wherein by successively altering some phonemes he obtained the right performance, this type of performance could not be rated as normal ones were. Even if they eventually succeed in fulfilling the task correctly, the way in which they proceeded pointed to a disorder and this was not to be overlooked.

Here are the criteria on which we based our estimates of the patients' performances.

Positive performances	Inadequate performances: Semantico-syntactical	Inadequate performances: Articulatory	Unspecific performances	Negative performances
Performances identical to those of normal subjects	a) Word substitutions b) Wrong grammatical usage c) Word omissions in syntagms	Deterioration of phonematic (graphemic) structure of words	a) Responses incongruous with the verbal stimulus b) Perseverations	Total lack of response

Material

The experiment bears upon 12 patients with aphasia who had been submitted to complete examination to establish the form of aphasia, the speech modalities involved and the severity of these disturbances. The test results showed that in two patients the disorder was too mild to be conclusive and that in another case the disturbance of speech was almost entirely of the articulatory type. These three cases were consequently not considered. The age, aphasia form and the clinical diagnosis of the patients are set forth in table 3.

Table 3. *The cases studied*

No.	Patient	Age	Aphasia form	Diagnosis
1	F. P.	42	Mixed predominantly expressive	Thrombosis of left middle cerebral artery Right-sided hemiplegia. Convulsive seizures following
2	R. B.	48	Mixed, predominantly expressive	Atrial fibrillation. Right-sided hemiplegia
3	R. N.	38	Mixed, predominantly expressive	Post-partum cerebral thrombophlebitis. Right-sided hemiplegia
4	P. P.	48	Mixed, predominantly expressive	Internal carotid thrombosis, Right-sided hemiplegia
5	G. G.	33	Expressive	Left temporoparietal cranio cerebral injury. Right sided hemiparesis
6	B. I.	47	Expressive	Ictus, Right-sides hemiparesis
7	V. M.	63	Expressive	Ictus without neurological signs
8	P. N.	65	Expressive	Ictus. Right-sided hemiparesis
9	M. I.	73	Mixed, predominantly expressive	Ictus. Hemiparesis on the right side, pyramidal signs

Results

The data reported here concern only 9 patients whose performances with the same words used both as single lexical units and within syntagms (10,800 words over the entire group) were oserved. The discussion refers to mean percent distributions of positive, negative and inadequate performances per word category and speech modality over the group as a whole. A close analysis is performed also, of some categories of inadequate performances.

Global results. Analysis of the mean percent values in the group as a whole showed the following (Table 4).

Positive performances were recorded with maximum mean values for word repetition, medium ones for reading and a very low mean percentage for dictated writing. An identical grading of positive performance over the whole group was also found when analysing each individual case.

Negative performance were never recorded on word repetition tests and only in a very low percentage on reading and dictated-writing tests. The group-percentage of dictated writing performances was influenced by the existence of total agraphia in 3 patients, while that of reading performances by total alexia in one patient, the remainder of negative performances being distributed among the other patients.

Table 4. *Global results (in %)*

	Positive performances	Inappropriate performances				Unspecific performances	Negative performances
		Substitutions	Omissions	Wrong grammatical usage	Articulatory errors		
Reading	40	23	2	3	13	6	13
Repetition	68	11	3	1	15	2	–
Dictated writing	18	4	2	1	37	25	13
General mean	42	13	2	2	22	11	8

Inadequate performances appeared in general to vary with each speech modality according to the complexity and degree of disorder. As 69% of all the possible errors in dictated writing were paragraphic errors and unspecific performances, these appeared to be the most characteristic in this speech modality. Reading performances were inappropriate in 47% of all the possible performances with substitution as the most characteristic error. Inappropriate repetition performances covered 32% of the total of possible performances with a distribution which did not preferentially involve a particular type of error.

Semantico-syntactical errors, namely, substitutions, wrong grammatical usage and word omission in syntagms which amounted to a rather low percentage – 17% in all – over the total of possible performances, covered all the same 34% of the total of inadequate performances.

Articulatory errors on reading and repetition tests were rather low and close in performance for either speech modality. Literal paragraphic errors, on the contrary, attained a rather high percentage over the group as a whole and they occurred in all our patients, though variable in number according to the severity of individual disturbance.

Unspecific performances attained a rather high percentage on dictated-writing tests, their most frequent form of manifestation being amorphous stereotypy.

Distribution of Global Performances per Lexical Category (Table 5)

A frequency-distribution analysis of the global results per lexical category showed that the behaviour of these categories of words varied with the speech modality studied. Thus, the conceptual-word category showed wide noun-verb differences in reading performance. While among the four categories of words it was with the noun that the highest percentage of positive and the lowest percentage of inadequate performances were obtained, with the verb the results were opposite. No such dissociation within the same category appeared in repetition performances where for conceptual words the results were similar and better

Table 5. *Distribution of global performances per lexical category (in %)*

	Prepositions			Conjunctions			Nouns			Verbs		
	+	±	–	+	±	–	+	±	–	+	±	–*
Reading	36	52	12	41	47	12	47	38	15	34	54	12
Repetition	62	38	–	63	37	–	73	27	–	69	31	–
Dictated writing	22	65	13	22	65	13	19	69	12	13	74	13

* + positive performances, ± inappropriate performances, – negative performances

Particular Aspects of Inadequate Performances (Table 6)

Table 6. *Global of substitutions, omissions, and errors in grammatical usage (in %)*

	Reading	Repetition	Dictated Writing
Substitutions	23	11	4
Omissions	2	3	2
Errors in grammatical usage	3	1	1

than for operational words, or on dictated-writing performance. In the latter case, however, operational words were better written than conceptual ones.

The results obtained showed that the inadequate performance category, though of rather unimportant weight over the total of possible performances, deserved a closer examination. Eliminating from the analysis the unspecific-performance and articulatory (graphemic) error categories, we focussed on semantico-syntactical errors, such as word substituion, word omission within syntagms and wrong grammatical usage.

It appears from the data presented that substitutions occurred more frequently with reading than with the other language modalities studied. As for omissions and changes in grammar usage, when compared to the number of stimuli presented to the group of patients as a whole, their mean global percentages were too low to deserve discussion.

More interesting aspects were revealed by analysis of the error-type distribution per lexical category (Table 7). It was thus noted that substituion and omission percentages were higher in the case of operational than in that of conceptual words regardless of the language modality. At the same time, on repetition and writing tests, prepositions and conjunctions, on the one hand, and nouns and verbs, on the other, yielded close values. In reading performances, however, there was a difference between the noun and the verb, which appeared both on analysis of global performances, positive performances being much more numerous with nouns than with verbs, and on analysis of the type of error substitutions of verbs being more frequent than those of nouns. Therefore, notwithstanding the fact that they belong to the same category – conceptual words – the noun and the verb showed some differ-

Table 7. *Distribution of semantico-syntactical errors per lexical category (in %)*

	Prepositions		Conjunctions		Nouns			Verbs		
	Substitutions	Omissions	Substitutions	Omissions	Substitutions	Omissions	Gram. wrong	Substitutions	Omissions	Gram. wrong
Reading	30	2	28	3	15	2	5	24	1	6
Repetition	17	3	16	7	7	1	2	8	2	2
Dictated writing	7	1	8	3	2	1	2	2	2	1

ences in behaviour. Our patients had usually greater difficulty in understanding a verb than a noun; the reason for this may lie in the different nature of what either lexical category stands for, the nouns corresponding to mentally representable objects appear less difficulty to evoke by the patient than the verb which comeys the meaning of action.

The difference in behaviour between operational and conceptual words was also apparent in the percentage of substitutions when simple or complex stimuli were used (Table 6). Thus, the substitution percentage increased in the case of operational words and decreased in the case of conceptual words with the complexity of the stimulus (two – or three – word syntagm). It appears therefore that aphasic patients can understand conceptual words better than operational ones within a semantico-syntactical context, the latter consequently providing a higher substitution rate.

Table 8. *Distribution of substitutions as a function of stimulus complexity (in %)*

	Reading				Repetition				Dictated writing			
	P*	C	N	V	P	C	N	V	P	C	N	V
Isolated words	28	24	19	28	9	7	5	4	4	8	2	2
Two-word syntagms	28	26	11	26	16	11	6	5	7	8	1	2
Three-word syntagms	33	35	12	18	26	27	9	12	11	10	2	2
General mean	30	28	14	24	17	15	6	7	7	9	2	2

* P = prepositions; C = conjunctions; N = nouns; V = verbs

A brief analysis of these substitutions showed that usually they occurred inside the same category, viz. N→N, V→V, N→V, V→N in the case of conceptual words or P→P, C→C, P→C, C→P in the case of operational words. We also noted substitution conceptual for operational but never of operational for conceptual words, however.

As for word omissions within syntagms (Table 9) two- and three -word syntagms yielded very close percentage. We assumed them to indicate a certain degree of agrammatism in certain patients. Omission of the preposition or conjunction in a syntagm, the remaining components of which were correctly understood and encoded, and the tendency to substitute operational words more than conceptual ones might be ex-

Table 9. *Distribution of omissions as a function of stimulus complexity (in %)*

	Reading				Repetition				Dictated writing			
	P*	C	N	V	P	C	N	V	P	C	N	V
Isolated words	–	–	–	–	–	–	–	–	–	–	–	–
Two-word syntagms	3	4	–	1	4	10	–	1	4	1	1	3
Three-word syntagms	3	4	4	2	5	11	2	3	1	7	1	3
General mean	3	4	2	2	4	11	1	2	3	4	1	3

* P = prepositions; C = conjunctions; N = nouns; V = verbs

plained by the fact that operational words have less meaning and less value informationally.

Inflection errors showed an uneven distribution in our patients. Their frequency was higher in only two cases. For nouns, for example, they consisted in shifts from the singular to the plural number or vice versa, and also in wrong case, lack of article, definite instead of indefinite article.

Conclusions

The comparison between operational and conceptual words presented as single verbal units and as parts of a syntagm to aphasic patients to read, write to dictation and utter enabled us to draw the following conclusions.

1) As emerges from the global mean values in our patients with either expressive or mixed predominantly expressive, aphasia, repetition was better preserved than reading and dictated writing. Reading errors were more numerous than repetition errors, the most numerous of all being however dictated writing errors in each patient.

2) Performance also was different with the two categories of words – operational and conceptual – as revealed both by the mean global values and, more particularly, by the distribution of some types of errors. Thus, both substitution and omission of words were more frequent in the case of prepositions and conjunctions – viz. operational words – than in the case of nouns and verbs – viz. conceptual words. These differences were more striking when the given word was part of a syntagm. The

substitution percentage of operational words increased with the complexity of the stimulus (two-and-three-word syntagms) while it decreased in the case of conceptual words.

The syntagm is a complex verbal structure possessing new components as compared to the single word. It makes up a whole wherein the semantic contents of its components merge with the result of a semantic content which is not the arithmetic sum of the semantic contents of the components. The syntagm components bear mutual-determination relationships to one another, viz. phonologic, semantico-syntactical, morphological and probabilistic relationships. Therefore, the syntagm caused the performance to change, that is, the aphasics' performances at words comprised within a syntagm differed from those at words presented as single units, for in the syntagm the words acquire a new attribute, determined by the semantico-syntactical part they are called to play. The operational character, the degree of integration, of the preposition and conjunction within the semantic context, their dependence on the sentence-structure were all factors rendering the performance in our patients more difficult. This appeared in the decreased number of positive performances and the increased number of errors when these categories of words were used within a syntactic context. The syntagm did not appear to exert any such 'inhibitory' influence on the nouns and verbs; on the contrary, it appeared to outline their semantical content and increase the number of positive performances concomitantly decreasing the number of inadequate semantico-syntactical performances.

3) The noun and the verb, though falling into the same category, did not always appear similar in behaviour. There was a smaller number of positive performances to the verb than to the noun, and also a greater number of semantico-syntactical errors to the verb than to the noun.

It appears therefore that the nature of the semantic content of the words and the degree of dependence of words upon the syntactic context have impact on performance in aphasics as revealed by the two categories of words, operational and conceptual.

⟨15⟩

E. WEIGL

Neuropsychological Studies of Structure and Dynamics of Semantic Fields with the Deblocking Method

The trend of neuropsychological research represented by the author is focused on problems directly related to semiotics. His *deblocking method* [⟨8⟩; ⟨9⟩; 179] developed roughly eight years ago and meanwhile considerably improved, permits the experimental study of the structure and dynamics of 'semantic fields' in cases of aphasic disturbances. The results gained with this method allow conclusions valid not only for pathology but also for normal semantic processes.

With our investigations we approach in a new way problems [21] dealt with 30 years ago by Raztran [139; 140], later by Riess [144], in recent times by Branca and others, and especially by the Soviet school: Luria and Vinogradova [118], Kogan [82], Bein [10], and others.

We use the term 'semantic field' in the sense of a system of ontogenetically developed connexions between 'meanings', i. e., 'object-meanings' as well as 'word-meanings'. In accordance with the assumption of Luria and Vinogradova [118], the real semantic field is not identical with a system of logical or linguistic categories, but can be of a broader or narrower character. Therefore, apart from the mentioned categories, there exist indivually generated connexions within each semantic field.

In aphasiacs the connexions between certain object-meanings, word-meanings or between object- and word-meanings can be disturbed, i. e., 'blocked', as a result of brain lesions. The phenomenon of deblocking in aphasiacs consists in the total or partial disappearance of disturbances of various verbal performances when the disturbed, i. e., 'blocked', verbal reaction is preceded by an unblocked adequate response. We have thus succeeded in deblocking disturbances like anomia, arepetition, alexia, agraphia, verbal deafness, etc. For instance, a patient with disturbances of word (or sentence) understanding can more or less temporarily acquire the ability of understanding a certain concrete word (sentence) provided he has previously seen the corresponding picture, an alexic patient succeeds in correctly reading a word (sentence) after hearing this word (sentence) uttered by the examiner, etc.

The effect of deblocking is based on the *Prestimulation* of certain semantic fields, using for this purpose an *intact*, 'non-blocked', channel as well as the existing connexion between the prestimulated and the blocked word (sentence).

In elaborating our method, we were led by the following principles. The patient is to be kept ignorant of both the object to be deblocked and the deblocking stimulus. The process must to a certain degree develop 'automatically', unconsciously. We intend, for example, to deblock troubles of verbal deafness in a patient by means of picture recognition (see fig. 1). In a previous test, a number of words which the patient cannot understand at all (auditory) have been established. In order to deblock the understanding of the word 'slippers', a group of pictures including a picture showing slippers is shown to the patient, who does not know which one corresponds to the word constituting the object of the deblocking experiment. After seeing these pictures the patient is confronted with several words (auditory) of which only one – 'slippers' in our case – corresponds to the previously given picture, meanwhile taken away. Thus the patient was unable to 'prepare' himself in advance by memorizing this picture.

DEBLOCKING OF VERBAL DEAFNESS THROUGH PICTURE-RECOGNITION

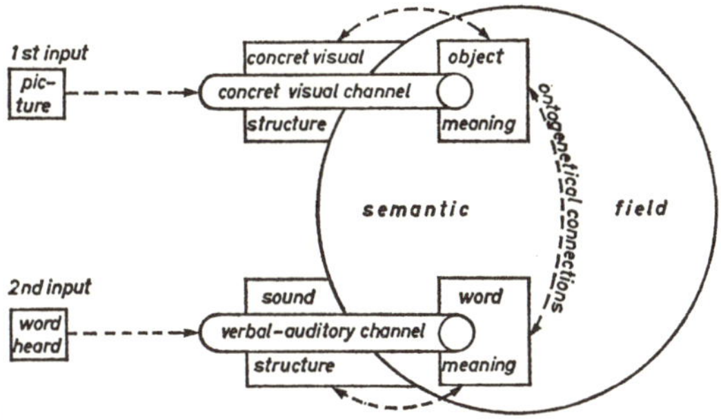

Fig. 1

We think the deblocking effect in this case is due to the fact that the ontogenetically developed connexion between the knowledge of the object (slippers) and the corresponding meaning of the word 'slippers' is reactivated by the exposition of this picture in the prestimulation phase, and that the otherwise blocked verbo-auditory channel can be deblocked in this way. From a neurophysiological point of view, this constitutes a process of summation between a liminal and subliminal stimulus [200].

With the help of this example we intend to illustrate briefly the mechanism of deblocking and its direct relation to the problem of meaning. The examination of the structure and dynamics of the great black box, called 'semantic field', is possible in the following way.

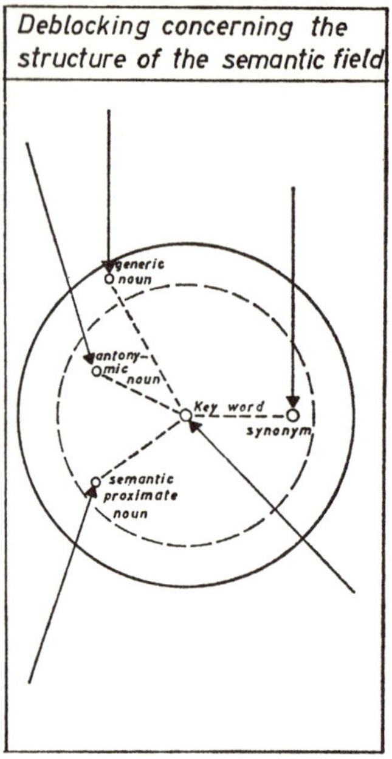

Fig. 2

We can prestimulate the respective semantic field (fig. 2):

(1) *Directly:* the key word appears in the prestimulation phase.

(2) *Indirectly:* instead of the key word the corresponding generic noun, the synonym, a semantically proximate word (*plate* instead of *cup*), an antonymical noun (*darkness* instead of *lightness*), etc. appears in the prestimulation phase.

(3) The *combination* between (1) and (2): in addition to the key word, the generic noun, or the synonym, a semantically proximate word, an antonymical noun, etc. appears also in the prestimulation phase.

These different models may have the following influences on the deblocking effect:

(1) *Reinforcing* of the d-effect: the d-rate *increases.*

(2) *Doubling* of the d-effect: in the response of the patient appear, apart from the key word, one or more of the 'field-words' given in the prestimulation phase; i. e., the patient must name the picture 'chair'; we ask him to repeat the words: stone – *chair* – fish – *furniture* – map; then we give him the picture 'chair'; he names: 'that is a chair – furniture'.

(3) *Deviation*-phenomenon: in the response of the patient appears, instead of the key word, another 'field-word' given in the prestimulation phase (i. e., *plate* instead of *cup*); he is convinced that his response is correct.

Among other things, the advantage of our investigation method consists in the fact that the results gained are both quantifiable and commensurable. In this way we can make statistical statements, for instance, on the correlations between the different deblocking models.

The Effect of Homonyms on Deblocking

A very interesting possibility for studying the relations between heterogeneous semantic fields is the use of homonyms. For instance, the German homonym 'Feder' has concrete meanings: pen, feather, and spring. In one of our experiments we asked an anomic patient to repeat several words, among them the word 'Feder'. After this we showed him different pictures, among them a pen, a feather, and a spring. And now, the patient was able to name all these three pictures correctly. Thus, it is possible to deblock several meanings contained in different heterogeneous semantic field with a single word stimulus.

With the help of this method, we have also succeeded in provoking certain 'conflicts' between heterogeneous semantic fields: i. e., we gave in the prestimulation phase the German homonym 'Flügel' (piano and wing), but we reinforce only one of the two meanings (piano); in this case we have noticed a *deviation* effect: the patient has named the picture 'wing' in the sense of the other, reinforced meaning, saying: 'a musical instrument . . . a guitar'.

We hope that this brief report not only indicates the part deblocking research is able to play in the study of semantic fields, but that it will, at the same time, stimulate close cooperation between neuro-psychologists and linguists in the large field of semiotics.

⟨16⟩

E. WEIGL

Neurolinguistic Research on Semantic Memory

The problem of memory in general and semantic memory in particular has become a field of contemporary interdisciplinary research. In particular linguistics, psychology as well as psycholinguistics and neurolinguistics endeavour to clarify the question of the storage and organisation of semantic factors of language in long-term memory (LTM)[1].

Our contribution to the problem of the storage and reactivation of lexical units in LTM is of a neurolinguistic nature. It applies to disturbances in *word-finding in naming* objects or pictures of objects, disturbances which appear especially in cases of semantic-amnestic aphasia. The 'non-remembering' of the correct word when somebody is shown the picture of an object indicates a greater or lesser impairment of certain mechanisms of semantic memory.

The study of such disturbances appears to us all the more important since they are by no means a sort of 'curiosity' completely outside the range of normal memory performance. The frequent use of the word 'thingamabob', which indicates the momentary inability of a normal speaker to locate the correct name for an object, shows the close connection with the word-finding disturbances of brain-pathological origin.

In the case of amnesic-aphasic patients, what is intact and what is impaired?

(1) They can decode semantically a perceived word structure, that is to say match the relevant sound structure to the corresponding word meaning in long-term storage.

(2) They can recognise the meaning of the object presented, that is they can assign it the adequate meaning structure from long-term storage.

(3) They can *not* find the sound structure of the word corresponding to the object perceived, although they possess the meaning structure upon which this word is based.

In other words, patients with amnesic-aphasic word-finding disturbances in naming objects are distinguished by the fact that they have no difficulty in understanding and enunciating words, or in recognising known objects, but that they do not have the ability to find spontaneously the sound structure of the word which identifies the given object. However, they have not 'lost' this sound structure; this is shown by the fact that they immediately accept this structure, also repeat it in certain cases, and can even write it when it is dictated.

A special access to the study of this memory problem is provided by the possibility of removing the centrally occasioned blocking of naming; that is to say to allow the patient to 'recall' the vainly sought word. The controlled use of such an experimental procedure, the *deblocking method,* provides a certain insight into the processes within the system of semantic memory. On the basis of the results of such a procedure it is possible to clarify further certain questions about the nature of the retrieval mechanism from the LTM, about possible 'fractures' in this mechanism.

The deblocking method which I developed, and which I have frequently described [see ⟨2⟩] is based, to put it briefly, upon the successive linking of certain performances of intact functions with the corresponding performances of disturbed functions, particularly in the speech field. In its simplest form, as used in the present research, a deblocking effect is produced when the access to a certain performance, which is blocked on one or more channels, is made available through one or more intact channels. This is achieved by evoking the unimpaired performance *prior* to the disturbed performance. Putting it concretely, if a patient is unable to find the name of a certain object with which he is familiar, one can help him to overcome this inability by allowing him previously to hear or read the word in question. In a very simplifeid form, this is the basis of the deblocking of anmesic-aphasic naming disturbances. That is to say the intact auditory word comprehension or word reading is used to remove the blocking of word finding.

The deblocking method thus has the task of setting free the blocked connection between meaning structure and sound structure.

The problem of freeing blocked memory content also raises the question of the stages which the deblocking stimuli pass through en route to the storage formations. The following research report shows that it is here necessary to take into acccount the connection between short-term memory (STM) and long-term memory. This distinction is based upon the concept that certain operative tasks, for instance the registration of input stimuli – in our case the perception of certain word material as well as pictured objects –, fall within the field of STM, whereas, for instance, the recognition of pictured objects and the semantic decoding of word meaning is a function of the experiences stored in LTM.

The deblocking process, that is the reactivation of the connection between pictured object and the relevant phonetic structure of the naming word, must, as is demonstrated below, be regarded as the result of a reciprocal cooperation between the two amnestic stages (LTM and STM).

In the following exposition we shall discuss, in the closest connection with the deblocking method, the problem of the organisation of lexical units in the form of semantic fields in LTM, a problem we have already explained in earlier works [187]. Luria and Vinogradova [118] did experimental research in the relationship between the representation of words of natural languages in LTM from the neurolinguistic viewpoint; and like them we set ourselves the task of studying from the same viewpoint – but with a different method – the stored *network* of object names. The method which we use gives us multifold possibilities in this connection, according to whether the blocked object naming should be set free by means of the direct supply of this word, or with the supply of a word standing in direct semantic-linguistic connection with it, or by both means. In this way we bring a certain naming word into relationship with other synonymous, hyperonymous superordinations, or lexically connected words, and thus attempt to obtain certain conclusions about the effectiveness of these connections. Here we are helped not only by those naming performances which are the result of direct deblocking, but also by those controlled misnamings which can tell us something about the mechanisms of misdirection in LTM.

In the attempt to interpret our test results we shall also discuss in outline certain signs for model concepts of naming under normal circumstances.

Deblocking auditory word comprehension disturbances

In the experimental research into amnestic-aphasic naming disturbances with the help of the deblocking method we have examined only patients with intact word comprehension. In addition we conducted a research variant with one case of sensory aphasia, in which we deblocked the faulty understanding of homonym meanings. In the former cases it was necessary to free access to the blocked sound structures; in the latter case the task was to make possible, starting from the sound structures provided, access to the corresponding blocked meaning structures. In both cases – as we shall see – semantic-lexical memory is affected in differing ways.

1. Experimental bases for deblocking experiments

Patients: The four patients involved in experiment variants A, B and C (picture naming) are all aphasics with a greater or lesser degree of *word-finding disturbance in naming pictures of various objects.* On the basis of their syndromes the patients can be classified as follows: patients Ni. and Mm. as semantic-amnestic; patient Br. as sensoric, and patient Schw. as efferent-motoric. Only in the case of Patient Ni. was a left-sided hemianopsy diagnosed, accompanied by slight picture-agnosic disturbances; however, naming difficulties arose in her case even with such pictures which she can be proved to have recognised correctly.[2] For the deblocking of *auditory word comprehension disturbances* with homonyms we selected patient Me., who displayed sensoric-aphasic impairment in speech perception.

The experimental conditions to show the deblocking phenomenon in its most elementary form ('simple deblocking' in distinction to 'chain deblocking', see [⟨9⟩; ⟨10⟩; ⟨2⟩]) have repeatedly been described in earlier works. For a better understanding of the deblocking process in connection with word-finding disturbance in naming pictures, some methodological pointers are given here.

Experimental methods:
Precontrol: before deblocking, a larger number of individual pictures were checked[3] to ascertain whether the patient was able to identify and name them, that is to say to find the corresponding word. For the deblocking experiments, a selection was made from the *non-named* pictures. On the basis of the repeated offer of one and the same picture, the fluctuation rate for the selected pictures was ascertained, this giving information as to the extent of fluctuation between positive and negative replies with regard to particular pictures (the last ones named were excluded).

The number of pictures which could not be correctly named spontaneously by the individual patients varied between 94% (patient Mm.) and 65% (patient Br.). Since the absolute number of pictures with which the patients failed totally was relatively great, we had available for the deblocking experiments a sufficient number of items from which a selection could be made for the differing variants.

Course of experiments: At the start, we pronounced or presented in writing to the patient a preliminary sequence of words (3–5); after he had perceived and understood them, he had to repeat them (or read them aloud); then the critical picture was presented for him to name. The result of the experiment was neither confirmed nor refuted by us.

Preliminary word sequences: These consist on the one hand of 'neutral' words which have no reference to the picture naming, and on the other hand of (a) words which directly designate the picture (i. e. the critical word 'nightclothes' for the relevant picture, or a pair of synonyms such as 'nightclothes' and 'pyjamas'); or (b) words which stand in more or less close semantic-lexical relationship with the picture (i. e. for the picture of pyjamas the hyperonym 'sleepwear', or the prarallel related words 'nightshirt', 'underpants', 'dressing gown', 'slippers', etc.) Table 1 (see p. 318) shows the differing variants in offering critical words and related words.

The modality of the preliminary word sequence was determined by which word comprehension function was intact in the patient concerned. In the case of patient Ni., who apart from her naming disturbance also suffered from receptive alexia (she could not comprehend the sense of words read), we offered the words auditorily, that is to say we pronounced the word sequences and had her repeat them (with this patient we also conducted homonym experiments).

With patient Mm., who also had intact auditory word comprehension and repetition, we utilised, to deblock the naming disturbances, as with patient Ni., these functions as deblockers.

In contrast, we offered the preliminary word sequences in writing to patient Br. and patient Schw., that is to say we had them read the individual words aloud, since in these cases word-reading comprehension and expressive reading were intact.

With patient Me., we conducted, instead of naming experiments, experiments with regard to the deblocking of auditory word comprehension (see homonym experiments, see p. 309). This patient had retained word-reading comprehension, so that we could offer him the preliminary word sequences in written form. After he had read these words and comprehended them, including the differing meanings of the homonyms, the homonymous word was pronounced to him; he had to indicate, either verbally or by gestures or drawing, whether he had understood correctly the homonym mean, this time auditorily.

Guaranteeing a non-conscious application of the deblocking procedure

In earlier works [⟨2⟩] I already indicated that a scientifically exact application of the deblocking method requires that a conscious intervention of the patient in the actual process of deblocking must be avoided; otherwise phenomena of pseudo-deblocking may easily arise. If a patient attempts, for instance, consciously to learn the preliminary word sequences, in order to repeat them when the pictures are subsequently presented, thus reproducing the corresponding word, this – even if the results are positive – had nothing to do with deblocking. What has taken place here is not a real naming, but a mechanical reproduction, a repetition of auditorily perceived linguistic utterances (insofar as disturbances in this field do not preclude such an effect).

In a multitude of experiments I have been able to ascertain, by questioning patients, that there has not been a conscious attitude to the deblocking process. For example, after one patient had promptly accomplished the correct naming after deblocking, we asked him how he located this word so promptly, though he had failed previously in namings of this nature. The patient answered very proudly that the word had 'simply occured to him'. Even when we asked him pointedly whether he had not heard this word before, or repeated it (read it aloud), the patient rejected this with conviction. Frequently the patients themselves express their astonishment that they have been able 'as from a clear sky' to name pictures, without becoming conscious of the connection with the preliminary word sequence. However, it certainly occured that in the course of the many naming tests a certain attitude of expectancy arose, which gave the patient the feeling that each time after the procedure of repeating (or reading aloud) he would be presented with a picture for naming, and that he would then be capable of overcoming his disturbance, though without knowing the basis for this 'miracle cure'.

To guarantee a non-conscious application, we introduced (selectively) a series of precautions:

(a) the *length of the preliminary word sequence,* that is the number of words, is if possible selected in such a way that a conscious and direct retention may be excluded as far as possible. Aphasics, as is well known, suffer in most cases from a narrow restriction of the extent of mechanical memory, so that the preliminary word sequence of four to five words generally used by us already exceeds this threshold.

(b) *intermediate non-deblocking word sequences:* an important insurance of the occurrence of a pure deblocking effect is provided by the word sequences which we insert, at irregular intervals, between the real preliminary sequences. The aim is to exclude in the patient the growth of a certain habituation; he should not become certain that each preliminary sequence with the critical word or a related word should inevitably be followed by the presentation of a picture corresponding to one of the preliminary words. In this manner we achieve an even greater degree of 'non-consciousness' in the experiment with regard to the deblocking method used.

Under these conditions the number of cases is extremely small in which the patient uses a word of completely different meaning from an interposed word sequence, in order to name the following picture which has no direct connection with the words of the preliminary sequence. Although patient Ni., for instance was completely able to understand auditorily and to repeat the words 'water-handkerchief-swallow-beetleowl', this had no effect on the following task, the naming of the picture 'leather bag'; the patient said: 'Write . . . you take in your hand'. Reference to one or more neutral preliminary words is therefore neither established in the gnostic identification of the pictures, nor in the search for the corresponding name.

(c) *neutral words:* The critical words or the related words are implanted in a sequence of neutral words, that is to say words which have no relationship with those needed in the picture naming (i. e. picture 'can', critical word in preliminary sequence: 'can', neutral words: *flowerbed, country, girl, riverbank*); here our aim was to leave the patient in ignorance as to which of the preliminary words would be critical. In this sense the registration of the preliminary words can proceed completely neutrally, that is without the marking of one word or another. Independently of their position in the preliminary sequence (at the beginning, middle or end), the neutral words were not used by the patients as a 'substitute' even when they were incapable of using the critical word or related word. It must be emphasised, however, that despite this neutrality these words are registered by short-term storage; this may be noted occasionally as when, for instance, a patient searching for the critical word is suddenly struck by a neutral word from a previous sequence.

2. *Hypotheses*

The experimental control of the deblocking of disturbed picture naming depends upon the composition of the preliminary word sequences. In this respect we had on the one hand the possiblity of *direct* control by including the critical word, that is the word needed for naming the picture, and on the other hand the *indirect* control by substituting in the preliminary sequence a related word for the critical word. Other possibilities were to present the critical word either alone in the preliminary sequence, or simultaneously with the corresponding related word, or the related word alone. Finally, we had the possibility of varying the related word, using either a synonym, a hyperonym, a related word, or a homonym.

With these differing variants we aimed at testing the effect of specific combinations of lexical units upon the deblocking. The presentation of one single critical word amongst a number of neutral words has the effect that the critical word offered provides direct 'punctiform' stimulation of the corresponding meaning structure in long-term storage (variant I); while the simultaneous offering of the critical word and a corresponding related word in the same sequence may provoke certain 'lexical conflicts' which leave open the possibility of a false naming with the related word.

Here we are confronted in addition with the question of the form of semantic concatenation of the critical word and the related word, that is to say according to the hierarchic levels of the lexicon where the coordination takes place (synonyms or adjacent related words such as chair – table, eagle – dove etc.), superordination (hyperonyms), the organisation of homonyms etc.

In automatic speech there are frequent word associations, such as *heaven-earth, man-wife, cat-dog,* which are often strengthened through stable idioms such as ' he moved heaven and earth' or 'it rained cats and dogs'; in distinction to such associations we have in our case lexical relations of a linguistic-logical nature between the critical word and the related word in the sense of class relations on the basis of mutual invariable conceptional coded features. This is true both for the relationship between the critical word and the attached related word (e. g. *window-door, vase-flowers, egg-ostrich,* etc.), and also between the critical word and its hyperonym (e. g. *icecream-confectionery, cannon-war material, book-printed matter,* etc.) or its synonym (e. g. *flag-standard*)[4].

These semantic linkings should appear particularly obvious in those variants (series B), in which the critical word in the preliminary sequence is replaced by one or more related words. Analysis of the influence of these related words upon the evocation of the critical word in picture naming is specially suited to provide certain insights into the relational structure of semantic memory.

In the framework of our research we devoted separate experimental series (C and D) to the problem of homonymics, a problem as yet relatively little studied in psycholinguistics.[5] Here we proceeded upon the assumption that by offering a homonym, that is one and the same sound structure, differing semantic fields would be excited (see [181]). This is, for instance, the case with the word *Schloss* which (in German, trans.) means both 'castle' – a splendid residence with all that goes with it, and 'lock' which may be understood in the widest sense of the word as an apparatus for closing. In our deblocking experiments we were guided by the remarkable fact that on the one hand there are patients who are able to identify a picture with the relevant word (e. g. door lock as *Schloss*), but who fail when they should use the same word for a different picture (e. g. *Schloss* in the sense of building); on the other hand certain patients can understand correctly a homonym in one meaning, but not in another. The deblocking of these naming disturbances or comprehension disturbances should give us a certain insight into particular aspects of the homonym problem.

Experimental series and variants (see Table 1)

1. Deblocking Picture-Naming Disturbances
Series A
The act of picture naming is *directly* stimulated by the critical word in the preliminary word sequence.

Variant I: The critical word alone is offered amongst a number of neutral words.

Variants II, III, IV: The critical word is offered in the preliminary sequence, simultaneously with one or more related words; these words can be hyperonyms (Variant II), synonyms (Variant III), or co-ordinate related words (Variant IV).

Series B
Cancellation of the disturbance in naming performances is *indirectly* aimed at by the sole presentation of related words the meaning structures of which are inter-relationally coupled with the critical words omitted from the preliminary sequence. These related words are on the one hand hyperonyms (Variant V), or on the other hand co-ordinate words, which in one case are presented in isolation amongst several neutral words (Variant VI), and in another case presented in the form of preliminary sequences entirely composed of words with a semantic relationship to the critical words (Variant VII); in Variant VIII the missing critical word in the preliminary sequence is replaced by a critical co-ordinate related word, the meaning of which is supported by the other related words (i. e. in the preliminary sequence the critical word 'owl' is replaced by the word 'crow', and this word meaning is reinforced by further descriptive words such as 'raven-swarm-black-shining-croaking').

Series C
The deblocking of naming disturbances with regard to differing pictured objects with one and the same name (homonyms) was partly undertaken by presenting the homonym name amongst a number of neutral words; sometimes the critical word was omitted from the preliminary sequence and replaced by related words which, however, strengthened only one of the two word meanings; this latter procedure was used in those cases in which in the procedure only one of the two objects pictured could be named (i. e. when the 'padlock' could be named as *Schloss* but not the castle; in this case the preliminary sequence gave the words 'building-pomp-court-king' before the picture of the building was presented).

2. Deblocking auditory word comprehension disturbances
Series D
In distinction to the previous experiments this series aimed at the

deblocking of auditory word comprehension disturbances with reference to the inability to understand varying homonym meanings; this should be done via intact word-reading comprehension. The following variants were applied in this case:

Variant D_1: In the written preliminary sequence a homonym was presented amongst neutral words; then this homonym was said to the patient, and he had to explain the meaning of the word (orally or with the help of gestures or of drawing).

Variant D_2: In the written preliminary sequence the critical word was presented, together with related words which reinforced only one of the homonym meanings. The patient must explain the word meaning.

Variant D_3: The same experiment, but with reinforcement of the other meaning of the same homonym.

3. Experimental results of the deblocking experiments

3.1 Picture naming disturbances

Before presenting quantitative results of the experiments, we should present some general conclusions on the dependence of the deblocking effect upon the prevailing experimental conditions. The dependences are as follows:

(a) Dependence upon the selection of word material: Word frequency: The assumption that the patient, in picture naming, is affected by the frequency of use of the words offered in the preliminary word sequence, was not confirmed. This can be demonstrated by the following examples: when for example patient Mm. identifies the picture of a brassiere with 'corsetry', patient Br. identifies the picture of a lipstick with 'cosmetics', patient Ni. the picture of icecream with 'confectionery', patient Schw. the picture of a book with 'printed matter', experience makes it clear that in this, and in many other cases, the less usual word has been chosen. The synonym experiments (Variant III) also do not allow the conclusion that there is a tendency to use the more usual synonym (for instance patient Br. prefers the word 'shrub' to the word 'bush', patient Ni. prefers the word 'vestibule' to the word 'corridor', etc.). In addition, the many double meanings (see page 299 also show that word frequency plays no significant role.

Phonological structure of the preliminary words (complexity, length, etc.)

The examples given in connection with word frequency show that the phonological structure of the words exercises no decisive influence on the word selection of the patient. For instance the word 'printed matter' is preferred to the word 'book', the word 'shrub' to the word 'bush', the word 'attic window' to the word 'skylight'.

(b) Positioning of the critical word or the related words in the prelimi-

nary sequence: We made special experiments to determine the influence on the deblocking effect of the positioning of the critical words or related words in the preliminary sequence, with the simultaneous presentation of both. We pursued this question systematically with two patients (Ni. and Mm.), using two parallel experimental series, in one of which the critical word was presented first and the related word later, and in the other vice versa. The results showed that it was not the positioning of these words but their status as critical word or related word which had the determining influence upon deblocking. Independent of its positioning, the critical word was named far more often than the related word.

(c) The length of the preliminary word sequence: As already noted, we were forced, dependent upon the situation of the patient, to vary the number of words offered between three and five. On the basis of a quantitative check on experimental results with longer or shorter word series, we were able to eliminate this factor as influencing the success rate in the experiments. This can also be shown by some examples: Preliminary sequence: 'bed-landscape-can-rain-girl'. Picture: can. Patient Mm.: 'That is the can'. Here, despite the relatively large number of preliminary words, the right name is found; the same occurs with a short run of words, for instance: 'leather-fish-book'. Picture: fish. Patient Br.: 'Fish'. However, a short run of words can lead to complete failure, or to false naming, for instance the preliminary words are 'beach-lipstick-cosmetics'. Picture: lipstick. Pat. Schw.: 'Cosmetics'.

3.2 Deblocking effects[6]

We regard as deblocking effect every case of picture naming which takes place on the basis of the induction brought about experimentally by the preliminary word sequence, irrespective of whether the critical word or the related word. In other words, in the case of patients who under normal circumstances remain silent when they see the picture, the naming of either the critical word or the related word is to be evaluated as the result of a deblocking effect.

Under our experimental circumstances a division into 'correct' and 'incorrect' namings can only be made with reservations. Naturally in our synonym experiments (Variant III), in which two words are given in the preliminary sequence, the meaning of which at least approximates to the same degree a given picture object, then the naming of either of the synonyms is quite correct; double namings with both synonyms must be regarded as unusual, particularly for patients with word-finding disturbances. In other variants, i. e. variants with hyperonyms (Variant II), it is not 'wrong' if a patient identifies a watering-can as 'garden implement', a snail as 'a mollusc', or a piece of soap as 'cleaning material'. It needs scarcely be emphasised that such namings can only be explained as a result of the experimental guidance, particularly with patients who are unable to find the names of the most everyday objects.

In the case of our patients there is complete inadequacy in the use of co-related words from the preliminary sequence, i. e. jacket instead of trousers, wolf instead of cat, slipper instead of boot, peas instead of carrots. Here it must be recalled that the choice of such words by the patient is incorrect, but not random; this is provoked by us, otherwise neutral words would be used just as frequently; but they are not.

In the following analysis we shall deal separately with the naming of the critical word, on the one hand, and the naming of related words on the other. We proceed not from the decision 'correct' or 'incorrect', but whether there is a deblocking effect which leads to the use of the critical word or a related word. In the second case we speak of *deviation effects;* such effects can naturally not arise either in Variant I, in which there are no related words in the preliminary sequence, nor in Variant III, in which the naming of one or the other synonym is equally adequate.

The following quantitative assessment of the results of our experiments is undertaken on the basis of these criteria: *Deblocking rates:* Sum of the frequency of all namings, independent of whether of the critical word or a related word. These rates are sub-divided into:

(1) d_{cw}*-rates:* sum of the namings of the critical word (cw), independently of whether this stands alone, or together with a related word.

(2) d_{rw}*-rates:* number of namings of a related word (rw), or simultaneously this and the critical word.

(3) *Double-naming-rates:* in these rates only the frequency of the double namings[7] is counted, minus the d_{cw} and d_{rw}-rates.

The average deblocking rate (see Table 2 column 1), that is to say the sum of the deblockings of naming-words (both critical words and related words) amounts to 90% (with a variation scale ranging from +10% to −45%). Compared to the zero level in the precontrol, these deblocking rates represent remarkable naming performances, both as regards the four patients and the differing variants. The total inability of the patients to react to the pictured object with an adequate – or even with an inadequate – word, could thus be overcome, totally or partially, on the basis of the deblocking method; the patient was then capable of naming the critical word, the related word, or both.

(2) d_{cw} *and* d_{rw}*-rates:* number of namings in which either the critical word or the related word alone is named. Following in brackets: number of namings applying either to the critical word or the related word, irrespective of whether the word in question appears in isolation or as part of a double naming.

(3) Double-naming rates: number of cases in which the critical word and one related word are used together in the naming.

In comparing the quantitative results of our deblocking experiments in Table 2 we have based ourselves upon the percentual placing system of Ludwig [104]. In addition, in those values which show only very low random samples, the difference in the experimental results of each two variants were determined in accordance with a non-parametric procedure for the comparison of two relative frequencies, described by Van Der Waerden [165]. The corresponding significance boundary was tested, in both methods, for an error probability of $\alpha = 5\%$.

3.2.1 Direct stimulation of picture naming by the critical word in preliminary word sequence (Series A)

The simplest form of direct stimulation by the critical word in the preliminary sequence consists in its isolated offering amongst several neutral words.

The d_{cw}-rates in Variant I (see Table 2): The percentage of cases in which the patient was able to name with the critical word the picture with which he had failed in the precontrol, lay at over 90% with two patients, and in two further cases at 44% and 77% (see Table 2, Variant I, column 1). The importance of these values can be appreciated in full measure if they are compared on the one hand with the zero values in the precontrol, and on the other hand with regard to the neutral words, where the values also approach the zero boundary: direct stimulation through the critical word corresponds with relatively high d_{cw}-rates. The patients are capable of using the critical word in all cases or in a great number of the cases.

Influence upon picture naming of the paired offer of critical word and related word (compare Variant I with Variants II, III and IV. See Table 2)[8].

Table 2 shows that the d_{cw}-rates can change on the basis of the simultaneous paired offers, on the one hand through an increase and on the other hand through a decrease in the d_{cw}-rates (increases: i. e. patient Mm. Variant I: 44%, Variant III: 100%; patient Schw. Variant I: 77%, Variant III: 100%; decreases: i. e. patient Ni.: Variant I: 92%, Variant II: 67%, Variant IV: 77%).

The increase in the d_{cw}-rates on the basis of the additional offer of certain related words admits the possibility of a facilitating influence of hierarchically superior lexical units (hyperonyms) or equally ranking lexical units (synonyms) on the deblocking of the critical word. Below we shall explain that this influence has effect on a certain processing stage in long-term storage (see p. 307).

The decrease of the d_{cw}-rates through the simultaneous offerings in the preliminary sequence indicates that in certain cases the presence of a related word hinders the evocation of the critical word, but this does not mean the same as a total lack of picture naming. This may be proved by the fact (see Table 2) that in all cases of a decrease in the d_{cw}-rate, the relevant related word is substituted for the critical word. The patients in question name the pictured object with the related word, and not the critical word (i. e. in Variant II. Preliminary sequence: 'beach-lipstick-cosmetics-collar'. Picture: lipstick. Pat. Ni.: 'Cosmetics').

The observation that the simultaneous offering of critical word and related word can lead on the one hand to a reinforcement of the deblocking effect, and on the other hand to a reduction shows for a start that the stimulation of the memory process by the critical word does not exclude the simultaneous effect of the related words also offered. The related words, connected with the critical word through hierarchically differing 'knots' can thus produce, at certain processing stages (see p. 307), favour or obstruct the release of the blocked evocation of the sound structure of the critical word, or they can lead to double meanings.

We aimed at a special form of deblocking by providing synonyms (Variant III). In the lexical structure, synonyms occupy one and the same knot with two or more word marks. In this way, during the evocation of the naming-word more alternatives are offered than when only one single critical word is given. The results achieved with Variant III in comparison with Variant I show that this offering can have results in two directions. On the one hand there is the increased chance of finding at least *one* picture naming (see Table 2, columns 1 and 2, patients Mm. and Schw.), but on the other hand the competition between the synonymous namings is so strongly stimulated that there can be a double naming, more or less involuntary on the part of the patient (see Table 2, column 3, pats. Ni. and Schw.).

3.2.2 Indirect stimulation by related words of the critical word missing in the preliminary word sequence (Series B)

Deblocking experiments carried out in the absence of the critical word in the preliminary sequence, solely on the basis of the offering of related words, provided a touchstone for the effectivity of the deblocking method. The determination that a patient can find the critical word when shown the picture, following the previous offer to this word, must be newly assessed now that we know that not only the critical word, but also a related word, can produce this deblocking effect. It may appear 'comprehensible' that a patient should be able to name correctly the picture of a woollen jacket, after previously having recognised this word earlier amongst others; but it appears less 'self-evident' when the claim is made that the same effect can be produced by offering the words 'knitted goods' or 'pullover'.

The special character of the indirect stimulation of picture naming is particularly to be seen in the fact that the related words offered are, to a certain extent, 'distant relations', i. e. they may be separated from the critical word, in the relevant semantic-lexical framework, by a series of hierarchically co-ordinated or super-ordinated knots. This is true, for instance, for the relationship between 'swallow' and 'eagle', between 'lamp-bulb' and 'candle', as well as between 'soap' and 'cleansing substance', and 'snail' and 'mollusc', etc. The discovery that even the reactivation of such complicated connections may form the basis for the deblocking effect, appears to us to give a certain insight into the structure and dynamics of the lexical organisation of semantic memory.

Influence upon naming performances of the presence or absence of the critical preliminary word:

Comparison of the deblocking rates (sum of all namings, including double namings, and faulty naming with a related word) *in Series A and B* (see Table 2, column 1):

The average deblocking rates in both series lie at an average of 90% (in the case of patient Mm. at 59% and 52%), that is to say that naming performance is not generally altered by the elimination of the critical word from the preliminary sequence. In other words, the deblocking effect is not dependent upon the direct offering of the critical word. *The* d_{cw}*-rates* (naming of the critical word, either alone, or together with a related word from the preliminary sequence), *under the conditions of Series B* (see Table 2, column 2, values in brackets):

Even when the critical word is missing in the preliminary sequence, the number of cases in which the critical word is used in naming often reaches relatively high values (up to 77%). This result shows that in Series B there can not only be a relatively high rate of namings (including faulty namings), but also a relatively frequent naming of the critical word.

Comparison of the d_{cw}*-rates and the* d_{rw}*-rates in the Series A and B* (Variants II and V) (Table 2, column 2, values in brackets): here we have, on the one hand, the paired offer of the critical word and the relevant hyperonym (i. e. 'dandelion' and 'meadow flower') (Variant II), and on the other hand the sole offer of a hyperonym (amongst neutral words) (Variant V).

Results:

1) In Variant II of Series A the d_{cw}-rates lie considerably higher than in Variant V of Series B (average 70% v. 35%) (see Table 2, column 2, values in brackets).

2) In contrast to the d_{cw}-rates in Variant V of Series B, the d_{rw}-rates, that is to say the number of cases in which use is made of a related word from the preliminary sequence, lie considerably lower in Variant II of Series A, averaging 22% v. 78% (see Table 2, column 2, values in brackets).

In other words, the influence of the presence of the critical word in

Series A makes itself felt through the fact that the patient uses this word much more frequently than the related word; in the absence of the critical word (Series B), the choice falls more frequently on the related word.

One might be tempted to dismiss the frequent namings of the pictures with related words as simply 'faulty namings'. In reality, however, as noted above, these deviations represent deblocking effects. Certain stages in long-term memory decide in favour of the choice of the sound structure of the relevant related word instead of the critical word: or there are 'conflicts' in which the decision is taken simultaneously for both words (double naming) (see Table 2, column 3).

Through the construction of Variant VIII (patient Ni.) we intended, by means of directed stimulation, to provoke competition between one co-related word and the missing critical word. For instance, where the critical word was 'owl', we stressed the importance of the co-related word 'crow' by the use in the preliminary sequence of words like 'ravens-swarms-black-shining-croaking'; in doing this, we aimed at making it more difficult to find the word 'owl', or even preventing it. The connection between the two species is transmitted through the knot 'birds'. In order, however, to establish a connection between the related word 'crow' and the picture of an owl, the hierarchically superior knot 'birds' must become effective. However, through this linking, the sound structure of the word 'crow' is so strongly re-activated that it not only inhibits the sound structure of the word 'owl', but becomes a complete substitute. Word alienation explains why patient Ni. – despite the possibility of recontrol with the help of the given picture – is firmly convinced that she named the correct word. Naturally, however, had the word 'crow' been offered by the examiner, the patient would firmly have rejected it.

The result of these guided deviations may be seen from the following results: the critical related word was named alone in 29% of the cases, and in 70% together with the critical word, or together with the other related words.

3.2.3 Paired use of the critical word and related word in picture naming. Double naming (see Table 2, column 3)

The deblocking effect, that is to say the removal of the inability of the patient to name certain pictures, is expressed in our investigations by the fact that the patients either react as normal subjects, designate the picture with one name, or they use in addition a second (or more) words, which are, however, also selected from the preliminary sequence. In this way, in many cases, not only the critical word, but also one or more of the offered related words are named. Double namings only occur in those variants which include related words; they do not appear in

Variant I, in which the critical word is accompanied exclusively by neutral words.

Table 2 shows that the double namings are distributed to very differing degrees amongst the various patients and variants. They are relatively frequent in the case of patient Ni., and partially relatively frequent with patient Schw., but in the cases of the two other patients they are rather infrequent. It is difficult to find a useful explanation for this difference with regard to the type of aphasia suffered. For example the spontaneous speech of patients Ni., Br. and Mm. is strongly logorrhoeic, while with patient Schw. it bears a motor-aphasic character. This would lead one to expect a higher rate of double namings from patients. Br. and Mm., too; on the other hand one is surprised by the relatively high rate of double namings from patient Schw.

In the case of patients Ni. and Schw. one is struck by the fact that with only a few exceptions, the frequency of double namings is greater than the use of the critical word alone to designate the picture; in the other two cases this is not the case.

In assessing the double namings, it must be taken into consideration that varying forms of behaviour are concealed behind this form of reaction:

(a) upon the presentation of the picture, the patient names the critical word simultaneously with a related word, without indicating a preference for one word or the other (i. e. preliminary sequence: 'milk-drink-ring', picture: milk. Patient Schw.: 'Milk, drink'); the critical word may be named first or second, independent of its position in the preliminary sequence.

(b) The double naming is spoken in the form of an alternative (i. e. preliminary sequence: 'note-bank-cheque-paper', picture: coins. Patient Schw.: 'Notes or money').

(c) The double naming expresses a correction, since the first naming is rejected, rightly or wrongly, by the patient himself (i. e. preliminary sequence: 'wool-knitted-put-on-handmade-cap', picture: head scarf. Pat. Ni.: 'Cap . . . actually a scarf, it's just put on, a cloth, a head scarf'.

(d) In other cases, related words from the preliminary sequence are used in sentence form for additional precision (i. e. preliminary sequence: 'newspaper-parcel-registered-loaded-delivery', picture: postman. Patient Ni.: 'The postman has to deliver the parcels').

In Variant III (synonyms) it should normally suffice, particularly for patients with word-finding disturbances, to select and name only one of the synonyms offered. But just in this Variant the values for double naming reach, for patients Ni. and Schw., the values of 93% and 73%. In these cases one could assume that the effectiveness of deblocking is 'too great'. We shall refer to this further below.

The inadequate character of the double namings is expressed most clearly in those variants in which the related words consist of co-ordinate lexical units (i. e. 'chair-table', 'horse-zebra'). Here these namings lead to a combination of correct and incorrect identification (i. e. preliminary sequence: 'brows-lashes-hair', picture: beard. Patient Schw.: 'Hair or beard'.

3.2.4 Results of deblocking picture naming through homonyms (Series C)

In the precontrol patient Ni., on whom these experiments were carried out, failed with 8 pictures: in 7 cases she identified only one of the two pictures, and in one case neither. Here are the details:

Correct	*Failed*
Schloß-Türschloß (lock)	*Schloß-Gebäude* (building)
Puffer-Kartoffelpuffer (pancake)	*Puffer-Eisenbahn* (railway)
Büchse-Konservenbüchse (can)	*Büchse-Gewehr* (shotgun)
Wolf-Tier (animal)	*Wolf-Fleischmaschine* (mincer)
Pflaster-Wundpflaster (plaster)	*Pflaster-Straße* (street)
Brause-Dusche (shower)	*Brause-Getränk* (lemonade)
	Anhänger-Schmuck (jewellery)
	Anhänger-Fahrzeug[9] (vehicle)

For the deblocking of these disturbances – analogously to Variant VII – the patient was given a preliminary word sequence without the critical word, and was then shown that picture for which she had been unable to provide the relevant homonym (i. e. preliminary sequence: 'metal-opening-door-key', picture: padlock; preliminary sequence: 'meat-grind-household-kitchen implement-hamburger', picture: meat mincer; preliminary sequence: 'village-street-cracks-road-bumpy', picture: cobbled paving).

Result of the experiments: in all cases the patient was able to name the picture with the corresponding homonym. For instance with the homonym 'trailer', in which the patient had failed in the precontrol with reference to both pictures (jewellery-vehicle), there was a direct deblocking, that is the critical word was offered amongst several neutral words (preliminary sequence: 'trailer-pencil-parcel'), and then presented successively with one of the two pictures. Both pictures were correctly named by the patient with the relevant homonym.

3.3 Results of the deblocking of disturbances of auditory word comprehension with homonyms (Series D)[10]

In the precontrol we ascertained that patient Me. was incapable of the auditory understanding of certain pairs of homonyms, though in the receptive reading of these words he had no comprehension difficulties.

Variant D_1: We registered that it was possible to deblock this disturbance in auditory semantic decoding, through prior receptive unvocaled reading of the optically-offered preliminary sequence. After the patient had read, for instance, the words 'bread-dew-give', and understood them correctly (his reading aloud was seriously disturbed) – the double meaning of the (German) homonym *Tau* in the sense of 'dew on the meadow' and of 'rope' was completely clear to him – the word *Tau* was spoken aloud to him, and he described its meaning either vocally or through gestures or drawings.

Experimental result: The patient was presented separately with 49 homonyms of this type; he was successful in 80% of the cases.

The considerations upon which the succeeding Variant $D_{2,1}$ and Variant $D_{2,2}$ are based run as follows: in the case of the auditory comprehension of a homonym based upon two or more different semantic fields, it must be possible systematically to facilitate one of the two fields and to suppress the other, through the utilisation of the deblocking method.

With the aid of the same process used in Variant VIII of our naming experiments, we reinforced one or the other meaning of the homonym by using a preliminary sequence of written words, excluding the critical word.

Variant $D_{2,1}$: the optical lexical preliminary sequence 'morning-grass-damp' reinforced the importance of the homonym *Tau* – which does not appear in the preliminary sequence – in the sense of 'dew on the meadow', while its sense as 'rope' remains unmentioned. When the examiner utters the word *Tau,* the patient understands it only in the first sense.

Results: In 55% of the cases it was shown that only the reinforced sense was understood, not the other.

Variant $D_{2,2}$: preliminary sequence: 'string-ship-make-fast'. When the word *Tau* is pronounced by the examiner, this is understood by the patient only in the sense of 'rope', and the sense 'dew on the meadows' is rejected by him.

Results: This effect could be registered in 73% of the cases, using 22 homonyms.

4. Speech behavior of the patients during the naming experiments

An impressive confirmation of our opinion with regard to the processes which take place during the deblocking experiments, apart from the quantitative results, may be found in the remarks made by the patients themselves during picture naming.

In a great variety of ways the patients, particularly during the precontrol, but also during the search phase of the experiment, stress that in their attempts to name pictures 'something is missing' – we would say 'blocked'. Shown the picture 'firs', one patient said: 'Ah, these here are missing now', but repeatedly declared that she 'knows' the word. The same tendency is shown by the self-addressed question: 'Well, what does one say now?' (patient Ni. to the picture 'violin'). However, such questions can also play a delaying role, giving the search process a chance of finding the name, whether correct or false (patient Ni., when shown the picture 'zebra': 'Well, what should we say to that now, I can't get the name . . . it's a horse . . .').

The mechanism of the return check, in which implemented naming is compared with optical reception, functions in very differing ways in the individual cases.

The patients are frequently convinced that the words used by them in the deblocking experiments are in fact correct, and cannot be persuaded to the contrary by the objections of the examiner. Patient Mm. reacted to the picture of a fork with the claim: 'This is a knife, yes there are other knives too, but this is a knife'. The same patient, giving the name 'jacket' to the 'trouser' picture, was absolutely convinced that she had chosen the right name: she replied rather crossly to our objections: 'But I said: jacket'. The same 'mistake', guided by the preliminary sequence, made her say 'shoes' instead of 'stockings'. When patient Ni. was shown the picture 'candle' the response was: 'A little lamp . . . electr . . . how do you say it? Electric lamp, it's not a lamp, that really is electric light . . . a light . . . little lamp . . . little bulb . . . twenty-fiver. (Here the short intercalated doubt 'it's not a lamp' is then rejected).

The insufficient strength of the control function may also be shown by the following case, involving patient Ni. Picture: 'sponge'. Patient: 'The facecloth (word of the preliminary sequence), you have it here . . . but that's actually a rubber cloth, so you can't really say facecloth . . . rubber . . . what do you say to that?'

Rejection of the selected naming can sometimes take a very sharp form, for instance when patient Ni. says instead of 'stags' the word 'ducks' (word of the preliminary sequence 'geese'), and finally states: 'But that is nonsense'.

Another form of deficient feedback is provided by the double namings (see p. 299). Patient Schw., faced with the picture of a 'watering can', searches for the correct name, finds only the word 'can', but simultaneously recalls the word of the preliminary sequence 'garden instrument' and repeats: 'can, garden instrument, can, garden instrument'.

Particularly interesting are the cases in which the differing processing stages are reflected in the statements made by the patients. Patient Ni., for instance, began with a word from the preliminary sequence, and only reached the critical word after a long search. Picture: bench, patient: "A chair (word of the preliminary sequence), no that isn't a chair any more, it's already . . . I can't say it, but now I have it on my tongue . . . I won't reveal it . . . a bench." In this case the return check was successful, though the critical word only emerged after a certain period of latency, in which the false naming was extinguished; this was followed by a momentary feeling of 'blocking' ('but now I have it on my tongue'), followed again by a slow working through to success (the expression 'I won't reveal it' should probably mean 'I can't say it yet'). With another picture (glasses), pat. Ni. first wandered through part of the preliminary sequence (Variant VIII: reinforced adjacent, semantically related word): 'coffee, hot, breakfast, cake', in which she omits precisely the reinforced word 'cups', then proceeds further 'coffee service, really quite nice', then reaches the false identification 'liqueur service', finally saying correctly 'wine glasses'.

The frequent failure of the return check shows the strength of the deblocking, in this case the deviation effect.

In other cases the feedback operates to the extent that the patients show a degree of uncertainty in their guided false namings, or they express their rejection of their own naming performance, even when they cannot relinquish the word they have once chosen. For instance pat. Br. described 'soap' as 'cleaning material', but added: "But it is called something else".

Examples of such false reports in the return check, without the possibility of correcting them, are very numerous amongst our patients. Patient Br., who instead of 'pansy' uses the word of the preliminary sequence 'garden flower' states with regret: "yes, but the pretty . . . I would always like to be the right one". Or patient Schw. looking at the picture of a cauliflower: "Vegetable (a word of the preliminary sequence) is right, but something more is missing."[11]

This 'clinging' to the word from the preliminary sequence was also noted in the case of patient Ni., who was searching for the word 'boot': "A shoe for a gentleman . . . also a debatable question (she meant whether this answer was right) a high shoe . . . tramping shoe for wet weather . . . leather shoe . . . but it's got a particular name . . . slipper (word of the preliminary sequence) . . . no, not slipper either." The same patient on the picture of a shirt: "Men's underpants (word of the preliminary sequence), it's not underpants, one day . . . not pants . . . the other one . . . pants are underneath . . . underclothing . . ." And patient Ni. is fully aware of her misnaming, since she ends her sentence: "but it is not quite what you want".

The patients' statements regarding the conflict within themselves in the search for the correct identification can be quite dramatic. Once again, the remarks made by patient Ni. are of importance. "Now I have got all the other words in my head, just not that one (the word in question was 'flag')." And: "Oh dear, everything is mixed up in my head now" (picture: glasses), or: "all sorts of animals I have on my lips" (picture: 'stags'). This last remark shows the patient to be aware of the semantic field 'animals', in which she seeks for the word 'stags'.

5. Discussion

Model concepts on the processing steps of deblocking word-finding disturbances in picture naming and disturbances in auditory word comprehension[12]

To understand better the processes which presumably lie behind the deblocking effects, it is necessary to stress once again that in the case of the semantic-amnesic disturbances in the naming of objects which we investigated, the correct gnostic identification did not lead at all, or only in limited measure, to the recall of the relevant sound structure in long-term memory. The connection between picture meaning and sound structure is blocked, although there is no impairment of the semantic decoding of word meaning.

Thus the deblocking of naming disturbances in our cases represents the removal of the blocking of this connection in long-term memory.

In the following we shall discuss the processing steps which are probably responsible.

5.1 Under the conditions of Variant I

Short-term storage of word structures, of the preliminary word sequences, and of the optical representation of the pictured object:

We proceed from the assumption that on the basis of the preliminary word sequence, for a start, only the sound structures of the individual words[13], and on the basis of the picture presentation only the optical image of the individual words have been fixed in short-term storage. Here we base ourselves upon the consideration that both the semantic decoding of the words of the preliminary sequence, and the recognition of the optical offerings, demand certain classification and selection processes which can only occur in long-term storage, and that only there can there be the relevant ontogenetically conditioned intra- and interrelational networks, and the strategies for their use.[14]

The assumption of reciprocal *transitions from long-term storage to short-term storage* appears to us to be basically necessary in cases involving semantic decoding or the grammatical processing of phonetic word structures.

The semantic decoding of the word structures offered in the preliminary word sequences assumes the evocation of the relevant meaning structures, which can certainly not be stored in short-term memory, but only in long-term memory: thus the transmission of these word structures from the short-term memory to the long-term memory constitutes, in our opinion, a basic condition for the deblocking process (here we ignore the grammatical processing of these structures).

Picture recognition also depends on the necessity of transmission from short-term storage to long-term storage, since the cognition or re-cognition of pictured objects must appeal to the storage of the relevant invariable feature sets which these objects represent in memory.

The semantic decoding of the word structures applies in the first place to all words of the preliminary sequence, and thus the disposition of their meanings, irrespective of their utility for the following process of naming.

Convergence: In our case this should be taken to mean, in the neuro-psychological view, the coincidence of excitation processes triggered by stimuli of varying modalities and levels (optical-auditory, verbal-nonverbal), and directed at one and the same meaning structure, that of the critical word and the pictured object.[15]

Under the conditions of Variant I, the deblocking effect here is based in the first place on convergence in long-term storage between the verbo-auditory and the optic-gnostic process, which leads to the identification and the common meaning structure behind the critical word and the pictured object.

As noted, this identification meets no difficulties in our patients, since both auditory word comprehension and picture recognition are intact. On the other hand, this convergence with regard to the common meaning structure does not suffice alone in order to cancel the blockage of the connection in long-term storage between meaning structure and the sound structure of the naming word. This demands further a simultaneous retrieval of the sound structure. Since the patient is not capable of doing this 'on his own', the sound structure must be provided from 'outside', in the form of the critical word offered in the preliminary sequence.[16]

The difference between the usual naming experiment in which the patient fails because of his word-finding disturbance, and naming under the conditions of deblocking is as follows: in the former case the patient can only rely upon his perception of the picture and its correct interpretation, in which he fails in verbalising its meaning – he is not capable of selecting the sound structure in long-term storage; but in deblocking experiments the patient has available to him the critical word, not only with regard to its meaning but also with regard to its phonetic structure, and by this means the blockage of the connection with the sound structure in long-term storage can be cancelled.

Marking: The processing which leads to the final naming requires certain marking stages to define precisely the relevant word structure. On the basis of the various structures offered in the preliminary word sequence, and the picture presented there must be – in the case of a successful deblocking – a marking of the critical word or related word, or both, first in long-term storage and then in short-term storage, too. At the same time there must be a far-reaching elimination of the other, the neutral, words.

Reporting back: In the 'reporting back' and 'checking back', discussed below, we proceed from the system character of neuro-psychological processes in memory in the case of self-regulating feedback systems (see [114]). Here short-term storage is regarded as a station which first registers the perceived information both with reference to the preliminary word sequence and to the object pictured; it then passes on this information to long-term storage, and receives in stages from long-term storage return reports on the process of meaning coordination (words, picture), of convergences and markings; short-term storage compares these with the data originally fixed, and refers the results of this comparison once again to long-term storage, and so on.

Checking back: The picture naming, either prepared in internal speech or already implemented, can be checked, consciously or unconsciously, with the picture presented, and if necessary corrected. Under some circumstances there must be a renewed run through the various processing stages. The question remains open as to whether, or how, the two storage stations are utilised in this checking back.

5.2 Additional model schemes

5.2.1 Offering the critical and related words in one and the same preliminary word sequence (Series A)

The variants of Series A, in which both critical and related words are presented in one and the same preliminary sequence (Variants II, III, IV), demand additional model schemes with regard to the operations upon which the deblocking process is based.

(1) This form of offering can lead, already at the stage of semantic

decoding in long-term storage, before perception of the picture, to a convergence of the meaning structures of the critical and related word, and their marking in distinction to the neutral words (i. e. picture: stag, preliminary sequence: 'dancer-bookcase-game-aunt-stag'. In this case there can be a 'closing-up' between the words 'stag' and 'game', in distinction to dancer, bookcase, aunt).

(2) The process of identifying the meaning structure of the pictured object in long-term storage then takes place under the conditions of the already decoded meaning structures of the critical and related word, including the sound structures which are placed ready.

(3) In the case of the successful deblocking of the critical word, the competition between this and the related word is decided in favour of the former, and this decision is conveyed to short-term storage, so that instructions may then be given to name the critical word.

5.2.2 Missing critical word in the preliminary word sequence (Series B, see Schema 2)

Even in those cases in which the patient is not offered the critical word directly before picture naming, the incidence of the deblocking effect throws a particular light on the mechanisms which form the basis for this process of word finding. Thus the blocking of the connection between picture meaning and the relevant sound structure can be removed *indirectly* in long-term storage with the aid of related words. This proves the effectivity of long-term storage of lexical connections between the critical word and the related word within the same semantic field.

The various stages of the deblocking process reveal themselves under these conditions in the following manner:

(1) Convergence in long-term storage between the meaning structure of the related word and that of the pictured object.

(2) Marking in long-term storage of the meaning structure of the related word and that of the pictured object.

(3) Not only the meaning structure of the related word and of the critical word, but also their sound structures, are ontogenetically connected in the relevant semantic field; this makes probable the assumption that the offered sound structure of the related word 'triggers' the blocked sound structure of the critical word, and thus releases its interrupted connection with the picture meaning.

(4) In this manner the marking of the related word can be cancelled in favour of the critical word, and the result of the reactivation of the sound structure of the critical word can be reported back to short-term memory.

(5) Under these conditions it becomes possible for the command to be given to the effector for the verbo-motoric implementation of the phonetic structure of the critical word.

5.2.3 Picture naming through homonyms (Series C)

The deblocking of naming disturbances by means of the use of homonyms does not differ basically, with regard to the processes involved, from the other word-finding disturbances. Since in this case (patient Ni.) there is no disturbance in understanding the various meanings of words with one and the same sound structure, but only in their coordination to, or better reactivation upon the presentation of differing pictured objects, this reactivation can take place along the paths of the deblocking process described above in connection with naming disturbances.

The fact that in certain cases this patient could name one object, but not a second object the word for which has the same sound structure, does not call for a supplementary model scheme. Here we have only an analogous case with that in which patients had to name different pictured objects represented by differing words; that is to say the naming disturbances of the patients are partial (in the preliminary check, patient Ni. was able to name correctly 35% of the pictures presented).

For this reason we utilised, for deblocking unilateral naming disturbances in homonyms, the technique applied in Variant VIII; in the preliminary word sequence, when the critical word was missing, we reinforced that meaning of the homonym which previously could not evoke the corresponding sound structure. As the results show, deblocking took place in this manner in most cases.

Thus the deblocking processes applicable here take their place with those previously outlined (Series B).

5.3 Disturbances of the auditory comprehension of homonyms (Series D)

In the case of the homonym experiments with patient Me., the conditions are rather different, since in this case we do not have a naming disturbance, but auditory word comprehension disturbance, with intact word reading comprehension. Thus there is not a disturbance of word comprehension *per se,* but only of the auditory modalities. The perceived sound structure can be registered in short-term storage, and under certain conditions be reproduced, that is to say repeated, but without comprehension. In other words, in this case long-term storage does not perform its function of semantically decoding the sound structure; it does this, however, when presented with the relevant *graphemic* structure, the written word.[17]

The blocking therefore lies in the transition from the sound structure to the meaning structure of the word, the opposite of what we see in cases of naming disturbances. In this case the deblocking method consists of utilising intact reading comprehension to cancel the disturbed comprehension of spoken words.

The results reported show (Variant D) that this form of deblocking was successful with patient Me., even with regard to the auditory comprehension of homonym meanings, in 80% of the cases. We ascribe this deblocking effect to the fact that, owing to intact perception and semantic decoding of the graphemic structure of the critical word in the preliminary word sequence, the subsequently perceived corresponding sound structure encounters an already pre-excited meaning structure in the relevant semantic field in long-term storage; in this way a connection is established between the meaning of the graphemic structure and of the sound structure, which releases the blocking of auditory word comprehension.

5.4 Deviation effects (model schemes)

5.4.1 Guided deviations in picture naming experiments

In the precontrol the patients failed, wholely or in part, in naming pictures, but as explained here it was possible, with the help of the deblocking experiments, to make the patients capable of naming either all of the pictures previously unnamed, or at least a considerable part. They did this either with the corresponding critical word, or – sometimes wrongly – with one of the related words from the preliminary sequence, or sometimes with both. Only the critical words or related words were used to name the pictured objects, and the neutral words used in the preliminary sequence; for this reason we regard all naming performances using related words as results of the applied deblocking method, just as with critical words.

In the first stage the related word, together with the other words of the preliminary sequence, is registered in short-term storage, and passed on to long-term storage for semantic decoding. At this stage there may be a marking of the related word which may be difficult to cancel in further processing. Here there are various alternatives:

(a) When both the critical word and the related word are present in the preliminary sequence (Variants II and IV), both word structures are semantically decoded in long-term storage, and the optical representation of the pictured object identified. In the optimal sense – as in Variant I – the offered sound structure of the critical word *per se* should suffice to remove the blocking of the connection between the meaning structure and sound structure of the critical word. In addition – and this happens in a majority of cases – the sound structure of the related word should produce a facilitating induction which reinforces the deblocking process with regard to the critical word. The fact that in a number of cases (up to 33%, see Table 2, Variants II and IV, column 2, h_w and a_{rw}) the related word and not the critical word is named, leads us to assume a competition between the relevant sound structures for the marking which leads to a command to the verbo-motoric effector. Thus the sound structure of the related word represents a genuine alternative, and a decision may sometimes be made in its favour.

It will be difficult to determine the reasons for such a result of the competition, particularly since word frequency and rank position (see above) appear to play no role here.

(b) When the critical word is missing in the preliminary word sequence (Series B): here the probability of deviations of the type named is considerably greater than in Series A, since the comprehension of meaning is concentrated on the one hand on the related word in the preliminary sequence, and on the other hand on the pictured object; thus differing but related meaning structures confront one another; in this way the structure of the critical word can be evoked; the deblocking of the sound structure corresponding to the meaning structure of the pictured object can be facilitated by the connection between critical word and related word, which is stored in long-term memory, but on the other hand there is the possibility of 'competition' between the two. The later evoked sound structure of the critical word is probably at a disadvantage compared to the phonetic structure of the related word, already fixed in the preliminary sequence; thus there is a bigger chance for the selection of the related word rather than the critical word. This explains the relatively high d_{rw}-rates (up to 95%) obtained.

(c) The double namings too, which appeared both in the variants of Series A and Series B, show the competition between the sound structures of the critical word and related word, reactivated in long-term storage. This is expressed in the relatively large number of usages of both words in picture naming. As soon as both words become available, the related word should be cancelled before the 'report back' to short-term storage. However, there appears to be a certain inertia in the structure of the related word previously evoked, so that the critical word 'pulls with it' the related word. The frequency of double namings can reach up to 95% of the cases.

5.4.2 Guided deviations in homonym experiments (Series C and D)

As our results in Series C and D show (see p. 302 f.), we were able to deblock both disturbances in the use of homonyms in picture naming, and also limitation in the comprehension of homonym meanings. In addition we were able to determine the direction in which this naming or comprehension operates. In both cases, a suitable semantic-lexical arrangement of the preliminary word sequence made possible guided deviations, although the psycho-linguistic processes upon which this is based are of differing types.

In the case of the amnestic-aphasic picture-naming disturbances of patient Ni., we were able to show that the selection of a particular homonym functioned correctly in the precontrol; however, when the experiment was repeated under suitable deblocking conditions, this led to the mis-performance which we intended. Thus, in the precontrol the patient was able to name correctly the picture of a stork's wing *(Flügel),* but not the picture of a grand piano (also *Flügel*), although she could identify the latter correctly gnostically. In the deblocking experiment we exposed auditorily the preliminary word sequence 'music-soloist-pianist-concert'. When presented with the picture of a grand piano the patient failed once again: "I know what it is . . . a musical instrument . . . really a piano, but a better sort"; on the other hand, when she was subsequently presented with the picture of a stork's wing, which she had named correctly in the precontrol, she now said: "Now the musical instruments are coming . . . I nearly said guitar".

Here it must be noted that the patient knew very well that the stork's wing was not a musical instrument. When queried on this she could give clear information; however, in her search for the relevant homonym *Flügel,* the perseverating influence of the semantic field *musical instrument,* which had been brought into readiness both by the preliminary word sequence and by the picture of the grand piano, made itself felt. However, this confusion was not of a semantic-notional nature, but can be explained by the fixation of the patient on the sound structures connected with the semantic field *musical instruments,* including *guitar.*

The deviations which we were able to produce in connection with the deblocking of auditory word comprehension disturbances concerning homonyms in patient Me. were of a basically different nature (see p. 302 f.). Here it was possible to inhibit the semantic decoding of one of the meanings of various homonyms by inducing the other meaning through the preliminary word sequence. These deviations in the correct comprehension of both meanings concern – in distinction to the deviations provoked in patient Ni. – the *semantic memory directly* (at least in the framework of one modality), in this case the stored homonym meanings. Such guided deviations came about in up to 73% of the cases.

5.4.3 Non-guided deviations

In the study of this type of mis-performance in aphasics, so-called semantic verbal paraphasia (see [4]) are suited to confirm and deepen our opinion of the character of deviations.

I. Weigl has investigated experimentally the problem of lexical mis-performances in aphasics among other things in connection with spontaneous substitutions in differing speech functions, etc. In a non-published work (on this see also ⟨3⟩), she reported on mis-namings and mis-readings of the following nature. Patient W. produced in expressive readings of single words mis-readings in 25% of the cases, such as *Schürze* instead of *Strümpfe* (apron instead of stockings), *Hose* instead of *Unterrock* (trousers-petticoat), *Badeanzug* instead of *Handtasche* (swim-suit-handbag), *Sandalen* instead of *Socken* (sandals-socks), *Krawatte* instead of *Manschette* (tie-cuff), *Mieder* instead of *Strickjacke* (corset-knitted jacket), *Pfirsiche* instead of *Apfelsinen* (peaches-oranges), *Banane* instead of *Ananas* (banana-pineapple), *Datteln* instead of *Feigen* (dates-figs), *Kartoffeln* instead of *Gemüse* (potatoes-vegetables), *Radieschen* instead of *Petersilie* (radishes-parsley), etc. In picture naming, the same patient produced misnamings in 47% of the cases, with *Erdbeeren* instead of *Kirschen* (strawberries-cherries), *Kohl* instead of *Salat* (cabbage-lettuce), *Dill* instead of *Petersilie* (dill-parsley), *Tomate* instead of *Mohrrübe* (tomato-carrot), *Bohne* instead of *Erbse* (bean-pea), etc. Patient We. named a glove *arm, finger,* a fur hat *knitted cap,* swimshorts *panties,* a headscarf *handkerchief,* a lion *bear,* etc.

Analogous findings are given in I. Weigl and Mihailescu [204] and in an extensive work by these authors now under preparation; this work describes a comparitive investigation on the reproduction of lexical units in reading aloud, repetition and writing to dictation, both with regard to isolated words and to these same words in syntagmas. In these cases, too, there were many cases of the substitution of lexically related words for the correct words (e. g. 'street' instead of 'corner', 'money' instead of 'gift', 'field' instead of 'turf', 'waiter' instead of 'hotel', etc.); this occured both with German-speaking and Roumanian-speaking patients.

The results of these experiments show that semantic-lexical deviations can occur both on the basis of experimental guidance and on the basis of spontaneous reproduction. This means that in both cases the coordination to a presented meaning structure of the sound structure or the graphemic structure of a certain word is blocked, and that as a result recourse may be taken to the sound structure of a word which is semantically-lexically related. The difference between the conditions of deblocking and the conditions of direct reproduction, by repetition, dictation writing or reading aloud, of words presented orally or in writing, is mainly the following: in the case of deblocking, the related word has been offered in the preliminary word sequence, whereas in the case of spontaneous reproduction the related word is 'supplied' by the patient himself.

In simple word reproduction – insofar as it is not absolutely mechanical, without comprehension[18] the auditorily or optically perceived semantically decoded word structure must be *transcoded,* first into its relevant sound structure and finally into the verbo-motoric structure (see also ⟨12⟩).

In the sense of our model scheme outlined above, misperformances of the type described must not be interpreted as semantic confusions, i. e. as substitutions of differing meaning structures, but as a fall-back upon non-blocked sound structures which, because of the ontogenetically stabilised semantic relationship between certain lexical units, are thus available in certain situations. In other words the patient who wishes to read the word 'cherry' aloud understands very well the meaning of this word as well as he knows the semantic difference to the word 'strawberry'; despite this, he uses the word 'strawberry' from the common semantic field 'fruit', since this word offers itself to him at this given moment instead of the blocked sound structure of the word 'cherry'.[19]

Thus the nature of aphasically motivated word finding disturbances in object naming presents itself as follows: it is not a question of 'gaps' in the lexicon' on the part of the patient, *not a question of the limitation of the semantic-lexical memory in the sense of 'meaning disturbance or name finding disturbance':* in fact *the ability of the patient is affected to reactivate the ontogenetically connected sound structures corresponding to certain meaning structures which he has at his command.*[20]

On the other hand, the results of the experiments with regard to disturbed auditory word comprehension in sensory aphasia (homonym experiment indicated that access to the semantic-lexical memory can be blocked to a greater or lesser degree, so that *the corresponding meaning structures cannot be found to the correctly perceived sound structures of the words.*

With the help of the deblocking method it is possible in principle, as we have shown above, to remove to a considerable degree the coordination disturbances in both cases, or to guide them in a specific direction (deviations).

Although the system of word finding disturbances *per se* has no clear localisation with regard to the cortex (see [1]; [12]; [53]; [61]) the authors are generally agreed that object naming is most often disturbed in cases of damage to the posterior regions of the left hemisphere, in particular the temporo-parieto-occipital intersection areas (gyrus angularis and supramarginalis): (see [43]; [47]).

Luria [115, p. 315 ff.] located object naming disturbances differingly, according to whether it was a case of impairment in optic-gnostic identification (parieto-occipital), auditory speech comprehension and speech production in sensory aphasia (temporo-occipital), Broca-aphasia (frontal), or semantic-amnestic aphasia (parieto-temporo-occipital).

The anomias occuring in the latter form of aphasia are ascribed by Luria [115, p. 9] to selectivity disturbances in which "a whole series of words with the same degree of probability are evoked".

In our case we are dealing with patients of differing aphasic types, and thus with differing localisation: the only thing they have in common is amnesic-aphasic failure in picture naming (with intact picture recognition, intact auditory or optical word comprehension, and a word production sufficient to judge naming performance). The possibility of strictly localising the word finding disturbances examined here is thus lacking.

Auditory word comprehension disturbances (acoustic-amnestic aphasia) is generally ascribed to damage to the upper region of the left temporal lobe.[21]

6. Comparison between the processes in the normal naming of pictured objects, and the deblocking of amnestic-aphasic disturbances in picture naming (model schemes)

The discussions above referred exclusively to model schemes on mnestic processes in the case of cortical damages. We are faced with the question of the basic differentiation from the normal processes in the semantic memory in the acts of naming. First of all, in the normal case of naming an object, there is the lack of the preliminary word sequences, characteristic of deblocking conditions. Under normal conditions the naming process requires only the presentation of the object, upon this basis the relevant phonetic word structure can be retrieved. What processing mechanisms participate in this?

First, there is the optical perception of the object, followed by its semantic decoding in long-term storage (possibly via short-term storage). Here the evocation of the relevant word-meaning structure and also the corresponding phonetic structure must take place. This evocation is based upon the connection between object meaning and sound structure, which became established in the course of childhood and later experience.

Insofar as it is only a question of the semantic decoding of the object, the processes can correspond under both pathological and normal conditions. However, the direct evocation of relevant sound structure through the decoded object meaning presumes a process which is blocked in the case of the anomic patients, and can only be deblocked by suitable previous offering.

As we have attempted to indicate, in the case of the deblocking experiments short-term storage plays an important part in the preliminary storage and marking, as well as for the registration of the 'report back' and the command to the verbo-motoric effector; the question is open to discussion as to whether, and to what extent, short-term storage has a role to play in the normal naming process. A special registration of the optically perceived object appears superfluous as long as the object itself is visible to the observer. In the same way the question remains open as to whether the command to the verbo-motoric effector does not proceed directly from long-term storage, even when for object naming there exists a choice of several, more or less synonymous words, from which the most suitable must be filtered.

From this standpoint – it seems to me – one of the main differences in the naming process under pathological (deblocking) conditions, compared to normal conditions lies in the role of short-term storage for word selection and phonetic word realisation in the case of naming disturbances.

7. *Summary*

The account given above is based upon an experimental method which serves to investigate certain aspects of semantic memory under pathological conditions, that is with patients with brain lesions (aphasics). The method used was developed by the author, and described in a number of publications: the *deblocking method*. In the present case this was carried out with four patients with word finding disturbances of a semantic-amnestic nature, regarding picture naming. The patients were capable of understanding auditorily perceived words, were able to recognise objects and show them when they heard the corresponding name; but they were not capable of naming these objects themselves.

With the help of this deblocking method, disturbances of this sort in naming performance can be cancelled either totally or to a very considerable degree.

In this way it becomes possible to influence, directly experimentally, processes which take place in semantic memory; these are processes affecting the reactivation of certain lexical connections, for instance the relations between synonyms, hyperonyms and hyponyms, between adjacent lexical units, and between varying meanings of homonyms. By utilising these connections inside particular semantic fields, deblocking effects can be achieved which relate either to the evocation of otherwise blocked picture names, or to guided mis-namings.

The quantitative evaluation of the results, made with the use of a series of experimental variants, enables us to analyse the conditions on the basis of which it is possible to release the blocked naming performances.

This study develops certain model concepts on presumed processes in short-term memory and long-term memory which play a part both in the deblocking of the interrupted connection between meaning structure (object-word) and sound structure, and in the guided production of mis-namings. Here we proceed from the systemic character of the mnestic processes which can play a part here in the sense of self-regulating feedback events, including the interaction between short-term memory and long-term memory. In the case of word-finding disturbances in the naming of pictured objects which we investigated, it is assumed that long-term storage has as its main task that of reactivating the connection between meaning structure and sound structure. This reactivation constitutes the central problem in the deblocking process used here, since without this the patient is incapable of transcoding the meaning of the pictured object into the phonetic-articulatory structure.

On the basis of the experimental results, *the word-finding disturbances in naming objects is not regarded as a difficulty in 'meaning finding' or 'concept finding', but as a difficulty in evoking the stored connection between sound structure and meaning structure.* The simultaneous presentation of a certain pictured object and of a word, the meaning structure of which is identical with the object or 'related' to it, can lead to the deblocking of the otherwise blocked convergence between the meaning structure and the sound structure of the critical word.

Semantic memory plays a certain role here, since the meaning structure is an important component in the reactivation of the sound structure. This shows itself in particular in the variants in which this reactivation takes place through a number of 'knots' in the semantic field.

In distinction to these word finding disturbances, the disturbances of auditory word comprehension investigated in a case of sensory aphasia resulted from a *direct blocking of the semantical-lexic memory;* there exists an *inability to reactivate the relevant meaning structure from the perceived sound structure.* In such cases, too, the disturbances (with homonyms) can be largely cancelled by deblocking methods, or guided in a particular direction (deviations).

I would like to take this opportunity to thank Renate Böttcher and Dr. Erika Metze for their active and painstaking work in helping with the experiments; Dr. Irina Weigl and Dr. Manfred Bierwisch for checking the manuscript and for their many helpful suggestions; and Jochen Neumann for his help in the statistical presentation.

Table 1
Scheme of the experimental series and variants

1. Deblocking word finding disturbances

	Variants	Preliminary sequence (examples)	Picture
Series A			
I	cw ∧ 4 nw	Korridor-Geschirr-*Kaninchen*-Bach-Stein (corridor-crockery-*rabbit*-stream-stone)	rabbit
II	cw ∧ 1 hw ∧ 3 nw	*Wiesenblume*-Schneider-Felle-Gitter-*Löwenzahn* (*wildflower*-tailor-hides-lattice-*dandelion*)	dandelion
III	cw_1 (s_1) ∧ cw_2 ∧ (s_2) ∧ 3 nw	*Flagge*-Fink-Staubtuch-*Fahne*-Herz (*standard*-finch-duster-*flag*-heart)	standard/flag
IV	cw ∧ 4 arw	*Störche-Schwalbe-Adler-Tauben-Meisen* *(storks-swallow-eagle-doves-tits)*	swallow
Series B			
V	1 hw ∧ 4 nw	Spaten-Maus-Dorf-Schreibheft-*Reinigungsmittel* (spade-mouse-village-notebook-*cleaning material)*	soap
VI	1 arw ∧ 4 nw	Apfel-Stempel-*Tasse*-Hafen-Hof (apple-stamp-*cup*-harbour-courtyard)	bowl
VII	5 arw	*Wald-Feld-Hain-Rain-Busch* *(wood-field-grove-grassstrip-bush)*	meadow
VIII	1 carw ∧ 4 arw	*Wiehern-Reiten-Schimmel-Pferd-Scheuklappen* *(neigh-ride-grey horse-horse-blinkers)*	zebra
Series C			
	1 homonym ∧ 4 nw	Bleistift-Paket-*Anhänger*-Bett-Haus (pencil-parcel-*pendant/trailer*-bed-house)	1. jewellery 2. vehicle
2. Deblocking auditory word comprehension disturbances			
Series D			
D_1	1 homonym ∧ 4 nw	(see Series C)	homonym spoken by the examiner
$D_{2.1}$	3 rw	*Morgen-Gras-feucht* *(morning-grass-damp)*	
$D_{2.2}$	3 rw	*Strick-Schiff-freimachen* *(rope-ship-cast off)*	rope

* Of the variants named, not all could be conducted with the 4 patients. Originially a smaller number of variants was planned. Two of our patients (pat. Br. and pat. Mm.) sadly did not survive for the expansion, and a third patient (pat. Schw.) was no longer available for other reasons. For this reason we must confine ourselves to pat. Ni. in assessments regarding all variants. Only pat. Ni. and pat. Me. are included in the homonym series.

Legend to Table 1

cw: critical word corresponding to the pictured object
nw: neutral words, with no direct connection with the critical word
hw: hyperonym (generic term) superordinate to the critical word
sw: synonymous words, thus doubling the critical word in preliminary sequence
rw: related words, that is words with a direct relation with the critical word (synonyms, hyperonyms, adjacent words)
arw: related word adjacent to the critical word
carw: critical adjacent related word, that is a related word in the preliminary sequence, the meaning of which is reinforced by the other related words, and thus distracts from the meaning of the critical word (see VIII).

The number of neutral words given above varies in certain cases.

Table 2

Percentual answer frequency (naming with critical word, related word, or double naming), based on the number of pictures submitted

	Variants	Pat. Ni.					Pat. Schw.					Pat. Mm.					Pati. Br.					Series
		Pic.	Deblockings				Pic.	Deblockings				Pic.	Deblockings				Pic.	Deblockings				
				1	2	3			1	2	3			1	2	3			1	2	3	
I	1 cw ∧ 4 nw	123	cw	92	–	–	141	cw	77	–	–	110	cw	44	–	–	50	cw	94	–	–	
II	1 cw ∧ 1 hw ∧ nw	15	cw hw	100	67 (67) 33 (33)	0	47	cw hw	100	28 (83) 17 (72)	55	50	cw hw	64	52 (54) 10 (12)	2	9	cw hw	100	77 (77) 23 (23)	0	
III	s_1w ∧ s_2w ∧ nw	30	s_1w s_2w	100	0 (0) 7 (93)	93	39	s_1w s_2w		10 (87) 13 (90)	77	23	s_1w s_2w	100	9 (22) 78 (91	13	30	s_1w s_2w	86	23 (36) 50 (63)	13	A
IV	1 cw ∧ 4 aw	17	cw aw	95	24 (77) 18 (71)	53	–	–	–	–	–	–	–	–	–	–	–	–	–	–	–	
V	1 hw ∧ 4 nw	23	cw hw	100	9 (26) 74 (91)	17	43	cw hw	100	14 (30) 70 (86)	10	50	cw hw	50	0 (0) 50 (50)	0	47	cw hw	100	23 (30) 70 (77)	7	
VI	1 aw ∧ 4 nw	34	cw aw	100	6 (53) 47 (94)	47	25	cw aw	91	71 (71) 20 (20)	0	11	cw aw	61	25 (25) 36 (36)	0	–	–	–	–	–	B
VII	5 aw	17	cw aw	100	12 (77) 23 (88)	65	–	–	–	–	–	–	–	–	–	–	–	–	–	–	–	
VIII	1 caw ∧ 4 aw	17	cw caw aw	100	12 (29) 29 (71) 18 (41)	41	–	–	–	–	–	–	–	–	–	–	–	–	–	–	–	

Legend to Table 2

cw:	critical word
nw:	neutral words
sw:	synonymous (critical) words
hw:	hyperonymous words (generic term)
arw:	adjacent related words, lexically co-ordinated to the critical word
carw:	critical adjacent related word, strengthened by the other related words when the critical word is missing in preliminary sequence
pic:	absolute number of pictures of objects submitted for naming in the deblocking experiment
rw:	related word, i. e. synonym, hyperonym and adjacent words

Columns

1: *deblocking rates:* total number of cases in which there is any sort of naming, i. e. the sum of the values given in column 2 (values not in brackets) and in column 3. In Variant I (without related word), only column 1 is concerned.

2: d_{cw} *and* d_{rw} *rates:* number of namings in which either the critical word or a related word were named alone. Following in brackets: total number of namings referring to either the critical word or the related word, regardless of whether such word occurred in isolation, or as part of a double naming.

3: *double naming rates:* number of cases in which the critical word and a related word were used together in naming.

Table 3

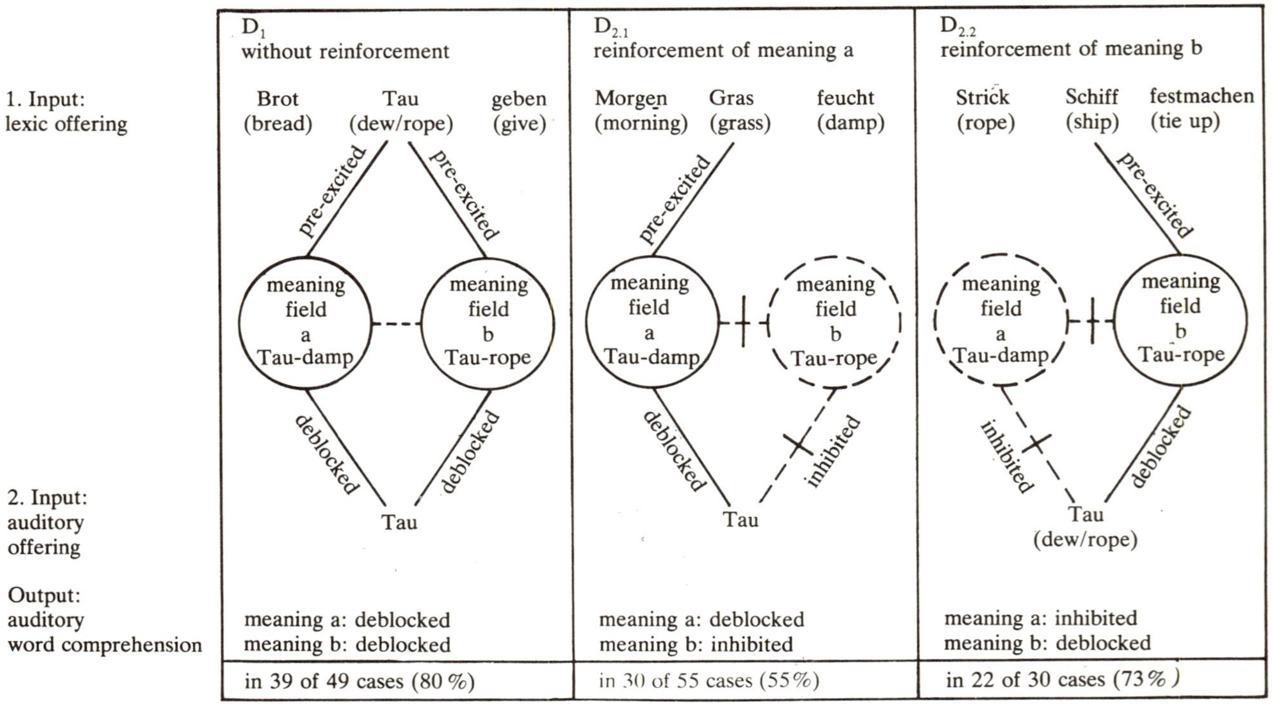
1. Input:
lexic offering
2. Input:
auditory
offering
Output:
auditory
word comprehension
D1
without reinforcement
Brot
(bread)
Tau
(dew/rope)
geben
(give)
pre-excited
pre-excited
meaning
field
a
Tau-damp
meaning
field
b
Tau-rope
deblocked
deblocked
Tau
meaning a: deblocked
meaning b: deblocked
in 39 of 49 cases (80 %)
D2.1
reinforcement of meaning a
Morgen
(morning)
Gras
(grass)
feucht
(damp)
pre-excited
meaning
field
a
Tau-damp
meaning
field
b
Tau-rope
deblocked
inhibited
Tau
meaning a: deblocked
meaning b: inhibited
in 30 of 55 cases (55%)
D2.2
reinforcement of meaning b
Strick
(rope)
Schiff
(ship)
festmachen
(tie up)
pre-excited
meaning
field
a
Tau-damp
meaning
field
b
Tau-rope
inhibited
deblocked
Tau
(dew/rope)
meaning a: inhibited
meaning b: deblocked
in 22 of 30 cases (73 %)

Table 4. *Examples for the Naming Reactions of Patients in Differing Variants*

1. Examples of successful deblocking

Var.	Picture	Preliminary sequence	Naming*	Pat.
I	Hühner (chickens)	*Hühner*-Kante-Stimme (*chickens*-edge-voice)	(precontrol: 'Coc-kadoodledoo') 'The Chickens'	Mei.
	Seile (ropes)	Würfel-*Seile*-Flieder (cube-*ropes*-lilacs)	(precontrol: 'You can tie up here') 'Ropes'	Ni.
	Kanne (can)	Bett-Landschaft-*Kanne*-Mäd-chen (bed-landscape-*can*-girl)	'That's the can'	Mm.
II	Löwenzahn (dandelion)	*Wiesenblume*-Schneider-Felle-Gitter-*Löwenzahn* (*wildflower*-tailor-hides-lat-tice-*dandelion*)	'That's the dan-delion'	Mm.
	Weintrauben (grapes)	*Weintrauben*-Karton-Obst (*grapes*-box-fruit)	'Grapes'	Schw.
III	Treppe-Stiege (staircase-steps)	*Treppe*-Student-*Stiege*-Peter-silie-Fische (*staircase*-student-*steps*-pars-ley-fish)	'Steps'	Br.
	Busch-Strauch (bush-shrub)	Melker-*Busch-Strauch*-Biene-Stiefel (milker-*bush-shrub*-bee-boot)	'Bush'	Br.
IV	Schwalbe (swallow)	*Störche-Schwalbe-Adler-Tauben-Finken (storks-swallow-eagle-doves-finches)*	'Swallows'	Schw.
	Meer (sea)	*Meer-Tuch-Fluss*-Pfütze-*Bach* (*sea-cloth-river*-puddle-*stream*)	'Sea'	Schw.
V	Radfahrer (cyclist)	*Sportler*-Salat-Petersilie-Kor-ridor-Rum (*sportsman*-lettuce-parsley-corridor-rum)	'The riders-cyclist'	Br.
	Wolljacke (wool jacket)	Bauklötze-Mauer-*Strickwaren*-Kissen (building stones-wall-*knitted goods*-cushion)	'Wool-wool jacket'	Schw.
VI	Elefant (elephant)	Hampelmann-Unterrock-Rosenblatt-Telegramm-*Giraffe* (puppet-petticoat-rose leaf-telegram-*giraffe*)	'Elephant'	Ni.

Var.	Picture	Preliminary sequence	Naming*	Pat.
	Vase (vase)	*Blumen*-Hafen-Gabel-Sosse-Lamm (*flowers*-harbour-fork-gravy-lamb)	'Vase'	Schw.
VII	Suppe (soup)	*Essen-Löffel-Schüssel (eat-spoon-bowl)*	'Soup'	Gre.
	Fön (hair-dryer)	*Haare-Trocknen-Warmluft-Friseur* (hair-dry-hot air-hairdresser)	'Hair-dryer'	Ni.
VIII	Kisten (crates)	*Eimer-Emaille-Wasser-Hausfrau-Aufwischen (bucket-enamel-water-housewife-wipe up)*	'Yes, a porter . . . like a worker, as though he was carrying two crates'	Ni.
	Hut (hat)	*schwarz-Zylinder-steif-Trauung-feierlich (black-tophat-hard-wedding-ceremonial)*	'A gentleman's hat'	Ni.

* The examples given come in part from patients not included in the available quantitive experiments.

2. Examples of Deviations

Var.	Picture	Preliminary sequence	Naming	Pat.
II	Büstenhalter (brassiere)	Küchentisch-*Büstenhalter*-Mülleimer-Telefon-*Miederware* (kitchen table-*brassiere*-dustbin-telephone-*corsetry*)	'That is a corsetry'	Mm.
	Lippenstift (lipstick)	Strand-*Kosmetik*-Uhr-*Lippenstift* (beach-*cosmetics*-watch-*lipstick*)	'Cosmetics'	Schw.
V	Buch (book)	Kanone-*Druckerzeugnis*-Turm (cannon-*printed matter*-tower)	'Printed matter . . . something missing . . . printed matter'	Schw.
	Kanone (cannon)	Hölle-Bauwerk-Schiff-*Kriegsgerät* (hell-building-ship-*war material*)	'That is war material'	Mm.
VI	Wasserhahn (watertap)	Junge-Mond-Magen-*Stöpsel*-Schnee (boy-moon-stomach-*plug*-snow)	'Plug'	Me.

Var.	Picture	Preliminary sequence	Naming	Pat.
	Schüssel (bowl)	Apfel-Stempel-*Tasse*-Hafen-Hof (apple-stamp-*cup*-harbour-courtyard)	'Cup'	Me.
	Mohrrüben (carrots)	Deckel-Haustür-Sonne-*Erbsen* (lid-front door-sun-*peas*)	'Peas'	Ha.
VIII	Augen (eyes)	*Nase-Mund-Ohren* *(nose-mouth-ears)*	'Ears'	Gre., Me.
	Sattel (saddle)	*sitzen-bequem-federn-verstellen-Leder* *(sit-comfortable-springy-adjust-leather)*	'A seat of leather'	Ni.
VIII	Eule (owl)	*Rabenvogel-Schwärme-schwarz-glänzend-Krähe-krächzen* *(raven-swarms-black-shiny-crow-croaking)*	'A crow . . . old crow, but it looks nice.'	Ni.
	Astern (asters)	*Rosen-Dornen-stechen-dunkelrot-teuer* *(roses-thorns-pricking-dark red-dear)*	"Well, I don't know, I don't regard it as a rose, which you just spoke about.'	Ni.
	Barometer (barometer)	*Fieber-Arzt-Thermometer-Bett-krank* *(fever-doctor-thermometer-bed-ill)*	'Thermometer? But it isn't a fever thermometer.'	Ni.

3. Examples of Double Naming

Var.	Picture	Preliminary sequence	Naming	Pat.
II	Milch (milk)	*Milch-Getränk*-Ring (*milk-drink*-ring)	'Milk . . . drink'	Schw.
	Augen (eyes)	*Augen*-Erde-Metall-*Körperteile*-Regenschirm (*eyes*-world-metal-*parts of the body*-umbrella)	'It's also parts of the body for eyes'	Mm.
III	Stiege-Treppe (steps-staircase)	*Stiege-Treppe*-Schreibmaschine (*steps-staircase*-typewriter)	'Steps, staircase'	Schw.
	Flagge-Fahne (standard-flag)	*Flagge-Fahne*-Fink-Staubtuch-Herz (*standard-flag*-finch-duster-heart)	'The big flag . . . standard'	Mm.

Var.	Picture	Preliminary sequence	Naming*	Pat.
IV	Staubsauber (vacuum cleaner)	*Teppich-elektrisch-Staubsauger-saubermachen-Hausfrau (carpet-electric-vacuum cleaner-clean up-housewife)*	"Vacu . . . vacuum cleaner . . . is carpet . . . clean up'	Br.
	Eichhörnchen (squirrel)	*Eichhörnchen-Nüsse-Wald-klettern-rotbraun (squirrel-nuts-wood-climb-red-brown)*	"Squirrel . . . it's in a tree . . . they climb . . . and make nuts"	Bri.
V	Bücklinge (bloaters)	Haselnuss-*Räucherware*-Läufer (hazelnut-*smoked foods*-carpet)	"Yes, smoked foods too . . . that's a bloater"	Ni.
	Elefant (elephant)	Handtasche-*Dickhäuter*-Bademantel (handbag-*pachyderm/thick skin*-dressing gown)	"Thick people . . . thick . . . elephant . . . pachyderm	Schw.
VI	Zigarette (cigarette)	Gesandter-Verlobung-*Zigarren*-Tulpen-Läufer (ambassador-engagement-*cigars*-tulips-carpet)	"Cigars . . . no that's not cigars, they are cigarettes'	Ni.
	Schaf (sheep)	Lampe-Sendung-Geschirr-*Ziege*-Säule (lamp-consignment-dishes-*goat*-column)	"A goat . . . no, actually a sheep"	Ni.
	Bart (beard)	*Brauen-Wimpern*-Haar (*eyebrows-lashes*-hair)	"Hair or beard"	Gre.
	Zylinder (tophat)	*Hut-Mütze-Kappe (hat-peaked cap-cap)*	"Hat or cap . . . top hat"	Schw.
VII	Geldmünzen (coins)	*Scheine-Bank-Scheck-Papier (notes-bank-cheque-paper)*	"Notes or money"	Schw.
	Kopftuch (headscarf)	*Wolle-gestrickt-aufsetzen-Handarbeit-Mütze (wool-knitted-put on-handmade-peaked cap)*	"Peaked cap . . . actually it's a muffler that's just put on, a scarf, a head scarf"	Ni.

Notes

1. The two psychological studies *Über Grundstrukturen und Funktionsprinzipien kognitiver Prozesse (Aspekte eines Zugangs zu Analyse und Synthese geistiger Leistungen)* and *Strukturelle und funktionelle Komponenten des menschlichen Gedächtnisses* by F. Klix in [81] appeared after the present study was completed. Apart from information on the latest experimental research in the field of the investigation of human memory, they contain basic theoretical considerations on the structure and function of the individual memory (as distinct from species memory) and references to the relevant literature of the past few years. Since these studies deal with normal psychological memory processes, a comparison can be made with the results and hypotheses of a clinical-neuropsychological type conveyed in the present report. The same applies to the basic study *Sprache und Gedächtnis: Ergebnisse und Probleme* by M. Bierwisch [15], in which the problem of semantic memory is discussed from a psycholinguistic standpoint.
2. In our experiments we took into account the left-sided hemianopsy of patient Ni., always presenting the pictures to the patient in her intact visual field. Those pictures which she had not recognised immediately in the preliminary examination because of her slight picture agnosis were not utilised in the main test.
3. Only clearly identifiable, graphically clear and mainly coloured reproductions were used: everyday objects (e. g. watering can, chair plaster), plants (e. g. pansy, cauliflower), animals (e. g. lion, zebra), and human figures (e. g. postman, cyclist), a total of about 150 pictures.
4. It should be emphasised that the patient is not expected – on the basis of his aphasic disturbance he cannot be expected – to undertake a conscious classification of critical word and related word in the sense of coordination or superordination. In fact such relations come about 'by themselves' in long-term memory, without the assistance of the patient.
5. Compare the homonym experiments in Cohen et al. ([32], p. II–6 ff.).
6. Here we must refrain from going into detail on the check experiments, which in most cases in this experimental series followed immediately afterwards or later. The quantitative results of these checks demonstrate that the long-term effect of the deblocking effect can be seen, not only on the same day, but also after several days or even weeks and months. A comparison between the presentation of new pictures and of pictures previously 'deblocked' sho this effect particularly clearly: the patients could not name the new pictures, but were in many cases able to name those pictures which they had been able to name in the deblocking experiment.
7. It occured in a number of cases that, after a series of related words had been offered in the preliminary sequence, not only the critical word but several related words were used. For the sake of simplicity we count such multiple namings as 'double-namings' only.
8. The values of the d_{cw}-rates may be found, for Variant I, in column 1. In the Variants II and IV the comparison refers to the d_{cw}-rates given in brackets in column 2, i. e. the number of namings with the critical word, both in isolation and in double namings. In Variant III the number of namings are quoted for comparison, in which one or both of the synonyms are used (column 1).
9. We cannot go further here in a qualitative analysis of the patient's failure in the use of

the homonyms in one of their two meanings. In any case these cannot be explained as random fluctuating naming disturbances, since the patient displayed the same differing reaction in repetition after the experiment; in addition, these differences were not governed by the effect of word frequency (see the examples above).

10. This experimental series, carried out under my supervision, has already been published (see [19]).
11. In the case of patient Schw. we were able to make this interesting observation: in one experiment, after a preliminary sequence in which instead of the critical word 'mussel' only the hyperonym 'mollusc' appeared amongst the neutral words, the patient promptly named the picture of a mussel with 'mollusc'. During a subsequent control with the same picture, which took place two years later, the patient once again stated, to his own regret, 'mollusc', and he was unable to find the correct word. Thus the deblocking of the hyperonym had persisted for a long time.
12. An attempt to derive the process of word finding from a series of semi-autonomous processing steps of a neurolinguistic kind may be found in Green [58]. Since the schema followed by this author includes, apart from the namig of objects, other forms of word finding, too, (for instance, word finding on the basis of a description of the objects by the examiner, or the finding of the word lacking in a sentence, etc.) this naturally has a much more general character than the model suggested by us.
13. The deblocking described can be complicated to some extent by the fact that the preliminary word sequence, in certain cases (for instance with patients with auditory word comprehension disturbances), must be given not acoustically but optically, that is to say the words are not spoken by the examiner, but presented in written form. This means that the patient is presented with graphemic word structures, not phonetic. This difficulty may be overcome by having the patient (as long as he has no expressive alexia) read the preliminary sequence of words aloud (i. e. patient Br.). In this way the graphemic word structures are transcoded into phonetic structures, so that the deblocking process described can proceed analogously to that after acoustic exposure.
14. The storage of sound structures mentioned here is abstracted from the fact that these structures, too, require, for their more exact determination, morphological-syntactical processing, which, for its part, stands in the closest connection with the semantic decoding in long-term storage.
15. I would like here to leave open the question as to whether meaning structures corresponding to such differing factors as object and word are coded 'together' or 'separate' in long-term memory; in the latter case, i. e. in channel-specific coding, it would be necessary to have an additional 'bringing-into-congruence' of these meaning structures, which are identical in content (on the problem of 'field-dependent' coding, see also [131], pp. 345 and 405).
16. One might object here that basically it should be sufficient to pronounce the critical word alone to the patient, so that he could use it in the following picture naming. Insofar as there are no visual agnosia, and no serious aphasic-motoric or sensoric disturbances, which could prevent a repetition, then such 'prompting' can in fact lead to a success, though mostly to a very short-lived one (see [114], p. 156). In contrast to this, our deblocking experiments, as already noted, are processes which occur on the *non-conscious* level, proceedings in which the long-term memory is tapped without conscious effort on the part of the patient. The special character of this form of retrieval displays itself particularly in the fact that deblocking is possible without providing the critical word, and that guided deviations and double namings are produceable.

17. Here we shall not go into the cortical localisation of these disturbances; here it is mainly damage to certain sections of the temporal lobe.
18. In the reproduction without comprehension of the heard or read word (i. e. in cases of auditory word comprehension disturbances of a sensoric-aphasic nature, or in receptive alexia), there are generally no mis-performances of this type. Goodglass et al. [51] and Weigl [192a-c] stated that the operation of speech production can be surprisingly independent of comprehension.
19. Certainly not all mis-performances of this sort should be understood in this way. There are also mistakes based upon phonological or graphemic resemblances or perseverations or connotative associations which can be held responsible for certain deviations.
20. Cohen et al. [32] and Benson and Geschwind [12], Wiegel-Crump and Koenigsknecht (1973) and others, agree that in the case of aphasically caused word finding disturbances "it is a question of the retrieval process . . . rather than a loss of words" ([32], p. VII–1). This assumption is confirmed by the experimental results of the latter authors; when their patients were presented for a second time with pictures previously not named, they were in most cases capable of finding the naming word when presented with a verbal context. For instance, when presented with the picture of a cupboard, and the simultaneous exposure of the incomplete sentence: "Hang the coat in the . . .", the patients can find the word 'cupboard'.

    In a subsequent test, the authors stated that renewed presentation of the picture (without sentence), produced significant post-effects.

    In her study *The Naming Process and its Impairment. A Multidisciplinary Approach,* Tsvetkova [164] ascribes the picture naming disturbances of semantic-amnestic and acoustic-amnestic aphasics to the impairment of differentiation on an optical-gnostic basis. According to the author, the imprecise information received in the perception of optically represented objects brings with it the retrieval of whole word series in the relevant semantic field (semantic verbal paraphasias in naming).

    Although an element of optical-gnostic differentiation disturbance cannot be excluded in our cases, particularly in patient Ni. (see p. 287, such an explanation can only be partially valid for the blocking of the connection between meaning structure and sound structure which we ascertained. From the 'sensory basis' [164] to the realisation of the verbo-motoric command given by the effector, the transcoding process from the meaning structure to the sound structure can be disturbed in many ways, depending upon the cortical localisation of the damage (see [192a-c]).
21. In this connection, particular interest attaches to the above-mentioned findings of Goodglass et al. [57] with regard to the difference between understanding and verbalising object namings. The authors found that these namings, independent of aphasia type, provided the easiest category for comprehension, but the most difficult category for naming. The function of speech comprehension showed itself surprisingly independent of speech production. In the opinion of the authors, these two functions are based upon differing psychic processes, and accordingly also on differing sorts of cortical localisations.

⟨17⟩

E. WEIGL

On Written Language: Its Acquisition and Its Alexic-Agraphic Disturbances

The acquistion and mastery of written language, in both receptive and expressive reading as well as the different forms of writing (spontaneous, to dictation, copying), is an extraordinarily complex process. The study of the neuropsychological and psycholinguistic preconditions of this sort of human transfer of information is still in its infancy in comparison with the study of spoken language. Important preliminary work has been done in this direction through psychological research into normal reading and writing[1], through investigations on alexia and agraphia, as well as on reading and writing disability among children[2], and recently through contributions made by linguistics and psycholinguistics[3]. Another source of insight into the processes underlying the acquisition of written language is our centuries-old experience with teaching reading and writing. In this chapter we shall discuss a number of basic psycholinguistic and neuropsychological aspects of the acquisition and mastery of written language, as well as the relevant sequelae to brain damage.

1. Psycholinguistic approaches

1.1 General Aspects

The ensemble of written symbols is not simply at late product of human society – to this day the number of those in the world who can read and write is far smaller than the number of illiterates – but is something which a child only learns long after he has mastered spoken language.

Our form of writing, with its many letters anc ombinations of letters, as well as its various type faces (e. g, printed and written letters, capitals and small letters, etc.), constitutes a signal system complete in itself and, with respect to its structure, entirely distinct from spoken language. The individual characters may be analyzed in terms of a limited number of basic elements (stroke, arch, loop, etc.) [see 37] whose combination makes it possible to produce any character of the alphabet. The combination of these basic elements does not occur randomly, but is governed by rules [14]. Both visual perception and writing depend on the efficiency of these basic rules.

These structural rules for alphabetically written language (unlike nonalphabetically written languages, e. g., Chinese) are not related in any way to factors of spoken language. Their acquisition is truly independent and is by no means facilitated by the earlier acquisition of spoken language. It would, however, be impossible to acquire an alphabetically written language merely by learning letters and their combinations. Alphabetically written languages can be learned only as a consequence of the rule-governed correspondence between graphemic and phonologic structures (we cannot discuss here the very intricate problem of the acquisition of written language by congenitally deaf children).

We are indebted to recent psycholinguistic investigations for important contributions to our understanding of the functional relationships between graphic and phonic structures. Gibson [48] investigating psychological problems, and Bierwisch [14], making a linguistic analysis, were able to show that the relationships between written and spoken language may be characterized, for any letter-writing system whatever, in terms of *grapheme-phoneme correspondence rules*. However, owing to the lack of an isomorphism between sound and written structures, there is no one-to-one correspondence between phonemes and graphemes. The graphic unit for reading and writing processes is not the individual letter, but letter clusters; each graphic unit stands in a specific, invariant, context-dependent relationship to a phonological unit, either phonemic or phonetic.

The exceptions to the rules are determined by lexical entries that indicate *graphemic idiosyncracies* [14]. Information of this sort in the lexicon is necessary in all those cases where the grapheme-phoneme correspondence rules fail to specify the graphemic structure. This is particularly true for the many *graphemic ambiguities* (that is to say those words with differing graphemic structures corresponding to one and the same phonetic structure; word pairs such as *raze-raise, beach-beech, altar-alter, sign-sine*).

In contrast to those graphemic structures that are assignable to phonemic structures according to specifiable rules and that therefore need no lexical entries, such graphemic irregularities must be specifically noted in the lexicon (and therefore marked accordingly in long-term memory).

Although *phonetically ambiguous* words are rarer, those that occur also require specific entries – for example, pairs such as *read* (present) and *read* (past); *permit* (noun) and *permit* (verb); *concrete* (noun) and *concrete* (adjective). (For these examples I am indebted to M. Bierwisch.)

Graphemic ambiguities (e. g., *sign-sine*) must be taken into account by the listener, the writer, and the receptive reader if they are to understand; in the transcoding of the graphemic input in the corresponding articulatory pattern (expressive reading) these ambiguities are ignored.

Phonetic ambiguities (e. g., *permit*) occur exclusively in the transcoding of graphemic structures in sound structures (reading aloud).

It is impossible to attribute to alphabetically written language a syntax and lexicon that is independent of spoken language. Written language assumes mastery of the phonology, morphology, syntax, and lexicon of the respective natural language. (A similar point of view has been expressed by Vygotsky, [169]). This means that knowledge of the grammar of a given language (Chomsky's [28] competence) is also at the root of the written performance – competence in oral language is an integral part of written language. Nevertheless, written language includes, in addition to the grammar rule-system of spoken language, its own structural and functional rules; it therefore seems reasonable to regard competence in alphabetically written language as *augmented* competence.

1.2 Genetic Aspects

It appears to us that the essential factor in acquisition of written language lies in this extension of competence, and not in the simple learning of the techniques of reading and writing. The prerequisites for such an extension are undoubtedly generically specific, that is, confined to man, in the same way as is the acquisition of spoken language competence.

The question as to whether this competence undergoes any qualitative change through such extension can scarcely be answered with a simple yes or no. From a linguistic point of view, the inclusion of a graphemic sign system derived from the phonemic system brings no change in principle.

From the psycholinguistic standpoint, however, the competence extension appears as a genuine restructuring of speech behavior. Spoken and written language differ mainly with regard to their differing communication character. The direct listener-speaker strategy in reception and emission on the spoken language level is replaced in written language by indirect reception (in repective reading) and indirect emission (in voluntary writing). This does not, however, apply to all application forms, since reading aloud and writing to dictation occupy a special position in this respect; reading aloud is addressed to one listener, and writing to dictation is linked with one speaker.

The competence expansion of written language is thus generally linked with a certain reduction in informational spoken language redundance

– the accompanying features of mimicry, gesticulation, intonation, accentuation, etc., are lacking in written information. This reduction in redundance forms an important difference between the two forms of language use.

Still largely unsolved is the problem of how the linking of features comes about in learning reading and writing, which forms the basis for classification, generalisation, and finally storage as rules; in this the situation is similar to that for many other cognitive processes[4].

Spoken language is acquired by the child unconsciously, that is to say without any systematic instruction, but written language is 'consciously' acquired by the pupil with the aid of a methodically constructed plan of instruction; this fact, however, is liable to hide the real character of this learning process.

If we proceed on the assumption that acquisition of both spoken and written language is based upon gaining speech competence, i. e., the necessary basic rules of a phonological, syntactical, semantic or structural, graphic and functional, graphemic-phonological nature, then the distinction 'unconsciously-consciously' disappears. Those who use these basic rules, as with the fundamental regular links in many other fields of human activity (e. g., logic), are generally not aware of them. As Chomsky [28] stated in connection with the rules of grammar, the application of these rules generally lies 'far beyond the stage of actual or even potential knowledge' (p. 18). Speakers and listeners, writers and readers, when using language behave as though these rules were 'known' to them, as though they 'applied' them consciously in the psychological sense. In general they behave towards phonological, graphemic, syntactic-semantic mistakes as though they consciously knew the rules against which they or others had offended (a feeling for the language). Since the terms 'knowledge', 'command, 'application', etc. are solely 'as-if' formulations, it would perhaps be better in psychology to speak rather of the 'becoming operative' of the rules, a term which does not a priori prejudice the level of their effectiveness.

This becomes particularly clear when we observe the process of *acquiring* these rules.

Miller [127b] wrote that "the child learns the language, but no one, least of all an average mother, knows how to teach it to him" (p. 346). Vygotsky remarks pertinently that the child possesses certain abilities in the field of speech, "but does not know that he has this command" [169, p. 208].

With regard to the process of learning to read and write, Gibson *et al.* [48] emphasize that the 'discovery' of the grapheme-phoneme correspondence (like the phonological and syntactical rules in acquiring spoken language) is made by the pupil himself 'without explicit instruction' in use of the written language; i. e., at a certain point in the learning process, he is capable of reading new words and sentences without any descriptive instructions.

From all this it is plain that for elementary instruction in reading or writing the aim cannot be to impart the complicated basic rules, research into which is a task for psycholinguistics. The main aim of this elementary instruction seems to be to create optimal conditions for the length and quality of the learning process with regard to unconscious rule formation, that is to say for the execution of the classification and generalisation processes of interiorised feature-linkage which takes place in the long-term storage. The main factor here is selection of the spoken-written-language supply which best satisfies this diversity of rules.

To avoid misunderstanding it should be emphasized that our understanding of the involuntary nature of rule acquisition does not stand in contradiction to the making conscious of certain aspects of the technique of reading and writing. In this respect there really is a difference between the learning processes in spoken language and in written language.

The small child has a situationally conditioned 'wish' for oral communication with his environment, and this has a completely different character from the conscious study motivation with regard to reading and writing as subjects of instruction.

A special psychological learning problem is acquisition of a variety of orthographical exceptions. In order to know the graphemic structure of words in this category, the elementary reader must, consciously or unconsciously, recognise their peculiarities. Let us take for a start a familiar case of graphemic ambiguity, the words 'raze' and 'raise'. They differ only in their meaning, not in their phonetical structure. The graphemic structure of the word 'raze' is self-evident, but the word 'raise' requires additional graphemic information in the lexicon, and the instruction for the 'ai' spelling of the diphthong must therefore be imparted separately in the learning process.

It is theoretically conceivable that these excpetions could be registered word for word in the school learning process, and thus fixed as additional information in the lexicon, but this assumption appears untenable. Naturally all systematic reading instruction aims at drawing the attention of the pupils to exceptions in orthography. But here, to a certain extent, the same thing applies as in the reception of orthographically regular words: the school does not have the time or means to present to the pupil in the course of instruction the entire vocabulary of the language. The orthographical exceptions can also be dealt with only to a relatively limited degree. The other cases must be acquired by the reading-learner himself as a result of more or less wide-ranging reading.

But this is the point at which a learning process begins which is involuntary to a very considerable extent, if not completely. The orthographic knowledge can only be reinforced by receptive reading, which makes possible the wide 'collection and sifting of material'. It is a well-known fact that even in persons practiced in reading and writing the passive knowledge of orthography is greater than the active use. The school is mainly able to assist this process of acquisition by awakening in the pupil a particular interest in independent observation of the way that words are written.

From the linguistic viewpoint, writing contains no basically new elements compared to reading and particularly to spoken language, with the exception of the internal linking rules upon which the basic elements of the letter structure of the alphabet are built. Orthography is no special problem of written production and reproduction, but primarily a question of written language perception and semantic decoding, i. e., receptive reading, which represents the basis for the acquisition of all written language application forms with regard to rule acquisition and the registration of the graphemic additional information. The main new acquisition in the field of writing is to be found in the creation of a writing-motor function entirely different from the verbo-motor function. The production or reproduction of graphemic structures with the help of the grapho-motor function represents an analogue to the production or reproduction of phonetic (articulatory) structures on the spoken language level. In both cases a synthesis is necessary between the relevant phonetic or graphemic units on the basis of the effectiveness of the specific basic rules of the spoken or written language. If it does not confine itself to mere parroting or imitation of alphabetical configurations displayed, the phonemic-graphemic corresponding rules and their exceptions must be learned by the elementary reader or writer. These rules permit an adequate transposition in the verbo-expressive or grapho-expressive processes.

2. Neuropsychological approaches

2.1 Genetic aspects

An important part of developmental neuropsychology is the study of the biological prerequisites, particularly those of a morphological and neurophysiological nature with the human brain as the material foundation, for the acquisition of higher psychic functions. Important beginnings of such research have been discussed by Lenneberg [97], especially in connection with the ontogenesis of the capacity for language acquisition. The importance of his work *Biological Foundations of Language* appears to us to lie mainly in the way in which he posed the question of a method which can be regarded as a guideline for genetic-neuropsychological research. As a preliminary for the eventual discovery of neuroanatomical and neurophysiological correlates of language acquisition, Lenneberg proposes the study of all those changes that take place in man's brain during and after the 'critical period' for perception and production of language acquisition.

> "It is not so much one or the other specific aspect of the brain thay must be held responsible for the capacity of language acquisition but the way the many parts of the brain interact. Thus it is mode of function rather than specific structures that must be regarded as the proper neurological correlate of language" [98, p. 170].

In this respect, Lenneberg approaches, in my opinion, the point of view expressed by Vygotsky and his disciples, Leontiev, Luria, Galperin, Zhinkin, and others, who maintain that one must understand the development of the higher psychic functions in general, and language in particular, as the result of integration of functional cerebral systems. According to this view, specific remote and highly differentiated cortical zones begin to interact and form unified *cerebral systems* during the course of ontogenesis, a process based on the child's communication with his environment and his handling objects. In other words, there are complicated intracerebral connections in dynamic interaction; however, each single zone makes a specific contribution to the entire function of the relevant system. The Soviet neuropsychologists refer to this as the system-specific character of higher cortical functions and their dynamic localization[5].

In the course of spoken or written language performances, many processes come together, particularly cognitive processes such as acoustic and optic perception, language comprehension, memory, inner speech, and also motor processes for speech production and reproducion. The complexity of the linguistic task, in which all of these are integrated, gives us an idea of the close and complex network of intracerebral connections. Since oral language comes prior to written language, we must assume that execution of the latter requires further cerebral zones that must be integrated with those already engaged in oral language. The zones in question are mainly those which on the one hand provide visual-spatial perception of letter signs and on the other hand ensure the course of the grapho-motor processes (certain frontal, parietal and occipital areas).

In addition, a number of spoken language functions become direct components in the process of reading and writing. Thus processes of the temporal lobe play a certain role in writing to dictation because of the verbo-auditory components of the letter. The premotor and sensory-motor segments of the cortex also enter into the task of reading aloud. Spontaneous, voluntary speech and writing are related to prefrontal cortical areas (for further details and bibliography, see [117]. Thus the cortical areas involved in reading and writing are larger than those involved in oral language and are based on the cooperation of most cerebral zones.

2.1.1 *Reduction of the connections of spoken to written language*

Once established, the higher psychic processes function differently from the way they functioned during the formative period. Whereas during acquisition various functional cerebral systems interacted, there is a *gradual reduction* in this functional complexity once a certain degree of mastery has been attained. Certain intracerebral connections are no longer needed once the function is perfected; however, such connections continue to be potentially available and may be reactivated in case of need. Vygotsky regards this type of modification in the interfunctional relationships as the most important aspect of psychological development [169, p. 148]. The notion of reduction in functions is of particular importance in understanding the transition from the learning phase to the mature stage of mastery of written language. This can be illustrated by consideration of the processes of acquisition and automatization of comprehension, reproduction, and production of graphemic structures.

In the acquisition of reading and writing, several aspects of oral language are involved, including the auditory perception of phonetic structures (the teacher pronounces the written word and explains its meaning) and their reproduction (the pupil articulates the word that he has heard and seen). At a later phase, the pupil himself must produce the sound pattern of the words he has learned to read, either by saying them to himself (inner speech) or by reading them aloud. Graphemic structures are paired with phonetic structures (as soon as the student has learned these correspondences, he will 'know' the meaning of the words). During primary education in reading, the phonological relations are further supplemented by pictorial material of the spelling book. A similar process is at work during the acquisition of writing.[6]

To begin with, learning to write is also closely connected with the spoken language level. The pupil co-articulates the word to be copied; when writing to dictation he hears the word and subsequently reproduces the phonetic structure for himself during the process of writing; in the independent writing of a known word, or at a later stage of a new word, the beginner either says it aloud or produces it on the inner speech level.[7]

In this connection, Nasarova's [129] investigations into coarticulation during the learning of writing are of importance. The author showed that a child's writing task becomes more difficult if he is forced to write with wide-open mouth and protruding tongue. Under these circumstances the incidence of writing mistakes increases appreciably. Thus written reproduction is facilitated by simultaneous speech movements; inhibition of these movements produces encoding difficulties.

In short, acquisition of written language requires the construction of a chain of interacting functions; a number of recoding processes are required between the various sensory modalities and the processes of inner speech and manifest articulatory or grapho-motor stereotypes. The latter may become complicated through feedback systems of an auditory and optic nature.[8] See Weigl et al. [194] for the distinctions between prearticulation, inner and outer speech level, between latent and manifest articulation. During the transition from reading or writing single words to reading or writing whole sentences, syntactic processes also begin to play a role.

In school, certain paradoxes may occur; a word that is well-known to the student may not be read correctly because he is fixed on individual letters (visual or phonetic), and thus the word or sentence may loose its identitiy. This happens when reading comprehension is preceded and overtaken by the recoding of the graphemic to the phonetic structures, which leads to reading without understanding, to mistakes, wrong accentuation and intonation, and so forth.

Later, reading becomes more automated, and the various recoding processes become reduced. The role of phonology is reduced to a minimum; it is no longer necessary to hear the words as internal speech or by manifest articulation in order to understand what is being read. Experiments [156; 180; 194] have shown that reading comprehension is not impaired by suppression of articulatory movements. This means that the semantic decoding of graphemic structures may take place immediately after optic perception and without a deviation via oral language. However, when difficulties in meaning arise, one falls back on phonological aids [157]. The same is true of writing.

It is sufficient to understand a word in order to reproduce it graphically. Normally in this process there is no strict copying or direct transcription, but an immediate recoding according to the sense and content (e. g., when the sample is given in print and must be reproduced in handwriting).

As we have been able to ascertain with the aid of our elimination process, copying in this manner proceeds completely normally even without the aid of latent articulation. The same is true with regard to voluntary writing.

Ordinarily, we need neither latent or manifest co-articulation nor conscious visual, auditory, or motor control when writing. However, this reduction may vary with the difficulty of the material to be written (for instance, the beginnings and ends of sentences, new paragraphs, punctuation, etc.). The free flow of writing processes requires the programming of a particular graphic picture and the evocation of a correlated pattern of innervation that will control the movements of the writing hand. In view of the little need for concentration during automatic writing and the rather high speed at which it is done, the following questions arise. Is there a new programming for every writing act and a new synthesis of grapho-motor impulses, or does the writing act proceed by means of the actualization of stored motor stereotypes (cf. Luria, [114], who speaks of kinaesthetic engrams)?

If there are stored motor stereotypes, are they limited to graphemic structures (words), or do they comprise only phonetic-graphemic sequences of structures? What is the relationship of the graphemic-phonologic correspondence rules to the grapho-motor stereotypes? Only future research can answer these questions.

Reduction in the area of psychic functions is important in the case of oral and written language because it implies a substantial reduction of the original tasks necessary for such activities. This results in a noticeable liberation of certain cerebral functional systems. The greater the independence of receptive reading from latent and manifest speech movements, the faster and more immediately may the process of semantic decoding of graphemic structures act.

Reduction of dependence on oral language does not imply an abandonment of the graphemic-phonemic relations that were built up in the course of learning. As the difficulty of the material increases – objectively or subjectively – the subject may return to their use.

Particularly instructive in this respect are those cases in which a graphemic structure must be matched with an adequate phonetic structure, without these words being semantically decodable. Such identification of senseless or unknown words, which are presented in written and spoken form, generally presents no problem to the normal practiced reader, insofar as these words belong to the sphere of his linguistic knowledge with respect to phonological structure. In a similar manner, a normal subject can write correctly to dictation senseless or unknown words (with the exception of possible orthographic ambiguities).

2.1.2 *Autonomous Partial Systems*

As a consequence of the completed development and automation of the higher psychic functions, relatively autonomous partial cortical systems take shape, which, despite their integration into the whole system, may operate absolutely independently from each other [⟨2⟩; 188]. Such an autonomy is also evident in the various forms of oral and written language, where comprehension and speaking, receptive and expressive reading, copying, writing to dictation, voluntary writing, and so forth, become completely independent. We shall return to this independence when discussing pathological conditions, which illustrate the point dramatically.

2.2 *Clinical aspects: disturbances of written language*

2.2.1 *Linguistic competence in alexia and agraphia*

The field of alexia and agraphia can serve as a proving ground for the validation of various hypotheses on the nature of graphemes and syntactic-semantic relationships and their respective psychological realities. On the other hand, the neuropsychological analysis of reading and writing disturbances raises a number of basic problems that require a new set of psycholinguistic hypotheses (see ⟨3⟩) that competence is not 'lost' even in severe cases of aphasic disturbances. We have furnished a number of arguments in support of this view based on aphasiological investigations. Of special importance were the following: even total aphasia may be completely or partially recovered; further, losses are usually confined to specific speech performances, such as comprehension or production; in the same patient the disturbances of language performances may fluctuate frequently; and finally, it is possible to deblock aphasic interferences [see ⟨2⟩, ⟨9⟩, ⟨10⟩]. Such facts make it unlikely that language disturbances are due to interference with the basic rules that govern verbal behavior.

A discussion of the problem of competence is of particular practical and theoretical importance when it comes to understanding cerebral language disorders. As shown by Lenneberg [98], there are temporal limitations imposed upon the effortless acquisition of language during childhood, which are conditioned by maturational processes of the brain and cerebral lateralization. During the 'critical period' of language acquisition, the immature brain has the capacity to acquire competence, that is knowledge and storage of the basic rules, a process that occurs spontaneously and is based on generalization and classification procedures. We agree with Lenneberg that at the close of the critical period, the human brain is no longer able to accomplish this.

If language competence were 'lost' in the case of aphasia, the patient would be faced with the task of forming *de novo* the respective basic rules, despite his damaged cortex. This would imply that language could, in fact, be reacquired from the start, which is precisely what is frequently attempted in the course of rehabilitation training. In view of the limited period of brain maturation, such an assumption is neuropsychologically untenable. We are in agreement with a number of authors (e. g., Lenneberg [98]; Wepmann [206], and to a certain degree also Luria,

Vinarskaya, Naydin, and Tsvetkova [117]) that the objective of aphasia therapy should not be a fresh start in primary language acquisition but, in contrast, should aim at reactualization of disturbed forms of language. We have been confirmed in this view by the results of our own research on deblocking, which we cannot discuss here [⟨2⟩, ⟨9⟩, ⟨10⟩]. Suffice it to say that it is possible to couple successively the use of specific intact and partially or completely disturbed speech performances and thus reactualize language usage that had been blocked. Our success implies that competence remains basically intact despite the partial disturbance of certain modalities, and this confirms the psychological reality of our assumptions. Our most recent experience with deblocking has shown that severely disturbed language functions may be rehabilitated and that the patient may regain the capacity for making syntactic transformations (see [16; 19]; these accomplishments do not signify *de novo* acquisition but are reactualizations of stored basic grammatical rules.

However, there are some additional problems of competence in the area of written language that are not easily solved. As already mentioned, competence underlying written language is augmented relative to the competence underlying spoken language. It is conceivable that in the case of alexia and agraphia, precisely this augmentation is affected and the storage of the graphemic-phonemic correspondences is thus compromised. There is no question that one must treat the problem of competence for written language separately from that of competence for spoken language. In this connection, it is particularly important that reading and writing can be learned after cerebral maturation is complete, that is, by adults; therefore, perhaps, the rules governing these later acquisitions are more labile and more subject to pathological interference than are the basic rules of spoken language.

The main evidence that would support such a view would be the existence of patients who have lost all aspects of written language – that is, a combination of alexia and agraphia – but whose spoken language has been completely spared. However, such patients are extremely rare.[9] Insofar as they do exist, one could argue that only the superstructure of additional rules for reading and writing has been affected. Such a hypothesis would never do for any of the other cases of alexia and agraphia, since in these cases – the vast majority – only one or the other form suffers. When losses are selective, we may not attribute them to interference with 'augmented competence'. Among the 55 aphasic patients of various types we examined, there was only one in whom every function of spoken language on the level of words (word understanding, repetition, oral naming) was intact, whereas receptive and expressive reading and copying were practically abolished. But even in this case, there was one graphic capacity that was almost completely spared:

writing to dictation. Moreover, alexic and agraphic disturbances may fluctuate considerably, and they are in general amenable to deblocking.

2.2.2 *Autonomy of the partial systems in alexia and agraphia*
From the foregoing, it is evident that the majority of aphasic, alexic, and agraphic disturbances must be regarded as a limitation of one or more aspects of performance. But how can this happen? What is the meaning in this case of selective aspects of performance? The short-sighted explanations in terms of cerebral localization can hardly be considered appropriate. Most aphasiologists are unanimous in believing that specific, localized cerebral lesions are not sufficient cause for selected losses in the presence of otherwise intact language functions. No doubt concepts such as 'disturbance of a fundamental nature' (Goldstein) or 'disturbances in the mode of action of given factors' (Luria – for instance, simultaneity or sequence; Lenneberg speaks of timing factors) are more suggestive. Nevertheless, it seems to us that the assumption of autonomous partial systems gets us still a step closer to a solution of the problem.

If it is correct that during the automation of certain functions there is a reduction in the interaction of various partial systems which had to interact in order to guarantee various performances, then it is possible that these systems might become 'protected' as they become independent each from the other; this then might clarify the nature of selected losses. In other words, the more autonomous a given partial system, the less likely would an interference with that system implicate other, even related systems, provided, naturally, that the common competence remains intact. Thus it becomes understandable that limitations of comprehension in spoken language need not affect comprehension in written language (acoustic sensory aphasia with receptive alexia) or that a patient with a motor aphasia may be able to read aloud correctly, etc.

In view of the problem of localized lesions the following hypothesis may not be unreasonable. Circumscribed disturbances of partial systems due to circumscribed cerebral lesions can occur only after reduction and automatization have taken place. In contrast to this are the results of lesions during childhood, at which time functions are in the process of acquisition and establishment, requiring the interaction of all of the partial systems at the same time, together with their respective cerebral structures and cerebral interconnections. See Vygotsky [170] and Luria [117] on the different consequences of cerebral lesions upon psychological functions at various developmental stages. During this period, there should be a very low probability that focal cortical lesions would produce selective disturbances. Of course, this hypothesis must be further verified on appropriate clinical material.

We propose a further hypothesis: disorders of written language due to cerebral lesions (alexia and agraphia) should have different symptomatology depending on whether the skills were acquired during infancy or adulthood; the augmented competence should be less susceptible to interference in the former case than in the latter.

2.3 *The efficiency of the graphemic-phonemic rules in cases of alexia and agraphia*

I should like to conclude this discussion of the neuropsychological problems of cortical disturbances of written language by reporting on some results of research on 55 aphasic patients of different types, undertaken in collaboration with my Rumanian colleagues A. Fradis, L. Mihăilescu, and N. Gheorghiţă [for the methodology of this work see 182; 197] and by interpreting these results in the light of the problem on the grapheme-phoneme correspondence rules.

To determine whether our alexic patients still had the necessary visual-gnosic prerequisites for the tasks of reading and writing, we asked them to select identical written letters from a long series of letters. Of the thirteen patients with partial or total receptive alexia, eleven were able to select these correctly. This means that despite their alexia, they had no disturbance in form perception.

In another experiment, we tried to determine whether the grapheme-phoneme correspondence rules were still effective among the alexic patients when semantics was excluded. We asked the patients to select equivalent words that were written in different type faces. In five cases of total or severe receptive alexia, the patients were able to perform the task correctly, even though they were unable to understand any of the meanings. Also, my collaborators, R. Böttcher and I. Weigl, were able to demonstrate the same thing on other patients with definite receptive alexia.

The significance of these results is less obvious than it may appear at first sight. A certain invariance must exist, which enables correct identification of written structures in the absence of semantic correspondences. The only common denominator in these different type faces is their relationship to their phonological values. The proper performance of this identification task by our patients serves as proof of the psychological reality of grapheme-phoneme relationships and their respective transformational rules.

In another set of experiments, we examined patients who were alexic and suffered from acoustic-sensory aphasia. There were eleven patients who presented both receptive alexia and word deafness. Different words were spoken to these patients, who then had to identify one of these words from a series of written words in front of them. Although they were unable to understand the words in either their auditory or their optic form, six patients were able to make correct identifications in about 75 to 100 percent of the cases (there were 20 words for each) [see ⟨12⟩]. In these cases, the correct matching in the absence of semantic understanding in either the acoustic or the graphic form could have been due only to the effective operation of the grapheme-phoneme correspondence rules, which, according to these findings, were apparently not affected.

Our method of deblocking offers a further opportunity for study of the relationship between written and spoken language. It is possible to deblock disturbed reading comprehension (receptive alexia) by first having the patient repeat orally given words and sentences or by having him copy the material or write it to dictation; the naming of the objects also helps; finally, a coupling of the remaining spared functions is brought about ⟨2⟩; ⟨10⟩. In these tasks, one deals not only with the grapheme-phoneme levels, but also with syntactic-semantic ones. At first, we believed that the results of these deblocking procedures were due only to the channeling of intact semantic models through different avenues. We must now add to this assumption; the semantic accomplishments have as prerequisite the intact operation of the different linguistic levels and of the grapheme-phoneme correspondence rules.

A final remark. In this article, I have tried to bring some neuropsycholinguistic views to bear upon alphabetically written language – a field relatively little investigated. I was most anxious to demonstrate the close relationships that exist between psychology, linguistics, and medical brain research.

The focus of this paper is on the basic graphemic-phonemic rules that relate written language to spoken language. Of particular interest are acquisition of these basic rules (linguistic competence) during maturity and their preservation even in cases of severe alexia and agraphia. The brain correlates of written language are discussed and are related to the theory of functional cerebral systems, in conjunction with the conceptualization of language acquisition and brain maturation.

Notes

1. For summaries of results, see [77], Results of Soviet Psychology (1967) (particularly Galperin, Kostjuk, Luria).
2. See Leischner's monography [95]; and also [106, 112; 117; 14; 42).
3. See [14; 42; 48; 147].
4. Certain hypothetical approaches with regard to a theory of rule acquisition (code learning) may be found in Bruner [23], who shows the relationship between the

acquisition by infants of extralingual rules in the fields of perception and motor, and linguistic rules. Bruner regards active cognitive integration of experience as most important for the formation of rule systems. Experiments on problem solving, in which subjects must discover certain rules, are only indirectly relevant to our topic. The same is true of concept-formation experiments. However, some of the theoretical models proposed in connection with problem-solving and concept-formation experiments, allied to the interrelation of distinctive features, the categorization and generalization processes, may be of value with regard to rule-formation in the process of acquisition dealt with here.

On the psycholinguistic side there are valuable indications, with regard to spoken language, in the works collected by F. Smith and G. A. Miller under the title 'The Genesis of Language' [153].

5. A thorough presentation of this view and a full bibliography can be found in Luria [114].
6. In the first instruction in reading there occur, apart from the spoken language connection, visual-gnosic factors. The reading book shows the picture corresponding to the word which has to be learned.
7. The investigations of Nasarova [129] on the role of coarticulation during writing on dictation in the learning phase make an important contribution in this connection. The author requires the children to write with mouths wide open and tongues extended, thus making co-articulation difficult. Under these circumstances there is a considerable increase in the number of mistakes. This demonstrates that simultaneous speech movements facilitate written reproduction; if these speech movements are inhibited, encoding disturbances appear.
8. For the relationship between inner and external speech, between latent and manifest articulation, between innerspeech processes on the prearticulatory and the latent-articulatory level, see [188].
9. Among the aphasics of various types examined by us – about 55 – we found no single patient in whom all spoken language functions (on the word level) were intact, while all functions connected with written language – receptive and expressive reading, copying and writing on dictation – were completely or largely cancelled.

Bibliography

[1] De Ajuriaguerra, J. and H. Hécaen
1960 *Le Cortex Cérébral.* Paris: Masson.

[2] Alajouanine, Th.
1960 The Principle of Baillarger-Jackson in Aphasia. *Journal Neurol. Neursurg. Psych.* 23: 191.

[3] Alajounanine, Th., Lhermitte, F., Ledoux and A. Vignolo
1964 Les composantes phonémiques et sémantiques de la jargonaphasie. *Rev. Neurol.* 110: 5.

[4] Alajouanine, Th. and Lhermitte, F.
1963 Les désorganisations des activités expressives du langage dans l'asphasie. *Encéphale* 5: 5.

[5] Alajouanine, Th. and Mozziconacci, P.
1948 *L'aphasie et la désintégration fonctionelle du langage.* Symposiums et monographies de la Sémaine des Hopitaus. L'expansion scientifique française. Paris.

[6] Alich, G.
1960 Zur Erkennbarkeit von Sprachgestalten beim Ablesen vom Mund. Diss. Bonn.

[7] Barbizet, J.
1966 La Reéducation du Langage. *La Presse Médicale* 74.

[8] Bassin, F. W. and Bein, E. S.
1957 *On the Application of Electromyographic Methods in Speech Research* (in Russ.) Izd. Akad. Pedagog. Nauk. Moscow.

[9] Bein, E. S.
1964 *Aphasia and its Therapy* (in Russ.) Izd. Medicina. Leningrad.

[10] 1966 Speech Dissociation in Aphasics as a Method of Studying the Relationships between Speech and Thought. In *XVIIIth International Congress of Psychology* Moscow. Symposium 26: 99.

[11] Beltjukov, W. I.
1967 Interactions of Analysators in the Process of Perception of Spoken Language (in Russ.). *Voprosy Psikhologii* 3: 19.

[12] Benson, F. and Geschwind, N.
1964 The Alexias. In *Handbook of Clinical Neurology,* edited by Vinken and G. De Bruyn, Amsterdam: Elsevier.

[13] Bierwisch, M.
1966 Strukturalismus, Geschichte, Probleme und Methoden, *Kursbuch* Frankfurt/ Main 5: 77.

[14] 1972 Phonologie und Schriftstruktur, *Probl. Erg. Psychol.* 43: 21.

[15] 1975 Sprache und Gedächtnis: Ergebnisse und Probleme. Linguistische Studien/ ZISW/A. 25. Also in *Psychologische Effekte sprachlicher Strukturkomponenten,* edited by M. Bierwisch. Berlin, Akademie Verlag. 1979.

[16] Bierwisch, M. and Weigl. I.
1976 Syntactic Transformations: Evidence from Aphasia. In *Abstracts of the XXIst International Congress of Psychology* Paris: 152.

[17] Blinkov, S. M.
1948 *On Writing Disturbances with Temporal Lobe Lesions* (in Russ.) Izd. Akad. Pedagog. Nauk. Moscow 15: 73.

[18] Böttcher, R.
1974 Zur Rolle von graphischen und semantisch-syntaktischen Faktoren beim Wortlesen. *Zeitschr. Psychol.* 182: 40.

[19] Böttcher, R., Metze, E., and Weigl. I.
1969 Untersuchungen der Beziehungen zwischen intakten und hirnpathologisch beeinträchtigten psychischen Funktionen im Dienste der Erforschung und Rehabilitierung aphasischer Störungen. *Probl. Erg. Psychol.* 28/29: 103.

[20] Brain, R.
1961 The Physiology of Speech. In *VIIth International Congress of Neurology,* edited by G. Alemá et al. International Congress Series: 38: 4. Amsterdam: Excerpta Medica.

[21] Branca, A. A.
1957 Semantic Generalization at the Level of the Conditioning Experiment, *American Journal of Psychology* 70: 541.

[22] Broca, P.
1888 *Mémoires sur le cerveau de l'homme et des primates.* Paris: Pozzi.

[23] Bruner, J. S.
1967 *Toward a Theory of Instruction.* Cambridge, Mass.: Harvard Univ. Press.

[24] Carterette, E. C. (ed.)
1966 Brain Function 3: *Speech, Language and Communication.*

[25] Chesher, E.
1937 Aphasia. *Bull. neurol. Inst.* N. Y., 6: 1.

[26] Chésni, Y.
1968 Méthode psychophysiologique appliquée à l'étude du langage. *Cab. Ét. Biol.*

[27] Chomskaya, E. D.
1967 Neuropsychology – a New Branch of Psychological Sciences (in Russ.) *Voprosy Psikhologii* 103.

[28] Chomsky, N.
1965 *Aspects of the Theory of Syntax.* Cambridge, Mass: M.I.T. Press.

[29] Chomsky, N. and Miller, G. A.
1963 Introduction to the Formal Analysis of Natural Languages, In *Handbook of Mathematical Psychology,* II, edited by R. D. Luce, R. R. Bush and E. Galanter New York: John Wiley.

[30] Chromov, N. A.
1949 Amnesia and Amnestic Aphasia (in Russ.) *Zhurnal Nevropat. Psich.*

[31] Cohen, D., Dubois, J., Gauthier, M., Hécaen, H. and Angelergues, R.
1963 Aspects du fonctionnement du code lingustique chez les aphasiques moteurs, *Neuropsychologia* 1: 165.

[32] Cohen, R. et. al.
1975 Experimentalpsychologische Untersuchungen zur linguistischen Erfassung aphatischer Störungen. Dritter Bericht an die Deutsche Forschungsgemeinschaft: Konstanz.

[33a] De Renck, A.V.S. and O. Connor, M. (eds)
1964 *Disorders of Language,* London: Churchill.

[33b] De Renzi, E., P. Faglioni, M. Savoiardo and L. A. Vignolo
1966 The Influence of the Hemispheric Side of the Cerebral Lesion on Abstract Thinking. *Cortex* 2: 339.

[34] Dobrow, G. M.
1969 *Wissenschaftswissenschaft.* Berlin: Akademie-Verlag.

[35] Dodge, R.
1896 *Die motorischen Wortvorstellungen.* Abh. Philos. Gesch. B. Erdmann 8: 30.

[36] Duncker, K.
1963 *Zur Psychologie des produktiven Denkens.* Berlin & New York: Springer-Verlag.

[37] Eden, M.
1961 On the Formalization of Handwriting. In *Structure of Language in its Mathematical Aspect.* edited by R. Jakobson. Providence, R. I.: American Math. Soc.

[38] Façon, E. and Wertheim, N.
1957 Pathophysiological Remarks on a Case of Aphasia (in Rom.) *Neurol.* Bucharest, 2: 147.

[39] Feuchtwanger, E.
1930 *Amusie: Studien zur Pathopsychologie der akustischen Wahrnehmung und Vorstellung und ihrer Strukturgebiete, besonders in der Musik und Sprache.* Berlin: Springer Verlag.

[40] Fonarev, A. M.
1957 *A Device for Electric Registering of Microspeech Movements on Latent Articulation* (in Russ.) Izd. Akad. Pedagog. Nauk. Moscow, 81: 99.

[41] Fradis, A.
1970 La capacité de réproduction orale et graphique des sons du langage et des lettres chez les aphasiques. *Actes du Xme Congrès International de Linguistiques* Bucharest, 3: 709.

[42] Fries, C. C.
1964 *Linguistics and Reading.* New York: Holt, Rinehart and Winston.

[43] Gardner, H.
1973 The Contribution of Operativity to Naming Capacity in Aphasic Patients. *Neuropsychologia,* 11: 218.

[44] Gelb, A.
1926 Die psychologische Bedeutung pathologischer Störungen der Raumwahrnehmung. *Ber. IX. Kongr. Psychol.* Jena.

[45] Gelb, A. and Goldstein, K.
1925 Über Farbennamenamnesie nebst Bemerkungen über das Wesen der amnesitischen Aphasie überhaupt und die Beziehungen zwischen Sprache und dem Verhalten zur Umwelt. *Psychol. Forsch.* 6: 127.
[46] Geschwind, N.
1967 Neurological Foundations of Language. In *Progress in Learning Disabilities,* edited by H. Mykelburst. New York: Grune and Stratton.
[47] 1974 The Varieties of Naming Errors. In *Selected Papers On Language and the Brain,* edited by N. Geschwind. Dordrecht: Reidel.
[48] Gibson, E. J., Pick, A., Osser, H. and Hammond, M.
1969 The Role of Grapheme-Phoneme-Correspondence in the Perception of Words. In *The Psychology of Language: Thought and Instruction,* edited by J. P. De Cecco. London: Holt, Rinehart and Winston.
[49] Goldstein, K.
1925a Zur Theorie der Funktion des Nervensystems. *Arch. Psychiat. Nervenkr.,* 74: 370.
[50] 1925b Das Symptom, seine Entstehung und Bedeutung für unsere Auffassung vom Bau und der Funktion des Nervensystems. *Arch. Psychiat. & Nervenkr. 76:* 84.
[51] 1926 Über Aphasie. Schweiz. *Arch. Neurol. Psychiat.* 19: 3.
[52] 1946 On Naming and Pseudonaming. *Word.* 2: 1.
[53] 1948 *Language and Language Disturbances.* New York: Grune and Stratton.
[54] 1954 Bemerkungen zum Problem Sprechen und Denken auf Grund hirnpathologischer Erfahrungen. In *Thinking Speaking.* Amsterdam: North-Holland.
[55] 1960 Thinking and Speaking. *Annals of the New York Academy of Sciences* 91: 38.
[56] Goldstein, K. and Scheerer
1941 *Abstract and Concrete Behavior.* An Experimental Study with Special Tests. Washington.
[57] Goodglass et al
1966 Specific Semantic Word Categories in Aphasia. *Cortex* 2: 74.
[58] Green, E.
1970 On the Contribution of Studies in Aphasia to Psycholinguistics. *Cortex* 6: 216.
[59] Guiraud, P.
1954 *Les caractères statistiques du vocabulaire.* Paris: Presses Universitaires de France.

[60] Hacker, W.
1973 *Allgemeine Arbeits- und Ingenieurpsychologie: Psychische Struktur und Regulation von Arbeitstätigkeiten.* Berlin: Deutscher Verlag der Wissenschaften.
[61] Head, H.
1926 *Aphasia and Kindred Disorders of Speech.* London: Cambridge Univ. Press.
[62] Hécaen, H.
1966 Développement de la Neuropsychologie comme champ de recherches disciplinaires. *XVIIIth International Congress of Psychology.* Moscow. Symposium 26: 110.
[63] 1969 Cerebral Localization of Mental Functions and their Disorders. In *Handbook of Clinical Neurology,* Vol. 3 (Disorders of Higher Nervous Activity), edited by P. J. Vinken and G. W. Bruyn. Amsterdam: Elsevier.

[64] Hécan, H., Angelergues, R. and Douzenis. J. A.
1963 Les agraphies. *Neuropsychologia* 1: 179.

[65] Heilbronner, K.
1912 Zur Psychologie der Alexie. *Mschr. Psychiat. Neurol.* 32: 461.

[66] Hermann, E. and Krolikowska, W.
1961 Untersuchungen der objektiven Äußerungen der inneren Sprache. Mitteilung auf dem Symposium über Aphasie in Bukarest. *World Neurol.* 2: 991.

[67] Hiebsch, H., Klix, F. and Vorwerg, M. (eds.)
1967 *Ergebnisse der sowjetischen Psychologie.* Berlin: Akademie Verlag.

[68] Hrbek, J.
1961 Neurophysiological Mechanisms of Speech. The Central Integrative Role of the Proprioceptive Analyser. In *Abstracts of the VIIth International Congress of Neurology,* edited by G. Alemá et al. International Congress Series 38: 20. Amsterdam: Excerpta Medica.

[69] Ivanov-Smolenski, A. G.
1951 On the Study of the Coordinated Functions of the First an the Second Systems of the Cerebral Cortex. (in Russ.). *Z. vyss. nerv. dejat.* 1.

[70] Jackson, H.
1932 *Selected Writings.* Vol. 2. London: Hodder & Stoughton.

[71] Jakobsen, R.
1964 Towards a Linguistic Typology for Aphasic Impairments, In *Disorders of Language,* edited by A.V.S. De Reuck and M. O'Connor. London: Churchill.

[72] 1966 Linguistic Types of Aphasia, In *UCLA Forum Med. Sci.,* University of California Press, 67–91.

[73] 1967 Linguistics and Adjacent Sciences. II. Natural Sciences. In *Xth International Congress of Linguistics:* Bucharest. Also in *Roman Jakobson: Selected Writings,* Vol. 2, The Hague: Mouton.

[74] 1969 *Kindersprache, Aphasie und allgemeine Lautgesetze.* Frankfurt/M.: Suhrkamp Verlag. Also in *R. Jakobsen: Selected Writings,* Vol. 1. The Hague: Mouton.

[75] Jusevič, I. S.
1954 Clinical Electromyography as an Instrument of Speech Pathological Reserarch (in Russ.) *Zhurn. Nevropat. Psych.:* 54.

[76] Kadočkin, L. K.
1955 The Role of Speech Kinaesthesy in the Acquisition of Orthographic Skills (in Russ.) *Voprosy Psikhologii* 3: 71.

[77] Kainz, F.
1956 *Psychologie der Sprache.* Vol. 4. Stuttgart: Enke.

[78] Kern, A.
1929 Vom inneren Sprechen. *Z. Kinderf.* 35: 420.

[79] Kintsch, W.
1972 Notes on the Structure of Semantic Memory. In *Organisation of Memory,* edited by E. Tulving and W. Donaldson, 249. New York: Academic Press.

[80] Klix, F.
1971 *Information und Verhalten.* Berlin: Deutscher Verlag der Wissenschaften.

[81] 1976 Strukturelle und funktionelle Komponenten des menschlichen Gedächtnisses. In *Psychologische Beiträge zur Analyse kognitiver Prozesse,* edited by F. Klix. Berlin: Deutscher Verlag der Wissenschaften.

[82] Kogan, W. M.
1963 Recovery Speech in Aphasia. (in Russ.) Diss. Moscow.
[83] Konorski, J., Kozniewska, H., Stepien, L.
1961 Analysis of Symptoms and Cerebral Localisation of Audio-Verbal Aphasia. In *Abstracts of the VIIth International Congress of Neurology,* edited by G. Aléma *et al.* International Congress Series 38: 22. Amsterdam: Excerpta Medica.
[84] Koževnikov, V. A. and Čistovič, L. A. (eds.)
1965 *Speech, Articulation and Perception* (in Russ.), Moscow.
[85] Kreindler, A.
1962 The Neurophysological Basis of Aphastic Studies. (in Rom.). *Stud. Cercet. Neurol.* 7: 7.
[86] 1968 Neuere Forschungsrichtungen auf dem Gebiet der Aphasie, *Nervenarzt.* 39: 145.
[87] Kreindler, A. and Fradis, A.
1961 The Bucharest International Symposium on Aphasia. *World Neurol.* 2
[88] 1968 *Performances in Aphasia,* Paris: Gauthier-Villars.
[89] Kreindler, A. and Ionăşescu, V.
1961 Clinical Comments on a Case of "pure" Wordblindness. *Journal Neurol. Neurosurg. Psych.* 24: 275.
[90] Kreindler, A. and Mihăilescu, L.
1970 Operational Words in Aphasics. *Journal Neurol. Sci.* 11: 275.
[91] Kroh, O. and Scholl, B.
1926 Über die teilinhaltliche Beachtung von Farbe und Form beim Haushuhn. *Zeitschr. Psychol.* 100.
[92] Krychova, N. A., und Schteinghart, K. M.
1960 État de l'Analysateur du Langage dans l'Aphasie. *Rev. neurol:* 103, 169.
[93] Ladîgina-Kots, N.
1923 *Investigations into the Recognition Abilities in Chimpanzees* (in Russ.) Moscow.
[94] Lang, E. and Lange, B.
1973 Was gehört zu einer Wissenschaftsdisziplin? (Ber. über zwei Bereichskolloquien zum Begriff der Wissenschaftsdisziplin und Beziehungen von Wissenschaftsdisziplinen). In *Wissenschaft im Sozialismus. Probleme und Untersuchungen.* (Autorenkollektiv). Berlin: Akademie-Verlag.
[95] Leischner, A.
1957 *Die Störungen der Schriftsprache* (Agraphie und Alexie). Stuttgart: G. Thieme.
[96] 1969 The Agraphias, In *Handbook of Clinical Neurology,* edited by P. Winken and G. De Bruyn. Amsterdam: Elsevier.
[97] Leischner, A. and Linck, H. A.
1967 Neue Erfahrungen mit der Behandlung von Aphasie. *Nervenarzt* 38.
[98] Lenneberg, E.
1967 *Biological Foundations of Language.* New York: J. Wiley & Sons.
[99] Leonhard, K.
1954 Innervatorische und ideokinetische Formen motorischer Aphasie. *Nervenarzt* 25: 177.

[100] Leontiev, A. A.
1967 *Problems of Speech Production and Language Teaching* (in Russ.) Izd. Mosk. Univ. 6.

[101] Leontiev, A. N.
1964 *Probleme der Entwicklung des Psychischen.* Berlin: Verlag Volk und Wissen.

[101] Liberman, A. M., Cooper, F. S., Harris, K. S. and MacNeilage, P. F.
1963 A Motor Theory of Speech Perception, In *Proceedings of the Speech Communication Seminar 2.* Stockholm: Royal Institute of Technology.

[103] Lotmar, F.
1933 Zur Pathopsychologie der erschwerten Wortfindung bei Aphatikern. *Schweiz. Arch. Neurol. Psychiat.* 30: 86–158; 322–379.

[104] Ludwig, R.
1968 Tafeln zur Signifikanzprüfung zweier Prozentzahlen. *Jugendforschung 6.*

[105] Luria, A. R.
1947 *Traumatic Aphasia* (in Russ.) Moscow: Izd. Akad. Med. Nauk. Also 1970 (in Engl.) The Hague: Mouton.

[106] 1950 *On the Psychophysiology of Writing.* (in Russ.) Moscow: Izd. Akad. Pedagog. Nauk.

[107] 1963 *Restoration of Brain Function after War Trauma.* Oxford: Pergamon.

[108] 1964 Factors and Forms of Aphasia, In *Disorders of Language,* edited by De Reuck, A. V. S. and O'Connor, M. London: Churchill.

[109] 1965 L. S. Vygotski and the Problem of Localization of Functions. *Neuropsychologia* 3: 381.

[110] 1966 Kurt Goldstein and Neuropsychology. *Neuropsychologia* 4: 311.

[111] 1967 Problems and Facts in Neurolinguistics. *Int. Rev. Soc. Sci.* 19: 36.

[112] 1970 *Die höheren kortikalen Funktionen des Menschen und ihre Störungen bei örtlichen Hirnschädigungen.* Berlin: Deutscher Verlag der Wissenschaften.

[113] 1973a The Future of Clinical Neuropsychology. *Bull. Intern. Neuropsychol. Society, Philadelphia,* November 5.

[114] 1973 *The Working Brain. An Introduction to Neuropsychology.* Hammondsworth: Penguin Education.

[115] 1974 Language and Brain. Towards the Basic Problems of Neurolinguistics. *Brain and Language* 1: 1.

[116] Luria, A. R. and Tsvetkova, L. S.
1968 The Mechanism of "Dynamic Aphasia", *Foundations of Language* 4: 296.

[117] Luria, A. R., Vinarskaya, E. N. Naydin, V. L. and Tsvetkova, L. S.
1969 Restoration of Higher Cortical Functions. In *Handbook of Clinical Neurology,* Vol. 3, edited by P. Winken and G. de Bruyn. Amsterdam: Elsevier.

[118] Luria, A. R., and Vinogradova, O. S.
1959 An Objective Investigation of the Dynamics of Semantic Systems. *Brit. Journal Psychol.* 50: 88.

[119] Marshall, J. C. and Newcombe, F.
1966 Syntactic and Semantic Errors in Paralexia, *Neuropsychologia* 4: 169.

[120] Marshall, M., Newcombe, F. and Marshall, J. C.
1969 The Microstructure of Wordfinding Difficulties in a Dysphasic Subject. In *Press. Proceed. Bressanone Conference,* Amsterdam: North-Holland.

[121] Maruszewski, M.
1966 *Aphasia, Theoretic Problems and Therapy* (in Polish) Warsaw.

[122] Meier, G. and Müller-Hegemann, D.
1955 Aphasiestudien. *Psychiat. Neurol. Psychol.* 7: 347.

[123] Meili, R.
1926 Experimentelle Untersuchungen beim Ordnen von Gegenständen. *Psychol. Forsch.* 7.

[124] Mihăilescu, L., Weigl, I., Weigl. E. and Kreindler, A.
1972 Performance an Aphasics at Conceptual and Operational Words used Single or within Syntagms. *Rev. Roum. Neurol.* 9: 181–195 (= 14 this Vol.)

[125] Mihăilescu, L., Voinescu, I. and Fradis, A.
1968 Aspects du vocabulaire chez les aphasiques. *Rev. Roum. Ling.* 13: 331.

[126] Miller, G. A.
1964 The Psycholinguists, *Encounter* 23: 29. Reprinted in *Psycholinguistics,* edited by E. Osgood and T. A. Sebeck. Bloomington: Ind. Univ. Press.

[127a] 1965 Speech and Language. In *Handbook of Experimental Psychology,* edited by S. S. Stevens. London: Wiley.

[127b] 1969 The Organisation of Lexical Memory: Are Word Associations Sufficient? In *The Pathology of Memory,* edited by S. A. Talland and N. C. Waugh. New-York, London: Acad.

[128] Myklebust, H. R.
1964 *The Psychology of Deafness.* New York-London: Grune and Stratton.

[129] Nasarova, L. K.
1952 On the Role of Kinaesthetics in Writing. (in Russ.) *Sovetskaya Pedagogika* 6: 24.

[130] Novikova, L. A.
1957 *Electrophysiological Investigations into Speech Kinaesthesy* (in Russ.) Moscow: Izd. Akad. Pedagog. Nauk.

[131] Oerter, R.
1974 *Moderne Entwicklungspsychologie.* Donauwörth: Verlag Ludwig Auer.

[132] Osgood, C. E. and Miron, M. S. (eds.)
1963 *Approaches to the Study of Aphasia.* Urbana, III: University of Illinois Press.

[133] Osgood, C. E. and Sebeok, T. A.
1965 *Psycholinguisties.* Bloomington, Ind.: Indiana University Press.

[134] Pick, A.
1909 *Über das Sprachverständnis.* Leipzig: Barth.

[135] 1913 *Die agrammatischen Sprachstörungen. Studien zur psychologischen Grundlegung der Aphasielehre.* Berlin: Springer.

[136] Pick, A. an Thiele, R.
1931 Aphasie. In *Handbuch der Norm. pathol. Physiologie,* edited by Bethe Berlin, Vol. 15 pp. 1464–1468. Berlin: Springer.

[137] Pribram, K. H.
1967 Steps Towards a Neuropsychological Theory In *Neurophysiology and Emotion,* edited by D. C. Glass. Rockefeller Univ. Press.

[138] Price, J. de Solla
1963 *Little Science, Big Science.* New York.

[139] Razran, G.
1936 Salivating and Thinking in Different Languages. *Journal of Psychol:* 1.
[140] 1949 Semantic, Syntactic and Phonetographic Generalization of Verbal Conditioning. *Journal of Experimental Psychol.,* 39: 642.
[141] Révész, G.
1925a Experimental Study in Abstraction in Monkeys. *Journal of comparative Psychol.* 5: 293.
[142] 1925b Abstraktion und Wiedererkennen. *Zeitschr. Psychol.* 98.
[143] 1928 *Über taktile Agnosie.* Haarlem: De Erven F. Bohn.
[144] Riess, B. F.
1949 Semantic Conditioning Involving the Galvanic Skin Reflex, *Journal of Experimental Psychol.* 26: 238.
[145] Rubin, E.
1921 *Visuell wahrgenommene Figuren.* Copenhagen: Gyldendalske Boghandel.
[146] Schilling, R.
1929 Zur Frage des inneren Sprechens. *Zeitschr. Psychol.* 111: 205.
[147] Schlesinger, I. M.
1968 *Sentence Structure and the Reading Process.* The Hague: Mouton.
[148] Scholl, R.
1926 Untersuchungen über teilinhaltliche Beachtung von Farbe und Form bei Erwachsenen und Kindern. *Zeitschr. Psychol.* 101.
[149] 1926 Zur Theorie und Typologie der teilinhaltlichen Beachtung von Form und Farbe. *Zeitschr. Psychol.* 101.
[150] Schuell, H.
1957 A Short Examination for Aphasia. *Neurology* 7: 625.
[151] Schulze, H. A. F.
1965 *Die klinische Analyse kombinierter hirnpathologischer Störungen (Aphasie, Apraxie, Agnosie).* Beiträge zur Neurochirurgie, Leipzig: Barth.
[152] Smith, A. and Schwartz, M. L.
1973 Editorial Postscripts. The Future of Neuropsychology: Training. *Bull. Intern. Neuropsychol. Society Philadelphia* 12.
[153] Smith, F. S. an Miller, G. A. (eds.)
1966 *The Genesis of Language. A Psycholinguistic Approach,* Cambridge Mass.: M. I. T. Press.
[154] Sokolov, A. N.
1941 *Inner Speech and Comprehension* (in Russ.) Moscow: Izd. Akad. Pedagog. Nauk. 2, 99.
[155] 1956 *On the Speech Mechanismus of Intellectual Activity.* Moscow: Izd. Akad. Pedagog. Nauk. Vol 81, p. 65.
[156] 1967 Untersuchungen zum Problem der sprachlichen Mechanismen des Denkens. In *Ergebnisse der sowjetischen Psychologie,* edited by H. Hiebsch, F. Klix and M. Vorwerg. Berlin: Akademie-Verlag.
[157] 1968 *Inner Speech and Thinking* (in Russ.), Moscow; Izd Prosveščenie.
[158] Sperry, R. W., Gazzaniga, M. S. and Bogen, J. E.
1969 Interhemispheric Relationships: The Neocortical Commissures, Syndromes of Hemisphere Disconnection, In *Handbook of Clinical Neurology,* edited by P. J. Vinken and G. W. Bruyn wl. 4 p. 273. Amsterdam: Elsevier.

[159] Steinbuch, K.
1965 *Automat und Mensch; Kybernetische Tatsachen und Hypothesen.* Berlin: Springer.

[160] Stevens, K. N. and Halle, M.
1967 *Remarks on Analysis by Synthesis and Distinctive Features: Models for the Perception of Speech and Visual Form,* pp. 88–102. Cambridge Mass.: M. I. T. Press.

[161] Szumska, J. and Celinski, M.
1970 Deblocking of the Disturbed Speech Function in Focal Brain Lesions (in Polish) *Zagdanenia Patofiziol. Wyszych Czymn. Nerv. Usz. Mosgu* 1: 157.

[162] Taylor, M. L. and Sands, E.
1965 Application of Programmed Instruction Techniques to the Language Rehabiliation on Severely Impaired Aphasic Patients. Paper presented at the American Speech and Hearing Association Annual Convention, Chicago.

[163] Teuber, H.-L.
1966 Kurt Goldstein's role in the Development of Neuropsychology. *Neuropsychologia,* 4: 299.

[164] Tsvetkova, L. S.
1975 The Naming Process and its Impairment. A Multidisciplinary Approach. In *Foundations of Language Development,* edited by E. Lenneberg, Vol. 2. New York: Academic Press Inc. and Paris: The Unesco Press.

[165] Van der Waerden, B. L.
1957 *Mathematische Statistik.* Berlin.

[166] Vendries, J.
1939 *Le langage. Introduction linguistique à l'histoire,* Paris: Albin Michel, p. 98–101.

[167] Vignolo, L. A.
1964 Evolution of Aphasia an Language Rehabilitation: A Retrospective Exploratory Study. *Cortex* 1: 344.

[168] Volkelt, H.
1926 Fortschritte der experimentellen Kinderpsychologie. *Ber. IX. Kongr. exper. Psychol.* pp. 80–135.

[169] Vygotsky, L. S.
1964 *Denken und Sprechen.* Berlin: Akademie-Verlag.

[170] 1965 Psychology and Localisation of functions. *Neuropsychologia* 3: 381.

[171] Weigl, E.
1927 Zur Psychologie sogenannter Abstraktionsprozesse. *Zeitschr. Psychol.,* 103: 2.

[172] 1941 On the psychology of so-called processes of abstraction. *Journal of Abnorm and Soc. Psychol.* 36, 3–33. (= 4 this Vol.).

[173] 1929 Übereinstimmende Verhaltensweisen von Menschen und Affen bei Wahlhandlungen. *Ber. XI. Kongr. exper. Psychol.* Fischer Jena, pp. 182–189.

[174] 1933 Sprache und Ordnen. Kritisches und Prinzipielles zu den von Kuenburgschen Zuordnungsversuchen bei Gesunden und Sprachgestörten. *Zeitschr. ges. Neurol.* Psychiat. 144: 507.

[175] 1961 The Phenomenon of Temporary Deblocking in Aphasia. *Zeitschr. Phonetik, Sprachwiss. Komm.,* 141 337 (= 9 this Vol.).

[176] 1962 An experimental Procedure for Mechanically Switching out the Specificaly Verbal Movements in Subjects with Normal and Impaired Speech (in Russ.). *Voprosy Psikhologii* 4: 138.

[177] 1963a Deblockierungen akustisch und optisch agnostischer Störungen. In *Ber. Tag. Oto-Neuro-Ophth.* p. 264–266. Leipzig: Thieme-Verlag.

[178] 1963b Deblockierung bildagnostischer Störungen bei einem Aphatiker. *Neuropsychologia* 1: 91.

[179] 1964 The Experimental Deblocking of Aphasic verbal Defects, a Method of Investigation of Processes of Cerebral Dynamics (in Russ.) *Voprosy Psikhologii* 4: 142.

[180] 1964 Die Bedeutung der afferenten, verbo-kinästhetischen Erregungen des Sprachapparates für die expressiven und rezeptiven Sprachvorgänge bei Normalen und Sprachgestörten. *Cortex* 1: 77 (= 7 this Vol.).

[181a] 1966a Neuropsychological Studies of Structures and Dynamics of Semantic Fields with the Deblocking Method. *XVIII*th *International Congress of Psychology.* Moscow: Abstr. 2: 424.

[181b] 1966b Neuropsychological Studies of Structure and Dynamics of Semantic Fields with the Deblocking Method. In Sign. Language. Culture , edited by A. J. Greimas *et al.* The Hague: Mouton 1970 p. 287–290 (= Janua Linguarum, Ser. Maior 1) (= 15 this Vol.).

[182] 1966c On the Construction of Standard Psychological Tests in Cases of Brain Damage. *Journal Neurol. Sci* 3: 123 (= 5 this Vol.).

[183] 1967 Neuropsychologische Beiträge zum Problem der Semantik *X*th *International Congress of Linguistics,* Bucarest Abstr. 401.

[184] 1968 On the Problem of Cortical Syndroms: Experimental Studies. In *The Reach of Mind. Essays in Memory of Kurt Goldstein,* edited by M. Simmel. New York: Springer. (= 10 this Vol.).

[185] 1969 Beiträge zur neuropsychologischen Grundlagenforschung, *Probl. Erg.Psychol.* 28/29: 87. Also in *Patholinguistics* edited by S. Penser. Vol. 4. München: Fink Verlag 1979 (= 2 this Vol.).

[186] 1969 Neuropsychological models of normal and pathological speech mechanisms. In *Abstracts of submitted papers, specially invited papers and films of the XIX*th *International Congress on Psychology* London. p. 30.

[187] 1970 A neuropsychological Contribution to the Problem of Semantics, in *Progress in Linguistics,* edited by M. Bierwisch and K. E. Heidolph. The Hague: Mouton.

[188] 1972 Zur Schriftsprache und ihrem Erwerb. Neuropsychologische und psycholinguistische Betrachtungen. *Probl. Erg. Psychol.* 43: 45.

[189a] 1974a Neuropsychologie als interdisziplinäre Wissenschaft. In *Psychodiagnostik. Probleme, Methoden und Ergebnisse* edited by H. R. Böttcher, A. Seeber and G. Witzlack, pp. 138–139. Berlin: Deutscher Verlag der Wissenschaften.

[189b] 1974b On the Future of Neuropsychology. In *Bulletin of the International Neuropsychology Society.* The Univ. of Michigan.

[190] 1976 Die Zukunft der Neuropsychologie. *Psychiat. Neurol. med. Psychol.* 28: 654. (= 1 this Vol.).

[191] 1974 Neuropsychological Experiments on Transcoding Between Spoken and Written Language Structures. *Brain and Language* 1: 227 (= 12 this Vol.).

[192a] 1975 Neuropsychological Approach to the Problem of Transcoding. *Linguistics* 1954/155: 105 (= 11 this Vol.)

[192b] 1975 Zur Schriftsprache, ihrem Erwerb und ihren alexisch-agraphischen Störungen. *Linguistics* 154/155: 137 (= 17 this Vol.).

[192c] 1975 On Written Language: Its Acpuisition and Its Alexic-Agraphic Disturbances. In *Foundations of Language Development,* edited by E. and E. Lenneberg. Vol. 2 New York: Academic Press Inc. and Paris: The Unesco Press.

[192d] 1979 Neurolinguistische Untersuchungen zum semantischen Gedächtnis. In *Psychologische Effekte sprachlicher Strukturkomponenten,* edited by M. Bierwisch. Berlin: Akademie Verlag. (= 16 this Vol.).

[193] Weigl. E. and Bierwisch, M.
1970 Neuropsychology and Linguistics: Topics of Common Research. *Foundations of Language* 6: 1 (= 3 this Vol.).

[194] Weigl, E., Böttcher, R., Lander, H.-J. and Metze, E.
1971 Neuropsychologische Methoden zur Analyse der Funktionen und Komponenten sprachfunktionaler Teilsysteme. *Zeitschr. Psychol.* 1979: 444 (= 6 this Vol.).

[195] Weigl, E. and Fradis, A.
1959 Semiological Approach to Alexia (in Russ.) *Zhurnal Nevropat. Psichiatr* 59: 1425.

[196] 1959 The Role of Kinaesthetic-Motor Analyser in the Compensation of Visual Analyser Disturbances in Reading (in Rom.) *Stud. Cercet, Neurol.* 4/385.

[197] 1960 Standard Examination for the Study of Verbal Alexia (in Rom.) *Stud. Cercet. Neurol.* 5: 517

[198] 1977 The Transcoding Processes in Patients with Agraphia to Dictation. *Brain and Language* 4: 11 (= 13 this Vol.).

[199] Weigl. E., Fradis, A., Mihăilescu, L. and Gheorghită, N.
1960 *Report at the Bucharest Symposium on Aphasia.*

[200] Weigl, E. and Kreindler, A.
1960 Beiträge zur Auffassung gewisser aphasischer Störungen als Blockierungserscheinungen. *Arch. Psychiat. und Zeitschr. f. d. ges. Neurol.* 200: 306. (= 8 this Vol.).

[201] Weigl, I.
1979a Neuropsychologische und psycholinguistische Grundlagen eines Programms zur Rehabilitierung aphasischer Störungen. In *Patholinguistica,* edited by G. Peuser. Vol. 4. München: Fink Verlag.

[202] 1979b Intedependenz neuropsychologischer und psycholinguistischer Faktoren in der Aphasie. In *Psychologische Effekte sprachlicher Strukturkomponenten,* edited by M. Bierwisch. Berlin: Akademie Verlag.

[203] Weigl, I. and Mihăilescu, L.
1973 Interdependence between the Syntactic Context and its Constituents, *Rev. Roum. Neurol.* 2: 12.

[204] 1974 Vergleichende neuropsychologische Untersuchungen an deutsch- und rumänischsprachigen Aphatikern. In *Psychodiagnostik. Probleme, Methoden und Ergebnisse,* edited by H. R. Böttcher. A. Seeber und G. Witzlack. Berlin: Verlag der Wissenschaften.

[205] Weisenburg, Th. and K. E. McBride.
1935 *Aphasia: A Clinical and Psychological Study*. New York: Commonwealth Fund.

[206] Wepman, J. M.
1951 *Recovery from Aphasia*. New York.

[207] Wepman, J. M., Bloch, R. D., Jones, L. V. and Pelt, D. van
1956 Psycholinguistic Study of Aphasia: A Revision of the Concept of Anomia. *Journal Speech and Hearing Disord.* 81: 468.

[208a] Wertheim, N. and Botez, M. I.
1961 Receptive Amusia: A Clinical Analysis. *Brain* 84: 19.

[208b] Wiegel-Crump, D.
1976 Agrammatism and Aphasia. In *Recovery in Aphasics,* edited bei Y. Lebrun and R. Hoobs pp. 243–253.

[209] Wolkow, G. N.
1970 *Soziologie der Wissenschaft,* Berlin: Dietz Verlag.

[210] Žinkin, N. I.
1958 *Speech Mechanisms.* (in Russ.) Moscow: Izd. Akad. Pedagog. Nauk.

[211] 1967 Zur Erforschung des Mechanismus der Sprache. In *Ergebnisse der sowjetischen Psychologie* pp. 406–429, Berlin: Akademie Verlag.

[212] Zipf, G. K.
1935 *The Psycho-biology of Language. Boston; Mass.:*

Sources

The permission to translate and/or reprint the articles from the following sources is gratefully acknowledged:

⟨1⟩ E. Weigl: On the Future of Neuropsychology. Original Title: Zur Zukunft der Neuropsychologie *Zeitschr. für Psychiatrie, Neurologie und medizinische Psychologie,* 1976, 28, p. 654–659. Translated and reprinted by Permission of S. Hirzel Verlag Leipzig.

⟨2⟩ E. Weigl: Contributions to Neuropsychological Basic Research. Original title: Beiträge zur neuropsychologischen Grundlagenforschung. *Probleme und Ergebnisse der Psychologie,* 1969, 28/29, p. 87–108. Translated and reprinted by Permission of VEB Deutscher Verlag der Wissenschaften, Berlin.

⟨3⟩ E. Weigl and M. Bierwisch: Neuropsychology and Linguistics: Topics of Common Research. *Foundations of Language,* 1970, 6, p. 1–18. Reprinted by Permission of D. Reidel Publishing Company/Dordrecht-Holland.

⟨4⟩ E. Weigl: On the Psychology of so-called Processes of Abstraction. Original title: Zur Psychologie sogenannter Abstraktionsprozesse. *Zeitschrift für Psychologie,* 1927, 103 S. 2–15. Translated in *Journal of Abnormal and Social Psychology,* 1941, edited by C. Landis, Columbia Univ. and K. Goldstein, Harvard Univ., p. 3–33.

⟨5⟩ E. Weigl: On the Construction of Standard Psychological Tests in Cases of Brain Damage. *Journal of the neurological Sciences,* 1966, 3 p. 123–127. Reprinted by Permission of Elsevier Publishing Company, Amsterdam.

⟨6⟩ E. Weigl, R. Böttcher, H. J. Lander und E. Metze: Neuropsychological Methods for Analysing the Functions and Components of Speech-Functional Partial Systems. Original title: Neuropsychologische Methoden zur Analyse der Funktionen und Komponenten sprachfunktionaler Teilsysteme *Zeitschrift für Psychologie,* 1971, 179, 4, p. 444–494. Translated and reprinted by Permission of Johann Ambrosius Barth Verlag, Leipzig.

⟨7⟩ E. Weigl: The Importance of Afferent, Verbo-Kinaesthetic Exitation of the Speech Apparatus for Expressive and Receptive Speech in Normal Subjects and Subjects with Speech Disturbances. Original title: Die Bedeutung der afferenten, verbo-kinästhetischen Erregungen des Sprachapparates für die expressiven und rezeptiven Sprachvorgänge bei Normalen und Sprachgestörten. *Cortex,* 1964, 64, 1, P. 77–90. Translated and reprinted by Permission.

⟨8⟩ E. Weigl und A. Kreindler: Contributions to the Interpretation of Certain Aphasic Disturbances as Blocking Phenomena. Original title: Beiträge zur Auffassung gewisser aphasischer Störungen als Blockierungserscheinungen. *Archiv für Psychiat-*

rie und Zeitschrift f. d. ges. Neurologie, 1960, 200, p. 306–323. Translated and reprinted by Permission.

⟨9⟩ E. Weigl: The Phenomenon of Temporary Deblocking in Aphasia. *Zeitschrift für Phonetik, Sprachwissenschaft und Kommunikationsforschung,* 1961, 14, 4, pp. 337–364. Reprinted by Permission of Akademie Verlag, Berlin.

⟨10⟩ E. Weigl: On the Problem of Cortical Syndromes: Experimental Studies. *The Reach of Mind: Essays in Memory of Kurt Goldstein,* edited by Marianne L. Simmel, 1968, p. 143–159. Reprinted by Permission of Springer Publishing Company, Inc. New York.

⟨11⟩ E. Weigl: Neuropsychological Approach to the Problem of Transcoding. *Linguistics,* 1975, 1954/155, p. 105–135. Reprinted by Permission of Mouton & Co. Publishers, The Hague.

⟨12⟩ E. Weigl: Neuropsychological Experiments on Transcoding Between Spoken and Written Language Structures. *Brain and Language,* 1974, 1, p. 227–240. Reprinted by Permission of Academic Press. Inc.

⟨13⟩ E. Weigl and A. Fradis: The Trancoding Processes in Patients with Agraphia to Dictation. *Brain and Language,* 1977, 4, p. 11–22. Reprinted by Permission of Academic Press. Inc.

⟨14⟩ L. Mihăilescu, I. Weigl, E. Weigl and A. Kreindler: Performance in Aphasics at Conceptual and Operational Words used Single or within Syntagms. *Revue Roumaine de Neurologie* 1972, 9, 3 p. 181–195. Reprinted by Permission of Editions de l'Académie de la République Socialiste Roumanie.

⟨15⟩ E. Weigl: Neuropsychological Studies of Structure and Dynamics of Semantic Fields with the Deblocking Method, *Sign. Language. Culture,* edited by A. J. Greimas et al. 1970, p. 287–290. Reprinted by Permission of Mouton & Co. Publishers, The Hague.

⟨16⟩ E. Weigl: Neurolinguistic Research on Semantic Memory. Original title: Neurolinguistische Untersuchungen zum semantischen Gedächtnis. *Psychologische Effekte sprachlicher Strukturkomponenten,* edited by M. Bierwisch, 1979, p. 269–331. Translated and reprinted by Permission of Akademie Verlag, Berlin.

⟨17⟩ E. Weigl: On Written Language: Its Acquisition and Its Alexic-Agraphic Disturbances. Original title: Zur Schriftsprache, ihrem Erwerb und ihren alexisch-agraphischen Störungen. *Linguistics,* 1975, 154/155, p. 137–160. Translated and reprinted by Permission of Mouton & Co. Publishers, The Hague.